Heath Grammar and Composition

with a Process Approach to Writing

Introductory Course

Authors
Carol Ann Bergman
J. A. Senn

D.C. Heath and Company
Lexington, Massachusetts / Toronto, Ontario

Series Titles

Heath Grammar and Composition: Introductory Course
Heath Grammar and Composition: First Course
Heath Grammar and Composition: Second Course
Heath Grammar and Composition: Third Course
Heath Grammar and Composition: Fourth Course
Heath Grammar and Composition: Fifth Course
Heath Grammar and Composition: Complete Course

Supplementary Materials (for each course)

Annotated Teacher's Edition
Teacher's Resource Binder
Writing Transparencies
Workbook
Tests

Acknowledgments: page 525

Design by Dawn Ostrer Emerson
Production Patrick Connolly

7   8   9   0

Introductory Course

Heath
Grammar and Composition

with a Process Approach to Writing

Series Consultant

Henry I. Christ
Former Chairman of the English Department
Andrew Jackson High School
St. Albans, New York

Reviewers

Arkansas

Joy Leatherwood
Lake Hamilton Junior High School
Pearcy, Arkansas

Elizabeth A. McDuff
Cloverdale Junior High School
Little Rock, Arkansas

California

Joan B. Greenberger
Jean Strauber
Suzanne M. Woods
Portola Junior High School
Tarzana, California

Linda Kay
Gompers Middle School
Los Angeles, California

Florida

Faithia T. Clayton
Sixteenth Street Middle School
St. Petersburg, Florida

Patricia A. Davey
Osceola Middle School
Seminole, Florida

Rebecca Hight Miller
Westridge Junior High School
Orlando, Florida

Illinois

Helen Glass Fulce
Haven Middle School
Evanston, Illinois

Iowa

Nathan James Weate
Lamoni Community School
Lamoni, Iowa

Louisiana

Diane Marusak
Campti Junior High School
Campti, Louisiana

New Jersey

Kathleen Kayser
Pequannock Valley School
Pompton Plains, New Jersey

Michael Napurano
Terrill Middle School
Scotch Plains, New Jersey

Jennifer Pasculli
Readington School
Readington, New Jersey

New York

Geraldine C. Charney
Center School
New York, New York

Carol S. Lotz
Booker T. Washington Junior High School
New York, New York

North Carolina

Ruth L. Hudson
Ligon Gifted and Talented Middle School
Raleigh, North Carolina

Wilma M. Roseboro
Kingswood Sixth Grade Center
Cary, North Carolina

Oregon

Vicki Jefferson
Briggs Middle School
Eugene, Oregon

Tennessee

Sheila A. Duncan
Margaret A. Moore
Central Middle School
Murfreesboro, Tennessee

Rebecca Harrelson
Brainerd Junior High School
Chattanooga, Tennessee

Washington

Steven Berry
Carmichael Junior High School
Richland, Washington

Evelyn Blatt
Islander Middle School
Mercer Island, Washington

Contents

UNIT 1 *Grammar*

UNIT 2   Usage

UNIT 3 Mechanics

UNIT 4

Composition

Part One

UNIT 5

Composition
Part Two

Chapter 20   Writing Descriptive Paragraphs   320

Chapter 21   Writing Explanatory Paragraphs   334

Chapter 22   Writing Opinion Paragraphs   350

UNIT 6

Composition

Part Three

Chapter 23 Writing Stories 364

Chapter 24 Writing Reports 382

UNIT 7 Related Language Skills

To the Student

This book is about communication—the act of expressing yourself. Think of how much of your day is spent speaking with your family, friends, and many others in your school and community. Speaking, however, is only one means of communication. Writing is another. Writing clearly is an important skill. In today's world more and more businesses are using computers to communicate information. The written word—whether displayed on a screen or printed on paper—is the backbone of communication.

The different units in this book have one main goal. That goal is to help you speak and write clearly. The first unit, on grammar, shows the structure of English and gives you choices for your speaking and writing. The next unit, on usage, explains ways to speak and write more clearly. The third unit, on mechanics, shows the importance of punctuation and capitalization in writing. The fourth, fifth, and sixth units show how to find, organize, and communicate your ideas in writing. The seventh unit gives important study tips and other language skills that you will need in school.

The composition units in this book are unique. The chapters include all the help you need to understand and write different kinds of compositions—from single paragraphs through reports. Within chapters you are taken step by step through the four stages of the writing process. In the *prewriting* stage, you choose and limit a subject and organize your ideas. In the *writing* stage, you learn how to write a draft based on your prewriting notes that includes a topic sentence and a concluding sentence. In the *revising* stage, you learn how to improve your work and to look at it from a reader's point of view. Finally, in the *editing* stage, you learn how to polish your work by applying what you have learned in the first three units.

Going through these writing stages is like having someone steady you as you learn to ride a bike. If you are unsure of yourself, there are many helps, including practice exercises, models, and checklists. These will show you exactly what to do, how to do it, and when to do it. Following these stages in the writing process will help you write well in tomorrow's world.

Special Helps

Your teacher will probably go through some of the chapters in this book with you. All of the chapters, however, have been written and organized so that you can refer to them and use them on your own throughout the year. You may find some of the following features of the book particularly helpful.

Keyed Rules All the rules are clearly marked with keyed blue arrows. An index at the back of the book tells you where to find each rule.

Tinted Boxes Throughout the text, important lists, summaries, and writing steps are highlighted in tinted boxes for easy reference.

Application to Writing These sections in the first three units of the book clearly show you how you can use the various grammatical concepts you have learned to improve your writing.

Diagnostic and Mastery Tests You can use the diagnostic and mastery tests to measure your progress. The diagnostic test at the beginning of a chapter will show you what you need to learn; the mastery test at the end will show you how well you learned it.

High-Interest Exercises Many of the exercises throughout the book are based on interesting topics. You will not only practice learning a particular skill, but you will also find the material in these exercises informative and interesting.

Composition Models Clearly marked models in the composition chapters provide interesting examples by professional writers.

Spotlight on Writing Fun activities at the end of each composition chapter give you many writing projects. Some ask you to write about a picture. Some give you information to work with. All of them give you more practice in growing as a writer.

Composition Checklists Almost all the composition chapters end with a checklist that you can follow—step by step—when you are writing a paragraph, an essay, or a report.

Standardized Tests Standardized tests, which follow all seven units, give you practice and build your confidence in taking tests.

Study Skills You will find information on note-taking, using the library, taking tests, and other topics that will help you succeed in school. A special chapter on speaking and listening will sharpen your oral skills.

Grammar

The Sentence

*D*iagnostic *T*est

Number your paper 1 to 10. Write each underlined word or words. Then label each one *subject* or *verb*.

EXAMPLE   Two loaves of bread <u>are baking</u> in the oven.
ANSWER   are baking—verb

1. An elephant's tusks <u>are</u> really giant teeth.
2. In March spring <u>begins</u>.
3. Raccoons <u>will eat</u> frogs, acorns, and many other things.
4. Some <u>flowers</u> do not have a sweet smell.
5. Doesn't the old <u>clock</u> on the bank tower work anymore?
6. Porcupines <u>can climb</u> trees.
7. Through the long tunnel roared the freight <u>train</u>.
8. Did <u>Lance</u> find his catcher's mitt?
9. A young <u>horse</u> is called a foal.
10. I <u>have</u> never <u>ridden</u> on a Ferris wheel.

A Sentence

Why do you speak or write? You have information or ideas you want other people to know. This information is so important you want to make sure people understand what you are saying or writing. To do this, you must be able to recognize complete thoughts and use them.

A **sentence** is a group of words that expresses a complete thought.

A group of words that does not express a complete thought is called a *fragment*. Notice in the following examples that fragments leave unanswered questions. More information must be added to make the fragments into sentences. (*See pages 21–23 for more information.*)

FRAGMENT   Listens to the radio. [Who listens?]

SENTENCE   **My older sister** listens to the radio.

FRAGMENT   A large black crow. [What did it do?]

SENTENCE   A large black crow **landed on the barn.**

EXERCISE 1   Recognizing Sentences

Number your paper 1 to 10. Then label each group of words *sentence* or *fragment*.

1. A visit to the newspaper office.
2. Lightning lit up the sky.
3. Watched a bulldozer scoop up the mound of dirt.
4. Rain and more rain every day this week.
5. The submarine explored the ocean floor.
6. The white horse in the center ring.
7. Sound travels one mile in about five seconds.
8. Hunted for treasure in the sunken ship.
9. The swing under the apple tree.
10. Bravely dove into the cold water.

Kinds of Sentences

All sentences are complete thoughts, but different sentences can have different purposes. Most sentences make a statement. Others ask a question or give a command, and a few sentences express strong feeling. To decide what punctuation mark should go at the end of a sentence, think about the purpose of that sentence.

1b ▶ A **declarative sentence** makes a statement or expresses an opinion. It ends with a period.

We spent five hours at an amusement park last weekend. [statement]

Amusement parks are so much fun. [opinion]

1c ▶ An **interrogative sentence** asks a question. It ends with a question mark.

Have you been to the new amusement park?

1d ▶ An **imperative sentence** makes a request or gives a command. It ends with either a period or an exclamation point.

Go to the amusement park with us next weekend. [This imperative sentence ends with a period because it is a mild request.]

Just think of all the excitement! [This imperative sentence ends with an exclamation point because it is a strong command.]

1e ▶ An **exclamatory sentence** expresses strong feeling. It ends with an exclamation point.

What a great time we'll have!

EXERCISE 2 Classifying Sentences

Number your paper 1 to 10. Write each sentence, using the correct end mark. Then label each sentence *declarative*, *interrogative*, *imperative*, or *exclamatory*.

EXAMPLE   Tigers live in the jungle.

ANSWER   Tigers live in the jungle. declarative

Bengal Tigers

1. Have you ever seen a live tiger
2. Look at this picture of a Bengal tiger
3. This tiger is about nine feet long and weighs over 600 pounds
4. That is an enormous animal
5. What do tigers eat
6. They eat other animals, fish, and even crocodiles
7. Listen to another fact about Bengal tigers
8. The design of black stripes is a different pattern on each side of the tiger
9. That's amazing
10. These beautiful animals have almost no enemies

EXERCISE 3 Classifying Sentences

Number your paper 1 to 10. Write each sentence, using the correct end mark. Then label each sentence *declarative*, *interrogative*, *imperative*, or *exclamatory*.

Great Inventors

1. Have you read about China in your history book
2. Look at this paragraph
3. The Chinese were great inventors
4. They invented paper
5. How did they make paper
6. They beat old rags, tree bark, and even fishing nets to a soft pulp
7. That sounds exhausting
8. Turn to the next page
9. The Chinese also invented the compass
10. The world would be very different today without paper and compasses

Subjects and Predicates

A sentence expresses a complete thought because it always has two parts. The first part of the sentence is the *complete subject*. The subject names the person, place, thing, or idea the sentence is about. The second part of the sentence is the *complete predicate*. The predicate tells what the subject is or does.

┌──────complete subject──────┐ ┌──────────complete predicate──────────┐
That large black cat is the mother of these kittens.
[*That large black cat* names the thing the sentence is about. *Is the mother of these kittens* tells what the complete subject is.]

┌──────────complete subject──────────┐ ┌──────complete predicate──────┐
The manager of the store orders the new supplies. [*The manager of the store* names the person the sentence is about. *Orders the new supplies* tells what the complete subject does.]

1f A **complete subject** includes all the words used to identify the person, place, thing, or idea that the sentence is about.

1g A **complete predicate** includes all the words that tell what the subject is doing, or that tell something about the subject.

COMPLETE SUBJECT	COMPLETE PREDICATE
(*names the person, place, thing, or idea the sentence is about*)	(*tells what the subject is or does*)
A famous actress	arrived in a limousine.
The deep growl of the dog	frightened the children.
Hot soup on a cold day	tastes delicious.
The grandfather clock	chimes every hour.
Every year our school	has a science fair.
The woman in that picture	is my aunt from Florida.
The light on the corner	blinks all the time.
Birds	fly.
I	love music.

EXERCISE 4 Finding Complete Subjects and Predicates

Number your paper 1 to 10. Write each sentence. Then draw one line under each complete subject and two lines under each complete predicate.

EXAMPLE   Your heart is about the size of your fist.

ANSWER   <u>Your heart</u> <u><u>is about the size of your fist.</u></u>

Your Body

1. The white cells in your blood fight disease.
2. Some of a baby's bones are soft at birth.
3. Most people over 21 have 32 permanent teeth.
4. Your liver stores extra vitamins and minerals.
5. Hair on your head grows a half inch each month.
6. A person's normal body temperature is 98.6° F.
7. Every cell in your body needs protein.
8. Your stomach stretches like a balloon.
9. People's voices get deeper around the age of 14.
10. Your rib cage protects your lungs.

EXERCISE 5 Combining Complete Subjects and Predicates

Number your paper 1 to 10. Match a subject in column A with a predicate in column B. Then combine them to form a sentence that makes sense. Sentences should begin with capital letters and end with appropriate end marks.

A	B
1. that blue Jeep	a. won the championship
2. the umpire	b. have feathers
3. the girls' team	c. is closest to the sun
4. Mercury	d. works at a shipyard
5. the heavy rain	e. has a powerful engine
6. several goldfish	f. gave me a headache
7. all birds	g. called a strike
8. Kermit the Frog	h. swam in the small bowl
9. the loud noises	i. spoiled our picnic
10. my oldest brother	j. is green

Simple Subjects

Most complete subjects include more than one word. Sometimes complete subjects are quite long. Other times they are quite short. Within each complete subject, however, there is one main word that tells what the sentence is about. This main word is called the *simple subject.*

1h ▶ A **simple subject** is the main word in the complete subject.

To find the simple subject, ask yourself *Who or what is doing something?* or *About whom or what is some statement being made?*

┌──────complete subject──────┐
The **train** through town stops every day at two o'clock. [What word answers the question *Who or what is doing something?*]

┌───────complete subject───────┐
The **man** in the next apartment is a deep-sea diver. [What word answers the question *About whom or what is some statement being made?*]

┌──complete subject──┐
Those black **pens** have my name on them. [What word answers the question *Who or what is doing something?*]

┌────────complete subject────────┐
Computer Wizard on Maple Road gave away two new computers. [*Computer Wizard* is the simple subject. Both words are the name of *one* place.]

┌──────complete subject──────┐
The Phantom Tollbooth tells a fantasy story about a boy named Milo. [*The Phantom Tollbooth* is the simple subject as well as the complete subject. All three words are the title of *one* book.]

A complete subject and a simple subject can be the same.

Water poured into the basement.

NOTE: Throughout the rest of this book, the simple subject will be called the *subject.*

EXERCISE 6 *Finding Complete and Simple Subjects*

Number your paper 1 to 10. Write each complete subject.
Then underline each subject.

EXAMPLE   White squirrels live in Olney, Illinois.
ANSWER   white squirrels

An Unusual Bridge

1. People in this town saw them first 80 years ago.
2. The white fur of these squirrels is unusual.
3. Their eyes are pink.
4. A law in Illinois protects these rare animals from careless drivers.
5. The highway through town has squirrel signs.
6. The police in Olney wear patches with squirrels on them.
7. Amos Peters built the world's narrowest bridge in Olney in 1963.
8. This unusual bridge is for the squirrels.
9. Nutty Narrows Bridge crosses Olympia Way, the main street in town.
10. Peanuts tempted the squirrels across the first time.

EXERCISE 7 *Finding Subjects*

Number your paper 1 to 10. Then write each subject.

The Incas

1. The Incas built a great empire in South America in the fifteenth century.
2. This mighty empire stretched 2,000 miles.
3. Many great roads connected the capital with other parts of the empire.
4. Runners for the government carried messages 600 miles in just five days on these roads.
5. The capital of the empire was in present-day Peru.
6. Some buildings there were covered with gold.
7. Six million Indians lived in the empire.
8. The people of this tribe were very smart.
9. Workers built irrigation systems and terraced farms.
10. Central governments in cities planned these projects.

9

Simple Predicates, or Verbs

Like complete subjects, most complete predicates contain more than one word. Within each complete predicate, however, there is one main word or phrase that tells what the subject is or does. This main word or phrase is called the *simple predicate,* or *verb.*

1i A **simple predicate,** or **verb,** is the main word or phrase in the complete predicate.

To find some verbs, ask *What is the subject doing?* or *What did the subject do?* These verbs show action.

┌──────────complete predicate──────────┐
The airplane **skidded** slightly on the wet runway.
[What word answers the question *What did the subject do?*]

Some verbs do not show action. Verbs of this kind tell something about the subject. Following is a list of verb forms that are used to make a statement about a subject.

Verbs That Make Statements				
am	are	is	was	were

┌──────────complete predicate──────────┐
The magazine **is** on the table beside the sofa.
┌──────complete predicate──────┐
The decorations **were** blue and silver.
┌──────complete predicate──────┐
The game **was** over before the rain.

A complete predicate and a simple predicate can be the same, as in the following examples.

The game **ended.**

My alarm clock **broke.**

The green light **changed.**

EXERCISE 8 *Finding Complete Predicates and Verbs*

Number your paper 1 to 10. Write each complete predicate. Then underline each verb.

EXAMPLE   Mars is a close neighbor of the earth.

ANSWER   <u>is</u> a close neighbor of the earth

Mars

1. Astronomers first looked closely at the planet Mars in 1965.
2. Mariner 4 flew by the planet.
3. They learned many new things about the "Red Planet" from this trip.
4. The red color of Mars is from rust.
5. Pictures of Mars show a solid surface.
6. The surface has many craters, volcanoes, canyons, and empty river beds.
7. The soil on Mars contains some water.
8. The temperatures on Mars are very low.
9. Dust storms block the sun's radiation.
10. Ice caps cover both of the poles on Mars.

EXERCISE 9 *Finding Verbs*

Number your paper 1 to 10. Then write each verb.

Surfing

1. A statue in Peru dates back to pre-Incan times.
2. This small figure is a surfer.
3. Polynesian surfers performed for Captain Cook in 1777.
4. These surfers used wooden canoes and boards up to 18 feet long.
5. People in California watched the first surfer in America in 1910.
6. Many early surfboards weighed over 100 pounds.
7. Tom Blake invented a lighter board in the 1920s.
8. He added a keel under a surfboard in 1935.
9. A keel gives a surfer more control of the direction of the surfboard.
10. Surfing was very popular in America in the 1960s.

Verb Phrases. Sometimes a verb needs other words to help it make a statement or to tell what action is taking place. Such words are called *helping verbs,* or auxiliary verbs. The main verb plus any helping verbs make up a *verb phrase.* Following is a list of the common helping verbs.

Common Helping Verbs	
be	am, is, are, was, were, be, being, been
have	has, have, had
do	do, does, did
other verbs	may, might, must, can, could, shall, should, will, would

┌─verb phrase─┐
The bicycles **are** racing around the track.

┌──── verb phrase ────┐
The temperature **has been** rising since noon.

Sometimes one or more words separate the parts of a verb phrase. The verb phrases in the example below are in heavy type.

I **have** always **made** my bed in the morning.

Did you **take** art? [You *did take* art.]

Our team **did** not **win** the game on Saturday in Middleton. [*Not* and its contraction *n't* are never part of a verb phrase.]

Some of the common helping verbs in the box can be main verbs. They are only helping verbs when they are part of a verb phrase.

MAIN VERB	Susan **is** my sister.
HELPING VERB	Susan **is** *playing* the piano.
MAIN VERB	Phil **does** the dishes every night.
HELPING VERB	Phil ***does*** *wash* the glasses carefully.

NOTE: Throughout the rest of this book, a verb phrase will be called a verb.

EXERCISE 10 Finding Verb Phrases

Number your paper 1 to 10. Then write each verb phrase.

1. A big white convertible was leading the parade.
2. The Eagles have won their first four games.
3. Two horses are galloping in this direction.
4. A chameleon can capture an insect 12 inches away.
5. I am singing a solo in the concert.
6. A blue whale may reach a length of over 100 feet.
7. Bottles with messages in them have traveled many thousands of miles from the points of their origin.
8. The picnic might be canceled.
9. A person's heart will beat about three million times in a lifetime.
10. We would like two seats in the balcony.

EXERCISE 11 Finding Verb Phrases

Number your paper 1 to 10. Then write each verb phrase.

1. He is not riding to the fair with us.
2. Does life exist on other planets?
3. I shall faithfully deliver your newspaper every morning by 6:00 A.M.
4. Betsy has always sat in this seat.
5. Did the mail arrive yet?
6. Jim is constantly making the Honor Roll.
7. Has everyone returned from the treasure hunt?
8. My sister has nearly missed the bus twice in the past week.
9. Could I answer that question?
10. Mark isn't answering his telephone.

EXERCISE 12 Writing Sentences

Write a five-sentence newspaper article that describes the construction of a building, a road, or a bridge in your town. At least two of the verbs should have a helping verb. When you are finished, underline each verb.

TIME-OUT FOR REVIEW • • • • •

Number your paper 1 to 20. Then write the subject and the verb in each sentence.

EXAMPLE Bob Martwick was looking for
     a very special cat in 1966.

ANSWER Bob Martwick was looking

Morris

1. This cat would star in TV commercials for a cat food company.
2. Pictures of hundreds of cats flooded Bob Martwick's office.
3. The cats were of every size, shape, and color.
4. This trainer of animals didn't see the right cat in any of the pictures.
5. The original Morris was living in an animal shelter in Chicago at the time.
6. This 15-pound tomcat eventually caught the eye of Martwick.
7. Stardom was his after only one audition.
8. A film with Burt Reynolds in 1973 made Morris even more famous.
9. An organization for animals gave Morris a Patsy Award that same year.
10. This trophy is like an Oscar for animal actors.
11. Fans of this finicky cat could buy Morris bowls, T-shirts, and calendars.
12. All kinds of Morris products were for sale.
13. Stores across the country were selling thousands of copies of his biography.
14. The book is called *Morris: An Intimate Biography.*
15. Morris's life was not always easy.
16. Catnappers often followed him.
17. Round-the-clock guards were always guarding him.
18. This famous cat died of heart failure in 1978.
19. He was 17 years old.
20. An understudy is now taking Morris's place on the TV commercials.

Position of Subjects

In most declarative sentences, the subject of the sentence comes before the verb. When the subject comes before the verb, the sentence is in its *natural order*. In the following examples of sentences in natural order, each subject is underlined once, and each verb is underlined twice.

Those storm <u>clouds</u> <u><u>are getting</u></u> darker.

The <u>forecaster</u> on television <u><u>predicted</u></u> rain today.

Once in a while, a declarative sentence is not written in natural order. When the verb comes before the subject, the sentence is in *inverted order*. To find the subject in an inverted sentence, turn the sentence around to its natural order.

INVERTED ORDER Around the fire <u><u>sat</u></u> the <u>campers.</u>

NATURAL ORDER The <u>campers</u> <u><u>sat</u></u> around the fire.

INVERTED ORDER Across the ice <u><u>skated</u></u> the <u>children.</u>

NATURAL ORDER The <u>children</u> <u><u>skated</u></u> across the ice.

Most interrogative sentences are written in inverted order. In those sentences part of the verb phrase usually comes before the subject. To find the subject in an interrogative sentence, change the question into a statement.

QUESTION <u><u>Are</u></u> many <u>ships</u> <u><u>docked</u></u> in the harbor?

STATEMENT Many <u>ships</u> <u><u>are docked</u></u> in the harbor.

QUESTION <u><u>Hasn't</u></u> <u>Jill</u> <u><u>called</u></u> yet?

STATEMENT <u>Jill</u> <u><u>hasn't</u></u> <u><u>called</u></u> yet. [<u>Jill</u> <u><u>has</u></u> not <u><u>called</u></u> yet.]

The subject of an imperative sentence is not stated in the sentence, but it is understood to be there. *You*, the person or persons receiving the command or the request, is always the *understood subject*.

COMMAND OR (<u>you</u>) <u><u>Wash</u></u> the dishes tonight.

REQUEST (<u>you</u>) Please <u><u>wait</u></u> for me in the library.

15

EXERCISE 13 *Finding Subjects and Verbs*

Number your paper 1 to 10. Then write the subject and the verb in each sentence. If the subject is an *understood you,* write *you* in parentheses.

EXAMPLE   Look at that huge waterfall.

ANSWER   (you) look

1. Can you tie a square knot?
2. Please answer the doorbell.
3. In the back of the drawer lay a gold coin.
4. Do all frogs croak?
5. Write clearly and neatly.
6. Has Frankie taken my catcher's mitt again?
7. Will the refreshments be served soon?
8. Make yourself a sandwich for lunch.
9. From the sidelines ran the defensive team in green and gold uniforms.
10. Is Clara making another model ship?

EXERCISE 14 *Finding Subjects and Verbs*

Number your paper 1 to 10. Then write the subject and the verb in each sentence. If the subject is an *understood you,* write *you* in parentheses.

1. Can monkeys swim?
2. Work quietly at your seats.
3. Across the floor spun the top.
4. Aren't the actors rehearsing for the play?
5. Set the alarm for six o'clock.
6. Did the Los Angeles Raiders win the Super Bowl last year?
7. From the attic came a strange noise.
8. Have the wild animals at the zoo been fed this morning?
9. Turn the calendar to March.
10. Don't put the newspapers and magazines on the kitchen table.

*C*ompound Subjects
and Compound Verbs

Sometimes a sentence is about more than one person or thing. For that reason, a sentence can have more than one subject. Two or more subjects that share the same verb are called a *compound subject*. The parts of a compound subject are usually joined by the conjunction *and* or *or*.

1j ▷ A **compound subject** is two or more subjects in one sentence that have the same verb and are joined by a conjunction.

In the following examples, each subject is underlined once and each verb is underlined twice. Notice that each subject shares the same verb—*make*.

ONE SUBJECT	Dogs make good pets.
COMPOUND SUBJECT	Dogs and cats make good pets.
COMPOUND SUBJECT	Dogs, cats, and fish make good pets.

Sometimes the subject is doing more than one thing, or more than one statement is being made about the subject. For those reasons, a sentence can have more than one verb. In a sentence where two or more verbs share the same subject, the sentence has a *compound verb*. The parts of a compound verb, like the parts of a compound subject, are usually joined by the conjunction *and* or *or*.

1k ▷ A **compound verb** is two or more verbs that have the same subject and are joined by a conjunction.

Notice that each verb in the following examples shares the same subject—*Jon*.

ONE VERB	Jon looked at me.
COMPOUND VERB	Jon looked and smiled at me.
COMPOUND VERB	Jon looked, smiled, and laughed at me.

17

EXERCISE 15 *Finding Compound Subjects and Verbs*

Number your paper 1 to 10.
Then write each compound
subject or compound verb.

EXAMPLE   Mercury and Venus
are closest to the sun.

ANSWER   Mercury, Venus

The Planets

1. Helium and hydrogen make up Mercury's atmosphere.
2. A spacecraft landed on Venus and sent pictures of the planet to the earth.
3. Within an hour the spacecraft was crushed and was destroyed by fire.
4. *Mariner 4* and other spacecrafts have visited Mars.
5. *Voyager 2* flew past Jupiter and Saturn and found no solid surface for a landing.
6. Telescopes and satellites have not learned very much about Jupiter and Saturn.
7. In 1610, Galileo looked through his telescope and discovered four of Jupiter's moons.
8. Ganymede and Europa are moons of Jupiter.
9. The great winds on Saturn blow constantly and form colorful bands of clouds.
10. Venus, Mars, Mercury, Saturn, and Jupiter are visible from Earth without a telescope.

EXERCISE 16 *Finding Compound Subjects and Verbs*

Number your paper 1 to 10. Write each sentence. Then underline each subject once and each verb twice.

Islands

1. Have you ever read or studied about islands?
2. A long time ago, volcanoes exploded and poured lava out of their tops.
3. Smoke and cinders filled the air.
4. Later the hot lava cooled and changed into islands.

5. Other islands were created or formed from erosion.
6. Oceans and streams were constantly washing some of the land into the water.
7. The wind loosened the soil and blew it away.
8. In other places the earth dried and sank.
9. Water from the ocean then filled the low places and made new islands.
10. England, Japan, and Greenland are islands.

EXERCISE 17 Writing Compound Subjects and Verbs

Number your paper 1 to 10. Rewrite each sentence, adding either a subject or a verb. The word in parentheses tells you whether the sentence should have a compound subject or a compound verb.

EXAMPLE   My brother swept the floor. (verb)
POSSIBLE ANSWER   My brother swept the floor and vacuumed the carpet.

1. Elephants are large animals. (subject)
2. The actresses bowed before the audience. (subject)
3. My friends were watching the movie . (verb)
4. Sue carefully cut out the red paper heart . (verb)
5. The potatoes are on the bottom shelf. (subject)
6. Bruce ran down the field . (verb)
7. Those apples look good. (subject)
8. Diamonds sparkle. (subject)
9. The bird flew to the feeder . (verb)
10. Mom bought a roast . (verb)

EXERCISE 18 Writing Sentences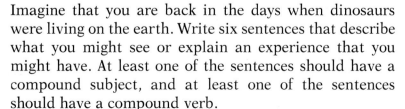

Imagine that you are back in the days when dinosaurs were living on the earth. Write six sentences that describe what you might see or explain an experience that you might have. At least one of the sentences should have a compound subject, and at least one of the sentences should have a compound verb.

19

TIME-OUT FOR REVIEW • • • • •

Number your paper 1 to 15. Then write the subject and the verb in each sentence. If the subject of a sentence is an *understood you,* write *you* in parentheses.

EXAMPLE   Do you enjoy gymnastics?
ANSWER   you, do enjoy

Early Training

1. The Greeks were building gymnasiums over 2,500 years ago.
2. Boys and young men in Greece trained very hard for the Olympics.
3. Healthy bodies were important to the early Greeks.
4. Teenagers would spend many hours in a gymnasium every day.
5. Around the track ran the eager runners many times.
6. These athletes also lifted weights and climbed ropes.
7. The Olympics was the goal of each boy.
8. Greek girls could not go inside the gymnasiums.
9. Do you agree with this rule?
10. Roman troops eventually entered Greece and conquered it.
11. One person in the Roman government canceled the Olympics.
12. The gymnasiums throughout Greece were officially closed in 392 A.D.
13. Would the Olympics ever begin again?
14. A man in Germany would finally begin the Olympics again in the 1800s.
15. Watch the gymnastics during the next Olympics.

EXERCISE 19   Writing Sentences

Write five sentences that describe a gymnastic event in the Olympics. You might tell about the side horse, the parallel bars, or the balance beam. If you have never seen these events, describe an exercise that could help an athlete build a stronger body.

Sentence Fragments

At the beginning of this chapter, you learned that an incomplete sentence is called a *fragment*.

1I ▶ A **sentence fragment** is a group of words that does not express a complete thought.

To express a complete thought, a sentence must have a subject and a verb. If either part is missing, the group of words is a fragment. In the following examples, each subject is underlined once, and each verb is underlined twice.

NO SUBJECT   Towered above the valley. [What towered above the valley?]

SENTENCE   The mountains towered above the valley.

NO VERB   A girl on the team. [What did she do?]

SENTENCE   A girl on the team injured her knee.

NO SUBJECT
OR VERB   Down the dusty road. [Who or what was on the dusty road? What happened there?]

SENTENCE   The old truck bumped down the dusty road.

EXERCISE 20 Recognizing Sentence Fragments

Number your paper 1 to 10. Then label each group of words *sentence* or *fragment*.

1. Flashed across the dark sky.
2. The puppy cried for its mother.
3. The lifeguard at the beach.
4. The runner on third base.
5. The waves beat against the rocks.
6. Inside the old shack by the railroad tracks.
7. Scratching at the backdoor.
8. The trophy on the mantle.
9. At eight o'clock sharp.
10. The South Pole is in Antarctica.

Ways to Correct Sentence Fragments

When you finish writing, always read your work aloud. Listen and look for fragments. If you find any, correct them. You can correct sentence fragments in one of two ways. One way is to attach a fragment to a nearby sentence. The other way is to make the fragment a separate sentence by adding words that make it a complete thought.

SENTENCE AND FRAGMENT	Tim made that birdfeeder. From an old milk carton.
ATTACHED	Tim made that birdfeeder from an old milk carton.
SEPARATE SENTENCES	Tim made that birdfeeder. He made it from an old milk carton.

EXERCISE 21   Correcting Sentence Fragments

Number your paper 1 to 10. Then correct each fragment by writing one complete sentence.

EXAMPLE	Judy got your postcard yesterday. And showed it to me.
POSSIBLE ANSWER	Judy got your postcard yesterday and showed it to me.

1. The Wright brothers made their first airplane flight. On December 17, 1903.
2. The crew members of the sinking ship.
3. I dropped the eggs. Onto the clean kitchen floor.
4. The mayor greeted us. And shook our hands.
5. In first place in the local basketball tournament this spring.
6. A large display of the students' science projects.
7. Bryan took the ball from the quarterback. And raced 70 yards for a touchdown.
8. Throughout the rain forests of Africa.
9. The horses on Mr. Potter's farm.
10. Nervously paced back and forth.

EXERCISE 22 Editing for Sentence Fragments

Rewrite the following paragraphs, correcting each sentence fragment. Start each sentence with a capital letter and end each sentence with a period.

EXAMPLE   This is a true story. About two unusual friends.

ANSWER   This is a true story about two unusual friends.

Unusual Friends

One day Frank and Ellen Hensel dug a one-acre pond. Near their Vermont home. Then, just for fun, they inflated a plastic toy dolphin. And floated it on the new pond. This blue and white beach toy had big eyes, long eyelashes, and a big broad smile. It bobbed in the breeze. And looked very much alive.

A large gray and black Canadian goose. Suddenly appeared on the pond one day. A breeze caught the dolphin, and it drifted across the pond. The goose quickly paddled. After the plastic fish.

Several days passed. The Hensels watched the goose. And worried about it. All the other geese were migrating to the South. Every day flocks of geese in V formations. Flew over their house.

One morning the Hensels heard the honking of the goose. And looked outside. A strong wind was blowing, and the dolphin was swirling in all directions. The goose was paddling as quickly as it could. But couldn't keep up with its friend.

The Hensels looked out the window. On the following morning. A branch had poked a hole. In the dolphin's side. It lay on its side, half under the water. Then the dolphin let out some bubbles. And sank to the bottom.

The goose was confused. It swam around its lost friend. In huge circles. It honked and flapped its wings. For two days the big bird watched over the blue and white form. At the bottom of the pond. Then finally, with a downward glance, the bird flapped its wings. And flew into the bright October sky.

Diagraming Subjects and Verbs

Throughout this chapter and the next six chapters of this book, you will read and *hear* how words are used in a sentence. Now you have a chance to *see* how they are used. Diagrams are pictures of sentences. Diagrams can help you easily find and identify all the parts of a sentence.

Subjects and Verbs in Declarative Sentences. Draw a straight baseline. Write the subject and the verb on this line. Then draw another line to separate the subject from the verb. Include capital letters but do not include the end mark.

Balloons broke.

| Balloons | broke |

Children are singing.

| Children | are singing |

Subjects and Verbs in Interrogative Sentences. Turn the question into a statement and diagram it like a declarative sentence.

Is Dad sleeping? (Dad is sleeping.)

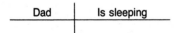

| Dad | Is sleeping |

Has traffic stopped? (Traffic has stopped.)

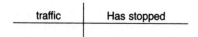

| traffic | Has stopped |

Subjects and Verbs in Imperative Sentences. Write the understood *you* in parentheses in the subject position on the diagram.

Wait!

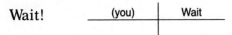

| (you) | Wait |

Compound Subjects and Verbs. Write the parts of a compound subject or a compound verb on parallel lines. Write the word that joins them on a broken line between them.

Men and women were talking.

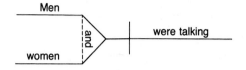

Andy draws and paints.

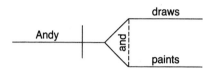

Wait and listen.

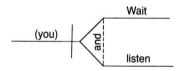

EXERCISE 23   Diagraming Subjects and Verbs

Diagram the following sentences or copy them. If your teacher tells you to copy them, draw one line under each subject and two lines under each verb. If the subject is an understood *you*, write *you* in parentheses.

1. Sand flew.
2. Leaves are falling.
3. Is water dripping?
4. Stop!
5. Ken was working.
6. Jerry and Martin are skating.
7. Flowers wilt and die.
8. Do fish sleep?
9. Speak.
10. Chipmunks and bears are hibernating.

_A_pplication to Writing

People do not always write the same way that they talk. When they write, they sometimes use short, choppy sentences. When they talk, however, they usually use longer, smoother sentences.

If you want to make your writing smoother, always read your written work aloud. If you see or hear two short, choppy sentences together, think about whether you can combine them. You can combine two sentences, for example, if they have the same verb but different subjects.

In the following examples, each subject is underlined once and each verb is underlined twice.

TWO SENTENCES	Vitamins build strong bones and teeth. Minerals also build strong bones and teeth. [These sentences can be combined with a compound subject.]
COMBINED	Vitamins and minerals build strong bones and teeth.
TWO SENTENCES	Stephanie picked some green apples. Margaret also picked some green apples. [These sentences can be combined with a compound subject.]
COMBINED	Stephanie and Margaret picked some green apples.

NOTE: Some repeated or unnecessary words can be dropped when sentences are combined.

You can also combine two short sentences that have the same subject but different verbs.

TWO SENTENCES	Kate lost her house key. Kate found it the next day. [These sentences can be combined with a compound verb.]
COMBINED	Kate lost her house key but found it the next day.

TWO SENTENCES The <u>detective</u> <u>discovered</u> a secret drawer in the desk. The <u>detective</u> <u>opened</u> it. [These sentences can be combined with a compound verb.]

COMBINED The <u>detective</u> <u>discovered</u> a secret drawer in the desk and <u>opened</u> it.

EXERCISE 24 Combining Sentences

Number your paper 1 to 10. Then combine each pair of sentences into one sentence with a compound subject or a compound verb. Use the word in brackets to join the compound subject or the compound verb.

EXAMPLE One type of jet makes a vertical take-off. It flies horizontally. [but]

ANSWER One type of jet makes a vertical take-off but flies horizontally.

1. Those chickadees eat at our birdfeeder. Those wrens also eat there. [and]
2. Some blackberries grow wild. Some raspberries also grow wild. [and]
3. Two raccoons turned over our trash can. The raccoons hunted for food. [and]
4. Al missed the bus. Al caught the next one. [but]
5. Crayfish are tasty snacks for raccoons. Snails are also tasty snacks for them. [and]
6. The rabbit stood on its hind legs. The rabbit listened carefully for any enemies. [and]
7. Crocodiles always live in warm places. Alligators also live in warm places. [and]
8. The dog chased the cat. The dog didn't catch it. [but]
9. The driver of the dog team sits on the sled. The driver gives the dogs orders. [and]
10. Elephants eat grass. Zebras eat grass. [and]

Chapter Review

A **Finding Subjects and Verbs.** Number your paper 1 to 10. Then write the subject and the verb in each sentence. If the subject of a sentence is an understood *you*, write *you* in parentheses.

1. My two friends are going to Washington, D.C. on their spring vacation.
2. The senator from Tennessee has not arrived at the airport yet.
3. Babe Ruth was a famous baseball player.
4. Do students in the sixth grade study China?
5. Look at that huge hornet's nest!
6. The reporter asked questions and took notes.
7. Behind our backyard runs a small stream.
8. The new stadium in town holds over 10,000 people.
9. Have the lakes and the streams frozen already?
10. The rain was quietly pattering on the tent all night.

B **Finding Subjects and Verbs.** Number your paper 1 to 10. Then write the subject and the verb in each sentence. If the subject of a sentence is an understood *you*, write *you* in parentheses.

Birds

1. Birds do not have teeth.
2. The colorful parrot can copy human words.
3. Most birds build nests and lay eggs in them.
4. Ducks, geese, and swans belong to the same family.
5. A male swan will choose a mate for life.
6. The brown pelican dives into the water and scoops fish into its beak.
7. Pigeons and doves have carried messages for people.
8. The biggest birds in the world are ostriches.
9. Does your family ever feed the birds in your yard?
10. Don't ever give birds anything salty.

C **Recognizing Sentence Fragments.** Number your paper 1 to 10. Then label each group of words *sentence* or *fragment*.

1. The supply room in the main office.
2. The honeybee went from flower to flower.
3. And called the local fire department as quickly as possible.
4. Wind your watch every morning.
5. Over the fence in the backyard.
6. The butterfly on that flower.
7. On the bottom of an old trunk.
8. Soared high into the air.
9. Young monkeys ride everywhere on their mothers' backs.
10. The emperor penguin lives in Antarctica.

*M*astery *T*est

Number your paper 1 to 10. Write each underlined word or words. Then label each one *subject* or *verb*.

1. The <u>light</u> in the window was shining.
2. The turtle and the <u>armadillo</u> have hard shells for protection.
3. A cottontail rabbit <u>will dig</u> a hole in the snow for warmth.
4. <u>Will</u> those squirrels in the yard <u>eat</u> these dried pumpkin seeds?
5. Does a <u>giraffe</u> have a black tongue?
6. Leroy borrowed my science book but <u>returned</u> it yesterday.
7. Up the stairs raced the two small Pekingese <u>puppies</u>.
8. Can a <u>cat</u> see in total darkness?
9. Barbara <u>has</u> never <u>found</u> her ring either at home or at school.
10. A zebra <u>is</u> a relative of the horse.

2

Nouns and Pronouns

Diagnostic Test

Number your paper 1 to 10. Write each underlined word. Then label each one *noun* or *pronoun*.

EXAMPLE <u>I</u> ride a subway to <u>school</u>.

ANSWER I—pronoun school—noun

1. <u>He</u> took a picture of the tallest <u>giraffe</u>.
2. This <u>letter</u> is addressed to <u>you</u>.
3. <u>Dad</u> is making <u>our</u> dinner tonight.
4. Was <u>she</u> the winner of the second <u>race</u>?
5. <u>My</u> friend wore a red <u>wig</u> in the play.
6. The <u>tire</u> on <u>his</u> new bicycle is flat.
7. Did <u>they</u> cross the border into <u>Canada</u>?
8. <u>I</u> will be an <u>astronaut</u> one day.
9. The dog has <u>mud</u> on <u>its</u> feet!
10. <u>We</u> have great <u>faith</u> in the future of the world.

*N*ouns

Like people, words have jobs. A job is what someone or something does. Each word in a sentence does a particular job. Each job is called a *part of speech*. In English, there are eight different parts of speech, as shown in the following list.

The Eight Parts of Speech

noun [names]   **preposition** [relates]
pronoun [replaces]   **conjunction** [connects]
verb [states action or being] **interjection** [expresses
adjective [describes, limits] strong feeling]
adverb [describes, limits]

Nouns are the most common of the parts of speech. Sometimes nouns are called naming words because they name people, places, things, and ideas.

2a ▶ A **noun** is a word that names a person, place, thing, or idea.

PEOPLE   Mary, Jake, doctor, boys, mechanics, chefs, Mr. Harrison, Ms. McInroy

PLACES   home, hospitals, forest, zoo, Philadelphia, Lake Michigan, France

THINGS   [*that can be seen, heard, or touched*] pen, whistle, blanket, animals, sky, earth, bells

[*that cannot be seen, heard, or touched*] memory, dreams, minutes, headache, life, heat, science, summer

IDEAS AND QUALITIES   friendship, honesty, kindness, freedom, hope, courage, ambition, love, independence, peace, respect, honesty

EXERCISE 1 Finding Nouns

Number your paper 1 to 10. Then write each noun. There are 25 nouns.

Still a Mystery

1. Explorers have covered most of the earth.
2. The ocean, however, is still a big mystery.
3. Today scientists are exploring deeper and deeper water in a bathysphere.
4. This is a big ball made of metal.
5. Divers can watch strange fish through its windows.
6. Some bathyspheres have doors.
7. People can go out and look around as long as they have a tank of air.
8. They have discovered high mountains and deep valleys under the water.
9. Oceans are very important.
10. They provide food for people, and they are highways for ships.

Common and Proper Nouns

Some nouns are the general names of people, places, and things. Nouns of this kind are called *common nouns.* Other nouns are the names of particular people, places, and things. These nouns are called *proper nouns.* A proper noun always begins with a capital letter.

COMMON NOUNS	PROPER NOUNS
girl	Karen
state	Tennessee
team	Chicago Bears
building	Empire State Building

NOTE: Some proper nouns like *Empire State Building* include more than one word. *Empire State Building* is still only one noun because it is *one* name of *one* building.

EXERCISE 2 Finding Common and Proper Nouns

Number your paper 1 to 10. Write each sentence. Then put a *C* over each common noun and a *P* over each proper noun. (A date is a common noun.) There are 20 nouns.

The First
1. The tallest mountain in the world is Mount Everest.
2. It is in the Himalayas between India and China.
3. English-speaking people first saw it in 1850.
4. One hundred years passed before it was conquered.
5. The first successful climber was Sir Edmund Hillary.
6. He faced constant danger.
7. Hillary often had to cling tightly to the steep cliffs.
8. He looked like an ant on a wall.
9. Icy winds hurt his eyes.
10. With great courage he finally reached the summit.

EXERCISE 3 Supplying Nouns

Number your paper 1 to 10. Then write a common or proper noun for each blank. (Add *a, an,* or *the* if needed.)

1. At the skating rink, I saw _____ and _____.
2. From the window I can see _____ and _____.
3. Neighboring states are _____ and _____.
4. At the store Mom bought _____ and _____.
5. The holidays I like best are _____ and _____.
6. Two things I like to eat are _____ and _____.
7. My doctor's appointment is on _____ or _____.
8. Some day I would like to be _____ or _____.
9. The colors I like best are _____ and _____.
10. Qualities I admire in people are _____ and _____.

EXERCISE 4 Writing Sentences

Write five sentences that describe various things you would put into a time capsule that would not be opened until one hundred years from today. Then underline each noun.

33

TIME-OUT FOR REVIEW • • • • •

Number your paper 1 to 10. Then write each noun. (A date is a noun.) There are 25 nouns.

**A School
for Frogs**

1. Bill Steed started college in 1970.
2. The students at his school are frogs.
3. The classes last 240 hours.
4. The little creatures work out in a pool.
5. They also lift tiny weights.
6. They eat centipedes and ladybugs to build up their strength.
7. A special snack that they like is bumblebees dipped in honey.
8. One pupil at the school was Grim Leaper.
9. He was owned by the governor of Arkansas.
10. Later this pet entered a race and became a winner.

Application to Writing

Your writing will be more lively and interesting if you substitute a specific noun like *poodle, cocker spaniel,* or *Irish setter* for a general noun like dog.

EXERCISE 5 Listing Specific Nouns

Number your paper 1 to 10. Then write at least two specific nouns for each general noun.

1. tool	6. food
2. plane	7. horn
3. state	8. city
4. bird	9. game
5. fruit	10. sport

EXERCISE 6 Writing Sentences

Write five sentences that tell about your most recent birthday. Use specific nouns whenever you can.

Pronouns

A *pronoun* is the part of speech that can be substituted for a noun. The second sentence in each pair of examples is shorter and clearer because pronouns have been substituted for nouns.

The horse swats flies off **the horse's** back with a swish of **the horse's** tail.

The horse swats flies off **its** back with a swish of **its** tail.

John asked Liz if **Liz** would help **John** fix **John's** bike.

John asked Liz if **she** would help **him** fix **his** bike.

2b A **pronoun** is a word that takes the place of one or more nouns.

Personal Pronouns

Personal pronouns are the kind of pronouns you use most often. Pronouns are divided into several groups, as shown in the following chart.

Personal Pronouns		
	SINGULAR	**PLURAL**
FIRST PERSON (speaker)	I, me my, mine	we, us our, ours
SECOND PERSON (person spoken to)	you your, yours	you your, yours
THIRD PERSON (person or thing spoken about)	he, him, his she, her, hers it, its	they, them their, theirs

NOTE: Do not confuse *its* with *it's* or *your* with *you're*. *It's* is a contraction for *it is; you're* is a contraction for *you are.*

35

FIRST PERSON PRONOUNS	**I** have **my** key with **me.**
	We must find **our** new scissors.
SECOND PERSON PRONOUNS	Are **you** wearing **your** new jacket?
	Yours are on the table.
THIRD PERSON PRONOUNS	**She** told **him** about **her** accident.
	They haven't written **their** reports yet.

EXERCISE 7 Finding Personal Pronouns

Number your paper 1 to 10. Then write each personal pronoun. There are 15 pronouns.

Cactus

1. My aunt gave me a book about plants last year in the spring.
2. I just loaned it to Judy.
3. She must be careful.
4. Too much water will hurt her cactus.
5. Its buds are very delicate.
6. Mark seldom waters his cactus plants.
7. He lets them dry out first.
8. The plants opened their buds, and they are beautiful.
9. I just love their color.
10. Unfortunately Judy overwatered hers.

Antecedents of Personal Pronouns

The word or words that a pronoun refers to, or replaces, is called an *antecedent*. An antecedent often comes before the pronoun. The antecedent may be in the same sentence or in another sentence. Sometimes a pronoun will have more than one antecedent. In the following examples, arrows point to the antecedent of each pronoun.

Stacy typed **her** report on a computer.

Nathan found a quarter. **It** was new and shiny.

The dog and the cat have had **their** shots.

36

*E*XERCISE 8 *Finding Pronouns and Antecedents*

Number your paper 1 to 10. Then write each personal pronoun and its antecedent.

EXAMPLE   Bill will bring his guitar.
ANSWER   his—Bill

1. Did Alma finish her homework?
2. Elephants love to spray water on their backs.
3. A raccoon always washes its food.
4. Kate and Jamie said they will call soon.
5. Chester to read his poem to the class.
6. Rico made a kite. Now he waits for a windy day.
7. Cindy left hers in the auditorium.
8. Lynn said, "I want to be a ballet dancer."
9. The parrot and the parakeets sing in their cages.
10. Gulls are good flyers. They are also good swimmers.

*T*IME-OUT FOR REVIEW • • • • •

Number your paper 1 to 10. Then write each personal pronoun and its antecedent.

1. Mother kangaroos carry their young in warm pouches.
2. David edited his story carefully.
3. A deer's antlers begin to grow in April or May. By the end of August, they are fully grown.
4. Watch out! That rose has a bee on it.
5. Baby seals sometimes ride piggyback on their mother's backs.
6. Laurie isn't here. She is babysitting tonight at the Johnsons.
7. Your boots and gloves have snow on them.
8. Lions weigh only about three pounds at birth. They are completely helpless for three weeks.
9. Paula and Susie are helping their English teacher.
10. Rob said, "The birthday party surprised me."

37

*C*hapter *R*eview

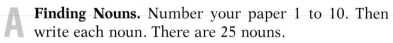

A **Finding Nouns.** Number your paper 1 to 10. Then write each noun. There are 25 nouns.

Giant
Clams

1. Most clams could fit in your hand.
2. The largest clams, however, weigh about 500 pounds!
3. One such clam could be a meal for many families.
4. Their shells are so big they could be used for a bed or a bathtub.
5. These giants are found in the Indian Ocean and in the Pacific Ocean near Australia.
6. Some people say that these mammoth creatures are their enemies.
7. Divers can get their legs or arms caught and drown.
8. These stories probably aren't true.
9. Their shells close very slowly.
10. Besides, these monsters of the ocean eat only plants.

B **Finding Pronouns.** Number your paper 1 to 10. Then write each personal pronoun. There are 20 pronouns.

1. Did you see that shooting star?
2. I have had my younger brother with me all day.
3. Theirs is the red car with yellow and blue stripes.
4. Our kitchen clock has stopped.
5. Turtles always carry their houses with them wherever they go.
6. We should take him with us.
7. She left her bag in the gym after volleyball practice today.
8. Your car is blocking ours.
9. Did he see his sister at the new mall on Farley Road?
10. A beaver steers with its tail as it swims through the water.

C **Finding Pronouns and Their Antecedents.** Number your paper 1 to 10. Then write each personal pronoun and its antecedent.

1. The quarterback injured his knee.
2. A robin makes its nest from grass and mud.
3. Carrie and Pete did their homework at the public library after school.
4. Has Regina bought her ticket yet?
5. For a while some birds lived in a nest on the porch. Then the cat discovered them.
6. Most monkeys make their homes in trees.
7. Andy said, "Save me a piece of watermelon."
8. Megan will lead her team in home runs this baseball season.
9. Farmers like ladybugs. They eat harmful insects.
10. Joshua and Nathan have bought their father a nice birthday present.

Mastery Test

Number your paper 1 to 10. Write each underlined word. Then label each one *noun* or *pronoun*.

1. On Sundays I like to read the comics in the morning newspaper.
2. Give me your new address.
3. Where did you find those wild blackberries?
4. Was he born in Connecticut?
5. They are expecting a large crowd of people at the fair on Saturday.
6. We must paint the rowboat this summer.
7. Does she have a pain in her side?
8. Mine is the umbrella with the broken handle.
9. The people in Iowa are proud of their state.
10. Does a zebra have white stripes or black stripes on its body?

3

Verbs

Number your paper 1 to 10. Write each verb or verb phrase. Then label each one *action* or *linking*.

EXAMPLE   This maple syrup is very thick.
ANSWER   is—linking

1. Oxen pulled the wagon along the pass.
2. Mr. Johnson is my piano teacher.
3. The streets were very slippery after the snowstorm.
4. Another mosquito has bitten me!
5. The ocean looks rough today.
6. The baby is always throwing the rattle on the floor.
7. Some senators have been astronauts.
8. Mom will take a plane to Memphis.
9. Do you like eggplant?
10. Those trees are 100-year-old oaks.

Action Verbs

A *verb* is one of the eight parts of speech. A verb is also a necessary part of a sentence. Without a verb, a group of words cannot be a sentence. Some verbs are called *action verbs* because they often show action.

An **action verb** tells what action a subject is performing.

To find an action verb, first find the subject. Then ask yourself *What did the subject do?*

The truck **rattled** noisily down the street. [The subject is *truck*. What did the truck do?]

Most action verbs show physical action, but some show mental action. A few verbs such as *have* and *own* show ownership or possession.

PHYSICAL ACTION   The audience **applauded** the actors.
                  The lamp **crashed** to the floor.
MENTAL ACTION   The principal **believed** our story.
                  We **wish** you much happiness.
OWNERSHIP   Andrew **has** a toothache.
                  I **own** four silver dollars.

EXERCISE 1   Finding Action Verbs

Number your paper 1 to 10. Then write each action verb.

EXAMPLE   Many people misunderstand bats.
ANSWER   misunderstand

Bats

1. Most bats eat insects or fruit.
2. Only the vampire bat drinks blood.
3. Bats see extremely well at night.
4. They also own a special type of radar.
5. Bats have very strong wings.
6. They sleep upside down.

7. Their hind feet hold objects tightly.
8. Many farmers like bats.
9. Some bats eat harmful insects on a farm.
10. A few people actually serve barbecued bats for dinner.

EXERCISE 2 Finding Action Verbs

Number your paper 1 to 10. Then write each action verb.

Glaciers

1. Glaciers shine like jewels on a mountain top.
2. Sometimes they sparkle like diamonds.
3. Over many years snow falls on mountain tops.
4. In the summer the sun melts the top layer of snow.
5. The water drips into the deep snow.
6. The water and snow freeze into a hard sheet of ice.
7. Eventually a glacier slides down a mountain.
8. Along its way it tears off large chunks of rock, some as big as houses.
9. Soon a glacier turns into icy water.
10. Then the water rushes into streams or lakes.

EXERCISE 3 Supplying Action Verbs

Number your paper 1 to 10. Then write an action verb for each blank.

EXAMPLE   The large tree _____ to the ground.
POSSIBLE ANSWER   crashed

1. Last night I _____ Mexican food for the first time.
2. The cat _____ onto the top of the refrigerator.
3. The batter _____ the ball to left field.
4. The bulldozer _____ a big hole in the backyard.
5. We _____ the school colors of blue and white.
6. Everyone _____ into the pool.
7. Mud _____ all over my new shoes.
8. Ugh! I _____ three tests on Friday.
9. My dog always _____ at strangers.
10. The speedboat _____ across the lake.

Helping Verbs

The verb of a sentence is not always one word. The main verb can be written with *helping verbs,* or auxiliary verbs. The main verb plus any helping verbs is called a *verb phrase.*

3b ▶ A **verb phrase** is a main verb plus one or more helping verbs.

Following is a list of common helping verbs.

Common Helping Verbs	
be	am, is, are, was, were, be, being, been
have	has, have, had
do	do, does, did
others	may, might, must, can, could, shall should, will, would

In the following sentences, the verb phrases are in heavy type.

The daffodils **are blooming** now.
The telephone **has been ringing** all day.

Sometimes a verb phrase is interrupted by other words, as in the following examples.

I **could**n't **walk** another step! [I *could* not *walk.* . . .]
Water **is** always **dripping** in the sink.

To find the verb phrase in a question, make the question a statement.

QUESTION Did you cook dinner tonight?
STATEMENT You **did cook** dinner tonight.

NOTE: Remember that a verb phrase is called a verb.

43

EXERCISE 4   *Finding Verb Phrases*

Number your paper 1 to 10. Then write each verb phrase.

1. Jamie is wearing her favorite T-shirt.
2. The doctor will see you in just a minute.
3. Everyone was quietly reading library books.
4. We have lived in Florida for six years.
5. Did the clock just strike six o'clock?
6. The quarterback hasn't made a successful pass yet.
7. I must have eaten some bad food.
8. Was the milk put into the refrigerator?
9. You should always walk in comfortable shoes.
10. People were training dogs in prehistoric times.

TIME-OUT FOR REVIEW • • • • •

Number your paper 1 to 10. Then write each action verb.

Talking Birds

1. Have you ever listened to a parrot?
2. Actually, parrots don't talk.
3. These beautiful birds can only imitate human sounds.
4. Many birds can mimic various sounds.
5. Some can even copy the songs of other birds.
6. Only the parrot, the crow, and the starling can actually copy human speech.
7. People must train these birds very slowly.
8. New words must be repeated over and over again.
9. Eventually these birds will learn the new words.
10. Then the birds will never forget the words.

EXERCISE 5   *Writing Sentences*

Make up your own superhero, someone like Superman or Wonder Woman. Then write five sentences that explain the powers of your superhero. What can he or she do that none of the other superheros can do? Then underline each action verb.

Direct Objects

The following groups of words each have a subject and a verb but do not make complete statements.

I want.   We took.

Another word, called a *complement,* is needed in each example above. It will make the meaning of the words in the examples complete.

I want **milk.**   We took **raincoats.**

A *direct object* is one kind of complement. A direct object always follows an action verb.

3c A **direct object** is a noun or pronoun that answers the question *What?* or *Whom?* after an action verb.

To find a direct object in a sentence, first find the subject and the action verb. Then ask yourself *What?* or *Whom?* after the verb. In the following examples, subjects are underlined once, and verbs are underlined twice.

DIRECT OBJECTS
Male <u>lions</u> <u>have</u> hairy **manes.** [Lions have what?]

My <u>uncle</u> <u>builds</u> **bridges.** [He builds <u>what</u>?]

<u>Joyce</u> <u>saw</u> **them** at the beach. [Joyce saw <u>whom</u>?]

To find the direct object in a question, change the question into a statement.

QUESTION   Did you read that book?

STATEMENT   <u>You</u> <u>did read</u> that **book.** [You did read <u>what</u>?]

Two or more direct objects following the same verb are called a *compound direct object.*

<u>Bess</u> <u>found</u> a gold **ring** and a digital **watch.** [Bess found <u>what</u>?]

EXERCISE 6   Finding Direct Objects

Number your paper 1 to 10. Then write each direct object.

Owls

1. Have you ever seen a real owl?
2. Owls have very big eyes.
3. Most owls make their nests in trees.
4. The burrowing owl lays its eggs underground.
5. The very small screech owl will often catch a mouse or a squirrel.
6. These owls carry their food to their homes.
7. The barn owl has a heart-shaped face.
8. You cannot see its ears.
9. However, these owls will hear even a tiny mouse.
10. Owls help farmers in many ways.

EXERCISE 7   Finding Direct Objects

Number your paper 1 to 10. Then write each direct object.

Farming in Japan

1. Japan has very little land for farms.
2. Huge mountains cover the islands.
3. The Japanese use the available soil to its maximum.
4. They plant only the best seeds.
5. They spread powerful fertilizers on the fields.
6. They use advanced tractors and other equipment.
7. The sea provides the Japanese with another source of food.
8. The Japanese eat much fish.
9. Fish contains protein for healthy diets.
10. The Japanese also raise seaweed for food.

EXERCISE 8   Writing Sentences

Number your paper 1 to 3. Write a sentence that answers each question. Then underline each direct object.

1. What is one thing you ate for breakfast?
2. What is one thing you have in your pocket?
3. What television program do you enjoy most? (Underline the title of the program.)

Indirect Objects

Many action verbs have direct objects. Some action verbs also have a second complement called an *indirect object*.

An **indirect object** is a noun or pronoun that answers the question *To or for whom* or *To or for what?* after an action verb.

To find an indirect object in a sentence, first find the direct object. Then ask yourself *To whom? For whom? To what?* or *For what?* about the direct object. Notice in the following examples that an indirect object always comes *before* a direct object in the sentence.

INDIRECT OBJECTS

Mr. Mason showed his **students** a film. [Mr. Mason showed a film *to whom?*]

We gave the **car** a nice shine. [We gave a shine *to what?*]

To find an indirect object in a question, change the question into a statement.

QUESTION   Did you give them a tour of the school?

STATEMENT   You did give **them** a tour of the school. [You gave a tour *to whom?*]

QUESTION   Has Joe shown you his picture?

STATEMENT   Joe has shown you his picture. [Joe has shown his picture *to whom?*]

Two or more indirect objects following the same verb are called a *compound indirect object*.

Paula told **Jeff** and **me** a riddle. [She told a riddle *to whom?*]

NOTE: Remember that in order to have an indirect object, a sentence must also have a direct object.

EXERCISE 9   Finding Indirect Objects

Number your paper 1 to 10. Then write each indirect object.

1. The mail carrier handed Linda three packages.
2. The library loaned the school some films.
3. Did you give Maria a birthday card?
4. The coach has read the athletes the new rules.
5. Grandfather told us stories about his childhood.
6. My older brother made me a model airplane.
7. The store is promising its customers free gifts.
8. Dad will cook the family a special Italian dinner.
9. Did you loan Teddy your bowling ball?
10. Cassie taught Billy and me some magic tricks.

EXERCISE 10   Finding Indirect Objects

Number your paper 1 to 10. Then write each indirect object.

1. Mr. Henderson will show us our grades today.
2. Denise handed the clerk her bankbook.
3. Dad has built Mugsy a new doghouse.
4. My math teacher assigned the class several problems for homework.
5. I told Mom and Dad the good news.
6. I have sent my grandparents an anniversary card.
7. We baked our neighbors some bread.
8. Please give me some more salad.
9. My brother read Mother his first poem.
10. The class brought Ms. Jacobs some white daisies.

EXERCISE 11   Writing Sentences

Write three sentences that include indirect objects. Use the verb *cooked* in the first sentence, the verb *showed* in the second sentence, and the verb *sent* in the third sentence. Then underline each indirect object.

EXERCISE 12 *Writing Sentences* ✒

Write five sentences about some sport that you like. It could be a sport like basketball, or it could be an event in a track and field meet. Your sentences should include at least one direct object and one indirect object. When you have finished, underline each complement and label it *d.o.* or *i.o.*

TIME-OUT FOR REVIEW • • • • •

Number your paper 1 to 15. Write each complement. Then label each one *direct object* or *indirect object*. (Some sentences do not have an indirect object.)

EXAMPLE   The coach gave the pitcher a signal.
ANSWER   pitcher—indirect object, signal—direct object

**The Big
Game**

1. The pitcher wiped his hands.
2. He gave the catcher a wink.
3. The catcher punched his glove with his hand.
4. The batter gripped the bat tightly.
5. He gave the pitcher a long, hard stare.
6. Then with the speed of lightning, the pitcher hurled the ball toward the batter.
7. The nervous batter swung his bat with all of his strength.
8. He missed the ball completely.
9. The umpire called the third strike.
10. The pitch had completely fooled the batter.
11. The crowd in the stands gave the pitcher a wild cheer.
12. The pitcher had practiced his curves the whole week before the game.
13. The Blue Eagles had won the state championship for the first time!
14. The band played the school song over and over.
15. The coach gave all the players much praise for a good season.

Linking Verbs

Not all verbs show action. Verbs that do not show action are called *state-of-being verbs*. These verbs make a statement about a subject.

Ronald **was** here a few minutes ago.

State-of-being verbs are often used as *linking verbs*. These verbs link, or connect, the subject with another word in the sentence. In English the most common linking verb is *be*.

3e A linking verb links the subject with another word that renames or describes the subject.

December **is** the last month of the year. [*Is* links *month* with *December*. *Month* renames the subject].

Last month **was** unusually cold. [*Was* links *cold* with *month*. *Cold* describes the subject—*cold month*.]

Following is a list of common linking verbs.

Forms of *Be*		Other Linking Verbs	
be	are	appear	look
am	was	become	seem
is	were	feel	smell

Those yellow flowers **are** tulips.

That shirt **looks** too big.

NOTE: Linking verbs can also have helping verbs.

That woman **might be** a famous actress.

Clouds **will appear** dark before a storm.

50

EXERCISE 13 Finding Linking Verbs

Number your paper 1 to 10. Write each linking verb. Then write the two words that the verb links.

EXAMPLE The weather yesterday was very hot.
ANSWER was—weather, hot

1. Snowflake is the name of the albino gorilla.
2. Thomas Jefferson became the third U.S. president.
3. Mary Ann looks sleepy.
4. I am a representative to the student council.
5. Some frogs are blue.
6. That medicine smells terrible.
7. Some dinosaurs were extremely small animals.
8. The ocean appeared unusually calm.
9. Baseball is my favorite sport.
10. The answer to that riddle seems easy.

EXERCISE 14 Finding Linking Verbs

Number your paper 1 to 10. Write each linking verb. Then write the two words that the verb links.

Tempura

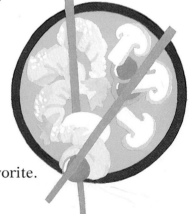

1. Tempura is a Chinese meal.
2. The carrots look crisp.
3. The mushrooms seem ripe.
4. These vegetables were inexpensive.
5. The shrimp smell very fresh.
6. Mom is the supervisor.
7. Dad was the chief cook last week.
8. The oil in the pan has become hot.
9. This dinner has always been our favorite.
10. The food was absolutely delicious!

EXERCISE 15 Writing Sentences

Write three sentences that include linking verbs. Use the verb *are* in the first sentence, the verb *was* in the second sentence, and the verb *looked* in the third sentence. Then underline the two words that each verb links.

Predicate Nominatives

The noun or pronoun that follows a linking verb and renames the subject is a complement called a *predicate nominative.*

3f ▶ A **predicate nominative** is a noun or a pronoun that follows a linking verb and identifies, renames, or explains the subject.

To find a predicate nominative in a sentence, first find the subject and the verb. Check to see if the verb is a linking verb. Then look for a noun or a pronoun that follows the linking verb and renames the subject. One way to check for a predicate nominative is to put an equal sign between it and the subject.

PREDICATE
NOMINATIVES

Lloyd is the team's new **manager.** [p.n.]
[manager = Lloyd]

That building will be the new **gymnasium.** [p.n.]
[gymnasium = building]

Two or more predicate nominatives following the same linking verb are called a *compound predicate nominative.*

The best runners on the team are **she** and **Scott.** [p.n.] [p.n.]

[she, Scott = runners]

EXERCISE 16 *Finding Predicate Nominatives*

Number your paper 1 to 10. Then write each predicate nominative.

1. St. Bernards are very large dogs.
2. Next Monday will be a school holiday.
3. Marie Curie became a famous scientist.
4. My best friends have always been Kate and Allen.
5. Pam should be the next captain of the cheerleaders at Barton Middle School.

6. Algeria is a large country in the northern part of Africa.
7. Usually I am a cheerful person.
8. Those people are workers at the nearby textile factory.
9. The birthday party may be a surprise.
10. Those lovely apartments were once abandoned warehouses.

EXERCISE 17 Finding Predicate Nominatives

Number your paper 1 to 10. Then write each predicate nominative.

Facts and Figures

1. Carlsbad Caverns are large caves in New Mexico.
2. High blood pressure is the most common disease in the United States today.
3. Galileo was the inventor of the thermometer.
4. Siberian tigers are the biggest cats in the world.
5. Chester Arthur was the 21st president of the United States.
6. Babe Ruth became the first player with 60 home runs in a single season.
7. The largest desert in the world is the Sahara.
8. Harvard was the first college in the United States.
9. Capitals of the United States have been Philadelphia and New York City.
10. Rice is the chief food for half of the people of the world.

EXERCISE 18 Supplying Predicate Nominatives

Number your paper 1 to 5. Then write a predicate nominative for each blank.

1. My favorite holiday is _____.
2. Elvis Presley was a famous _____.
3. Those green vegetables are _____.
4. I am a good _____.
5. My teacher last year was _____.

TIME-OUT FOR REVIEW • • • • •

Number your paper 1 to 25. Write each verb. Then label each one *action* or *linking*.

EXAMPLE A moose is a large animal in the deer family.
ANSWER   is—linking

A True Story

1. For 800 years no moose had lived in Sweden.
2. Then a female moose and two male moose swam to Sweden from a nearby country.
3. Their new lives seemed happy.
4. Then suddenly the female moose died.
5. The Swedish people were very upset about the loss of their only female moose.
6. Quickly they hunted for another female.
7. Eventually a man in Denmark offered them Hildy.
8. He had raised her on his farm.
9. She was a very gentle animal.
10. A forest in Sweden became Hildy's new home.
11. For a while, Hildy appeared content.
12. Then one day she marched into town.
13. All the people looked fearful.
14. A full-size moose can be very dangerous.
15. It can kill a person with one strike.
16. Poor Hildy felt very sad.
17. She was only looking for some new friends—human friends.
18. Some people were brave.
19. After all, this moose didn't look mean.
20. Hildy was so happy!
21. Within a short period of time, she was friends with all the people in town.
22. For the rest of her days, she lived at the zoo.
23. However, she could easily jump across a wide ditch around the zoo.
24. Then she would visit people in the town outside the zoo every day.
25. All the townspeople became Hildy's best friends.

Diagraming Complements

Most complements are written on the baseline of a diagram, along with the subject and the verb. An indirect object is the only exception. An indirect object is written on a line attached to the baseline.

Direct Objects. Write a direct object on the baseline right after the verb. Then draw a short, straight line to separate the direct object from the verb. Write the parts of a compound direct object on parallel lines. Then write the word that joins the parts of the compound direct object on a broken line between them.

We ate watermelon.

She reads books and magazines.

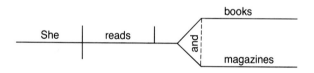

Indirect Objects.   Indirect objects are written on horizontal lines below the baseline. These horizontal lines are connected to the verb on the baseline by a slanted line. The parts of a compound indirect object are also written on parallel horizontal lines. The conjunction is placed on a broken line.

Sally promised us prizes.

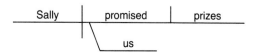

Give Tim and John paper.

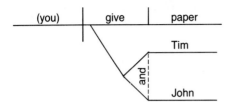

Predicate Nominatives. Write a predicate nominative on the baseline after the verb, and use a slanted line to separate it from the verb. Write the parts of a compound predicate nominative on parallel lines.

Teenagers become adults.

Women are managers and executives.

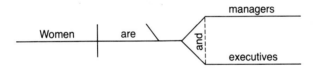

EXERCISE 19 *Diagraming Complements*

Diagram the following sentences or copy them. If your teacher tells you to copy them, draw one line under each subject and two lines under each verb. Then label each complement *d.o., i.o.,* or *p.n.*

1. Dad paints houses.
2. We gave her roses.
3. Mavis likes dogs and cats.
4. Tadpoles become frogs.
5. Mom bakes us apples.
6. Computers are machines.
7. Pedro taught Barry and me Spanish.
8. Mr. Rogers coaches basketball.
9. Grandmother sends me cards.
10. Those dogs are collies and poodles.

Application to Writing

Have you ever listened to a radio announcer give a play-by-play description of a baseball game? Even though players are constantly *throwing* the ball, an announcer seldom uses the verb *throw*. Announcers know that overused verbs like *throw* do not create a clear picture in the minds of their listeners. As a result, announcers are constantly using colorful, action-packed substitutes such as *fire, hurl, propel,* and *thrust*.

You can learn from these sports announcers. When you write, always look for colorful, action-packed verbs. Stretch your mind for substitutes for overused verbs or look in the dictionary or a thesaurus.

EXERCISE 20   Supplying Colorful Verbs

Number your paper 1 to 5. Then write an answer to each question. Include two colorful verbs in each answer.

EXAMPLE   Did the stars shine?
POSSIBLE ANSWER   No, they sparkled and twinkled.

1. Did the hawks fly?
2. Did the athletes run?
3. Did the people walk?
4. Did the glass break?
5. Did the rain fall?

EXERCISE 21   Using Colorful Verbs

Use each of the following colorful verbs in a sentence.

1. swerved   2. scattered   3. toppled   4. clutched

EXERCISE 22   Writing Sentences

You are a radio announcer, reporting on a demonstration of jet planes. In your five-sentence report, include colorful verbs instead of overused verbs like *fly*.

Chapter Review

A **Finding Action Verbs.** Number your paper 1 to 10. Then write each action verb.

1. The squirrel leaped up the tree.
2. A flock of pigeons was circling overhead.
3. The fire in the old warehouse has been blazing for two hours.
4. The band is playing my favorite song.
5. Did you walk to school today?
6. The red paint on the front porch has now dried completely.
7. The puppy could be catching a cold.
8. The clock in my bedroom isn't ticking anymore.
9. Will you visit your grandparents this summer?
10. Some kinds of large whales reach lengths of a hundred feet or more.

B **Finding Linking Verbs.** Number your paper 1 to 10. Write each linking verb. Then write the two words the verb links.

Modern Balloons

1. Balloons are balls of air.
2. They look colorful at birthday parties.
3. The purpose of some modern balloons appears quite different.
4. One new helium-filled balloon is a great tool for farmers.
5. The picture on the balloon looks familiar to people and to birds.
6. It is a hawk.
7. The black hawk with its large wings seems real to birds.
8. Real birds are fearful of hawks.
9. The balloon is really a trick.
10. This balloon has become the modern scarecrow.

C **Identifying Complements.** Number your paper 1 to 10. Then label each underlined complement *direct object, indirect object,* or *predicate nominative.*

1. Colorado became a <u>state</u> in 1876.
2. We found some beautiful <u>shells</u> along the beach near Park Street.
3. Some sharks have no natural <u>enemies</u>.
4. The Adams family of Massachusetts gave their <u>country</u> two presidents.
5. The animal with the longest life is the giant <u>tortoise</u>.
6. Mr. Granger promised <u>Terry</u> extra help after school today.
7. Have you ever thrown a <u>boomerang</u>?
8. In the winter snow, monkeys eat <u>vines</u> and tree <u>bark</u>.
9. Jerry eagerly showed his <u>mother</u> his first report card of the school year.
10. Elephants are excellent <u>swimmers</u>.

Mastery Test

Number your paper 1 to 10. Write each verb. Then label it *action* or *linking.*

Not True

1. Over the years people have given pigs a bad reputation.
2. Pigs are not dirty animals.
3. Often pigs must live in dirty pens.
4. In the wild, however, they seem quite clean.
5. On hot days pigs will wallow in mud.
6. They have a good reason for this behavior.
7. Pigs don't perspire.
8. The wet mud feels cool on their bodies.
9. Pigs are also very smart.
10. Their intelligence is greater than that of dogs, cats, horses, or sheep.

4

Adjectives and Adverbs

Diagnostic Test

Number your paper 1 to 10. Write each underlined word. Then label each one *adjective* or *adverb*.

EXAMPLE   Our <u>new</u> stove was delivered <u>recently</u>.
ANSWER   new—adjective   recently—adverb

1. The <u>red</u> banner <u>slowly</u> fluttered in the wind.
2. The <u>unusual</u> dodo bird has <u>completely</u> disappeared.
3. <u>Then</u> Hank's <u>forward</u> pass was intercepted.
4. Mary's <u>silver</u> bracelet has <u>just</u> been found!
5. I have <u>always</u> liked <u>old</u> coins.
6. Put <u>these</u> plants <u>outside</u>.
7. The <u>winter</u> wind <u>sometimes</u> howls like a wolf.
8. <u>African</u> jungles are <u>often</u> quite dense.
9. <u>Occasionally</u> the local bus is <u>late</u>.
10. <u>Recently</u> heavy snow fell for 12 <u>straight</u> hours.

*A*djectives

RAY: Please hand me the book on the shelf.
SUE: Which book?
RAY: The green one.
SUE: There are two green books on the shelf.
RAY: I want the big green book.
SUE: Oh, yes, now I see which one you want.

Without the words *big* and *green,* Sue would have never known which book Ray wanted. *Big* and *green* are adjectives. An *adjective* is an important part of speech. Adjectives add color and exactness to your writing.

4a ▸ An **adjective** is a word that modifies, or describes, a noun or a pronoun.

To find an adjective, look for each noun or pronoun. Then ask the question *What kind? How many?* or *How much?* In the following examples, an arrow points to the word each adjective describes. Notice that an adjective usually comes before the word it describes.

WHAT KIND?	**red** suspenders	**light** rain
	sturdy, old barn	**tall, thin** boy
HOW MANY?	**three** mice	**many** fish
HOW MUCH?	**no** rain	**much** sleep

NOTE: The words *a, an,* and *the* form a special group of adjectives called *articles.* Use *a* before a word that begins with a consonant sound. Use *an* before a word that begins with a vowel sound.

a watch   **a** cat   **an** hour ago   **an** apple

Since articles are used so often, you do not have to list them in the following exercises.

EXERCISE 1 Finding Adjectives

Number your paper 1 to 10. Write each adjective. Then beside each adjective, write the word it describes. (Remember, do not list the articles *a, an,* and *the.*)

A Chicken Farm

1. Grandad Jones raises baby chicks.
2. He has a small farm.
3. He has many chicks.
4. The chicks need a warm home.
5. Grandma places them in a large brooder.
6. The chicks have a nutritious diet.
7. Grandad feeds them special grain.
8. The home of the chicks has a constant temperature.
9. A trough provides them with clean water.
10. A pen will be the next shelter for the chicks.

EXERCISE 2 Finding Adjectives

Number your paper 1 to 10. Write each adjective. Then write the word each adjective describes. There are 15 adjectives.

EXAMPLE   Deserts get less than ten inches of rain in a whole year.

ANSWER   ten—inches   whole—year

The Largest Desert

1. North Africa is a dry, harsh land.
2. In North Africa is the Sahara, the largest desert in the world.
3. It is about the same size as the United States.
4. Often hot, dry winds create ridges of sand, called dunes.
5. Dunes sometimes look like huge mountains of sand.
6. The Sahara has hot days and cold nights.
7. There is little water in the desert.
8. Years can pass with no rain.
9. Most water in the desert comes from underground streams.
10. In the desert, people wear long, loose robes as protection from the heat, cold, and sandstorms.

Proper Adjectives

Africa is a proper noun. It is the name of a particular place. *African* is a *proper adjective* because it is formed from the proper noun *Africa*. A proper adjective, however, is used to describe a noun or a pronoun—*African villages*. A proper adjective always begins with a capital letter.

PROPER NOUNS	PROPER ADJECTIVES
America	**American** culture
Mars	**Martian** creatures
Great Britain	**British** trade

EXERCISE 3 Finding Proper Adjectives

Number your paper 1 to 10. Write each proper adjective. Then write the word it describes.

1. The English people speak with an accent.
2. I enjoy Mexican food.
3. Did you have to stop at the Canadian border before entering Montreal?
4. We watched a Hawaiian dance.
5. New York is on the Atlantic coast.
6. How long is an Alaskan winter?
7. A severe snowstorm will hit the Midwestern states tomorrow.
8. Have you studied European history in any of your classes?
9. Is that German money?
10. The President ordered the Congressional committee to investigate the matter.

EXERCISE 4 Writing Sentences

Number your paper 1 to 3. Write the proper adjectives that are formed from the following proper nouns. Then use each one in a sentence.

1. China   2. South America   3. France

Adjective or Noun?

A word's part of speech depends on how it is used in a sentence. *Computer* and *flower,* for example, can be either nouns or adjectives. Each of these words is a noun if it is the name of something, but it is an adjective if it describes a noun or a pronoun.

NOUN Do you own a **computer?**

ADJECTIVE I go to the **computer** room every afternoon.

NOUN The **flower** was a pale yellow rose.

ADJECTIVE Here is a package of **flower** seeds.

EXERCISE 5 Distinguishing between Adjectives and Nouns

Number your paper 1 to 10. Write each underlined word. Then label it *adjective* or *noun.*

EXAMPLE Are you meeting him at the *bus station?*
ANSWER bus—adjective

1. Did you go to the <u>basketball</u> game on Saturday?
2. Please give me a <u>glass</u> of water.
3. There's a <u>spring</u> in the meadow.
4. Is the <u>team</u> ready for the big game?
5. The building was constructed with <u>steel</u> beams.
6. <u>Spring</u> flowers are blooming everywhere.
7. Is that <u>basketball</u> made of leather?
8. How much of that car is made of <u>steel</u>?
9. Who broke the <u>glass</u> pitcher?
10. Harvey is the new <u>team</u> captain.

EXERCISE 6 Writing Sentences

Write two sentences for each of the following words. First use the word as a noun. Then use the word as an adjective.

1. orange   2. car   3. television

This, That, These, and Those

This, that, these, and *those* can be used as adjectives. Words like these answer the adjective question *Which one?*

ADJECTIVES   I just read **that** book. [*Which book?*]

We like **those** chairs best. [*Which chairs?*]

This, that, these, and *those* can also be used as pronouns. They are adjectives when they come before nouns and pronouns and describe those nouns or pronouns. They are pronouns when they stand alone and take the place of nouns.

PRONOUNS   I just read **that.** [*That* takes the place of the noun *book.*]

We like **those** best. [*Those* takes the place of the noun *chairs.*]

EXERCISE 7   Using *This, That, These,* and *Those*

Number your paper 1 to 10. Write each underlined word. Then label it *adjective* or *pronoun.*

1. These are very juicy oranges.
2. Try on this jacket next.
3. Is that too expensive?
4. Those mistakes must be corrected.
5. Do these TV dinners take long to cook?
6. This month has 31 days.
7. Who said that?
8. You should try this. It's delicious!
9. I'll take a few of those.
10. Why did he buy this?

EXERCISE 8   Writing Sentences

Write two sentences for *this* and *these.* Use each word as both an adjective and a pronoun. Then label the use of each word.

Predicate Adjectives

An adjective does not always come in front of the word it describes. An adjective can also follow a linking verb and describe the subject of a sentence. Such an adjective is a complement called a *predicate adjective*. (*See pages 45, 47, and 52 for more information about the other complements—direct objects, indirect objects, and predicate nominatives.*)

4b A **predicate adjective** is an adjective that follows a linking verb and modifies, or describes, the subject.

A predicate adjective always follows a linking verb.

Forms of *Be*		Other Linking Verbs	
be	are	appear	look
am	was	become	seem
is	were	feel	smell

To find a predicate adjective, first find the subject and the verb. Check to see if the verb is a linking verb. Then find the adjective that follows the verb and describes the subject.

PREDICATE ADJECTIVES The <u>claws</u> of tigers <u>are</u> very **sharp**. [*Sharp* describes the subject—*sharp claws.*]

At midnight the <u>street</u> <u>appeared</u> **empty**. [*Empty* describes the subject—*empty street.*]

Two or more predicate adjectives following the same linking verb are called a *compound predicate adjective.*

The <u>road</u> to the old farmhouse <u>is</u> **long** and **narrow**. [*Long* and *narrow* both describe the subject—*long, narrow road.*]

EXERCISE 9 Finding Predicate Adjectives

Number your paper 1 to 10. Then write each predicate adjective.

Monkeys

1. Monkeys usually look friendly.
2. They are often very noisy.
3. In trees, they seem safe from enemies.
4. The hair of some monkeys is red.
5. Their fur can be long or short.
6. Their fur, however, feels very coarse.
7. Of all monkeys in the world, the Red Howler is the largest.
8. The tail of this monkey is extremely long and strong.
9. Most monkeys appear quite smart.
10. Some monkeys have even become popular as actors.

EXERCISE 10 Supplying Predicate Adjectives

Number your paper 1 to 10. Then write a predicate adjective for each blank.

1. I am _____.
2. That bread seems rather _____.
3. Deer are usually _____.
4. Before my speech I became _____.
5. The story about the ghost was very _____.
6. That stew smells _____.
7. Daniel looks _____ in his new suit.
8. That movie was _____.
9. Those new exercises were _____.
10. The fresh air felt _____ and _____.

EXERCISE 11 Writing Sentences

Write two sentences for each of the following adjectives. In the first sentence, place each adjective in its normal position before a noun. In the second sentence, use each adjective as a predicate adjective.

1. young   2. famous   3. warm

67

TIME-OUT FOR REVIEW • • • • •

Number your paper 1 to 15. Then write each adjective. (Remember to include predicate adjectives.) There are 20 adjectives.

Buried Treasure

1. After searching for 11 years, Mel Fisher discovered the *Atocha* in the summer of 1985.
2. The *Atocha* is an old Spanish ship.
3. It sank during a terrible hurricane in 1622.
4. The search for the treasure was long and difficult.
5. Fisher first read old records in Seville, Spain.
6. The information was extremely valuable.
7. Modern sonar also helped Fisher find the *Atocha*.
8. Fisher has already found silver bars, gold coins, and jewelry.
9. An American archaeologist is working with Fisher.
10. To him, this discovery is extremely important.
11. From the wreckage, the archaeologist hopes to learn many things.
12. How were Spanish galleons built?
13. How did European sailors live and work 350 years ago?
14. Years might go by before these facts are finally learned.
15. Meanwhile, the treasure site will be constantly guarded against thieves.

EXERCISE 12 Writing Sentences

Look very carefully at your right shoe. Then describe it in five or six sentences. For example, you might include its color, any marks on it, and the condition of the shoestrings. Your description should be so accurate that anyone could find your shoe if it were placed in a pile with 20 other shoes. When you have finished writing, underline each adjective.

Application to Writing

Adjectives make a big difference in whatever you write. Adjectives can create a mood by making a room *dark* and *gloomy* or *bright* and *sunny*. They can also make a description exact. A *tasty, Italian* meal is very different from a *rich, French* meal.

When you write, always choose fresh, specific adjectives that will create clear pictures in the minds of your readers. Use the dictionary or a thesaurus to look for colorful substitutes for dull, overused adjectives such as *good, nice, bad,* and *awful.*

EXERCISE 13 Finding Fresh, Specific Adjectives

Number your paper 1 to 5. Then write at least two specific adjectives that could describe each noun.

1. person 2. storm 3. car 4. jungle 5. lake

EXERCISE 14 Supplying Fresh, Specific Adjectives

Write a specific adjective for each blank.

On a _____ day, the _____ boy climbed into his _____ boat. The sea was very _____, but the boy was _____. The currents were _____, and the boat seemed too _____. The _____ waves made the boy feel _____. The boy had to return quickly to the _____ shore.

EXERCISE 15 Writing Sentences

Pretend that you own a diner. You serve home style food like meatloaf, spaghetti, and baked chicken, but you want your menu to sound very enticing. Using colorful adjectives, write short descriptions of two meals. Then read your menus aloud and see if anyone knows what the meal really is.

Adverbs

Like an adjective, an adverb is a *modifier*. An adverb modifies, or describes, another word in the sentence. Unlike an adjective, however, an adverb describes a verb, an adjective, or another adverb.

4c An **adverb** is a word that modifies, or describes, a verb, an adjective, or another adverb.

Adverbs are important words because they make your writing more precise or exact. Notice, for example, how the second example is more precise just because two adverbs were added to the first example.

The car stopped.
Then the car stopped **abruptly.**

You can easily recognize some adverbs because they end in *-ly.*

Usually the newspaper arrives **promptly** at six o'clock.

Following are common adverbs that do not end in *-ly.*

Common Adverbs			
again	ever	outside	somewhere
almost	here	quite	soon
already	just	rather	still
also	never	seldom	then
always	not	so	there
away	now	sometimes	too
down	often	somewhat	very

NOTE: *Not* and its contraction *n't* are always adverbs.

This lamp is**n't** working. [This lamp is **not** working.]

✓

Adverbs That Describe Verbs

Most adverbs describe verbs. To find these adverbs, ask yourself *How? When? Where?* or *To what extent?* about each verb. Notice that some of the following adverbs come before the verb and others come after the verb.

HOW?   He drove **carefully.**

WHEN?   **Now** we wait.

WHERE?   The dog went **outside.**

TO WHAT EXTENT?   Karen **almost** fell twice on the ice.

More than one adverb can describe the same verb.

I **always** sleep **soundly.**

An adverb always describes the main verb plus any helping verbs. Notice in the second example that an adverb sometimes interrupts a verb phrase.

You should meet us **here** in ten minutes.

I have **never** answered his letter.

EXERCISE 16 Finding Adverbs

Number your paper 1 to 10. Write each adverb. Then write the word or words it describes.

Glice

1. Now someone has invented Glice.
2. Because of Glice, Southerners can skate outside.
3. Surprisingly, Glice is a plastic substitute for ice.
4. It seldom needs any upkeep.
5. Workers vacuum it lightly after each use.
6. Electricity is never used—except for lights.
7. Soon people in all states will skate in Glice rinks.
8. One rink has just opened in New York.
9. More rinks will be opening continually.
10. Europe already has 28 rinks with nonmelt Glice.

EXERCISE 17 Finding Adverbs

Number your paper 1 to 10. Write each adverb. Then write the word or words each one describes. There are 15 adverbs.

EXAMPLE Now tiny radios are greatly helping scientists.
ANSWER now—are helping greatly—are helping

Tiny Radios

1. In the past scientists couldn't really help some animals.
2. They never knew all the habits or homes of these animals.
3. With modern technology, that has already changed.
4. Now scientists can accurately track most animals through their daily activities.
5. However, they couldn't do their studies without the help of tiny radio transmitters.
6. Often these transmitters are securely attached to collars around animals' necks.
7. A scientist will quietly track a black bear, for example.
8. Then dogs will bark loudly.
9. Immediately the bear will quickly climb a tree.
10. Finally the scientist will shoot the bear with a tranquilizing drug and attach the collar.

EXERCISE 18 Writing Sentences

Number your paper 1 to 5. Using one or more adverbs, write a sentence that answers each question. Then underline each adverb.

EXAMPLE How do fire fighters put out a fire?
POSSIBLE ANSWER They <u>usually</u> put out a fire <u>quickly</u>.

1. How do you play your radio?
2. How does a skater glide across the ice?
3. How or how often do you read comic books?
4. How do you sing?
5. How do elephants walk?

*A*dverbs That Describe Adjectives and Other Adverbs

An adverb—such as *quite, rather, so, somewhat, too,* or *very*—can describe an adjective or another adverb. When it does, it usually comes before the word it describes.

DESCRIBING AN ADJECTIVE
The lake is **rather** choppy. [*Choppy* is a predicate adjective that describes *lake. Rather* is an adverb that tells how choppy the lake was.]

DESCRIBING AN ADVERB
He left **quite** rapidly. [*Rapidly* is an adverb that describes the verb. *Quite* is an adverb that tells how rapidly he left.]

*E*XERCISE 19 Finding Adverbs

Number your paper 1 to 10. Write each underlined adverb. Then write the word it describes.

EXAMPLE   Brenda started the marathon <u>too</u> quickly.
ANSWER   too—quickly

1. <u>Very</u> soon the senator will begin his speech.
2. The storm developed <u>quite</u> suddenly.
3. The temperatures today were <u>rather</u> mild.
4. The skaters were circling the rink <u>very</u> rapidly.
5. Some new jets are <u>remarkably</u> fast.
6. Our <u>extremely</u> slow clock must be fixed.
7. The company's reply came <u>almost</u> immediately.
8. Our new puppy is <u>somewhat</u> small.
9. Everyone in the mayor's office is <u>so</u> helpful.
10. Don't arrive at the surprise party <u>too</u> early.

*E*XERCISE 20 Writing Sentences

Write sentences that follow the directions below.

1. Include an adverb that describes a verb.
2. Include an adverb that describes an adjective.
3. Include an adverb that describes another adverb.

TIME-OUT FOR REVIEW • • • • •

Number your paper 1 to 10. Then write each adverb. There are 15 adverbs.

Alive!

1. Recently two California women amazingly survived an adventure of a lifetime.
2. These brave women were completely lost in the Indian Ocean.
3. They were extremely lucky.
4. They were having a very good time on a vacation in Indonesia.
5. On a 16-foot boat, they excitedly headed for a nearby wildlife preserve.
6. They never made it.
7. Suddenly the boat's engine stopped abruptly.
8. Soon their water supply was totally gone.
9. Then their boat crashed against a reef.
10. Luckily helicopters rescued them rather quickly.

Application to Writing

To make your writing more interesting, begin some of your sentences with adverbs. If all your sentences begin the same way, your writing sounds dull.

REGULAR ORDER   The door opened **suddenly.**

VARIETY   **Suddenly** the door opened.

EXERCISE 21 Creating Sentence Variety

Number your paper 1 to 10. Use each word as an adverb in a sentence. Then change five of the sentences around so that they begin with the adverb.

1. lately	3. often	5. patiently	7. now	9. gently
2. slowly	4. soon	6. silently	8. here	10. seldom

Diagraming Adjectives and Adverbs

Adjectives and adverbs are both diagramed on slanted lines below the words they describe. Adverbs that describe adjectives or other adverbs are connected to the words they describe.

Those very young children often talk too quickly.

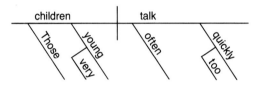

Predicate Adjectives. Diagram a predicate ad) tive exactly as you do a predicate nominative. (*See page*)

That puzzle was easy.

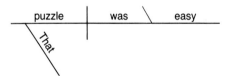

EXERCISE 22 Diagraming Adjectives and Adverbs

Diagram sentences or copy them. If you copy them, draw one line under each subject and two lines under each verb. Then label each modifier *adjective* or *adverb*.

1. Many violets are blooming.
2. That doctor works tirelessly.
3. Several monkeys were chattering noisily.
4. The old dog was romping happily.
5. The coach seemed angry.
6. Four white horses galloped away.
7. Those books are old.
8. Then the scouts marched outside.
9. The extremely heavy rain has ended.
10. Rabbits run rather quickly.

*C*hapter *R*eview

A **Finding Adjectives.** Number your paper 1 to 10. Write each adjective. Then write the word each adjective describes. There are 15 adjectives.

The
Moon

1. By 1972, twelve American astronauts had landed on the surface of the moon.
2. They returned with large samples of soil and rocks.
3. What have we learned from these explorations?
4. The surface of the moon is covered with a fine powdery dust.
5. Sometimes this dusty surface is deep.
6. Moon rocks are made of minerals and gases.
7. With no wind on the moon, these rocks hardly ever change.
8. The many footprints of the astronauts will probably never change either.
9. The astronauts left several instruments on the moon.
10. The information from the instruments will be extremely valuable.

B **Finding Adverbs.** Number your paper 1 to 10. Write each adverb. Then write the word or words each adverb describes. There are 15 adverbs.

1. Paula jumped high and cleared the pole.
2. Seldom do you see such a brilliant sunset.
3. A bear will always fight bravely for its young.
4. Must we watch that program again?
5. Then everyone was laughing heartily.
6. Did you close the door tightly?
7. Sometimes we walk slowly along the beach.
8. You must jump down now.
9. Tommy is pitching quite carelessly.
10. Those unusually large balloons are colorful.

C **Noun, Pronoun, or Adjective?** Number your paper 1 to 10. Write each underlined word. Then label each one *noun, pronoun,* or *adjective.*

1. We have a <u>dog</u> named Max.
2. Everyone should know <u>that</u> information.
3. The <u>movie</u> reviews weren't very good.
4. Did anyone buy any of <u>these</u>?
5. That strange <u>telephone</u> is in the shape of a mallard duck.
6. <u>That</u> is my correct address.
7. This canned <u>dog</u> food is on sale.
8. I saw a wonderful <u>movie</u> last week at the Plaza Cinema.
9. I like <u>these</u> more than the red ones.
10. Did the <u>telephone</u> bill arrive yet?

Mastery Test

Number your paper 1 to 10. Write each underlined word. Then label each one *adjective* or *adverb.*

1. The <u>cool</u> breezes of autumn are coming to New England <u>soon</u>.
2. The group has <u>just</u> recorded several familiar <u>Spanish</u> songs.
3. Woodpeckers <u>often</u> build <u>small</u> nests in trees.
4. <u>Already</u> I have <u>successfully</u> completed two of my swimming tests.
5. <u>This</u> sweater will be quite <u>warm</u>.
6. The sheep <u>carefully</u> climbed the <u>steep</u> cliffs.
7. A <u>very</u> <u>expensive</u> diamond ring was lost.
8. Orangutans <u>usually</u> travel through the dense jungle <u>alone</u>.
9. That <u>large</u> warehouse is <u>empty</u>.
10. The home of a harbor seal is <u>almost</u> <u>always</u> cold and snowy.

5

Prepositions, Conjunctions, and Interjections

Diagnostic Test

Number your paper 1 to 10. Write each underlined word. Then label each one *preposition, conjunction,* or *interjection.*

EXAMPLE Hang the sheets <u>on</u> the clothes line.
ANSWER on—preposition

1. Wasps <u>and</u> hornets are extremely nearsighted.
2. <u>From</u> the lighthouse we could see across the bay.
3. Let's run <u>around</u> the track a couple times.
4. Monkeys live <u>in</u> every tropical climate except Australia.
5. <u>Yes!</u> I accept the nomination for class president.
6. The tree <u>across</u> the road fell during the storm.
7. Seagulls can drink fresh water <u>or</u> saltwater.
8. The prize <u>inside</u> that cereal box is a package of stickers.
9. The book is long <u>but</u> interesting.
10. <u>Wow!</u> People blink once every two to ten seconds.

*P*repositions

Pretend that someone has just asked you for directions to your school. A small word such as *before, at, across,* or *after* could make all the difference in whether that person finds the school based on your directions or not.

The building
$$\begin{cases} \textbf{before} \text{ the intersection} \\ \textbf{at} \text{ the intersection} \\ \textbf{across} \text{ the intersection} \\ \textbf{after} \text{ the intersection} \end{cases}$$
is the school.

The words *before, at, across,* and *after* show the relationship of the building to the intersection. These words are called *prepositions*.

5a ▶ A **preposition** is a word that shows the relationship between a noun or a pronoun and another word in the sentence.

Following is a list of the most common prepositions.

Common Prepositions			
about	behind	from	over
above	below	in	through
across	beneath	inside	to
after	beside	near	toward
against	between	of	under
along	beyond	off	up
around	by	on	with
at	during	out	within
before	for	outside	without

Close the windows **during** the storm.
The person **on** the horse is my instructor.
Lean the rake **against** the barn.
With the extra help, we should finish soon.

79

EXERCISE 1 Supplying Prepositions

Number your paper 1 to 10. Then write a preposition for each blank. Do not use the same preposition more than once.

EXAMPLE Julio is sitting _____ Raymond.
POSSIBLE ANSWER beside

1. The brown house _____ ours on Maple Street is for sale.
2. Is the dog sleeping _____ your sister's bed again?
3. _____ Friday I don't have tests in any of my classes.
4. Our car stalled _____ a gas station on Lincoln Highway.
5. The name _____ that locker is his.
6. Can you jump _____ that low fence at the edge of the park?
7. _____ the ocean on the other side of the island are several public beaches.
8. Put those receipts _____ your mother's brown checkbook.
9. That old dirt road leads _____ the lake.
10. _____ the rocks we could see a small nest full of chirping baby birds.

Prepositional Phrases

A preposition is always the first word of a group of words called a *prepositional phrase*.

> **5b** A **prepositional phrase** is a group of words made up of a preposition, its object, and any words that describe the object.

PREPOSITIONAL
PHRASES

prep.   obj.
During intermission no one left
             prep. obj.
They will take us **with them.**
                      prep.   obj.
The cat was hiding **inside an old box.**

80

A prepositional phrase can have two or more objects. Such a phrase has a *compound object of the preposition.*

COMPOUND OBJECT OF A PREPOSITION	The movie **about** (prep.) **spiders** (obj.) **and insects** (obj.) was quite interesting.
	We will go **to** (prep.) **the aquarium** (obj.) **or the zoo.** (obj.)

A sentence can have more than one prepositional phrase, as shown by the following examples.

During (prep.) **our school's basketball season,** (obj.) I went **to** (prep.) **every home game.** (obj.)

The tip **of** (prep.) **the highest mountain** (obj.) **in** (prep.) **that range** (obj.) is taller than the Empire State Building.

EXERCISE 2 *Finding Prepositional Phrases*

Number your paper 1 to 10. Write each prepositional phrase. Then underline the preposition once and its object twice. There are 12 phrases.

EXAMPLE   Do you want property on the moon?
ANSWER   on the moon

Selling the Moon

1. A museum in Boston once had a wonderful idea.
2. It sold land on the surface of the moon.
3. The prices started at 25 dollars.
4. All the lots had a good view of Earth.
5. All owners received "deeds" to their lunar property.
6. These unofficial deeds came with certain property rights.
7. Property owners can walk, land, and settle on the moon.
8. For these rights owners made a promise.
9. They would respect any little green men or other creatures within their property.
10. The museum used the money from these lunar sales for additional exhibits and programs.

EXERCISE 3 *Finding Prepositional Phrases*

Number your paper 1 to 10. Then write each prepositional phrase. There are 15 phrases.

Fancy Shoes for Men

1. The open-toed purple boots of Roman emperors were decorated with jewels and gold thread.
2. Some years later leather shoes from Africa arrived in Europe.
3. These shoes had long tips, and people often fell over them.
4. Eventually people fastened the tips of their shoes to their knees or waist.
5. These shoes, for all their problems, lasted through four centuries.
6. Then people wore wide shoes on their feet.
7. These shoes sometimes stretched beyond 10 inches.
8. Inside them was wool, hair, or hay.
9. Because Louis XIV was short, he ordered high heels under his shoes.
10. These fancy shoes on the king's feet had bows and flowers across the tops.

EXERCISE 4 *Expanding Sentences*

Number your paper 1 to 10. Then add at least one prepositional phrase to each sentence.

EXAMPLE   The train just left.
POSSIBLE ANSWER   The train for Baltimore just left.

1. Jim finished his homework.
2. The bird flew away.
3. The baseball team has won the championship.
4. Fresh fruit is delicious.
5. Someone is waving.
6. Students visited the science museum.
7. These roller skates are too small.
8. The author is signing autographs.
9. Our neighbor brought us flowers.
10. A bright light is shining.

***E*XERCISE 5** *Writing Sentences*

If you live in a cold climate, write a description of a snowman or an ice sculpture you would like to build one day. If you live in a warm climate, write a description of a sand castle you would like to construct one day. Your descriptions should be five or six sentences long. When you have finished, underline each prepositional phrase.

***T*IME-OUT FOR REVIEW** • • • • •

Number your paper 1 to 15. Then write each prepositional phrase. There are 20 phrases.

An Unusual Winter

1. By October the first snow falls in Yellowstone National Park.
2. Soon temperatures drop below zero.
3. Strong winds swirl the snow along the ground.
4. Winter at Yellowstone will last for six long, cold months.
5. Around the park visitors will see some very unusual sights.
6. During the winter the geysers still erupt.
7. Underground steam explosions force hot water through a narrow opening.
8. Castle Geyser shoots water 90 feet into the air for nearly 20 minutes.
9. Old Faithful faithfully erupts on a fairly regular schedule.
10. After an eruption a geyser is quiet.
11. A geyser's spray changes from steam to ice almost instantly.
12. The frozen spray suddenly turns to strange-looking shapes.
13. Clouds of steam hang above warm ponds.
14. Colorful algae still grow around the hot springs.
15. All these things happen only at Yellowstone National Park.

Diagraming Prepositional Phrases

A prepositional phrase is diagramed underneath the word it describes. Often that word is directly in front of the prepositional phrase in the sentence.

The team of eight horses was beautiful.

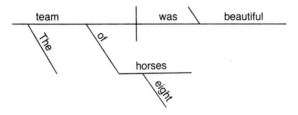

We walked along the river.

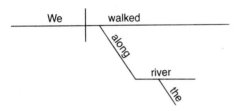

EXERCISE 6 Diagraming Prepositional Phrases

Diagram the following sentences or copy them. If your teacher tells you to copy them, draw one line under each subject and two lines under each verb. Then circle each prepositional phrase.

1. That tube of toothpaste is empty.
2. The cowboy rode across the prairie.
3. The temperature inside the house is high.
4. We were swimming in the lake.
5. The barn near the house is old.
6. The flowers in the vase have died.
7. Everyone dove under the table.
8. The telephone in the kitchen is broken.
9. The cat has crawled under the car.
10. Jim climbed up the ladder.

Application to Writing

Normally, people write the way they talk. They usually begin a sentence with the subject. That is the normal order for a sentence. You can create some variety in your writing by beginning some of your sentences with prepositional phrases.

NORMAL ORDER   We had a fire drill **during first period.**

VARIETY   **During first period** we had a fire drill.

NOTE: Put a comma after a prepositional phrase at the beginning of a sentence if the prepositional phrase has four or more words in it.

EXERCISE 7 Creating Sentence Variety

Number your paper 1 to 10. Find the prepositional phrase in each sentence. Then rewrite each sentence so that it begins with the prepositional phrase.

EXAMPLE   A typist's fingers travel 12.6 miles in a normal workday.

ANSWER   In a normal workday, a typist's fingers travel 12.6 miles.

1. Blue and white are the most common school colors in the United States.
2. Yellow is the most visible color on most roads.
3. Light can circle the earth nearly seven and one-half times in a single second.
4. Mosquitoes don't bother people in cool weather.
5. A dollar bill is worn out after 8,000 folds.
6. The average person walks 65,000 miles in a lifetime.
7. Leopards and tigers are endangered species in Asia.
8. Smell is the least developed of all the human senses.
9. Hong Kong is the noisiest city in all the world.
10. A rooster can crow 85 times in half an hour.

Conjunctions and Interjections

Conjunctions and interjections are parts of speech. Conjunctions connect words, and interjections show strong feeling.

5c A **conjunction** connects words or groups of words.

Following is a list of the most common coordinating conjunctions. These conjunctions connect single words and groups of words.

Coordinating Conjunctions		
and	but	or

WORDS — Eat a *plum* **or** a *pear*. [connects nouns]
It's for *him* **and** *her*. [connects pronouns]
The dog *growled* **and** *barked*. [connects verbs]
Dan is *tall* **but** *thin*. [connects adjectives]
She works *fast* **and** *neatly*. [connects adverbs]

GROUPS OF WORDS — The rake is *in the garage* **or** *on the back porch*. [connects prepositional phrases]
Rena and Jon *left the house early* **but** *arrived late at the airport*. [connects complete predicates]

5d An **interjection** is a word that expresses strong feeling.

An interjection at the beginning of a sentence is followed by an exclamation point or a comma.

Oops! I dropped a full pitcher of orange juice on the floor.
Well, no one could have done better!

EXERCISE 8 Finding Conjunctions

Number your paper 1 to 10. Then write each conjunction.

1. Black bears climb trees for nuts or honey.
2. Our new car's engine works quietly and efficiently.
3. The detective waited and listened.
4. All those divers are strong but graceful.
5. Walk the dog to the park or around the block.
6. My soup spilled on the table and dripped on the floor.
7. This small but cozy house belongs to my sister.
8. He or she should become the club president.
9. An alligator's nest is a big pile of mud and grass.
10. We wrote to the newspaper a month ago but have not received a reply.

EXERCISE 9 Writing Sentences

Number your paper 1 to 5. Then write five sentences that follow the directions below.

1. Use <u>and</u> to connect two nouns.
2. Use <u>or</u> to connect two verbs.
3. Use <u>but</u> to connect two adjectives.
4. Use <u>and</u> to connect two adverbs.
5. Use <u>or</u> to connect two prepositional phrases.

EXERCISE 10 Writing Sentences

Number your paper 1 to 5. Then write a sentence for each of the following interjections.

1. Aha!   2. Ouch!   3. Yes!   4. Ugh!   5. Wow!

EXERCISE 11 Writing Sentences

Pretend that you are exploring a newly found island with a group of scientists. You come across a strange animal that does not exist anywhere else in the world. Write five sentences that describe that animal. Use at least one conjunction and one interjection.

Chapter Review

A **Finding Prepositional Phrases.** Number your paper 1 to 10. Then write each prepositional phrase. There are 15 phrases.

Getting a Cat

1. Does everyone in your home want a cat?
2. Does anyone get sick around cats?
3. A cat can live for 18 years and will need your care during all those years.
4. Kittens shouldn't be taken from their mother before eight weeks.
5. Look for a kitten with bright eyes.
6. At your home you need bowls for food and water.
7. Never place a little tray near the cat's bed.
8. A good toy is an empty spool on a piece of string.
9. Make your cat a nice, warm bed inside a box.
10. Shots will protect your cat against diseases.

B **Finding Prepositional Phrases.** Number your paper 1 to 10. Then write each prepositional phrase. There are 15 phrases.

The New Godspeed

1. In 1985, the *Godspeed* sailed across the Atlantic.
2. The first *Godspeed* came to America in 1607.
3. The people on the first *Godspeed* settled the Jamestown colony.
4. The new ship was built by funds from Virginia.
5. The original sailors would find some surprises below the decks of the new *Godspeed*.
6. The new ship is equipped with a radio.
7. The cooks make delicious meals for the sailors.
8. The sailors on the original *Godspeed* went without these modern comforts and conveniences.
9. The first settlers did not land at Plymouth.
10. The Plymouth settlers landed 13 years after the Jamestown settlement.

C **Finding Conjunctions and Interjections.** Number your paper 1 to 10. Write each conjunction and interjection. Then label each one *conjunction* or *interjection*.

1. Smith and Chang are the most common names in the world.
2. The clouds were dark but beautiful.
3. Hurrah! I made an A on my English test.
4. We will find him and her a seat.
5. Wow! An ostrich egg is bigger than my father's hand.
6. My homework must be in my locker or at home.
7. Is your birthday in June or July?
8. The children talked fast and excitedly.
9. Penguins are birds but cannot fly.
10. Aha! I caught you with your hand in the cookie jar.

Mastery Test

Number your paper 1 to 10. Write each underlined word. Then label each one *preposition, conjunction,* or *interjection*.

1. Ten cities <u>across</u> the nation have more telephones than people.
2. Tonight I have math homework <u>and</u> history homework.
3. <u>Yes</u>! Nearly half the people in the United States over the age of three wear glasses.
4. Don't look <u>inside</u> the box.
5. Each eyelash lasts <u>for</u> only four months.
6. The movie was long <u>but</u> funny.
7. This letter is <u>from</u> your grandmother.
8. <u>Eek</u>! You scared me.
9. The mouse found its way <u>through</u> the maze.
10. One out of three adults cannot read <u>or</u> write.

Parts of Speech Review

Diagnostic Test

Number your paper 1 to 10. Write each underlined word. Then beside each word, write its part of speech: *noun, pronoun, verb, adjective, adverb, preposition, conjunction,* or *interjection.*

EXAMPLE   The tarantula <u>is</u> a large, fierce <u>spider</u>.
ANSWER   is—verb   spider—noun

1. He <u>carefully</u> folded the letter and put <u>it</u> into a small envelope.
2. He <u>painted</u> his room with red <u>paint</u>!
3. Fresh blueberries <u>or</u> strawberries are delicious <u>with</u> cereal.
4. Paul and <u>I</u> often <u>shoot</u> baskets after school.
5. The <u>Hawaiian</u> lei is a symbol of <u>friendship</u>.
6. Did you buy <u>those</u> skates at the <u>mall</u>?
7. We <u>always</u> pay the rent <u>on</u> time.
8. <u>Ugh</u>! That chicken is still <u>raw</u> on the inside.
9. The horses of the <u>Comanches</u> were small <u>and</u> powerful animals.
10. <u>Those</u> are the best <u>paint</u> brushes.

*P*arts of Speech Review

This chapter reviews the eight parts of speech. Remember that a word does not become a part of speech until it is used in a sentence. The word *iron,* for example, can be used as three parts of speech.

NOUN   Watch out! The **iron** is hot.
VERB   **Iron** your shirt tonight.
ADJECTIVE   Those **iron** rods are very strong.

The following series of questions will help you determine a word's part of speech.

NOUN   Is the word naming a person, place, thing, or idea?
Jan values the **book** of **poems.**

PRONOUN   Is the word taking the place of a noun?
These are the books **he** wanted.

VERB   Is the word showing action?
I **rode** the Ferris wheel three times.

Does the word link the subject with another word in the sentence?

The soup **is** very hot!

ADJECTIVE   Is the word describing a noun or a pronoun? Does it answer the question *What kind? How many? How much?* or *Which one?*

Those two kitchen chairs are **new.**

ADVERB   Is the word describing a verb, an adjective, or another adverb? Does it answer the question *How? When? Where?* or *To what extent?*

Usually our athletes run **quite fast.**

PREPOSITION   Is the word showing a relationship between a noun or a pronoun and another word in the sentence? Is it part of a phrase?
  ***After* school** come ***to* my house.**

CONJUNCTION   Is the word connecting words or groups of words?
  For breakfast I had juice **and** cereal.
  Pedro can visit the library before school **or** after school.

INTERJECTION   Is the word expressing strong feeling?
  Ouch! A bee just stung me.

EXERCISE 1   *Identifying Parts of Speech*

Number your paper 1 to 10. Write each underlined word. Then beside each one, write its part of speech: *noun, pronoun, verb, adjective, adverb, preposition, conjunction,* or *interjection.*

EXAMPLE   Lotus plants <u>are</u> water <u>plants</u> with pink flowers.
ANSWER   are—verb   plants—noun

From Long Ago

1. Hundreds of years ago, lotus plants were growing <u>in</u> a lake in <u>China</u>.
2. <u>Eventually</u> the <u>lake</u> dried up.
3. Somehow many <u>of</u> the lotus seeds were preserved in the hardened <u>mud</u>.
4. A <u>Japanese</u> scientist <u>carefully</u> dug some of the seeds out of the mud.
5. He put <u>them</u> into a box and forgot about them for <u>30</u> years.
6. In 1951, <u>he</u> gave two seeds to an <u>American</u> scientist.
7. Then that man <u>returned</u> to <u>America</u>.
8. He <u>put</u> the seeds on damp cotton <u>under</u> a glass cover.
9. <u>Surprise</u>! The seeds soon sprouted <u>and</u> grew into lotus plants.
10. <u>Now</u> the descendants of those seeds <u>thrive</u> in the Kenilworth Aquatic Gardens in Washington, D.C.

EXERCISE 2 *Identifying Parts of Speech*

Number your paper 1 to 10. Write each underlined word. Then beside each one, write its part of speech: *noun, pronoun, verb, adjective, adverb, preposition, conjunction,* or *interjection.*

Migration

1. Twice a year <u>many</u> animals make long <u>journeys</u>.
2. <u>They</u> migrate from place <u>to</u> place.
3. Swallows <u>are</u> <u>great</u> travelers.
4. Each spring they leave Africa <u>and</u> fly to <u>Europe</u>.
5. <u>Faithfully</u> salmon migrate <u>from</u> the sea to rivers.
6. <u>Wow</u>! The <u>European</u> eel swims nearly 3,000 miles.
7. <u>After</u> its long journey, <u>it</u> lays its eggs.
8. Reindeer <u>live</u> <u>near</u> the North Pole.
9. In <u>winter</u> their food supply grows <u>short</u>.
10. They <u>travel</u> hundreds <u>of</u> miles to the south.

EXERCISE 3 *Identifying Parts of Speech*

Number your paper 1 to 10. Write each underlined word. Then beside each one, write its part of speech: *noun, pronoun, verb, adjective, adverb, preposition, conjunction,* or *interjection.*

The Names of the Planets

1. All the planets, except the earth, were named <u>for</u> a <u>god</u> or goddess in mythology.
2. <u>Mercury</u>, the planet closest <u>to</u> the sun, is named for the Roman god of travel.
3. Mercury <u>travels</u> around the sun in only <u>88</u> days.
4. Venus is named for the goddess of love <u>and</u> <u>beauty</u>.
5. <u>She</u> was beautiful, and to people on earth, Venus <u>is</u> the most beautiful planet.
6. It <u>shines</u> very <u>brightly</u> in the morning or evening.
7. <u>Sometimes</u> Venus looks like a beacon <u>or</u> the taillight on an airplane.
8. <u>Yes</u>! Jupiter is named for the <u>king</u> of the gods.
9. <u>It</u> is the <u>largest</u> planet.
10. The moons <u>around</u> Jupiter are <u>also</u> named after mythological characters.

EXERCISE 4 *Identifying Parts of Speech*

Number your paper 1 to 20. Write each underlined word. Then beside each one, write its part of speech: *noun, pronoun, verb, adjective, adverb, preposition, conjunction,* or *interjection.*

Is Anyone Out There?

What do (1) <u>you</u> think? Does extraterrestrial (2) <u>life</u> exist? (3) <u>Some</u> scientists say yes (4) <u>but</u> are looking for proof. This job cannot be done (5) <u>by</u> spaceships. A spaceship would (6) <u>not</u> reach the nearest (7) <u>star</u> for (8) <u>40,000</u> years. What (9) <u>is</u> the answer? Scientists are (10) <u>now</u> using (11) <u>giant</u> antennas. (12) <u>They</u> are listening for signals from a far-off (13) <u>civilization</u>.

One 84-foot antenna is called META (Megachannel Extraterrestrial Assay). (14) <u>It</u> is located at the Oak Ridge Observatory in (15) <u>Massachusetts</u>. (16) <u>Wow</u>! In 1985, its powerful scanning system (17) <u>tuned</u> in to some 400 billion stars in our galaxy.

Scientists are planning a whole group of antennas. They will stretch 5,000 miles (18) <u>across</u> the United States from Hawaii to the Virgin Islands. The scientists also (19) <u>want</u> antennas on the moon (20) <u>or</u> on satellites in space.

EXERCISE 5 *Determining Parts of Speech*

Number your paper 1 to 10. Write each underlined word. Then beside each one, write its part of speech: *noun, pronoun,* or *adjective.*

1. <u>This</u> is my favorite dinner.
2. Tim and Jill made a <u>magazine</u> rack for the library.
3. Granddad planted this <u>tree</u> 50 years ago.
4. Take a picture of <u>those</u> horses.
5. Have you ever read <u>this</u> book?
6. My <u>birthday</u> is the first of March.
7. Several <u>tree</u> limbs must be pruned.
8. <u>Those</u> are the grapes without seeds.
9. The subscription to the <u>magazine</u> is for one year.
10. Light the <u>birthday</u> candles.

*E*XERCISE 6 *Determining Parts of Speech*

Number your paper 1 to 10. Write each underlined word. Then beside each one, write its part of speech: *noun, pronoun, verb, adjective, adverb, preposition, conjunction,* or *interjection.*

1. <u>That</u> is my favorite <u>vegetable</u>.
2. Does <u>she</u> take <u>piano</u> lessons?
3. <u>Yikes</u>! The <u>garden</u> hose just sprung a leak.
4. What kind of <u>music</u> does <u>he</u> enjoy?
5. Several trout were jumping <u>above</u> the <u>water</u>.
6. <u>I</u> enjoyed your <u>vegetable</u> casserole.
7. <u>Suddenly</u> the lights went <u>out</u>.
8. The <u>piano</u> in the <u>music</u> room is old.
9. Are <u>you</u> growing pumpkins in your <u>garden</u>?
10. Do you want a <u>water</u> glass <u>or</u> a juice glass?

*E*XERCISE 7 *Labeling Parts of Speech*

Number your paper 1 to 5. Copy the following sentences. Then above each word, write the abbreviation for its part of speech. Remember that the articles *a, an,* and *the* are adjectives.

noun = *n.*	adjective = *adj.*	conjunction= *conj.*
pronoun = *pron.*	adverb = *adv.*	interjection = *interj.*
verb = *v.*	preposition = *prep.*	

EXAMPLE   They will make some posters for the dance.
ANSWER   They will make some posters for the dance.
           pron. v.   v.   adj. n.   prep. adj. n.

1. December begins in three days.
2. Those boys and girls are from the high school.
3. Hurrah! We have beaten our rivals.
4. I have finally finished the last math problem.
5. The French students will soon return to Paris.

*E*XERCISE 8 *Writing Sentences*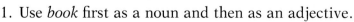

1. Use *book* first as a noun and then as an adjective.
2. Use *this* first as an adjective and then as a pronoun.

*C*hapter *R*eview

A **Identifying Parts of Speech.** Number your paper 1 to 10. Write each underlined word. Then write its part of speech: *noun, pronoun, verb, adjective, adverb, preposition, conjunction,* or *interjection.*

Bees

1. A <u>beehive</u> is about the size of a <u>small</u> doghouse.
2. <u>In</u> summer <u>it</u> houses up to 60,000 bees.
3. The queen bee <u>has</u> only <u>one</u> job.
4. <u>She</u> lays about <u>1,500</u> eggs each day.
5. Worker bees <u>do</u> all the household chores <u>and</u> bring in all the food.
6. The youngest bees <u>always</u> stay <u>inside</u> the hive.
7. They <u>clean</u> the cells <u>or</u> care for the eggs.
8. <u>After</u> three weeks <u>they</u> graduate to outside jobs.
9. Workers <u>usually</u> stay <u>within</u> two miles of the hive.
10. <u>Ah</u>! In six weeks they wear out their <u>wings</u> and die.

B **Identifying Parts of Speech.** Number your paper 1 to 10. Write each underlined word. Then write its part of speech: *noun, pronoun, verb, adjective, adverb, preposition, conjunction,* or *interjection.*

One of a Kind

1. Would <u>you</u> live in an underground <u>house</u>?
2. Baldasare Forestiere <u>liked</u> the <u>idea</u> very much.
3. In 1906, he <u>dug</u> a <u>huge</u> underground home.
4. He carved <u>it</u> out of clay near Fresno, <u>California</u>.
5. <u>He</u> used only <u>hand</u> tools such as a pick and a shovel.
6. <u>Originally</u> he scooped out only a kitchen and a bedroom <u>but</u> then dug more and more.
7. <u>Amazing</u>! He <u>eventually</u> had <u>65</u> rooms.
8. Most rooms had holes <u>in</u> the roof for light <u>and</u> air.
9. He <u>planted</u> shrubs and tropical trees and added a fish pond and a fireplace <u>for</u> chilly nights.
10. <u>Now</u> this unusual home is open <u>to</u> visitors.

C **Determining Parts of Speech.** Number your paper 1 to 10. Write each underlined word. Then write its part of speech: *noun, pronoun,* or *adjective.*

1. WDRC is my favorite <u>radio</u> station.
2. Read <u>these</u> two poems for your homework.
3. I got a new <u>camera</u> for my birthday.
4. My sister just got a <u>diamond</u> engagement ring.
5. We should discuss <u>that</u> as soon as possible.
6. This <u>camera</u> lens must belong to you.
7. Listen to the special program on the <u>radio</u> tonight.
8. Is that a real <u>diamond</u>?
9. How did <u>these</u> get into the laundry basket?
10. I baked <u>that</u> loaf of bread myself.

Mastery Test

Number your paper 1 to 10. Write each underlined word. Then beside each word, write its part of speech: *noun, pronoun, verb, adjective, adverb, preposition, conjunction,* or *interjection.*

1. The <u>French</u> waiter was <u>extremely</u> polite.
2. <u>With</u> its trunk, an elephant can uproot a tree, pick up a pin, <u>or</u> untie a slipknot.
3. I have <u>never</u> owned a ten-speed <u>bicycle</u>.
4. <u>These</u> fresh oranges are quite <u>juicy</u>.
5. <u>She</u> takes great <u>pride</u> in her children.
6. Four of the first five United States presidents <u>came</u> from <u>Virginia</u>.
7. We discovered that the heart <u>of</u> a blue whale weighs about 1,200 <u>pounds</u>.
8. We <u>found</u> an old <u>bicycle</u> pump in the garage.
9. <u>Well</u>! I certainly don't like <u>these</u>.
10. The Bolas spider spins its own rope <u>and</u> throws it <u>around</u> its prey.

Simple and Compound Sentences

Diagnostic Test

Number your paper 1 to 10. If a sentence is a simple sentence, write *simple*. If a sentence is a compound sentence, write *compound*.

EXAMPLE   We saw a mouse, but it ran outside.
ANSWER   compound

1. Asia and Europe are attached, and sometimes these two continents together are called Eurasia.
2. Terry slugged the ball and ran to first base.
3. We can buy the film now, or Jeff can get it later.
4. Spices are used in medicine and perfumes.
5. Most deer are the size of a pony, but the musk deer is the size of a small dog.
6. My birthday and my brother's birthday are on the same date in March.
7. We will wait for you here or meet you in the gym.
8. Earthquakes roll big stones around and sometimes uncover fossils.
9. The mail just arrived, and you have two letters.
10. Toads live on land, but frogs can live in the water.

Simple Sentences

There are different kinds of sentences. Including different kinds of sentences in your writing will give your writing more variety and make your writing more interesting. One kind of sentence is called a *simple sentence.*

A **simple sentence** is a sentence that has one subject and one verb.

In the following examples, each subject is underlined once, and each verb is underlined twice.

ONE SUBJECT, <u>Batman</u> <u><u>has</u></u> super powers.
ONE VERB <u>He</u> <u><u>lives</u></u> in Gotham City.

In a simple sentence, either the subject or the verb can be compound.

COMPOUND SUBJECT The <u>Joker</u> and the <u>Penguin</u> <u><u>are</u></u> Batman's enemies. [Both subjects share the verb <u><u>are</u></u>.]

COMPOUND VERB <u>Batman</u> <u><u>rides</u></u> in his speedy Batmobile and <u><u>flies</u></u> in his swift Batplane. [Both verbs share the subject <u>Batman</u>.]

EXERCISE 1 Writing Sentences

Number your paper 1 to 10. Then use the following compound subjects and compound verbs to write ten simple sentences.

EXAMPLE ate and drank
POSSIBLE ANSWER I ate some toast and drank some juice.

1. July and August
2. carrots or peas
3. planes and helicopters
4. dogs or cats
5. purple and orange
6. ran and hid
7. sat and waited
8. tossed and turned
9. slipped and fell
10. rode and jumped

Compound Sentences

Two or more simple sentences can be placed together to make another kind of sentence, a *compound sentence.*

A **compound sentence** is made up of two simple sentences, usually joined by a comma and the coordinating conjunction *and, but,* or *or.*

If the comma and the conjunction are dropped from a compound sentence, two simple sentences remain.

COMPOUND SENTENCE	I <u>have fed</u> the chickens, and <u>David</u> <u>has</u> <u>brought</u> the cows in.
SIMPLE SENTENCES	I <u>have fed</u> the chickens. David <u>has brought</u> the cows in.
COMPOUND SENTENCE	The <u>computer</u> <u>is working</u>, but the <u>printer</u> <u>is</u> <u>broken</u>.
SIMPLE SENTENCES	The <u>computer</u> <u>is working</u>. The <u>printer</u> <u>is broken</u>.
COMPOUND SENTENCES	Tonight I <u>will read</u> a book, or my <u>brother</u> <u>will</u> <u>take</u> me to a movie.
SIMPLE SENTENCES	Tonight I <u>will read</u> a book. My <u>brother</u> <u>will take</u> me to a movie.

NOTE: Use the conjunction *and* when the second part of a compound sentence adds more information. Use *but* when it shows a contrast or gives a different point of view. Use *or* when it gives a choice.

Do not confuse a compound sentence with a simple sentence that has a compound verb.

COMPOUND SENTENCE	I <u>ran</u> very fast, and the <u>kite</u> <u>soared</u> into the blue sky. [The two subjects are *I* and *kite*.]
COMPOUND VERB	I <u>ran</u> very fast and <u>loosened</u> the string on the kite. [There's only one subject, *I*.]

EXERCISE 2 Understanding Compound Sentences

Number your paper 1 to 10. Copy each compound sentence. Underline each subject once and each verb twice. Then circle each conjunction.

EXAMPLE   Monday is the third, and Friday is the seventh.
ANSWER   <u>Monday</u> <u><u>is</u></u> the third, (and) <u>Friday</u> <u><u>is</u></u> the seventh.

1. My bicycle has a flat tire, and I lost my pump.
2. I will write my report carefully today, or I will type it tomorrow.
3. Birch leaves turn yellow, but maple leaves turn red.
4. The bulldozer dug a hole, and we poured cement.
5. I will make a meatloaf, or you can make spaghetti.
6. John is tall, but his parents are short.
7. Monday is a holiday, and our school is closed.
8. The movie was dull, but I stayed until the end.
9. For hours the rain poured, and the thunder boomed.
10. His temperature is high, but his pulse is normal.

EXERCISE 3 Recognizing Compound Sentences

Number your paper 1 to 10. Then label each sentence *simple* or *compound*.

Laser Beams

1. A beam of light hits a diamond, and it splits.
2. Light strikes a needle, and instantly a hole appears.
3. This light is a laser beam, and it is amazing.
4. Workers cut and weld metal with laser beams.
5. With laser beams scientists send signals into space and measure distances to other planets.
6. Laser beams read price codes on items in a grocery store and transfer the prices to the cash register.
7. Ordinary light is weak, but lasers are stronger.
8. Ordinary light spreads and fades in short distances.
9. Light from a laser moves in a straight line and travels long distances.
10. The power of a laser can be controlled, and scientists can adjust a laser for different jobs.

Punctuating Compound Sentences

If the parts of a compound sentence are joined by a conjunction, add a comma. If the parts of a compound sentence are *not* joined by a conjunction, add a semicolon.

COMMA WITH A COMPOUND SENTENCE	Katie's parakeet is yellow**, but** my parakeet is blue.
SEMICOLON WITH A COMPOUND SENTENCE	Parakeets are small birds**;** parrots are much larger.

No comma comes between the parts of a compound verb.

NO COMMA WITH A COMPOUND VERB	We put our parakeet into its cage and covered the cage for the night.

---

*E*XERCISE 4 *Punctuating Compound Sentences*

Number your paper 1 to 10. Write each compound sentence and punctuate it correctly with a comma or a semicolon. If a sentence does not need any punctuation, write *none* after the number.

Animal Facts

1. An elephant is the largest land animal a blue whale is the largest sea animal.
2. An aardvark lives in Africa and eats termites.
3. A panda looks like a bear but the raccoon is its closest relative.
4. Male tigers always live and hunt alone.
5. Indian rhinoceroses have one horn African rhinoceroses have two horns.
6. Female lions watch the cubs and hunt for food.
7. A kangaroo measures $4\frac{1}{2}$ feet but its tail measures another $3\frac{1}{2}$ feet.
8. A mother sheep is a ewe a father sheep is a ram.
9. A giraffe can be 13 feet tall and weigh 4,000 pounds.
10. Gorillas sleep 14 hours a day but elephants sleep only 2 hours.

*T*IME-OUT FOR REVIEW • • • • •

Number your paper 1 to 15. Then label each sentence *simple* or *compound*.

Meteors and Meteorites

1. Shooting stars are not stars, and they do not shoot.
2. People see meteors and call them shooting stars.
3. A meteor shines brightly, but meteors are not stars.
4. Stars are suns far out in space, but meteors are bits of metal or rock.
5. Sometimes these bits of metal and rock streak through the earth's atmosphere and burn.
6. Meteors glow brightly, but we can see them for only a few seconds
7. Most meteors burn up in the earth's atmosphere.
8. Others fall to the earth's surface; those meteors are called meteorites.
9. Scientists have collected and examined several thousand meteorites.
10. Most meteorites are very small, but some are large.
11. The American Museum of Natural History in New York has a meteorite on display; it weighs 31 tons.
12. It fell thousands of years ago in Greenland, and scientists brought it to the museum in 1906.
13. Only about 150 meteorites a year make it through the atmosphere and land on the earth.
14. In 1971, a meteorite went through the roof of a Connecticut home, but no one was hurt.
15. Eleven years later a meteorite hit another Connecticut house—less than a mile away.

*E*XERCISE 5 *Writing Sentences*

Write five or six sentences that describe a UFO. At least two sentences should be compound sentences.

Run-on Sentences

When a compound sentence is written without a conjunction or proper punctuation, the result is a *run-on sentence*. Run-on sentences are confusing to read. One sentence runs into another. A reader is never sure where one idea ends and another idea begins.

7c A **run-on sentence** is two or more sentences that are written as one sentence. They are separated by a comma or have no mark of punctuation at all.

Some run-on sentences have only a comma and no conjunction. Other run-on sentences have neither a comma nor a conjunction.

RUN-ON SENTENCES

The fire is dying out, we have no more wood. [only a comma and no conjunction]

Our grades are posted I made an *A*. [no comma and no conjunction]

There are two ways to correct run-on sentences. You can write the two sentences as separate sentences.

SEPARATE SENTENCES

The fire is dying out. We have no more wood.

Our grades are posted. I made an *A*.

You can also write the two sentences as a compound sentence with a comma and the conjunction *and, but,* or *or*.

COMPOUND SENTENCES

The fire is dying out, **but** we have no more wood. [The conjunction *but* was added.]

Our grades are posted**, and** I made an *A*. [The conjunction *and* and a comma were both added.]

NOTE: Only combine closely related sentences in a run-on sentence into a compound sentence. If the sentences are not closely related, make them into separate sentences.

104

EXERCISE 6   Correcting Run-on Sentences

Number your paper 1 to 15. Then correct each run-on sentence (1) by writing two separate sentences, or (2) by writing a compound sentence. Remember to use capital letters, commas, and end marks correctly.

EXAMPLE   A survey was conducted, Americans rated cycling as the fourth most enjoyable sport.

ANSWER   A survey was conducted, and Americans rated cycling as the fourth most enjoyable sport.

Bicycles

1. Bicycles became popular between 1890 and 1900 these years were The Golden Age of the Bicycle.
2. The automobile arrived   the bicycle craze ended.
3. Then around 1960, the bicycle staged a comeback, cycling is still growing in popularity today.
4. Today millions of people are riding bicycles every year more bicycles are sold than cars.
5. Why do so many people ride bicycles   there are many reasons.
6. Some people ride to school or work,   others ride for pleasure.
7. Bicycle competitions are springing up across the country people enjoy the challenge of these events.
8. Some events are local road races,   the most challenging is Olympic speed racing.
9. Cycling is a healthful exercise,   you get somewhere at the same time.
10. Look at expert cyclists they are all thin.
11. Cycling is good exercise   it is also one of the best diets in the world.
12. Cycling burns up calories they are burned up in a pleasant way.
13. General riding burns up 500 to 800 calories an hour, faster riding burns up even more.
14. Bicycles haven't changed much over the past 20 years,   the future may have some big surprises.
15. Engineers are testing new models they will be enclosed, high-speed bicycles.

EXERCISE 7 Editing for Run-on Sentences

Rewrite the following paragraphs, correcting each run-on sentence. Remember to use capital letters, commas, and end marks correctly.

Lost: A True Story

Second officer Harry Kindall first noticed the black and white terrier it was coming up the gangplank of the *Proud Lady*. Once on board the dog stood perfectly still and looked all around. The deck was loaded with lumber, the dog sniffed it carefully.

Then the dog returned to shore and boarded the next ship. Kindall watched the dog it repeated this same routine on each ship at the port. Soon Kindall got busy, at noon the *Proud Lady* left Canada for Japan.

Kindall found the dog early the next morning it was lying outside the captain's cabin. It had come aboard again and had stowed away. The sailors were friendly toward the terrier, it seemed indifferent to them.

For 18 days the *Proud Lady* plowed across the Pacific then the coast of Japan was sighted. The ship eventually reached the harbor and stopped between two other ships.

The terrier ran from one side of the ship to the other and looked at the other ships. Its tail switched back and forth, its nostrils quivered nervously. The nearest ship was a Dutch ship workers were unloading lumber from it.

Just then a rowboat with two men in it was lowered from the Dutch ship, the boat headed toward the shore. Suddenly the dog barked frantically, the rowboat stopped. The men looked up and saw the terrier.

One of the men in the rowboat jumped to his feet and called out excitedly to the dog. The rowboat turned back and headed toward the *Proud Lady*. The rowboat came alongside the ship, the dog leaped into the water. The man pulled the dog from the water and hugged him. The dog whined and licked his face the dog and its master were reunited. How had the dog picked the *Proud Lady* to find its master? No one knows—except, perhaps, the black and white terrier.

Diagraming Compound Sentences

A compound sentence is diagramed like two simple sentences with the subject and verb on the baseline. The direct object is also on the baseline as in the example below. The two diagrams are connected by a broken line. The broken line joins the two verbs. The conjunction that joins the two sentences is written on the broken line.

Jerry caught a fish, and Dad cooked it.

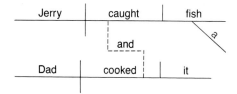

EXERCISE 8 Diagraming Compound Sentences

Diagram the following sentences or copy them. If your teacher tells you to copy them, draw one line under each subject and two lines under each verb. If your teacher tells you to diagram them, follow the example above.

1. Lea read the poem, and we listened.
2. Andy made a home run, and the Warriors won.
3. You must row, or the boat will drift.
4. I like basketball, but Pam prefers football.
5. Sue lit the birthday candles, and everyone sang.
6. I opened a bank account, and now the money is earning interest.
7. We attended the dance, and the band played many old songs.
8. I rang the doorbell, but nobody answered it.
9. You can drive me, or I will take the bus.
10. The electricity went out, and we could not find any candles.

A pplication to Writing

Combine some simple sentences to add variety to your writing. Two sentences with the same subject can be combined into a simple sentence with a compound verb.

TWO SIMPLE SENTENCES The <u>horse</u> <u>jumped</u> over the fence.
The <u>horse</u> <u>grazed</u> in the pasture.

COMPOUND VERB The <u>horse</u> <u>jumped</u> over the fence and <u>grazed</u> in the pasture.

Two closely related simple sentences with different subjects can be combined to form a compound sentence. Add either a comma and a conjunction or a semicolon.

TWO SIMPLE SENTENCES The <u>doctor</u> <u>examined</u> the patient. The <u>nurse</u> <u>assisted</u> her.

COMPOUND SENTENCE The <u>doctor</u> <u>examined</u> the patient, and the <u>nurse</u> <u>assisted</u> her. [comma and conjunction added]
The <u>doctor</u> <u>examined</u> the patient; the <u>nurse</u> <u>assisted</u> her. [semicolon added]

EXERCISE 9 Combining Sentences

Combine the following pairs of sentences into simple sentences with compound verbs or compound sentences.

1. Carol is a musician. Her brother is an artist.
2. The movie's plot was realistic. The acting was bad.
3. I will take the bus. I will walk to school.
4. She jogs each morning. She swims every weekend.
5. Our dog is old. Our cat is only six weeks old.
6. The hare took a nap. The tortoise crawled slowly on.
7. The popcorn looks stale. The popcorn tastes stale.
8. We must bail out some water. The boat will sink.
9. He found a coded message. He figured out the code.
10. Dark clouds blocked the sun. Huge hail stones fell.

Chapter Review

A **Recognizing Compound Sentences.** Number your paper 1 to 10. Read each sentence. Then label each sentence *simple* or *compound*.

The Giant Sequoias

1. A race of giants lives on this earth, but these giants do not walk.
2. These giants grow in California and are firmly rooted in the ground.
3. They are the giant sequoias, and many people visit them every year.
4. The largest sequoia measures more than 100 feet around its base and is over 270 feet tall.
5. Its largest branch is seven feet thick, and a full-grown man could lie across it.
6. The roots of a sequoia are shallow but spread out over three acres, the size of four football fields.
7. The bark of the sequoia is thick and protects it.
8. Fires have burned some sequoias, but they have grown new wood over the scars.
9. Many sequoias are 3,000 to 4,000 years old, and these trees are still producing new seeds.
10. Many of these giant trees have been cut down; only a small number of them remain.

B **Correcting Run-on Sentences.** Number your paper 1 to 10. Then correct each run-on sentence by writing two separate sentences or a compound sentence.

1. Egyptians built the first nation, other nations conquered it many times.
2. I bought a sweater, it's too small for me.
3. My pen ran dry I don't have another one.
4. A bird is building a nest it looks like a sparrow.

109

5. The giant squid has the largest eyes   each eye is as big as a basketball.
6. I studied for my social studies test for three hours it is tomorrow.
7. Water is necessary for life,   no water was found on the moon.
8. The earth is slowing down in 600,000,000 B.C., a day was only 21 hours.
9. I like funny movies,   my older sister likes romances.
10. In its early days, China was many small kingdoms the country was finally united in 221 B.C.

*M*astery *T*est

Number your paper 1 to 10. If a sentence is a simple sentence, write *simple*. If a sentence is a compound sentence, write *compound*.

1. James Watt invented the steam engine, and his invention greatly changed life in the 1800s.
2. A thermometer measures the temperature, but a barometer measures air pressure.
3. I have made dinner and will serve it at six.
4. The airplane circled the small airport and then landed on the single runway.
5. Most birds avoid darkness, but more than half of the world's mammals hunt at night.
6. Fire heats the air, and the warm air heats you.
7. The moon has changed over millions of years and is still changing.
8. The hurricane is getting stronger, and the waves are getting higher.
9. I ran to the bus stop and still missed the bus.
10. The dolphin jumped from the water and snatched a fish from its trainer's hand.

Standardized Test

Directions: Decide which description best fits each group of words. In the appropriate row on your answer sheet, fill in the circle containing the same letter as your answer.

SAMPLE   At the pool with Jamie.

     A fragment   **B** run-on   **C** sentence

ANSWER   Ⓐ Ⓑ Ⓒ

1. The top of the mountain.

   A fragment   **B** run-on   **C** sentence

2. The gym is crowded.

   A fragment   **B** run-on   **C** sentence

3. Marcie frowned.

   A fragment   **B** run-on   **C** sentence

4. The dogs barked, and the cat ran away.

   A fragment   **B** run-on   **C** sentence

5. Below the surface of the water.

   A fragment   **B** run-on   **C** sentence

6. Dinner was almost ready, we were hungry.

   A fragment   **B** run-on   **C** sentence

7. The alligator chased the small boat for two miles.

   A fragment   **B** run-on   **C** sentence

8. The phone rang, nobody was there.

   A fragment   **B** run-on   **C** sentence

9. Ran from the window to the door.

   A fragment   **B** run-on   **C** sentence

10. Red gym shoes with black and gold laces on them.

   A fragment   **B** run-on   **C** sentence

Directions: Decide which underlined part is the subject in each sentence. On your answer sheet, fill in the circle containing the same letter as your answer.

SAMPLE   The <u>bull</u> <u>jumped</u> over the <u>fence</u>.
              A   **B**   **C**

ANSWER Ⓐ Ⓑ Ⓒ

11. The <u>cook</u> <u>stirred</u> the <u>soup</u>.
     A   **B**   **C**

12. <u>Has</u> <u>Pat</u> talked to <u>you</u>?
    A **B**   **C**

13. <u>On</u> the <u>branch</u> sat a small brown <u>bird</u>.
    A   **B**   **C**

14. <u>Three</u> <u>sailboats</u> floated on the <u>water</u>.
    A   **B**   **C**

15. A <u>piece</u> of <u>fruit</u> makes a good <u>snack</u>.
      A   **B**   **C**

Directions: Decide which underlined part is the verb in each sentence. On your answer sheet, fill in the circle containing the same letter as your answer.

SAMPLE   The <u>sun</u> <u>shone</u> <u>brightly</u>.
              A   **B**   **C**

ANSWER Ⓐ Ⓑ Ⓒ

16. The <u>wall</u> <u>fell</u> <u>down</u>.
     A   **B** **C**

17. <u>He</u> <u>was</u> a <u>good</u> artist.
   A **B**   **C**

18. <u>Through</u> the hoop <u>jumped</u> the <u>dog</u>.
    A   **B**   **C**

19. The top <u>drawer</u> <u>often</u> <u>sticks</u>.
        A   **B**   **C**

20. She <u>has</u> <u>done</u> the <u>dance</u> <u>step</u>.
        A   **B** **C**

Usage

8

Using Verbs

Diagnostic Test

Number your paper 1 to 10. Then write the correct verb form for each sentence.

EXAMPLE Jill (threw, throwed) the ball.
ANSWER   threw

1. My sister has (wrote, written) several poems and a children's story.
2. Have you ever (saw, seen) a live chimpanzee?
3. The hurricane has (blew, blown) out to sea.
4. My mother (drove, drived) us to the movies.
5. The Bennetts have (came, come) to each hockey game.
6. Dan (ringed, rang) the doorbell.
7. Megan (swam, swum) from the boat to the dock.
8. Amy has (chose, chosen) basketball and tennis as her favorite sports.
9. The rainy season in Africa has (began, begun).
10. Daniel has (went, gone) to the aquarium with his sister and brother.

Principal Parts of Verbs

As you know, a verb shows action or gives information about a subject. Another thing the verb does is tell when the action happens.

PRESENT ACTION   I **write** in my journal every day.

   PAST ACTION   I **wrote** in my journal yesterday.

FUTURE ACTION   I **will write** in my journal tomorrow.

In order to show when the action happens, a verb changes its form. The different forms are made from the basic parts of the verb. These basic parts are called *principal parts.*

8a Three of the **principal parts** of a verb are the *present,* the *past,* and the *past participle.*

Regular Verbs

Most verbs form their past and past participle in a regular way. These verbs are called *regular verbs.*

8b The past and the past participle of a **regular verb** are formed by adding *-ed* or *-d* to the present.

The principal parts of the regular verbs *stretch, note, lift,* and *jog* are listed below. Notice that some words, like *jog,* double the final consonant before *-ed* is added.

PRESENT	PAST	PAST PARTICIPLE
stretch	stretch**ed**	(have) stretch**ed**
note	note**d**	(has) note**d**
lift	lift**ed**	(has) lift**ed**
jog	jog**ged**	(had) jog**ged**

NOTE: A helping verb such as *have, has,* or *had* is always used with the past participle.

115

*E*XERCISE 1 *Writing the Principal Parts of Regular Verbs*

Make three columns on your paper. Label them *present, past,* and *past participle*. Then write the three principal parts of each of the following regular verbs. Use *have* when you write the past participle.

1. walk   3. drop   5. jump   7. listen   9. remember
2. save   4. plan   6. dream   8. count   10. watch

Irregular Verbs

Some verbs do not form their past participle by adding *-ed* or *-d*. They are called *irregular verbs*.

8c ▸ An **irregular verb** does not form its past and past participle by adding *-ed* or *-d* to the present.

The following irregular verbs are grouped according to the way their past and past participles are formed.

Group 1

These irregular verbs have the same form for the present, the past, and the past participle.

PRESENT	PAST	PAST PARTICIPLE
burst	burst	(have) burst
hit	hit	(have) hit
put	put	(have) put

Group 2

These irregular verbs have the same form for the past and the past participle.

PRESENT	PAST	PAST PARTICIPLE
bring	brought	(have) brought
catch	caught	(have) caught
hear	heard	(have) heard
say	said	(have) said
tell	told	(have) told
think	thought	(have) thought

116

*E*XERCISE 2 *Using the Correct Verb Form*

Number your paper 1 to 10. Then label each underlined verb form *past* or *past participle*. Remember that *have, has*, or *had* is used with the past participle.

1. Ann <u>brought</u> sweaters and jackets for the children.
2. I have <u>thought</u> about several names for my new puppy.
3. Nancy has <u>caught</u> a very bad cold.
4. Tim's father had already <u>told</u> him the answer to the riddle.
5. The balloon <u>burst</u> with a loud bang.
6. David <u>caught</u> two perch and a trout.
7. I have <u>heard</u> that story before.
8. Mrs. Yates <u>said</u> the directions twice.
9. Sue has <u>hit</u> the ball into left field three times.
10. Carlos has <u>put</u> the poster on the bulletin board.

Group 3

These irregular verbs form the past participle by adding *-n* to the past.

PRESENT	PAST	PAST PARTICIPLE
break	broke	(have) broken
choose	chose	(have) chosen
freeze	froze	(have) frozen
speak	spoke	(have) spoken
steal	stole	(have) stolen

Group 4

These irregular verbs form the past participle by adding *-n* to the present.

PRESENT	PAST	PAST PARTICIPLE
blow	blew	(have) blown
drive	drove	(have) driven
give	gave	(have) given
grow	grew	(have) grown
know	knew	(have) known
see	saw	(have) seen
take	took	(have) taken
throw	threw	(have) thrown

117

E*XERCISE 3* *Determining the Correct Verb Form*

Number your paper 1 to 10. Then write the correct verb form for each sentence. Remember that *have, has,* or *had* is used with the past participle.

EXAMPLE   I have (saw, seen) the Grand Canyon.
ANSWER   seen

1. The wind has (blew, blown) all the leaves off the maple tree outside my window.
2. Have you (spoke, spoken) to your guidance counselor about the change in your schedule?
3. Michael has (growed, grown) at least four inches in the past year.
4. Tom's sister has (drove, driven) him to band practice twice this week.
5. Katie (knew, knowed) all the answers on the math test last Friday.
6. Rob (broke, breaked) his glasses yesterday.
7. The choir has (gave, given) a concert every December for ten years.
8. Jane's father (took, taked) her to the museum.
9. Elaine (choose, chose) broccoli with her chicken at the cafeteria.
10. I (threw, throwed) the jackets into the blue car.

E*XERCISE 4* *Using the Correct Verb Form*

Number your paper 1 to 10. Then write the past or the past participle of each verb in parentheses. *Have, has,* or *had* is used with the past participle.

EXAMPLE   The quarterback (throw) two touchdown passes.
ANSWER   threw

1. Donna has (see) the school play twice this week and twice last week.
2. I have (know) about the surprise party for two weeks now.

3. In *Alice in Wonderland,* Lewis Carroll (speak) of "ships and shoes and sealing wax."
4. Ms. Tyler has (drive) us to many softball practices and games.
5. You (know) the answers on the math test, didn't you?
6. Orchids have (grow) successfully on every continent but Antarctica.
7. My older brother Fred has (take) several engineering courses at the University of Wisconsin.
8. Karen has (choose) a pirate's costume for the masquerade party next Saturday at school.
9. Mark has (break) the school record for rebounds.
10. The daisies (freeze) last night.

Group 5

These irregular verbs form the past and past participle by changing a vowel.

PRESENT	PAST	PAST PARTICIPLE
begin	began	(have) begun
drink	drank	(have) drunk
ring	rang	(have) rung
sing	sang	(have) sung
swim	swam	(have) swum

NOTE: In these verbs the *i* in the present changes to an *a* in the past and a *u* in the past participle.

Group 6

These irregular verbs form the past and past participle in various ways.

PRESENT	PAST	PAST PARTICIPLE
come	came	(have) come
do	did	(have) done
eat	ate	(have) eaten
fly	flew	(have) flown
go	went	(have) gone
ride	rode	(have) ridden
run	ran	(have) run
write	wrote	(have) written

119

EXERCISE 5 *Determining the Correct Verb Form*

Number your paper 1 to 10. Then write the correct verb form for each sentence. Remember that *have, has,* or *had* is used with the past participle.

1. The geese (flew, flown) south early last year.
2. Ken hasn't (began, begun) his homework yet.
3. The school choir (sang, sung) several popular songs at the music festival.
4. We had already (ate, eaten) by then.
5. Dr. Seuss has (wrote, written) many children's books.
6. Emily (swam, swum) in the county meet last year.
7. Eric has (rode, ridden) his bike to school all year.
8. Six students have (did, done) the science project.
9. John (drank, drunk) two glasses of tomato juice.
10. Terry has (ran, run) in two regional track meets.

EXERCISE 6 *Using the Correct Verb Form*

Number your paper 1 to 10. Write the past or the past participle of each verb in parentheses. Remember that *have, has,* or *had* is used with the past participle.

1. Exploration of China (begin) in the 1200s.
2. Corrie (do) a funny sketch of me.
3. Joanna has (sing) that song in several concerts.
4. The clock tower bells have (ring) every hour.
5. Columbus (come) to the Americas in 1492.
6. Paul (write) a letter to the local newspaper.
7. Vicky has (go) to the North Woods for a hike.
8. Tom (run) for student council president last year.
9. People have (swim) around Manhattan Island.
10. Carmen (eat) an apple for dessert.

EXERCISE 7 *Writing Sentences*

Write sentences using each principal part of the irregular verbs *put, say, choose, see,* and *swim.*

TIME-OUT FOR REVIEW • • • • •

Number your paper 1 to 20. Write the past or the past participle of each verb in parentheses. (This exercise includes both regular and irregular verbs.)

Pecos Bill

1. Surely you have (hear) about Pecos Bill.
2. Many writers have (write) about his enormous size and super strength.
3. Over the years people have (know) him as the most famous legendary cowboy.
4. Pecos Bill (begin) his life in an unusual way.
5. He (play) with bears and wildcats, instead of other children.
6. He (live) and (eat) with coyotes.
7. As an adult, Pecos Bill once (catch) a ride on an Oklahoma cyclone across three whole states.
8. Eventually the cyclone (come) to a stop and (rain) on him instead.
9. Over the years, many cowboys have (speak) about that tremendous rainstorm.
10. The huge washout from that storm (create) the Grand Canyon!
11. Once an enormous mountain lion had (see) Pecos Bill in the canyon below.
12. The lion (wait) and (jump) him.
13. Soon fur (fly) in all directions.
14. The lion (beg) Pecos Bill for mercy.
15. Instead he (ride) the lion like a horse.
16. Bill (go) everywhere on his real horse.
17. He had (give) his horse nitroglycerin and dynamite as a colt.
18. A friend of Bill's (take) a ride on Bill's horse one day.
19. The horse (throw) the man into the air as high as Pikes Peak.
20. These sentences have (tell) you only a few of Pecos Bill's many amazing adventures.

Problem Verbs

This section will cover four problem verbs. They are considered problems because sometimes people confuse their meanings.

Learn and Teach

Learn means "to gain understanding" or "to find out how something is done or what something means." *Learn* is a regular verb. Its principal parts are *learn, learned,* and *(have) learned.*

PRESENT	I **learn** new songs easily.
PAST	I **learned** a new song last night.
PAST PARTICIPLE	I **have learned** three new songs this past week.

Teach means "to instruct" or "to show how something is done or what something means." *Teach* is an irregular verb. Its principal parts are *teach, taught,* and *(have) taught.*

PRESENT	Mrs. Brown **teaches** history.
PAST	Mrs. Brown **taught** history last year.
PAST PARTICIPLE	Mrs. Brown **has taught** me about the Greek and Roman empires.

EXERCISE 8   Using Problem Verbs

Number your paper 1 to 10. Then write the correct form of *teach* or *learn.*

1. My sister has just (taught, learned) a new dance.
2. Carlos (taught, learned) me several Spanish words.
3. My uncle will (teach, learn) me some magic tricks.
4. In civics I will (teach, learn) about the government.
5. My parrot has (taught, learned) the word *hello.*
6. She (taught, learned) us the colors of the spectrum.

7. Mom has (learned, taught) me several exercises.
8. Public television (learns, teaches) children numbers.
9. My sister (learned, taught) the alphabet from *Sesame Street*.
10. The cheerleaders (learned, taught) us a new cheer.

Let and Leave

Let means "to allow or permit." *Let* is an irregular verb. Its principal parts are *let, let,* and *(have) let.*

PRESENT	I **let** the dog inside every evening.
PAST	I **let** the dog inside last night.
PAST PARTICIPLE	I **have let** the dog inside every night this week.

Leave means "to go away from" or "to fail to take along." *Leave* is also an irregular verb. Its principal parts are *leave, left,* and *(have) left.*

PRESENT	I **leave** the house at eight each morning.
PAST	I **left** the house at eight yesterday.
PAST PARTICIPLE	I **have left** the house at eight each day this week.

EXERCISE 9 Using Leave and Let

Number your paper 1 to 10. Then write the correct form of *leave* or *let.*

1. Wade always (lets, leaves) Tim use his football.
2. Mom has (let, left) Betsy make dinner.
3. We (let, left) our dogs at home on Saturday.
4. Beth (let, left) her gym clothes at school.
5. My sister never (lets, leaves) me into her room.
6. A guard (let, left) the students into the museum.
7. (Let, Leave) the dancers practice now.
8. We (let, left) for the airport after dinner on Friday.
9. My mother will (let, leave) me take drum lessons.
10. Please (let, leave) me give you a sandwich.

Verb Tenses

Tense is the form a verb takes to show time. The three most commonly used tenses are the *present tense,* the *past tense,* and the *future tense.* The principal parts of a verb are used to form the tenses.

The *present tense* expresses action that is going on now.

PRESENT   The dogs **play** outside. [regular verb]
  TENSE   I **ride** the bus to school. [irregular verb]

The *past tense* expresses action that took place in the past. Except for irregular verbs, the past tense is formed by adding *-d* or *-ed* to the present.

PAST   The dogs **played** outside yesterday.
TENSE   I **rode** the bus to school yesterday.

The *future tense* expresses action that will happen in the future. The future tense is formed by adding the helping verb *will* to the present. If the subject of a sentence is *I* or *we, shall* can also be used as the helping verb.

FUTURE   The dogs **will play** outside tomorrow.
  TENSE   I **shall ride** the bus to school tomorrow.

EXERCISE 10 *Identifying Verb Tenses*

Number your paper 1 to 10. Decide whether the tense of each underlined verb is *present, past,* or *future.* Then write the tense.

EXAMPLE   The moon *reflects* light from the sun.
ANSWER   present

Facts and Figures

1. The skeleton of an insect <u>grows</u> outside its body.
2. Alexander Graham Bell <u>invented</u> the telephone.
3. Babe Ruth <u>scored</u> 741 home runs during his career.
4. A full moon <u>appears</u> only once every 29 days.
5. Halley's Comet <u>will pass</u> near Earth again in 2062.

6. Thomas Jefferson and John Adams <u>died</u> on July 4.
7. Usually crocuses <u>will bloom</u> in March.
8. The Smithsonian Institution <u>contains</u> more than 100 million items.
9. Isaac Newton <u>discovered</u> the principle of gravity.
10. Gulls <u>will fly</u> in all kinds of weather.

EXERCISE 11 Identifying Verbs and Tenses

Number your paper 1 to 10. Write each verb. Then label its tense: *present, past,* or *future.*

1. Strong huskies pull Eskimo sleds.
2. The ducklings followed their mother across the pond.
3. Jeffery drank the medicine in one gulp.
4. I wash my own clothes every weekend.
5. That saucer of milk will spill onto the floor.
6. Jake swiftly added the numbers in the column.
7. Mark Twain wrote *The Adventures of Tom Sawyer.*
8. The students in industrial arts will make bookends for the library.
9. Usually black bears look for food at night.
10. The candle will burn all night.

EXERCISE 12 Writing Verbs in the Correct Tense

Number your paper 1 to 10. Then write each underlined verb in the tense that is written in parentheses.

EXAMPLE   Anne <u>choose</u> *(past)* a new notebook yesterday.
ANSWER   chose

1. The baby <u>play</u> *(past)* with the stuffed elephant for 15 minutes.
2. My grandparents <u>visit</u> *(future)* us at Thanksgiving.
3. Eric <u>go</u> *(past)* on a bicycle trip through Wisconsin last summer.
4. Lance accidentally <u>throw</u> *(past)* the ball into Mr. Peterson's front window.

5. In the spring the Stewarts <u>build</u> *(future)* an additional room onto their house.
6. Raccoons <u>turn</u> *(past)* over our garbage cans again.
7. Grandmother <u>freeze</u> *(future)* those extra tomatoes.
8. A bird <u>fly</u> *(past)* into our house.
9. Last Saturday I <u>ride</u> *(past)* a horse for the first time.
10. Everyone on the hike <u>bring</u> *(future)* a lunch.

EXERCISE 13   Writing Sentences

Reread the examples of the present, past, and future tenses on page 124. Then write a sentence for each tense of the regular verb *talk* and the irregular verb *go*.

TIME-OUT FOR REVIEW • • • • •

Number your paper 1 to 10. Write each verb. Then label its tense: *present, past,* or *future.*

Facts and Figures

1. A swan will mate only once in its lifetime.
2. The Brooklyn Bridge, the world's first steel-wire suspension bridge, opened on May 24, 1883.
3. Sometimes bears will get cavities from too much honey.
4. A woman once pitched to the Boston Red Sox in spring training.
5. A blue whale weighs as much as 30 elephants.
6. George Washington chose the site of the nation's capital.
7. New York State established the first dog license law in 1894.
8. Lightning will strike the ground around the world an average of 100 times each second.
9. A wolf eats as much as 20 pounds of meat at a single feeding.
10. Crickets chirp less on cool days.

Application to Writing

Looking for errors in your use of verbs should be part of the editing stage of your writing. One way to find verb errors is to read your work aloud. Hearing what you have written will sometimes alert you to an error. If you find any errors, always take the time to correct them.

EXERCISE 14 Editing for Verb Errors

Read the following paragraphs and find the ten verb errors. Then write the paragraphs, using the correct verb forms.

American Chop Suey

You probably have ate chop suey many times at home or in restaurants. You also probably think of chop suey as a Chinese meal. It isn't. Chop suey actually begun in the United States in 1896.

In that year, the emperor of China choose Li Hung-Chang as his ambassador to the United States. Li Hung-Chang come to New York on August 28. He had bringed with him 3 cooks, 5 valets, his personal barber, and 22 household servants.

President Grover Cleveland gived Li Hung-Chang a very warm welcome. Immediately the Chinese ambassador made plans for a grand gesture of some sort. He thought about several ideas. Finally he decided on a huge dinner party at the Chinese embassy the following evening. Quickly he rung for his three cooks and speaked to them. He ordered an entirely new dish. Both Americans and Chinese must like it.

Chop suey was the result of this order. Soon, however, the new dish catched on across the United States and even in China. Today it is prepared almost the same as it was on the night of August 29, 1896.

Chapter Review

A **Using the Correct Verb Form.** Number your paper 1 to 10. Write the past or the past participle of each verb in parentheses.

1. I have (know) Marcia for five years.
2. A tall man in a suit (ring) the doorbell.
3. Karen and Sandy have (blow) up 100 balloons for the dance.
4. The robin (fly) into a nearby tree.
5. Mr. Franklin (write) a book about the history of the printing press.
6. Todd isn't home; he has (go) to the store.
7. Leslie has (throw) two strikes so far.
8. A nightingale has (sing) outside my window for the past few nights.
9. My grandparents have (come) for a short visit.
10. Jack's mother (drive) us to the large public library in Centerville.

B **Using the Correct Verb Form.** Number your paper 1 to 10. Find and correct each verb form that is used incorrectly in the following sentences. If the verb form is correct, write *C* after the number.

1. I never seen a more colorful sunrise.
2. Brian went to Joe's house yesterday.
3. Dee has chose the winning ticket.
4. Yesterday Eric run two miles.
5. Ellen has done the puzzle correctly.
6. Nick stealed second base.
7. We drived for six hours without a stop.
8. I speaked as softly as possible.
9. Darcie has already went to the picnic with her friends.
10. The sunflowers growed higher than my head.

C **Identifying Tense.** Number your paper 1 to 10. Write each verb. Then label its tense *present, past,* or *future.*

1. Some birds migrate thousands of miles each year.
2. Kevin raked the leaves in the backyard.
3. Harvey ate two cheese sandwiches for lunch.
4. Suzanne will write an editorial for the school newspaper.
5. My cat always sleeps in the bottom drawer of my dresser.
6. The concert will begin with a lively song.
7. Kansas contains large salt reserves.
8. Mickey Mantle broke the American League strikeout record in his first season with the Yankees.
9. Hot lava poured out of the top of the volcano.
10. More than a million people will visit the National Air and Space Museum each year.

Mastery Test

Number your paper 1 to 10. Then write the correct verb form for each sentence.

1. I have already (spoke, spoken) to Jan.
2. Jim (gived, gave) his mother a book.
3. At the parade they (threw, throwed) confetti into the air.
4. The mirror has (broke, broken) into a million pieces!
5. Donna (took, taked) her raincoat with her.
6. Brian (telled, told) me the contest rules.
7. I have (drank, drunk) all the cranberry juice.
8. Cris has (wrote, written) a wonderful story.
9. The phone has (rang, rung) six times today.
10. Pat (came, come) early to the rehearsal.

9

Using Pronouns

Diagnostic Test

Number your paper 1 to 10. Then write the correct word in parentheses.

EXAMPLE   Linda will draw Sara and (I, me).
ANSWER   me

1. (She, Her) and the dolphin jumped at the same time.
2. The mayor gave the children (his, their) first-aid certificates.
3. The players can't wear (they're, their) blue uniforms for Saturday's game.
4. Dad took James and (she, her) to the fair.
5. Aunt Helen gave each of (us, we) a glass of juice and a snack.
6. (He, Him) and Kyle studied very hard for the science test.
7. We'll meet at (your, you're) house after school.
8. (They, Them) wear helmets to ride bicycles.
9. Each book has (its, it's) place on the shelf.
10. Stan and (I, me) left the game early.

Kinds of Pronouns

Pronouns are words that take the place of nouns. They make it possible to avoid using the same nouns over and over again. *His* and *him* are personal pronouns. In the first example, these pronouns take the place of *Roberto*. In the second example, *she* and *her* are personal pronouns that take the place of *Gwen*.

Roberto carried **his** trumpet with **him** on the plane.
Gwen said **she** likes **her** new bicycle.

Different personal pronouns can take the place of the same noun because there are different kinds of pronouns. In English there are three kinds of pronouns: *subject pronouns, object pronouns,* and *possessive pronouns.* Each one of these kinds of pronouns is used in a different way in a sentence.

Subject Pronouns

	Singular	Plural
FIRST PERSON	I	we
SECOND PERSON	you	you
THIRD PERSON	he, she, it	they

Object Pronouns

	Singular	Plural
FIRST PERSON	me	us
SECOND PERSON	you	you
THIRD PERSON	him, her, it	them

Possessive Pronouns

	Singular	Plural
FIRST PERSON	my, mine	our, ours
SECOND PERSON	your, yours	your, yours
THIRD PERSON	his, her, hers, its	their, theirs

131

Subject Pronouns

The list below shows all the personal pronouns that are subject pronouns. *(See pages 35–36 for a review of person.)*

Subject Pronouns		
	Singular	Plural
FIRST PERSON	I	we
SECOND PERSON	you	you
THIRD PERSON	he, she, it	they

Subject pronouns are used two ways in sentences.

9a ▶ Subject pronouns are used for subjects and predicate nominatives.

Pronouns Used as Subjects. A subject pronoun names the person, place, or thing the sentence is about.

SUBJECTS   **She** collects insects.
          They have arrived.

Sometimes more than one word is the subject of a sentence. In such a sentence, the subject is called a *compound subject*, as in the following example.

COMPOUND SUBJECT   Patty and (he, him) fish on weekends during the summer.

To decide which is the correct pronoun, say each one separately. Say the sentence as if each pronoun were a simple subject.

CORRECT   **He** fishes on weekends during the summer.

INCORRECT   **Him** fishes on weekends during the summer.

CORRECT   Patty and **he** fish on weekends during the summer.

EXERCISE 1 *Using Subject Pronouns*

Number your paper 1 to 10. Then write the correct personal pronoun in parentheses.

EXAMPLE Joshua and (we, us) sing in a quartet.
ANSWER we

1. Kelly and (I, me) went to the game together.
2. Harold and (she, her) both wore green.
3. On Sunday Angela and (he, him) made breakfast.
4. The Chargers and (we, us) play on Saturday.
5. Antonio and (they, them) won several prizes.
6. Monica and (she, her) both take violin lessons.
7. After school Bret and (I, me) played soccer.
8. Your parents and (they, them) should bring refreshments to open house at school.
9. Pat and (he, him) always read science fiction.
10. Marla and (I, me) saw a film about puffins.

Pronouns Used as Predicate Nominatives. A predicate nominative is a word that follows a linking verb—such as *is, was,* or *has been*—and identifies or renames the subject. *(See page 50 for a list of common linking verbs.)* Subject pronouns are used as predicate nominatives.

PREDICATE NOMINATIVES My swimming teacher is **she**.
That's **they** in the boat.

To find the correct pronoun in a compound predicate nominative, turn the sentence around. Make the predicate nominative the subject. Then say the sentence as if each pronoun were a simple subject.

Jessica's helpers were Jamie and (I, me).

Jamie and (I, me) were Jessica's helpers.

CORRECT **I** was Jessica's helper.

INCORRECT **Me** was Jessica's helper.

CORRECT Jessica's helpers were Jamie and **I**.

EXERCISE 2 Using Subject Pronouns

Number your paper 1 to 10. Then write the correct personal pronoun in parentheses.

1. I thought the officers were Sue and (they, them.)
2. It was Stephanie and (I, me) at the gate.
3. At the rink the best ice skater is (he, him).
4. The best person for the job is (she, her).
5. The leaders for this exercise are (we, us).
6. The winners were Mark and (I, me).
7. That is (us, we) in the picture.
8. The best painters are Michele and (he, him).
9. The best players are the Dodgers or (they, them).
10. Tomorrow the speaker will be Tim or (she, her).

EXERCISE 3 Supplying Subject Pronouns

Number your paper 1 to 10. Then complete each sentence with a subject pronoun. (Do not use *you* or *it*.)

1. _____ hope the suit fits.
2. Felicia and _____ played a song together.
3. It will be _____ at the finish line.
4. Ryan and _____ are absent today.
5. The candidates for the lead are Jo and _____.
6. The class president should be _____.
7. Jackie and _____ left the party early.
8. The coaches and _____ met before the game.
9. _____ is my favorite baseball player.
10. The Tigers or _____ will win the tournament.

EXERCISE 4 Writing Sentences

Write sentences that follow the directions below.

1. Use *he* as a subject.
2. Use *Marcy and she* as a compound subject.
3. Use *judges and I* as a compound subject.
4. Use *he* as a predicate nominative.
5. Use *Jo and I* as a compound predicate nominative.

Object Pronouns

The following list shows the personal pronouns that are object pronouns.

Object Pronouns		
	Singular	Plural
FIRST PERSON	me	us
SECOND PERSON	you	you
THIRD PERSON	him, her, it	them

Object pronouns are used in three ways in a sentence.

9b Object pronouns are used for direct objects, indirect objects, and objects of prepositions.

Pronouns Used as Direct and Indirect Objects. Object pronouns are used for direct objects and indirect objects. A direct object follows an action verb and answers the question *Whom?* or *What?*

DIRECT OBJECTS Nick calls **him** every day at six o'clock. [Nick calls whom?]

Nancy has always liked **them** very much. [Nancy has always liked whom?]

An indirect object comes before a direct object and answers the questions *To whom?* or *For whom?*

INDIRECT OBJECTS Samantha told **us** a joke. [Samantha told a joke to whom?]

Susan made **him** some socks. [Susan made some socks for whom?]

To find the correct pronoun in a compound direct object or indirect object, say the sentence as if each pronoun were the only object.

135

DIRECT OBJECT	Rick invited Kim and (I, me) to dinner.
INCORRECT	Rick invited **I** to dinner.
CORRECT	Rick invited **me** to dinner.
CORRECT	Rick invited Kim and **me** to dinner.

EXERCISE 5 Using Object Pronouns

Number your paper 1 to 10. Then write the correct personal pronoun in parentheses.

1. Aunt Mildred gave (she, her) that sweater.
2. Emily brought (they, them) to school.
3. Mom gave Johnny and (I, me) some medicine.
4. Terry saw Tina and (she, her) at the mall.
5. Eric told David and (we, us) about his trip.
6. The crowd cheered Irene and (he, him).
7. That movie gave Terry and (I, me) nightmares.
8. Donna should have called the Masons or (we, us).
9. Tad wrote Pat and (they, them) thank-you notes.
10. The teacher asked Marcia and (she, her) a question about the homework.

Pronouns Used as Objects of Prepositions. A prepositional phrase begins with a preposition—such as *to, for, near,* or *with*. A prepositional phrase ends with the object of a preposition. An object pronoun is used as an object of a preposition.

OBJECTS OF PREPOSITIONS	The phone call is for **her**. [*For her* is the prepositional phrase.]
	Monica found a seat near **me**. [*Near me* is the prepositional phrase]

To find the correct pronoun in a compound subject of a preposition, say each pronoun separately.

OBJECT OF A PREPOSITION	These circus tickets are for you and (she, her).
INCORRECT	These circus tickets are for **she**.
CORRECT	These circus tickets are for **her**.
CORRECT	These circus tickets are for you and **her**.

EXERCISE 6 *Using Object Pronouns*

Number your paper 1 to 10. Then write the correct personal pronoun in parentheses.

1. Many students voted for (she, her).
2. Show the pictures to Ginny and (he, him).
3. The next song was written by Pam and (I, me).
4. The story was about Warren and (he, him).
5. Don't look at Paula or (they, them) for a minute.
6. Stand behind Tim and (we, us).
7. Everyone else arrived before Wayne and (she, her).
8. The Morrisons live near Janice and (I, me).
9. Henry went with Matt and (us, we) in the truck.
10. Take two steps toward Paula and (he, him).

EXERCISE 7 *Supplying Object Pronouns*

Number your paper 1 to 10. Then complete each sentence with an object pronoun. (Do not use *you* or *it*.)

1. The lawyer gave _____ a curt look.
2. Sylvia told Raymond and _____ about the book.
3. The Schmidts asked Lee and _____ to dinner.
4. Vincent threw the ball to _____.
5. I always sing with _____ at parties.
6. Paula looked everywhere for Bob and _____.
7. Robert lifted Pete and _____ to safety.
8. Dana told Robert and _____ several riddles.
9. Charles was with Nancy and _____ last night.
10. The school awarded Liz and _____ a trophy.

EXERCISE 8 *Using Object Pronouns*

Number your paper 1 to 10. Write the correct personal pronoun. Then label the use of each pronoun: *direct object, indirect object,* or *object of a preposition.*

1. Jeremy will eat lunch with Jeff and (I, me).
2. Pedro gave Amanda and (he, him) good directions.
3. He bought tickets for Carrie and (we, us).

4. The director invited Bill and (they, them) backstage after the show.
5. Uncle Aaron showed Mom and (we, us) photographs of his trip to Colorado.
6. All night long the cat sat beside Mrs. Monroe and (I, me).
7. I invited Joel and (she, her) to the party at my house.
8. Martin threw the ball behind Bob and (he, him).
9. Dad bought Marvin and (she, her) rubber fins for skindiving.
10. The team won the championship game without Buddy and (I, me).

EXERCISE 9 *Writing Sentences*

Number your paper 1 to 5. Then write sentences that follow the directions below.

1. Use <u>her</u> as a direct object.
2. Use <u>Jenny</u> and <u>him</u> as a compound direct object.
3. Use <u>us</u> as an indirect object.
4. Use <u>you or me</u> as a compound indirect object.
5. Use <u>Katherine</u> and <u>her</u> as a compound object of the preposition <u>with</u>.

Possessive Pronouns

The following list shows the personal pronouns that are possessive pronouns.

Possessive Pronouns		
	Singular	Plural
FIRST PERSON	my, mine	our, ours
SECOND PERSON	your, yours	your, yours
THIRD PERSON	his, her, hers, its	their, theirs

9c **Possessive pronouns** are used to show ownership or possession.

Possessive pronouns can be used before nouns or alone.

BEFORE A NOUN   **Your** shoes are untied.
ALONE   The untied shoes are **yours.**

The possessive forms of personal pronouns are never written with an apostrophe.

POSSESSIVE   The kitten with the gray face and white
PRONOUN   paws is **hers** [Not *her's.*]

Sometimes people confuse possessive pronouns with contractions. *Its, your, their,* and *theirs* are possessive pronouns. *It's* (it is), *you're* (you are), *they're* (they are), and *there's* (there is) are contractions.

POSSESSIVE PRONOUN   **Your** hands are cold.
CONTRACTION   **You're** (you are) a good person.

EXERCISE 10 *Using Possessive Pronouns*

Number your paper 1 to 10. Then write the correct word in parentheses.

1. Is this (your, you're) home?
2. Miners cover (their, they're) heads with helmets.
3. My parrot does not like (its, it's) new cage.
4. (Hers, Her's) is the prettiest smile in the picture.
5. (Their, They're) cats eat table scraps.
6. (Your, You're) parents were at the play.
7. Most of the plants are (ours, our's).
8. Do chickens lay (their, they're) eggs at night?
9. Maureen thought the shoes were (hers, her's).
10. The painting fell out of (its, it's) frame.

EXERCISE 11 *Writing Sentences*

Write sentences for each of these possessive pronouns.

1. our   2. your   3. its   4. my   5. his

139

TIME-OUT FOR REVIEW • • • • •

Number your paper 1 to 25. Then write and correct any error. If a sentence is correct, write *C* after the number.

EXAMPLE   Lenny and him walked to the pool.
ANSWER   him—he

1. Melinda carried the sandwiches to Larry and she.
2. Ken wants Joan and her at the ceremony.
3. Alicia joined the club with Raul and I.
4. Diana and us have learned about hot-air balloons.
5. This is they're favorite restaurant.
6. Before sunrise each day, Ginny and her go for a long run.
7. Allan and her sang on the radio today.
8. The coach drove the players and them to the game in an old school bus.
9. The strongest competitors are Joe and him.
10. That was Betty and he at the back door.
11. I like talking with George and they.
12. The fire engine was flashing its red lights.
13. The rumbling noise alarmed Bryan and her.
14. Douglas gave Billy and her a lecture about the danger of roller skating without a helmet.
15. You're best effort will be good enough.
16. Maria fixed we some peanut butter and banana sandwiches for lunch.
17. Roger called they're house at noon.
18. You should go to the play with Chris and me.
19. Cheryl urged Miles and them to follow the rules.
20. Jerry and her left for the bus station at the same time.
21. Katie was looking at you and he in the balcony.
22. Sheep give us wool for warm clothing.
23. Yesterday Timothy and me went for a ride in a helicopter.
24. A snake sheds it's skin.
25. Shani's brother showed Dad and we his new jacket.

Pronouns and Antecedents

The word that a pronoun refers to is called the pronoun's *antecedent*. The antecedent of a pronoun can be a noun or another pronoun. In the following examples, *Ralph* is the antecedent of *his,* and *she* is the antecedent of *her.*

PRONOUNS AND ANTECEDENTS

Ralph quickly gave **his** cap to Jo Ann at the school gym.

She passed **her** coat to Tony during the school play.

Because a pronoun and its antecedent refer to the same person, place, or thing, they must agree.

9d A pronoun must agree in number and gender with its antecedent.

Number indicates whether a noun or a pronoun is singular (one) or plural (more than one). A pronoun must be singular if its antecedent is singular. It must be plural if its antecedent is plural.

SINGULAR **Ramona** enjoys **her** piano lessons.

PLURAL Most **trees** lose **their** leaves in the fall.

A pronoun must also agree with its antecedent in gender. *Gender* indicates whether a noun or a pronoun is masculine, feminine, or neuter.

Pronoun	Gender
MASCULINE	he, him, his
FEMININE	she, her, hers
NEUTER	it, its

MASCULINE **Theodore** waited for **his** parents.

FEMININE **Ellen** quickly glanced at **her** watch.

NEUTER My **turtle** hides in **its** shell.

Other personal pronouns—*I, me, mine, you, yours, they, theirs*—can refer to either masculine, feminine, or neuter antecedents.

EXERCISE 12 *Making Pronouns and Antecedents Agree*

Number your paper 1 to 10. Then write the personal pronoun that correctly completes each sentence.

1. Jay took _____ radio along on the camping trip.
2. The raccoon washed _____ paws in the stream.
3. Mother took me to _____ eye doctor.
4. The poets read _____ poems aloud.
5. Brad took care of _____ brothers and sisters.
6. The children rode _____ sleds down the icy hill.
7. Donna washes _____ hair every morning.
8. Paul broke _____ hockey stick last night.
9. The bird ruffled _____ feathers.
10. Chorus members must turn in _____ music now.

TIME-OUT FOR REVIEW • • • • •

Number your paper 1 to 10. Then write the personal pronoun that correctly completes each sentence.

1. Melinda showed me _____ new bike.
2. Most students were pleased with _____ grades.
3. Each girl in the chorus gave _____ name.
4. The runners took _____ places.
5. Ginger must have forgotten _____ keys.
6. The jukebox played _____ last tune.
7. All the boys offered _____ help.
8. Glen looked sadly at _____ broken computer.
9. I read the next chapter in _____ science book.
10. My brother likes _____ milk very cold.

142

A pplication to Writing

When you finish writing anything from a letter to a science report, always edit your work. Check to see if you have used the correct form of each pronoun. Then make sure that each pronoun agrees with its antecedent in number and gender. If you find any mistakes, take the time to correct them. A pronoun error can cause a reader to misunderstand what you are writing.

EXERCISE *13 Editing for Pronoun Errors*

Read the following paragraphs and find the ten pronoun errors. Decide what pronouns are needed to make the sentences correct. Then write the paragraphs, using the correct pronouns.

Elephants

My friend Katie and me went to the library today. Katie took several books off the shelf and showed them to I. They were all about elephants. We are writing about elephants for her science report.

One book had some interesting facts in them. For example, at birth baby elephants are 3 feet tall and weigh 200 pounds. Each elephant gains another 550 pounds in their first nine months.

I called to Katie, and her and I read the next few sentences together. Elephants walk on its toes! Much of the weight of an elephant is supported by pads on their feet. Elephants sometimes walk 300 miles in search of food and water. Normally, them and their calves walk at a speed of four to five miles an hour. For short distances, however, elephants can run as fast as 24 miles an hour. My brother is a fast runner, but even he can't run that fast!

Katie and I learned so much about elephants today. We must tell Jenny about elephants tomorrow at lunch. Jenny and us will have a good time.

*C*hapter *R*eview

A **Using the Correct Kinds of Pronouns.** Number your paper 1 to 10. Then write the correct personal pronoun in parentheses.

1. Janet and (she, her) won bicycles in the town raffle.
2. Ted invited the twins and (they, them) to the fair.
3. My parents and (we, us) are going to the open house at the high school.
4. That book must be (your, yours).
5. The school reporters are Leslie and (he, him).
6. Alice taught Brenda and (we, us) several new skills.
7. Fernando and (she, her) went to the theater by subway.
8. Candice handed (he, him) some celery and carrots.
9. Carlos told Mike and (I, me) the directions to his house.
10. Francine always sits with Patty and (I, me) at lunch.

B **Correcting Pronoun Errors.** Number your paper 1 to 10. Then write and correct any error. If a sentence is correct, write *C* after the number.

1. Melinda and me have been good friends for years.
2. The typists are Lance and she.
3. Barbara showed Gretchen and I her portrait of Thomas Jefferson.
4. Give the results of the class election to Gretchen or him.
5. The band and us travel by bus to the games.
6. The news surprised Sally and she.
7. The dog watched Carla and him suspiciously.
8. Denny passed Michael and her the test papers.
9. You should buy a used bicycle from the bike shop or we.
10. Judy and them eagerly joined the game.

C **Making Pronouns and Antecedents Agree.** Number your paper 1 to 10. Then write the personal pronoun that correctly completes each sentence.

1. Fran told Dennis about _____ friend's horse.
2. I can't find _____ math book.
3. Each boy on the track team recently had _____ uniform altered.
4. Tanya is holding _____ little brother's hand.
5. My grandparents have just sold _____ house.
6. Several runners have blisters on _____ feet.
7. Allen stopped by the fruit stand on _____ way home from band practice.
8. Laurie swallowed _____ juice with a gulp.
9. Sales clerks stand on _____ feet all day.
10. That bird is building _____ nest in our garage.

*M*astery *T*est

Number your paper 1 to 10. Then write the correct word in parentheses.

1. Steve and (she, her) passed the diving test.
2. The fire warmed (their, they're) cold hands.
3. Those flowers must be (your, yours).
4. Band members must pay (his, their) instrument rental fees today.
5. The cold water gave Jan and (I, me) leg cramps.
6. The coach put (your, you're) name on the list.
7. Ron and (we, us) ran to the gym yesterday.
8. A camel stores water in (its, it's) hump.
9. Mona told Tim and (I, me) a funny story.
10. Carol took (they, them) to the school librarian.

Subject and Verb Agreement

Diagnostic Test

Number your paper 1 to 10. Then write the form of the verb in parentheses that agrees with each subject.

EXAMPLE   My cat (jumps, jump) at yarn and ribbons.
ANSWER   jumps

1. Mercury (is, are) the closest planet to the sun.
2. I (was, were) the only volunteer.
3. My grandfather (doesn't, don't) ski anymore.
4. Nitrogen and oxygen (is, are) the most common elements in the atmosphere.
5. (Does, Do) Carol take ballet lessons?
6. Dinosaurs (was, were) roaming the earth 65 million years ago.
7. You (has, have) our total support.
8. (Isn't, Aren't) nine justices serving on the United States Supreme Court?
9. Mr. Swanson or his assistants (teaches, teach) my art class.
10. From the attic (was, were) coming strange noises.

*A*greement of Subjects and Verbs

If you have ever played dominoes, you know that you must match the number of dots on one of your tiles with a tile that has the same number of dots. A six goes with a six, and a two goes with a two. Subjects and verbs must match just like the tiles in dominoes.

Subjects and verbs match when there is *agreement* between them. One basic rule applies to all subjects and verbs.

10a A verb must agree with its subject in number.

*N*umber

All nouns, pronouns, and verbs have number. *Number* is the term that is used to indicate whether a word is *singular* (one) or *plural* (more than one). In this chapter you will learn how the number of a verb must agree with the number of its subject, which will be either a noun or a pronoun.

Number of Nouns and Pronouns. The plural of almost all nouns is formed by adding *-s* or *-es* to the singular form. A few nouns, however, form their plurals in other ways. (These irregular plurals are always listed in the dictionary.)

SINGULAR computer tomato tooth
PLURAL computer**s** tomato**es** **teeth**

Since pronouns take the place of nouns, pronouns also have number.

SINGULAR I, he, she, it
PLURAL we, they

NOTE: The pronoun *you* can be either singular or plural.

147

EXERCISE 1 *Determining the Number of Nouns and Pronouns*

Number your paper 1 to 20. Then label each word *singular* or *plural*.

1. candles	6. he	11. women	16. vase
2. we	7. feet	12. cities	17. Nancy
3. Maine	8. flies	13. tulip	18. desks
4. plate	9. apple	14. it	19. mice
5. tables	10. they	15. bricks	20. he

Number of Verbs. In the present tense, most verbs add -*s* or -*es* to form the singular. Third person plural forms in the present tense usually drop the -*s* or -*es*.

	SINGULAR		PLURAL
	jump**s.**		jump.
My dog	beg**s.**	My dogs	beg.
	watch**es.**		watch.

The verbs *be, have,* and *do* have special singular and plural forms in the present tense. *Be* also has special forms in the past tense.

Forms of *Be, Have,* and *Do*

	SINGULAR	PLURAL
be	is (present)	are (present)
	was (past)	were (past)
have	has	have
do	does	do

In the examples throughout this chapter, each subject is underlined once, and each verb is underlined twice.

SINGULAR   He is the star of the school play.
              Kathy has a twin sister.
  PLURAL   They are at the basketball game.
              The girls have English this period.

EXERCISE 2   Determining the Number of Verbs

Number your paper 1 to 10. Then label each item *singular* or *plural*.

1. Jason studies
2. cabbages are
3. she was
4. worms have
5. we were

6. players exercise
7. helicopter lands
8. it is
9. they do
10. Vermont has

Singular and Plural Subjects

The number of a verb must agree with the number of its subject, whether the subject is a noun or a pronoun.

10b A singular subject takes a singular verb.

10c A plural subject takes a plural verb.

To make sure a verb agrees with its subject, ask yourself two questions: *What is the subject?* and *Is the subject singular or plural?* Then choose the correct verb form.

SINGULAR   She sings in the chorus.
PLURAL   They sing in the chorus.

SINGULAR   Tracy is on the swimming team.
PLURAL   Her brothers are on the swimming team.

EXERCISE 3   Making Subjects and Verbs Agree

Number your paper 1 to 10. If the item is singular, write it in the plural form. If the item is plural, write it in the singular form.

1. light shines
2. horses race
3. they dance
4. he reads
5. candles flicker

6. trees grow
7. bell rings
8. she works
9. pictures hang
10. bull charges

EXERCISE 4 *Making Subjects and Verbs Agree*

Number your paper 1 to 10. Write each subject and label it *singular* or *plural*. Then write the form of the verb in parentheses that agrees with the subject.

EXAMPLE   Some animals (grows, grow) new limbs.
ANSWER   animals, plural—grow

New Parts for Old

1. A small lizard (darts, dart) through the woods.
2. It (looks, look) for insects for its dinner.
3. Suddenly two birds (attacks, attack) the lizard.
4. One bird (grabs, grab) the lizard by the tail.
5. Instantly the tail (falls, fall) off.
6. Then the tailless lizard (runs, run) to safety.
7. Within 8 to 12 weeks, it (has, have) a new tail.
8. Some worms (grows, grow) new sections.
9. Some snails even (gets, get) new eyes.
10. The name of this process (is, are) *regeneration*.

You and I as Subjects

The singular pronouns *you* and *I* are exceptions to the two rules for agreement between subjects and verbs.

You is *always* used with a plural verb.

PLURAL
VERBS

Jim, <u>you</u> <u>are</u> a good reader.
Girls, <u>you</u> <u>sing</u> well together.

I usually takes a plural verb.

PLURAL
VERBS

<u>I</u> <u>make</u> good grades in science.
<u>I</u> <u>have</u> a test tomorrow.

The singular verbs *am* and *was* are also used with *I*.

SINGULAR
VERBS

<u>I</u> <u>am</u> on the track team.
<u>I</u> <u>was</u> at the pool all day on Saturday.

EXERCISE 5 *Making Verbs Agree with* You *and* I

Number your paper 1 to 10. Then write the form of the verb in parentheses that agrees with the subject.

1. I (has, have) two older brothers.
2. You (is, are) a fantastic soccer player.
3. Today you (looks, look) very tired.
4. I (has, have) a new kitten.
5. You (needs, need) more help with the computer.
6. I (am, are) taking piano lessons.
7. You (has, have) a lovely smile.
8. I (was, were) playing basketball over the weekend.
9. You (was, were) a great help to me yesterday.
10. I (wants, want) a calculator for my birthday.

TIME-OUT FOR REVIEW • • • • •

Number your paper 1 to 15. Then write the form of the verb in parentheses that agrees with the subject.

1. The sun (is, are) 93 million miles from the earth.
2. Some ferns (grows, grow) 50 feet tall.
3. Jonathan (has, have) a new 10-speed bicycle.
4. I (am, are) an Eagle Scout.
5. Spiders (is, are) not insects.
6. They (has, have) eight legs.
7. My friends (is, are) good at trivia games.
8. You (was, were) the leader for this group yesterday.
9. A toad (eats, eat) about 100 insects a day.
10. I (irons, iron) my own clothes.
11. He (makes, make) good pancakes.
12. Modern birds (has, have) no teeth.
13. Dinosaur names (comes, come) from Greek words.
14. They (owns own) the hardware store on Elmwood Avenue.
15. We (builds, build) snow castles every winter in front of the house.

Common Agreement Problems

The agreement between subjects and verbs in some situations needs a little extra attention. This section covers agreement problems that people commonly have with verb phrases, compound subjects, sentences in inverted order, and contractions.

Verb Phrases

A verb phrase is a main verb plus one or more helping verbs. (*See page 43.*) If a sentence includes a verb phrase, the subject must agree in number with the first helping verb.

10d The helping verb must agree in number with its subject.

SINGULAR Jennie **is** studying in her room.
PLURAL My friends **are** planning a surprise party.

Following is a list of singular and plural forms of some common helping verbs.

Common Helping Verbs	
SINGULAR	**PLURAL**
am, is, was, has, does	are, were, have, do

SINGULAR Phil **is** feeding the pigs.
PLURAL My parents **are** milking the cows.
SINGULAR Jody **has** mowed the lawn.
PLURAL They **have** trimmed all the hedges.
SINGULAR Kevin **was** typing very fast.
PLURAL His brothers **were** watching him.

152

EXERCISE 6 *Making Subjects and Verbs Agree*

Number your paper 1 to 10. Write each subject. Then write the form of the helping verb in parentheses that agrees with the subject.

1. My cat (is, are) constantly catching mice.
2. Four large deer (was, were) licking the salt block.
3. Those new yellow curtains (does, do) look nice in my bedroom.
4. The telephone (was, were) ringing all day today.
5. Several students (has, have) made decorations for the school dance.
6. The Wildcats (is, are) playing the Falcons tomorrow.
7. The card store (has, have) moved to a new location on Greenwood Avenue.
8. The tree (was, were) covered with ants.
9. The judge (does, do) follow the rules exactly.
10. Peanuts (is, are) used in ink, paper, shoe polish, and some floor cleaners.

Compound Subjects

Some sentences have two subjects that share the same verb. Such a subject is called a *compound subject*. Usually the parts of a compound subject are joined by a single conjunction such as *and* or *or,* or by a pair of conjunctions such as *either/or* or *neither/nor*.

10e When the parts of a compound subject are joined by *and,* the verb is usually plural.

When a subject is more than one, it is plural. The verb, therefore, must also be plural to agree with the subject.

PLURAL VERBS   <u>Katya</u> **and** <u>Tamara</u> <u>help</u> the art teacher each day after school.

This <u>book</u> **and** these <u>magazines</u> <u>contain</u> useful information for my science report.

When the parts of a compound subject are joined by *or,* *either/or,* or *neither/nor,* agreement between the subject and the verb follows a different rule.

10f ▶ When the parts of a compound subject are joined by *or,* *either/or,* or *neither/nor,* the verb agrees with the subject closer to it.

SINGULAR VERB <u>Monday</u> **or** <u>Tuesday</u> <u>is</u> the deadline. [The verb is singular because *Tuesday,* the subject closer to it, is singular.]

PLURAL VERB **Either** the <u>skirts</u> **or** the <u>jackets</u> <u>are</u> on sale. [The verb is plural because *jackets,* the subject closer to it, is plural.]

This rule applies even when one subject is singular and the other subject is plural.

SINGULAR VERB **Neither** the <u>stars</u> **nor** the <u>moon</u> <u>was</u> visible tonight. [The verb is singular because *moon,* the subject closer to it, is singular.]

PLURAL VERB **Neither** the <u>moon</u> **nor** the <u>stars</u> <u>were</u> visible through the clouds. [The verb is plural because *stars,* the subject closer to it, is plural.]

EXERCISE 7 *Making Verbs Agree with Compound Subjects*

Number your paper 1 to 10. Then write the correct form of each verb in parentheses.

1. Marty and Chris (has, have) taken riding lessons for several years.
2. Either broccoli or corn (goes, go) with chicken.
3. Spruce trees and Douglas firs (does, do) not lose their needles in the fall.
4. My sister or my cousins (is, are) going to the concert.
5. My sneakers and uniform (is, are) in my locker.
6. Neither the red shirt nor the yellow shirt (looks, look) good with those pants.

7. Celery and cheese (makes, make) a good snack after school.
8. Neither tape nor staples (is, are) holding this book together.
9. Pat and Max (is, are) playing checkers in the family room downstairs.
10. Either the Turners or Ivan (was, were) organizing a paper drive.

EXERCISE 8 Writing Sentences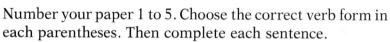

Number your paper 1 to 5. Choose the correct verb form in each parentheses. Then complete each sentence.

1. Balloons and streamers (was, were) . . .
2. Peaches or strawberries (is, are) . . .
3. Natalie and Mindy (writes, write) . . .
4. Either carnations or one red rose (is, are) . . .
5. Neither the shirt nor the pants (needs, need) . . .

Inverted Order

A sentence is in natural order when the subject comes before the verb. In some sentences, however, the verb or part of a verb phrase comes before the subject. Such a sentence has *inverted order*. A verb always agrees with its subject, whether the sentence is in natural order or in inverted order.

10g The subject and the verb of a sentence in inverted order must agree in number.

When you are looking for the subject of an inverted sentence, turn the sentence around to its natural order. Once you know the subject, you can easily check to see if the verb agrees with it.

INVERTED ORDER   On that shelf <u>are</u> the new library <u>books</u>.
NATURAL ORDER   The new library <u>books</u> <u>are</u> on that shelf.

155

When you are looking for the subject in a question, turn the question into a statement.

QUESTION   Have the actors learned their lines?
STATEMENT   The actors have learned their lines.

EXERCISE 9   Making Verbs Agree with Subjects in Inverted order.

Number your paper 1 to 10. Write each subject. Then write the form of the verb in parentheses that agrees with the subject.

1. (Is, Are) your glasses lost again?
2. (Has, Have) the potatoes cooked too long?
3. On the living room rug (was, were) several dirty footprints.
4. (Does, Do) a touchdown count for seven points?
5. At the top of the mountain (is, are) a nice Italian restaurant.
6. (Has, Have) the principal made an announcement of the contest winners?
7. (Does, Do) the Newton twins dress alike?
8. At the beach (is, are) many unusual seashells.
9. (Was, Were) Ben and Scott at practice today?
10. Over our heads (was, were) flying a helicopter.

Doesn't and Don't

You already know that *does* is singular and *do* is plural. Sometimes, however, these words are used in contractions: *doesn't* (does not) and *don't* (do not). When a contraction is used, agreement with a subject can be confusing. There is an easy way to solve this problem. Always say the individual words of a contraction when you are checking for agreement.

10h The verb part of a contraction must agree in number with the subject.

INCORRECT   My <u>backpack</u> **do**n't <u>hold</u> all my books.
  CORRECT   My <u>backpack</u> **does** not <u>hold</u> all my books.
INCORRECT   My <u>brothers</u> **does**n't <u>like</u> football.
  CORRECT   My <u>brothers</u> **do** not <u>like</u> football.

Rule 10h applies to all contractions. Keep in mind which contractions are singular and which are plural.

SINGULAR   **is**n't, **was**n't, **has**n't
  PLURAL   **are**n't, **were**n't, **have**n't

EXERCISE 10   Making Subjects Agree with Contractions

Number your paper 1 to 10. Write each subject. Then write the contraction in parentheses that agrees with the subject.

1. My alarm clock (doesn't, don't) work anymore.
2. Female birds (isn't, aren't) as colorful as male birds.
3. My classroom (doesn't, don't) have a calendar on the wall.
4. The altos (hasn't, haven't) rehearsed their part for this song yet.
5. The art supplies (wasn't, weren't) delivered yet.
6. The pigs (doesn't, don't) need a bigger pen.
7. The iron (wasn't, weren't) turned on.
8. I (doesn't, don't) read the newspaper every day.
9. (Isn't, Aren't) the play tryouts tonight?
10. My uncle and aunt (hasn't, haven't) arrived yet.

EXERCISE 11   Writing Sentences

Number your paper 1 to 5. Choose the correct verb form in each parentheses. Then complete each sentence.

1. The music (doesn't, don't) . . .
2. These oars (isn't, aren't) . . .
3. Those tall trees (doesn't, don't) . . .
4. (Isn't, Aren't) the players . . .
5. Megan and her brothers (wasn't, weren't) . . .

TIME-OUT FOR REVIEW • • • • •

Number your paper 1 to 20. Then write the form of the verb in parentheses that agrees with each subject.

Sports Cards

1. (Does, Do) you collect anything?
2. Some people (saves, save) postcards, buttons, comic books, or spoons.
3. One person even (has, have) a collection of 735 oil rags!
4. (Is, Are) money the main reason for a collection?
5. No, most collectors (doesn't, don't) look for profit.
6. They (is, are) looking for fun.
7. Sports cards (is, are) collected by many people.
8. These cards (wasn't, weren't) printed until some time in the 1880s.
9. Cereal, meat, and even macaroni (has, have) been sold with sports cards in their packages.
10. Then in 1951, the Topps Chewing Gum Company (was, were) putting their cards in with their bubble gum.
11. Today it (is, are) still making the cards.
12. Baseball, football, basketball, and hockey (is, are) the only sports on the cards.
13. (Is, Are) baseball or football the most popular sport today?
14. For years boys and girls (has, have) preferred the baseball cards.
15. Famous players (is, are) always on cards.
16. The first Mickey Mantle card (wasn't, weren't) printed until 1952.
17. Today it (is, are) worth around 3,000 dollars.
18. Card prices (is, are) printed in the book *The Sports Collector's Bible.*
19. Across the country (is, are) many conventions for card collectors each year.
20. (Isn't, Aren't) you interested now in a sports card collection?

A pplication to Writing

You write to communicate your thoughts and ideas to someone else. A breakdown in that communication can occur if your writing includes errors in subject and verb agreement. To make sure that your readers fully understand what you are writing, always take the time to edit your work. When you edit, read each sentence carefully and correct any mistakes in subject and verb agreement.

EXERCISE 12 Editing for Subject and Verb Agreement

Read the following paragraphs and find the ten verbs that do not agree with their subjects. Decide what verbs are needed to make the sentences correct. Then write the paragraphs, using the correct verbs.

Unidentified Flying Objects

Has you ever seen a UFO? Through the centuries people has seen many unusual objects in the sky. From about 1950, these stories were given much publicity in the newspapers.

In 1964, a police officer was chasing a speeding car in New Mexico. Then instantly in front of him were a blue flaming ball. The officer pulled off the road and investigated. Two human-looking beings were standing near an oval, silvery-white object. They was about the size of 10-year-old children.

The officer was terrified. He ran back to the car. An ear-splitting noise stopped him. Then suddenly the object were rising into the air. Later investigators was looking over the landing spot. They found burn marks on the ground.

Most UFO stories isn't true. Some people has made up stories. Airplanes or a distant planet are the explanation for other stories. Still, a few unsolved mysteries remain. Does UFOs really exist?

*C*hapter *R*eview

A **Making Subjects and Verbs Agree.** Number your paper 1 to 10. Then write the form of the verb in parentheses that agrees with each subject.

1. One field hockey player (has, have) sprained her knee.
2. I (am, are) getting braces on my teeth next week.
3. The ship's sails (was, were) billowing in the wind.
4. (Does, Do) the winters get very cold in Georgia?
5. The scouts (doesn't, don't) meet at the school.
6. You (has, have) the next turn at bat.
7. Dad and my sisters (is, are) flying kites today.
8. (Wasn't, Weren't) the rules changed?
9. On the front of the package (was, were) pasted an unusual seal.
10. A large truck or a car (is, are) stalled at the corner.

B **Finding Errors in Subject and Verb Agreement.** Number your paper 1 to 10. Find and write each verb that does not agree with its subject. Then write each sentence correctly. If a sentence is correct, write *C* after the number.

EXAMPLE   Does flowers grow in that shady spot?
ANSWER   Do flowers grow in that shady spot?

1. Ralph have a basketball hoop over his garage.
2. Some butterflies are attracted to clover.
3. Ivy have been growing on our house for 20 years.
4. My cousin or my brothers has a catcher's mitt.
5. You was the best singer at the concert.
6. This video recorder don't work very well.
7. Wasn't our report cards handed out on Friday?
8. I was shaking during my report.
9. Does squirrels hibernate in the winter?
10. The train and the plane leaves at the same time.

C **Editing for Subject and Verb Agreement.** Read the following paragraphs and find the ten verbs that do not agree with their subjects. Decide what verbs are needed to make the sentences correct. Then write the paragraphs, using the correct verbs.

Most Legs

Has you ever seen a millipede? Millipede means "thousand-legged." This unique insect, however, don't live up to its name. A few millipedes has 200 legs. Still, 200 legs makes the millipede a record-breaking insect. The 30 legs of centipedes doesn't even come close.

How does millipedes walk with so many legs? They move each pair of legs in turn down the length of their bodies. Baby millipedes doesn't have hundreds of legs. At birth they has only three pairs of legs. Most millipedes is vegetarians. However, mice and birds eats millipedes.

Mastery Test

Number your paper 1 to 10. Then write the form of the verb in parentheses that agrees with each subject.

1. The name Margaret (has, have) many nicknames.
2. The boys (is, are) chopping wood for the fireplace.
3. I (has, have) just read the book *Black Beauty*.
4. (Do, Does) that music sound familiar to you?
5. Near the lake (was, were) standing three bears.
6. Stickers (doesn't, don't) come off the wall easily.
7. A crow or several blue jays (is, are) making much noise outside.
8. You (is, are) never absent from school.
9. (Isn't, Aren't) your sister on the swimming team?
10. Spring and autumn (is, are) my favorite seasons.

11

Using Adjectives and Adverbs

*D*iagnostic *T*est

Number your paper 1 to 10. Then write the correct word in parentheses.

EXAMPLE   Who is (taller, tallest), Bob or Ryan?
ANSWER   taller

1. This morning's sunrise was (more, most) colorful than yesterday's.
2. There isn't (no, any) milk in the refrigerator.
3. That cool shower felt so (good, well).
4. Which subject do you find (harder, more harder), geography or math?
5. Jeff plays the piano quite (good, well).
6. Of Lee's four dogs, which barked (louder, loudest)?
7. Do beeswax candles or ordinary candles burn (more slowly, most slowly)?
8. Haven't you (never, ever) seen a laser show?
9. Which season do you like (better, best)?
10. In the race on Saturday, who ran (faster, fastest), my older sister or my younger sister?

Comparison of Adjectives and Adverbs

When you write a description, you often use adjectives or adverbs to compare one person, place, thing, or action with another. Most adjectives and adverbs have three forms that you will need to know when you make such comparisons.

11a Most adjectives and adverbs have three degrees of comparison: the *positive*, the *comparative*, and the *superlative*.

The *positive* degree is used when a person, place, thing, or action is being described and no comparison is being made.

ADJECTIVE   The elm tree is **tall.**
ADVERB   I swim **often.**

The *comparative* degree is used when two people, places, things, or actions are being compared.

ADJECTIVE   The elm tree is **taller** than the oak.
ADVERB   I swim **more often** than Kelly.

The *superlative* degree is used when more than than two people, places, things, or actions are being compared.

ADJECTIVE   The elm tree is the **tallest** tree in our yard.
ADVERB   Of all my friends, I swim **most often.**

Regular Comparison

How an adjective or an adverb forms its comparative and superlative degrees usually depends on the number of syllables in the word.

11b Add *-er* to form the comparative degree and *-est* to form the superlative degree of one-syllable modifiers.

163

	POSITIVE	COMPARATIVE	SUPERLATIVE
ADJECTIVE	smart	smart**er**	smart**est**
	big	bigg**er**	bigg**est**
ADVERB	soon	soon**er**	soon**est**

NOTE: A spelling change sometimes occurs when *-er* or *-est* is added to certain words such as *big*.

Many two-syllable adjectives or adverbs are formed exactly the way one-syllable adjectives or adverbs are formed. You add *-er* or *-est* to the positive.

A two-syllable adjective such as *playful,* however, would be difficult to say with *-er* or *-est—playfuler* and *playfulest.* For such two-syllable adjectives and adverbs, you should add *more* and *most* to form the comparative and superlative forms—*more playful* and *most playful. More* and *most* should also be used with adverbs that end in *-ly.*

11c Use *-er* or *more* to form the comparative degree and *-est* or *most* to form the superlative degree of two-syllable modifiers.

	POSITIVE	COMPARATIVE	SUPERLATIVE
ADJECTIVE	narrow	narrow**er**	narrow**est**
	easy	easi**er**	easi**est**
	harmless	**more** harmless	**most** harmless
ADVERB	often	**more** often	**most** often
	early	earli**er**	earli**est**
	quickly	**more** quickly	**most** quickly
	bravely	**more** bravely	**most** bravely

NOTE: A spelling change occurs in many modifiers that end in *-y,* such as *easy* and *early.* The *y* changes to *i* before *-er* or *-est* is added.

Form the comparative and superlative degrees of adjectives and adverbs with three or more syllables by adding *more* and *most.*

11d Use *more* to form the comparative degree and *most* to form the superlative degree of modifiers with three or more syllables.

	POSITIVE	COMPARATIVE	SUPERLATIVE
ADJECTIVE	serious	**more** serious	**most** serious
ADVERB	carefully	**more** carefully	**most** carefully

EXERCISE 1 Forming the Regular Comparison of Modifiers

Number your paper 1 to 20. Copy each adjective or adverb. Then write its comparative and superlative forms.

1. steep	6. slowly	11. quick	16. hot
2. long	7. little	12. light	17. near
3. steady	8. happily	13. smart	18. rapidly
4. curious	9. difficult	14. cold	19. neatly
5. tall	10. frequently	15. heavy	20. delicious

EXERCISE 2 Using the Correct Form of Modifiers

Number your paper 1 to 10. Then write the correct form of the adjective or adverb in parentheses.

1. Which star is (brighter, brightest), Rigel or Pollux?
2. Who finished his chores (more quickly, most quickly), Jake or Roger?
3. Of all Stevenson's books, I think *Kidnapped* is the (more enjoyable, most enjoyable).
4. Which is the (quicker, quickest) of your four favorite games?
5. The cheetah is the (faster, fastest) of all the land animals.
6. Who was (earlier, earliest), Lucy or Susan?
7. Which moves (more slowly, most slowly), a snail or a garter snake?
8. Of all the fruits in the salad, I found the strawberries (tastier, tastiest).
9. Which is (colder, coldest), the North Pole or the South Pole?
10. I think baseball is the (more interesting, most interesting) game we play in gym class.

165

Irregular Comparison

A few adjectives and adverbs are compared in an irregular manner. Those in the following list are very common. You will need to use them often.

Irregularly Compared Modifiers		
Positive	Comparative	Superlative
bad	worse	worst
good (and) well	better	best
little	less	least
much (and) many	more	most

POSITIVE	I have too **much** homework.
COMPARATIVE	It is **more** homework than I had last week.
SUPERLATIVE	It is the **most** homework I've ever had.

EXERCISE 3 Using the Correct Form of Modifiers

Number your paper 1 to 5. Read the first sentence in each group. Then write the comparative and superlative forms of the underlined adjective or adverb.

EXAMPLE   Today's lunch was <u>good</u>.
It was _____ than yesterday's lunch.
It was the _____ lunch we've had all week.
ANSWER   better, best

1. Lauren is a <u>good</u> writer.
   She is a _____ writer than I am.
   In fact she is the _____ writer in the school.
2. Roger watches too <u>much</u> TV.
   He watches even _____ TV than Aaron does.
   He watches the _____ TV of anyone I know.
3. I have <u>little</u> interest in football.
   I have even _____ interest in soccer.
   I have the _____ interest in wrestling.

4. The movie at Cinema T is <u>bad</u>.
   It is _____ than last month's movie.
   In fact it is the _____ movie I've ever seen.
5. <u>Many</u> people strolled along the river.
   _____ people watched the parade.
   _____ people attended the concert.

*T*IME-OUT FOR REVIEW • • • • •

Number your paper 1 to 20. Find and write each incorrect adjective or adverb. Then write the correct form. If a sentence is correct, write *C* after the number.

EXAMPLE This is the longest of the two books.
ANSWER longest—longer

1. Which are more fragrant, violets, roses, or tulips?
2. Of my five cousins, I have seen Debbie more recently.
3. Which ocean is deeper, the Pacific or the Atlantic?
4. Who works hardest, Katie or Emily?
5. Which do you like most, Monopoly or Scrabble?
6. The second movie in science class was better than the first one.
7. Which is biggest, an elephant or a blue whale?
8. This has been the worse week of my life.
9. Of all sports, basketball is my least favorite.
10. When did the band play best, today or Tuesday?
11. Is Ramona most talented at fielding or at hitting?
12. Which player on the wrestling team is stronger?
13. Of the three colors, which do you like better?
14. Which is softer, a cat's fur or a rabbit's fur?
15. Is March or April the longest month?
16. When did Andy feel worst, yesterday or last Monday?
17. Which is least expensive, the hat or the tie?
18. Of all creatures, cats seem most curious.
19. Which sounds best, Tina's radio or Don's radio?
20. Of the four rooms in our apartment, the kitchen is bigger.

Problems with Modifiers

The following section shows some special problems you should watch for when you are making comparisons.

Double Comparisons

Use only one method of forming the comparative or the superlative form of an adjective or an adverb. Using both methods—for example, *-er* and *more* together—results in a *double comparison*.

11e Do not use both *-er* and *more* to form the comparative degree, or both *-est* and *most* to form the superlative degree.

DOUBLE COMPARISON	No one studies **more harder** than Jane.
CORRECT	No one studies **harder** than Jane.
DOUBLE COMPARISON	Steve is the **most tallest** player.
CORRECT	Steve is the **tallest** player.

EXERCISE 4 Correcting Double Comparisons

Number your paper 1 to 10. Then write the following sentences, correcting each error.

1. Who is the most greatest player in baseball?
2. This down coat is more warmer than my wool coat.
3. Choir practice took more longer than usual today.
4. Forsythias usually bloom more earlier than lilacs.
5. Shep is the most cutest puppy I've ever seen.
6. I like math more better than science.
7. Is China or the Soviet Union the most biggest nation?
8. Eric can run more faster than Mark.
9. Sloan Avenue is the most steepest hill in town.
10. The icy wind was more stronger today than it was yesterday.

Double Negatives

Following is a list of common negative words. Notice that all of these words begin with *n*.

Common Negatives

never	none
no	not (and its contraction, *n't*)
no one	nothing

Two negatives should not be used together to express the same idea. When they are, the result is a *double negative*.

11f Avoid using a double negative.

DOUBLE NEGATIVE	We **don't never** go to the lake.
CORRECT	We **don't** go to the lake.
CORRECT	We **never** go to the lake.

*E*XERCISE 5 *Correcting Double Negatives*

Number your paper 1 to 10. Then write the following sentences, correcting each error.

1. We don't have no extra fuses.
2. Sarah hasn't never been to the art museum before.
3. The planet Mercury hasn't no moons.
4. Lewis doesn't know nothing about computers.
5. There isn't no playground near our house.
6. We haven't nothing to do tomorrow.
7. Al hasn't never been on a roller coaster or a giant Ferris wheel.
8. There aren't no pearls in the Great Lakes.
9. There wasn't no one at the skating rink or the basketball court in the park.
10. Mozart never composed no polkas.

169

Good and Well

Good is always an adjective. Sometimes *good* comes before a noun, as most adjectives do. Other times *good* is used as a predicate adjective. A *predicate adjective* describes the subject and follows a linking verb such as *am, is, are, was, were, appear, feel, look, seem,* and *smell.* (*See page 66.*)

Well is usually used as an adverb. When *well* means "in good health," however, it is an adjective.

ADJECTIVE   This bread smells **good.** [*Good* is a predicate adjective that describes *bread.*]

ADVERB   Jocelyn drew the map **well.** [*Well* is an adverb that tells how Jocelyn drew the map.]

ADJECTIVE   Larry doesn't feel **well.** [*Well* means "in good health."]

EXERCISE 6   Using Good and Well

Number your paper 1 to 20. Then write *good* or *well* to complete each sentence correctly.

1. He learns _____.
2. The salad is _____.
3. The sun feels _____.
4. The team played _____.
5. I feel quite _____.
6. She paints _____.
7. His car runs _____.
8. His voice is _____.
9. The play was _____.
10. The boat sails _____.
11. Your plan seems _____.
12. He dances _____.
13. That shirt looks _____.
14. The meat appears _____.
15. The breeze feels _____.
16. The robot works _____.
17. The roast smells _____.
18. My dog behaves _____.
19. He types _____.
20. Your room looks _____.

EXERCISE 7   Writing Sentences

Write a six-sentence comparison of an eagle and a person flying a glider. Make sure that you use the correct forms of all adjectives and adverbs.

TIME-OUT FOR REVIEW • • • • •

Number your paper 1 to 25. Then write the following sentences, correcting each error. If a sentence is correct, write *C* after the number.

1. Mount Everest is the most tallest mountain in the world.
2. Marsha skies good on the high slopes.
3. Generally apes are more larger than monkeys.
4. I didn't get no books from the library.
5. Of the three dancers, which one is most graceful?
6. A frog's skin is more smoother than a toad's skin.
7. The talent contest this year was better than the one last year.
8. This camera hasn't never been used before.
9. Which is worst, a rainy vacation or no vacation at all?
10. The fresh air smells so good.
11. Who can throw the football farther down the field, Ben or Yuri?
12. Is Ralph more taller than me?
13. We couldn't find no cans of soup in the kitchen cabinet.
14. I'm a more faster walker than my sister.
15. The hygienist cleaned my teeth good yesterday.
16. Which of the five Great Lakes is deeper?
17. Muskrats don't never cut down trees like beavers do.
18. Indian elephants are usually more smaller and easier to train than African elephants.
19. Which shines brightest, a diamond or a ruby?
20. I haven't never visited Washington, D.C.
21. Of all the colors, purple is my least favorite.
22. Does that feather pillow feel good?
23. Moths have more heavier bodies than butterflies.
24. Of all my friends, I sit nearer the front of the room.
25. There wasn't no one in the auditorium after school yesterday.

A pplication to Writing

When will you ever write comparisons? In geography you might be asked to compare the size or the exports of two countries. In science you might be asked to compare two planets or two different types of clouds. In English you might be asked to compare two books or two authors. These are just a few of the many assignments you might get during your school years.

When you write comparisons, always edit your work to make sure that you have used the correct forms of adjectives and adverbs for comparison. Also check to see that you have not included any double comparisons or double negatives, and that you have used *good* and *well* correctly. If you find any errors in your writing, always take the time to correct them.

*E*XERCISE 8 *Editing for the Correct Use of Modifiers*

Read the following paragraphs and find the five errors. Then write the paragraphs correctly.

Seals and Sea Lions

If you went to Sea World, would you see seals or sea lions? Some people can't never tell them apart. Both are mammals, and both have rounded, streamlined bodies. Both animals swim very good. However, they are both awkward on land.

There are many differences, nevertheless, between seals and sea lions. A seal has the smallest head of the two. The seal also has a more shorter neck. If you saw these animals on land, you would notice the most biggest difference. A seal moves by pulling its body forward with only its front flippers. A sea lion, on the other hand, moves by "walking" on all four flippers. By the way, seals rarely perform.

*C*hapter *R*eview

A **Using the Correct Form of Modifiers.** Number your paper 1 to 10. Then write the correct word.

1. Which do you like (better, best), fiction or nonfiction?
2. This is the (biggest, most biggest) flower vase I could find.
3. Roberta draws very (good, well).
4. Derek is the (thinner, thinnest) twin.
5. Which is the (taller, tallest) building, the Sears Tower or the Empire State Building?
6. There aren't (no, any) pencils in the drawer.
7. Does tonight's dinner look (good, well)?
8. Which is (prettier, prettiest), the blue jacket or the gray jacket?
9. This hill is (steeper, more steeper) than the one we climbed earlier.
10. Of my three sisters, Jenny is the (older, oldest).

B **Correcting Errors with Modifiers.** Number your paper 1 to 10. Then write the following sentences, correcting each error. If a sentence is correct, write *C* after the number.

1. Who is the best singer, Patty or Sharon?
2. I haven't never practiced this hard before.
3. Which do you like less, gymnastics or track?
4. This box is more lighter than the first one.
5. Of all your classmates, who writes more neatly?
6. I can't never remember which planet is farthest from the sun.
7. I do the dishes more oftener than my sister does.
8. Which is taller, a redwood tree or a sequoia tree?
9. My little brother behaved good at the party.
10. Which burns brightest, the thick candle or the thin one?

C **Forming the Comparison of Modifiers.** Write the correct form of each adjective or adverb written below. Then use each word in a sentence.

1. the comparative of *fast*
2. the superlative of *smart*
3. the superlative of *bravely*
4. the comparative of *good*
5. the superlative of *often*
6. the comparative of *easy*
7. the superlative of *delicious*
8. the comparative of *much*
9. the superlative of *difficult*
10. the comparative of *soon*

Mastery Test

Number your paper 1 to 10. Then write the correct word in parentheses.

1. The muffins are (fresher, more fresher) than the bread.
2. Doesn't (no one, anyone) know what time the game will start?
3. Which runs (faster, fastest), a tiger or a fox?
4. Of the four brown puppies, which one do you like (better, best)?
5. This soft towel feels (good, well) next to my sunburn.
6. Who got the (higher, highest) grade on the math test last Friday, Ann or you?
7. Which do you like (more, most), Italian food, Chinese food, or French food?
8. Isn't there (no, any) gas in the car?
9. Who is the (stronger, more stronger) swimmer, Tracy or Jill?
10. James plays the flute (good, well).

Standardized Test

Directions: Choose the word or words that best complete each sentence. In the appropriate row on your answer sheet, fill in the circle containing the same letter as your answer.

SAMPLE   The batter _____ the ball.

    A hit   **B** hitted   **C** hitten

ANSWER   Ⓐ Ⓑ Ⓒ

1. Gino has _____ up all the balloons.

    A blew   **B** blown   **C** blowed

2. The water in the pond _____ last night.

    A froze   **B** freezed   **C** frozen

3. One puppy was _____ than the others.

    A big   **B** bigger   **C** biggest

4. During the party we _____ the piñata.

    A broken   **B** breaked   **C** broke

5. Of the three little mice, which is _____?

    A small   **B** smaller   **C** smallest

6. Has Paulette _____ all the milk?

    A drinked   **B** drunk   **C** drank

7. Toby did _____ than John in math.

    A good   **B** better   **C** more better

8. Everyone in the class watched and _____ the movie.

    A hear   **B** heard   **C** hearred

9. The clown is _____ than the acrobat.

    A happier   **B** more happier   **C** happiest

10. He is the _____ of the three weight lifters.

    A weaker   **B** most weakest   **C** weakest

Directions: Decide which underlined part in each sentence contains an error in usage. On your answer sheet, fill in the circle containing the same letter as the incorrect part. If there is no error, fill in *D*.

SAMPLE   <u>We</u> <u>doesn't</u> have our dog with <u>us</u>. <u>No error</u>
       A   **B**   **C**   **D**

ANSWER   Ⓐ Ⓑ Ⓒ Ⓓ

11. <u>She</u> <u>don't</u> see <u>him</u>. <u>No error</u>
    A   **B**   **C**   **D**

12. <u>Have</u> you <u>given</u> the present to <u>she</u>? <u>No error</u>
    A   **B**   **C**   **D**

13. The frogs <u>is</u> <u>jumping</u> into <u>deep</u> water. <u>No error</u>
         A   **B**   **C**   **D**

14. <u>He</u> <u>doesn't</u> want <u>no</u> more books today. <u>No error</u>
    A   **B**   **C**   **D**

15. Sam and <u>I</u> <u>are</u> going to <u>our</u> class together. <u>No error</u>
       A B   **C**   **D**

16. The tuba and the flute <u>is</u> <u>playing</u> <u>well</u> together. <u>No error</u>
                A   **B**   **C**   **D**

17. Each girl in the scout troop <u>is</u> <u>making</u> <u>her</u> project this
                     A   **B**   **C**

    week. <u>No error</u>
       D

18. That girl and <u>her</u> <u>pet</u> monkey <u>has</u> entertained the crowd.
             A   **B**   **C**

    <u>No error</u>
    D

19. Which one of <u>your</u> two jobs is <u>more</u> <u>harder</u>? <u>No error</u>
            A   **B**   **C**   **D**

20. <u>Him</u> and Stash <u>have</u> <u>worse</u> colds than the other students.
    A   **B**   **C**

    <u>No error</u>
    D

Mechanics

12

Capital Letters

Diagnostic Test

Number your paper 1 to 10. Then write each word that should begin with a capital letter.

EXAMPLE   was paul born in january or february?
ANSWER   Was, Paul, January, February

1. her family just got an apartment on pine road.
2. my brother and i often swim at franklin lake.
3. my grandparents will visit us on thanksgiving.
4. do you get the magazine *ranger rick*?
5. your doctor's appointment is next tuesday.
6. the henderson hospital is adding a new wing.
7. i liked the short story "stone stalkers."
8. is jupiter the biggest planet?
9. is mr. pollock the manager of the first national bank in memphis?
10. in july 1776, the declaration of independence was signed.

*F*irst Words and the Pronoun *I*

Imagine how difficult it would be to read a simple set of directions if the directions did not include any capital letters or end marks. It would be very confusing. Without capital letters and end marks, one sentence would run into another.

12a Capitalize the first word in a sentence.

SENTENCES **M**y thumb hurts.

Tomorrow is my birthday.

The pronoun *I* is also always capitalized.

12b Capitalize the pronoun *I*, both alone and in contractions.

ALONE Since yesterday **I** have read two chapters.

CONTRACTION In ten minutes **I**'ll clean my room.

*E*XERCISE 1 *Capitalizing First Words and I*

Number your paper 1 to 20. Then write each word that should begin with a capital letter.

My Science Project

next week my science project is due. for a while i couldn't think of anything. then i decided i'd make a wind vane and record the direction of the wind.

first i got some heavy paper, a straw, some glue, and a pair of scissors. i also found a pin, a compass, and a pencil with an eraser. i cut an arrow point and tail out of the heavy paper and made an even cut at each end of the straw. next i carefully slid the tail and the point into the cuts and added glue. then i pushed a pin through the middle of the straw. finally i pushed the pin into the eraser of the pencil.

tomorrow i'll take the wind vane outside. with my compass, i'll record the direction of the wind.

179

Proper Nouns

A *common noun* is the name of any person, place, or thing. A *proper noun* begins with a capital letter because it is the name of a particular person, place, or thing.

COMMON NOUN   girl, city, day
PROPER NOUNS   Cindy, Fort Myers, Tuesday

12c Capitalize proper nouns and their abbreviations.

Most proper nouns fit into one of the following groups. Use these groups to check the capitalization of proper nouns. Always do this when you edit your written work.

Names of Persons and Animals.   Capitalize the names of particular persons and animals.

PERSONS   Andrea, Charles, Chen Loo, Elvin **A.** Brooks
ANIMALS   Lassie, **M**ax, **M**uffin, **B**aron, **P**eter **R**abbit

Geographical Names.   Capitalize the names of particular places and bodies of water.

STREETS, HIGHWAYS	Lindsay Avenue (**A**ve.), **R**oute 34 (**R**t.) **O**hio Turnpike, **G**rove **S**treet (**S**t.)
CITIES, STATES	Trenton, New Jersey; **W**ashington, **D.C.**
COUNTRIES	Soviet Union, **N**igeria, **N**orway, **I**taly
MOUNTAINS	Rocky Mountains, **M**ount **E**verest
PARKS	Dinosaur National Park, **R**eed **P**ark
ISLANDS	Philippine Islands, **M**anhattan **I**sland
BODIES OF WATER	Baltic **S**ea, **I**ndian **O**cean, **G**ulf of **M**exico, **L**ake **H**uron, **O**hio **R**iver

NOTE: Words such as *street, mountain,* and *city* are capitalized only when they are part of a proper noun.

The **N**ile **R**iver is the longest **r**iver in the world.

180

EXERCISE 2 Using Capital Letters

Number your paper 1 to 10. Then write each word that should begin with a capital letter.

1. about 1,600 years ago, india was divided into many small kingdoms.
2. sometimes my dad and i fish in the chesapeake bay.
3. which is larger, north america or south america?
4. without the nile river, egypt would be nothing but a lifeless desert.
5. next week i'll catch the bus at morton road.
6. how many ships pass through the panama canal each year?
7. i have a cousin who lives in bigfoot, texas.
8. all of lake michigan is in the united states; parts of the other great lakes are in canada.
9. i have an orange-striped cat that looks like morris.
10. the united states purchased alaska from russia in 1867.

EXERCISE 3 Using Capital Letters

Number your paper 1 to 10. Then write each word that should begin with a capital letter.

1. gold was discovered in california in 1848.
2. take route 34 to the pennsylvania turnpike.
3. alaska is surrounded by the arctic ocean, the bering sea, and the gulf of alaska.
4. the capital of south carolina is columbia.
5. james watt, the inventor of the steam engine, was born in scotland.
6. the sahara desert, the largest desert in the world, is in africa.
7. what states border the pacific ocean?
8. there are about 3,000 geysers and hot springs at yellowstone national park.
9. is mt. rainier in washington or oregon?
10. my family and i have visited the hawaiian islands.

EXERCISE 4 *Writing Sentences*

Write five sentences about a city or a country you have studied recently in social studies. Give its location and describe some of its rivers, lakes, mountains, or parks.

Specific Time Periods and Events. Capitalize the days of the week, the months of the year, civil and religious holidays, and special events. Also capitalize the following abbreviations: A.D., B.C., A.M., and P.M.

DAYS, MONTHS	**M**onday, **T**uesday, **A**pril, **D**ecember
HOLIDAYS	**N**ew **Y**ear's **D**ay, **F**ourth of **J**uly
SPECIAL EVENTS	**B**oston **M**arathon, **O**range **B**owl **P**arade
CERTAIN ABBREVIATIONS	By about 1100 **B.C.**, Egypt had lost its great empire.

NOTE: Do *not* capitalize the seasons of the year.

I like **s**pring more than **s**ummer.

Nouns of Historical Importance. Capitalize the names of historical events, periods, and documents.

EVENTS	**K**orean **W**ar, **B**attle of **B**unker **H**ill
PERIODS	**I**ndustrial **R**evolution, **M**iddle **A**ges
DOCUMENTS	**C**onstitution, **D**eclaration of **I**ndependence

NOTE: Prepositions, such as *of* in *Declaration of Independence,* are not capitalized.

EXERCISE 5 *Using Capital Letters*

Number your paper 1 to 10. Then write each word that should begin with a capital letter.

1. the garnet is the birthstone for january.
2. julius caesar ruled rome around 50 b.c.
3. the united states participated in world war II.
4. did delaware ratify the constitution?

182

5. did you know that mother's day is next sunday?
6. king john of england, signed the magna charta in 1215.
7. early in the middle ages, nobles controlled most towns in europe.
8. the french and indian war lasted for eight years, from 1755 to 1763.
9. the first day of winter is next wednesday.
10. abraham lincoln made thanksgiving a national holiday in 1863.

EXERCISE 6 Using Capital Letters

Number your paper 1 to 10. Then write each word that should begin with a capital letter.

1. at the age of 13, andrew jackson fought in the american revolution.
2. the golden age of athens lasted from 461 b.c. to 429 b.c.
3. all book reports are due on friday.
4. did the industrial revolution take place at the same time in england and the united states?
5. my friends from seattle will arrive at 6:45 p.m.
6. the last monday in may is always memorial day.
7. the battle of lexington took place in massachusetts on april 19, 1775.
8. next summer i'm taking swimming lessons at the local swimming pool.
9. the treaty of versailles officially ended world war I.
10. the first labor day was celebrated on september 5, 1882.

EXERCISE 7 Writing Sentences

Write five sentences that tell about your favorite holiday. Include the date of the holiday and where you usually celebrate that holiday. Be sure to capitalize all proper nouns.

Names of Groups and Businesses. Capitalize the names of groups, such as organizations, businesses, institutions, and government bodies.

ORGANIZATIONS	Chicago Bears, American Red Cross
BUSINESSES	First State Bank, Tony's Restaurant
INSTITUTIONS	Conway School, Parkington Hospital
GOVERNMENT BODIES	House of Representatives, Supreme Court, Department of Agriculture

NOTE: Words such as *bank, restaurant, school,* and *hospital* are not capitalized unless they are part of a proper noun.

The oldest university in England is Oxford University.

Names of Planets and Stars. Capitalize the names of the planets, stars, constellations, and galaxies. Do *not* capitalize *sun* and *moon.*

PLANETS	Mercury, Venus, Saturn
STARS	North Star, Sirius, Vega
CONSTELLATIONS	Great Dog, Big Dipper
GALAXY	Milky Way

NOTE: Do not capitalize *earth* if the word *the* comes in front of it.

CAPITAL	The third planet from the sun is Earth.
NO CAPITAL	The moon rotates around *the* earth.

Other Proper Nouns. Capitalize all other proper nouns.

AWARDS	Nobel Peace Prize, Oscar, Emmy
BUILDINGS	Empire State Building, Kennedy Center
LANGUAGES	English, Spanish, Russian, Hebrew
MONUMENTS, MEMORIALS	Washington Monument, Mount Rushmore, Lincoln Memorial, Vietnam Memorial
NATIONALITIES	an American, the French, an Italian
RELIGIONS	Christianity, Judaism, Islam, Buddhism

EXERCISE 8 *Using Capital Letters*

Number your paper 1 to 10. Then write each word that should begin with a capital letter.

1. most of mars looks very much like the desert in arizona.
2. are the white sox playing the yankees tonight?
3. my older sister goes to cloverdale high school.
4. the headquarters of the united nations is in new york city.
5. the sears tower in chicago has 110 floors.
6. each year the outstanding college football player receives the heisman trophy.
7. my uncle owns franklin hardware store.
8. can you pick out the little dipper in the sky?
9. we wrote to the internal revenue service.
10. the methodists are holding two services on sunday.

EXERCISE 9 *Using Capital Letters*

Number your paper 1 to 10. Then write each word that should begin with a capital letter.

1. the planet pluto orbits the sun every 247.7 years.
2. we sent her flowers at the cambridge memorial hospital.
3. my parents always buy food for us at molly's grocery on elm street.
4. how wide is the earth around the equator?
5. in its first 10 years, the top of the empire state building was struck by lightning 68 times.
6. a woman was first appointed to the united states supreme court in 1981.
7. the dutch first settled along the hudson river.
8. for many years astronomers believed that the sun moved around earth.
9. people in brazil speak portuguese.
10. in england, the parliament is divided into the house of lords and the house of commons.

185

TIME-OUT FOR REVIEW • • • • •

Number your paper 1 to 15. Then write each word that should begin with a capital letter.

Who's Who?

1. who helped dorothy get back to kansas?
2. who was the first woman to fly solo across the atlantic ocean?
3. who created mickey mouse and donald duck?
4. who lives on paradise island and has super powers?
5. who is buried at mount vernon, virginia?
6. who lives at 1600 pennsylvania avenue, washington, d.c.?
7. who was marie antoinette, a queen of france or a queen of england?
8. who won four gold medals in track at the 1936 olympics, jesse owens or arthur ashe?
9. who owned a horse named trigger, the lone ranger or roy rogers?
10. who wrote the declaration of independence, thomas jefferson or john adams?
11. who receives the cy young award, a baseball player or a football player?
12. who is on the five-dollar bill, george washington or abraham lincoln?
13. who is the cat in the comics on sunday who eats too much, morris or garfield?
14. who gave christopher columbus the money for his voyage to america, italians or spaniards?
15. who played for the atlanta braves and broke the long-standing record set by babe ruth, hank aaron or lou gehrig?

Other Uses for Capital Letters

Most words you capitalize are proper nouns. There are, however, a few other uses for capital letters. Proper adjectives are capitalized. Titles of people and titles of written works and other works of art are also capitalized.

Proper Adjectives

Proper adjectives are formed from proper nouns. Since proper nouns begin with capital letters, most proper adjectives also begin with capital letters.

12d Capitalize most proper adjectives.

PROPER NOUNS	PROPER ADJECTIVES
Egypt	Egyptian pyramids
Russia	Russian songs
South America	South American people

EXERCISE 10 Capitalizing Proper Adjectives

Number your paper 1 to 10. Then write the following items, adding capital letters only where needed.

1. british explorers
2. european nations
3. asian history
4. french perfume
5. roman leaders
6. danish farmers
7. japanese imports
8. african plains
9. chinese customs
10. north american lakes

EXERCISE 11 Writing Sentences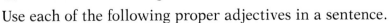

Use each of the following proper adjectives in a sentence.

1. Australian
2. English
3. Korean
4. American
5. South American

*T*itles

Certain titles are capitalized to show that they are the particular titles of people or things.

12e Capitalize the titles of people and works of art.

Titles Used with Names of People. Capitalize a title showing office, rank, or profession when it comes before a person's name. The same title is usually not capitalized when it follows a person's name.

BEFORE A NAME   Can **C**aptain Morris speak to us?
AFTER A NAME   James Morris is a **c**aptain in the Navy.
BEFORE A NAME   Please welcome **A**mbassador Reid.
AFTER A NAME   Mr. Reid is the new **a**mbassador.

Other titles or their abbreviations—such as *Mr., Rev.,* and *Sgt.*—should also be capitalized when they come before a person's name.

I have an appointment with **D**r. Simpson.
Do you know **M**rs. O'Reilly?

*E*XERCISE 12   *Capitalizing Titles of People*

Number your paper 1 to 10. Then write each word that should begin with a capital letter. If a sentence is correct, write *C* after the number.

1. Is senator Murphy running for a second term?
2. My sister is taking a course from professor Kyle.
3. Grace Silverman became a lieutenant before she retired from the Army.
4. I would like you to meet doctor Foster.
5. The letter was addressed to mrs. Robert Taylor.
6. Give this message to governor Weeks right away.
7. Carlos Rivera is a senator from my state.
8. Hata Mori is the doctor in the next office.
9. I have known rev. Bolaway for three years.
10. Is lieutenant Johnson your brother?

Titles of Written Works and Other Works of Art. Capi-
talize the first word, the last word, and all important
words in the titles of books, newspapers, magazines, short
stories, poems, plays, musical compositions, and other
works of art, such as names of paintings and sculptures.

Do not capitalize a preposition, a coordinating conjunction, or an article (*a, an,* or *the*) unless it is the first or last
word in a title.

BOOKS AND CHAPTER TITLES	The test will cover the chapter "**E**urope in the **M**iddle **A**ges" in your textbook *Our World from Past to Present.*
NEWSPAPERS, MAGAZINES	My mother gets the *Washington Post* and the *National Geographic*. [Generally, you do not capitalize *the* as the first word of a newspaper or a magazine title.]
MOVIES	Did you ever see the movie *The Purple Rose of Cairo?*
MUSICAL COMPOSITIONS	I liked the song "**T**he **R**ain in **S**pain" from the musical *My Fair Lady.*

*E*XERCISE 13 *Capitalizing Titles*

Number your paper 1 to 10. Then write each word that
should begin with a capital letter.

1. Have you read the story "the city of the ancients"?
2. We placed an ad in the *chicago tribune.*
3. I like the song "feed the birds" from the musical *mary poppins.*
4. The chapter "the rise of rome" in my history book was very interesting.
5. I enjoyed reading *the book of baseball greats.*
6. We read the poem "after the fireworks" in my English class.
7. My sister gets the magazine *children's digest.*
8. "odysseus and the cyclops" is a good myth.
9. I played Captain Jane Evan in the play "the aliens."
10. For my book report, I read *the earth and space.*

TIME-OUT FOR REVIEW • • • • •

Number your paper 1 to 15. Then write each word that should begin with a capital letter.

What's What?

1. in what movie would you hear the song "somewhere over the rainbow"?
2. what nation once ruled india, england or russia?
3. which planet is closer to the earth, mars or saturn?
4. what is the name of the largest state, california, texas, or alaska?
5. what kind of animal was thumper in the movie *bambi*?
6. what is the capital of ohio, cincinnati or columbus?
7. what was julius caesar's nationality, greek or roman?
8. on what continent would you find mount kilimanjaro, south america or africa?
9. what holiday is celebrated every year on july 4, labor day or independence day?
10. what occurs more often, an eclipse of the moon or an eclipse of the sun?
11. what is the largest country in south america, brazil or argentina?
12. what did general dwight d. eisenhower become in 1953, a senator or a president?
13. the missouri river is the second longest river in the united states. what is the longest river?
14. what language do the people in austria speak, german or english?
15. the congress is made up of the senate and what other legislative body?

Application to Writing

An important part of your editing should be checking to see that you have included capital letters everywhere they are needed. You should also check to see if you have used capital letters for some words, such as *moon* and *winter*, that do not need to be capitalized. As you edit your work, refer to the rules and the examples in this chapter, and correct errors when you find them.

EXERCISE 14 Editing for Proper Capitalization

Read the following paragraphs and find the 25 words that should begin with a capital letter. (Do not include words that are already capitalized.) Then rewrite the paragraphs correctly.

A Fantasy Come True

For centuries the moon has fascinated people. In 1865, the french novelist jules verne, who wrote the book *20,000 leagues under the sea,* wrote a story about a man walking on the moon. His fantasy became a fact 104 years later.

It was president john f. kennedy who got the space program going in 1961. By 1968, american scientists felt they knew enough about the moon to send astronauts there. In december 1968, a spacecraft carried three astronauts ten times around the moon.

Then on july 16, 1969, a spacecraft took off from cape canaveral, florida. On july 20, neil armstrong and edwin aldrin landed on the sea of tranquillity on the moon. They spent over $2\frac{1}{2}$ hours on the surface and collected 46 pounds of stones and dust. Their every move was watched on television by people across the united states and around the world. Four days later they splashed down in the pacific.

*C*hapter *R*eview

A **Using Capital Letters.** Number your paper 1 to 10. Then write each word that should begin with a capital letter.

1. martin luther king, jr. won the nobel peace prize.
2. our sun is about 5,000 years old.
3. the world trade center in new york city is taller than the eiffel tower in paris, france.
4. in mexico i learned a few words of spanish.
5. the muslims first invaded spain in a.d. 711.
6. has governor kline flown to washington, d.c.?
7. all the doctors at the local hospital belong to the american medical association.
8. the rhine river flows through germany.
9. on june 1, 1954, congress changed the name of armistice day to veterans day.
10. the story "the luck of pokey bloom" was good.

B **Using Capital Letters.** Number your paper 1 to 10. Then write each word that should begin with a capital letter.

1. the french people donated money for the statue of liberty.
2. my grandfather can speak polish and russian.
3. martin luther was a roman catholic, but he started a new church in 1520.
4. in many ways mercury resembles the moon that orbits the earth.
5. my sister works at murphy's market.
6. the japanese use their rivers to irrigate their land.
7. have you ever read the bill of rights?
8. last winter glen road was closed for two months.
9. the pacific ocean is larger than the atlantic ocean.
10. the chinese ruled vietnam for over 1,000 years.

C **Editing for Proper Capitalization.** Number your paper 1 to 10. Read the following paragraphs and find the 20 words that should begin with a capital letter. (Do not include words that are already capitalized.) Then write the paragraphs correctly.

Eastward, Ho!

In the early 1400s, prince henry of portugal wanted a better route to asia. He believed it was possible to reach india and china by sailing around africa. At the time no one knew if he was right.

In 1419, one of his ships reached madeira, a group of islands off the coast of morocco. For the next 15 years, his sailors refused to go much farther south. They had heard that beyond cape bojador were man-eating monsters.

Finally 54 years later, bartholomeu dias, a portuguese sea captain, reached the cape of good hope, the southernmost tip of africa. prince henry's plan had worked.

Mastery Test

Number your paper 1 to 10. Then write each word that should begin with a capital letter.

1. ten moons orbit the planet saturn.
2. the first indoor football game in the national football league was played on december 18, 1932.
3. kate could be the next senator from this state.
4. my brother wants to go to yale university in new haven, connecticut.
5. during the middle ages, few europeans visited china.
6. suzuki just got her american citizenship.
7. when did the civil war begin?
8. we watched the old movie *lawrence of arabia*.
9. point out the big dipper to me.
10. the city of troy was located in what is now turkey.

13

End Marks and Commas

*D*iagnostic *T*est

Number your paper 1 to 10. Write each sentence, adding a comma or commas where needed. Then put the correct end mark after each sentence or question.

EXAMPLE   I was born in Pittsburgh Pennsylvania
ANSWER   I was born in Pittsburgh, Pennsylvania.

1. We are collecting old clothes food and blankets
2. Dad have you seen the dog
3. Inside the small box we heard a little meow
4. Is Andy doing his homework watching TV or talking on the telephone
5. Listen class to the special announcement
6. On June 6 1970 my parents were married
7. Well this party was the biggest surprise of my life
8. Falmouth Massachusetts is a lovely town
9. Watch out for the falling ladder Bruce
10. I'm busy after school but Connie will help you

End Marks

There are four different kinds of sentences. Each one has a different purpose. The purpose of a sentence determines its end mark. (*See page 4 for a review of the different kinds of sentences.*)

13a Place a **period** after a statement, after an opinion, and after a command or request made in a normal tone of voice.

PERIODS   The Tigers are playing the Boxers. [statement]
This has been a great game so far. [opinion]
Watch the coach on the sidelines. [command]

13b Place a **question mark** after a sentence that asks a question.

QUESTION MARK   Who is up at bat next?

13c Place an **exclamation point** after a sentence that states strong feeling and after a command or request that expresses great excitement.

EXCLAMATION POINTS   Terry just hit the ball over the fence! [a sentence that expresses strong feeling]
Look at it soar through the air! [a command said with great excitement]

EXERCISE 1   Using End Marks

Add end marks to the following sentences.

Cooking Dinner

1. Tonight I'm cooking dinner for the family
2. Where's a baking pan, Mom
3. Peel the potatoes for me, Jeff
4. I must cook the meatloaf
5. Turn the oven on for me, Nancy

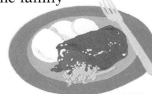

6. The temperature is much too high
7. How long should I cook the meatloaf
8. Dinner will be ready in 30 minutes
9. Dad, will you cut the meatloaf
10. What a wonderful meal I cooked

Periods with Abbreviations

Abbreviations are shortened forms of words. You should use abbreviations for notes and messages, but most abbreviations should not be used in formal writing like stories or reports.

13d Use a **period** with most abbreviations.

Following is a list of some common abbreviations. Notice that many abbreviations begin with capital letters. (*For a list of state abbreviations, see page 411.*)

Common Abbreviations	
DAYS	Sun. Mon. Tues. Wed. Thur. Fri. Sat.
MONTHS	Jan. Feb. Mar. Apr. Aug. Sept. Oct. Nov. Dec. [Other months are not abbreviated.]
STREETS	St. Rd. Ave. Dr. Blvd. Pl. Rt.
TITLES WITH NAMES	Mr. Mrs. Ms. Dr. Rev. Gov. Gen. Lt. Capt. Sgt. Jr. Sr. [Initials are also followed by periods—Mr. R. M. Rawlings.]
TIMES WITH NUMBERS	450 B.C. [before Christ] A.D. 80 [*anno Domini*—in the year of the Lord] 5:30 A.M. [*ante meridiem*—before noon] 9:45 P.M. [*post meridiem*–after noon]

NOTE: A colon (:) comes between the hours and the minutes when time is written in numbers.

EXERCISE 2 Writing Abbreviations

Number your paper 1 to 10. Then write the abbreviations that stand for the following items.

1. Tuesday
2. Mister
3. before Christ
4. Street
5. Doctor

6. Captain
7. Avenue
8. after noon
9. December
10. Junior

EXERCISE 3 Writing Sentences

Number your paper 1 to 10. Rewrite each item below, substituting a complete word for each abbreviation. Then use each item in a sentence of your own.

1. Gen. Adams
2. Paul Simms, Sr.
3. Mon.
4. Mullins Rd.
5. Sat., June 3

6. Aug. 6, 1987
7. Park Blvd.
8. the first of Jan.
9. Gov. Richardson
10. Rt. 64

TIME-OUT FOR REVIEW • • • • •

Number your paper 1 to 10. Then write each sentence, adding any periods for abbreviations and a correct end mark.

1. Davis Rd is being repaved
2. Is Lt Robertson in charge of this barracks
3. At 4:00 PM we are meeting in the cafeteria
4. Gov Simpson invited me to the governor's mansion
5. By about 500 BC the Chinese way of life was over a thousand years old
6. Last Dec my school had five snow days
7. Is Mrs T R Dickerson the new superintendent
8. On Fri bring your books to class
9. Last Sat I won a trip to Hawaii
10. Dr Tunner is my sister's arm hurt badly

Commas

Commas (,) help you understand what you read. They keep words and some sentences from running together and causing confusion.

Dates and Addresses

Use a comma to separate the date from the year and to separate a city from a state or country.

13e Use commas to separate elements in dates and addresses.

DATES   My brother was born on August 20, 1974.

ADDRESSES   Have you ever visited Miami, Florida?

If the year, the state, or the country does not come at the end of the sentence, use a comma to separate it from the rest of the sentence.

DATES   On March 6, 1985, we moved into our house.

ADDRESSES   Some people in Charleston, South Carolina, have homes along the ocean.

EXERCISE 4   Using Commas in Dates and Addresses

Number your paper 1 to 10. Then write each sentence, adding a comma or commas where needed.

Young Record Breakers

1. An 18-year-old boy set the world record for sit-ups on December 19 1977.
2. An 11-year-old boy became the organist at Leeds' Cathedral in West Yorkshire England.
3. Five-year-old Cory Orr of Littleton Colorado was the youngest golfer to shoot a hole-in-one.
4. Twelve-year-old Gertrude Ederle broke the women's 880-yard freestyle swimming world record in Indianapolis Indiana.
5. Gertrude was born on October 23 1906.

198

6. Jeanette La Bianca was born on May 12 1934.
7. Born in Buffalo New York she became the youngest opera singer at age 15.
8. A 15-year-old boy from Ontario Canada built a house of cards—39 stories high.
9. On August 17 1974 a 13-year-old girl swam the English Channel.
10. An 8-year-old boy rode his bicycle from San Francisco California to Atlantic City New Jersey.

Items in a Series

A series is three or more similar words or groups of words listed one after another. Commas are used to separate the items in a series.

13f Use commas to separate items in a series.

WORDS	We need balloons, streamers, and banners for the party decorations. [nouns]
	Contestants in the talent show sang, danced, and yodeled. [verbs]
GROUPS OF WORDS	Everyone listened carefully, took notes, and asked questions. [complete predicates]
	The hikers went down Route 70, across the meadow, and into the woods. [prepositional phrases]

EXERCISE 5 Using Commas in a Series

Number your paper 1 to 10. Then write each sentence, adding commas where needed.

1. Snow leopards pumas and lynxes often live high in the mountains.
2. The raccoon found some food washed it and ate it.
3. We looked around the mall in two stores and in a catalog for Mom's birthday present.
4. They grow soy beans corn and wheat on their farm.

5. On week nights I eat dinner wash the dishes and finish my homework.
6. Famous redheads are Mark Twain George Washington and Thomas Jefferson.
7. The small boat rolled pitched and tossed in the ocean.
8. Look for the car keys along the driveway under the car and inside the garage.
9. Garnets amethysts and aquamarines are the birthstones for the first three months of the year.
10. The robin caught a worm flew to its nest and fed it to its young.

Introductory Elements

When certain words or certain prepositional phrases come at the beginning of a sentence, a comma is used to separate them from the rest of the sentence.

13g Use a comma after certain introductory elements.

Usually a comma follows words such as *no, oh, well,* and *yes* when they begin a sentence. Usually when these words come at the beginning of a sentence, they are being used as interjections. (*See page 86 for more information about interjections.*)

WORDS   Yes, you are on the right road.
        Oh, it's time to leave.

A comma follows an introductory prepositional phrase that has four or more words. A comma also follows two or more prepositional phrases that come at the beginning of a sentence.

PREPOSITIONAL   During social studies class, we watched a
PHRASES   film about Japan. [four-word phrase]
                In the corner of the room, we saw several
                large boxes. [two phrases]

EXERCISE 6 *Using Commas with Introductory Elements*

Number your paper 1 to 10. Then write each sentence, adding a comma where needed. If a sentence does not need a comma, write *C* after the number.

Facts and Figures

1. Well I never knew that the heart pumps 2,000 gallons of blood a day.
2. Throughout the United States 34 percent of the land is owned by the federal government.
3. Without our sun the temperature on Earth would fall to minus 459 degrees Fahrenheit.
4. No owls are not the smartest birds.
5. At the beginning of first grade most students already know about 6,000 words.
6. In a lifetime the average person will eat about 60,000 pounds of food—the weight of 6 elephants.
7. During its first six months a baby doubles the size of its brain.
8. Yes a bloodhound can track a scent through water.
9. With one normal breath you take in a pint of air.
10. Oh vandalism costs schools $600 million a year.

Direct Address

When you talk to someone, you sometimes call that person by name. Such a name is called a noun of *direct address*.

13h ▸ Use a comma or commas to separate a noun of direct address from the rest of the sentence.

Julie, tonight you can help me with the dinner.
Tonight you can help me with the dinner, Julie.

Use two commas with a noun of direct address that comes in the middle of a sentence.

Tonight, Julie, you can help me with dinner.

201

EXERCISE 7 *Using Commas with Direct Address*

Number your paper 1 to 10. Then write each sentence, adding a comma or commas where needed.

1. Jessie is a zebra a white animal with black stripes or a black animal with white stripes?
2. Smile for the camera Ellis.
3. Did you know Laurie that the crow is probably the smartest of all birds?
4. Adela please eat lunch with me today.
5. There are about 9,000 taste buds on your tongue Lee.
6. Bruce did you feed the cat?
7. There are 206 bones in your body Dawn.
8. Do you know how to get to the stadium Barry?
9. Andrea please turn down your radio.
10. Yes Charles modern blood tests can diagnose 2,000 different diseases.

Compound Sentences

A *compound sentence* is two or more simple sentences usually joined by the coordinating conjunction *and, but,* or *or.* A comma usually comes before the conjunction. (*See pages 100–102 for a review of compound sentences.*)

13i Use a comma before a coordinating conjunction that joins the parts of a compound sentence.

Dad is in the basement, and Pete is outside.
The teams waited, but the referee never showed up.

Do not confuse a compound sentence with a simple sentence that has a compound verb.

COMPOUND SENTENCE   The captain blew the whistle, and the ship left the dock. [A comma is needed.]

COMPOUND VERB   The captain blew the whistle and steered the ship from the dock. [No comma is needed.]

EXERCISE 8 Using Commas with Compound Sentences

Number your paper 1 to 10. Then write each sentence, adding a comma where needed. If a sentence does not need a comma, write *C* after the number.

1. Orange juice is the most popular fruit juice in the United States and prune juice is the least popular.
2. Jerry finished his book and wrote his book report.
3. The front window is broken and rain is pouring in!
4. First-born children are usually the smartest but last-born children are usually the most popular.
5. The bell rang and all the students sat down.
6. King Arthur formed the Knights of the Round Table and served as their leader.
7. Today is a holiday but tomorrow is school as usual.
8. Chimpanzees learn faster than gorillas but chimpanzees forget things sooner.
9. The horse ran to the fence but didn't jump over.
10. Women generally see better at night and men generally see better in the daytime.

EXERCISE 9 Writing Sentences

Number your paper 1 to 10. Then write sentences that follow the directions below. Add commas where needed.

1. Include your city and state.
2. Include the date and year of your birth.
3. Use a series of nouns.
4. Include a series of complete predicates.
5. Begin with *yes.*
6. Begin with the prepositional phrase *in an hour.*
7. Begin with the prepositional phrase *during last night's basketball game.*
8. Begin with a noun of direct address.
9. End with a noun of direct address.
10. Join two simple sentences with *and* to form a compound sentence.

TIME-OUT FOR REVIEW • • • • •

Number your paper 1 to 20. Then write each sentence, adding a comma or commas where needed. If a sentence is correct, write *C* after the number.

Strange Contests

1. Today class I'm going to tell you about contests.
2. Who runs the fastest and who jumps the highest?
3. Well people are always taking part in contests to find answers to these questions.
4. Throughout history people have competed in contests of many kinds.
5. People in ancient Greece held the Olympic Games, and children in ancient Rome held tugs-of-war.
6. Before the European discovery of America American Indians competed in ball games and footraces.
7. Today many contests are serious tests of athletic abilities but some are just for fun.
8. People race their pet crabs worms and turkeys.
9. Others race down a street and flip pancakes.
10. Yes some even slide down ski slopes on inner tubes.
11. Every year people in Albuquerque New Mexico hold the world's largest hot-air balloon contest.
12. Hundreds of balloonists compete.
13. One silly race is held in British Columbia Canada.
14. Off Vancouver Island contestants cross the Strait of Georgia in power-driven bathtubs!
15. This annual race began on August 25 1967.
16. No this is not a joke.
17. The contestants mount fiberglass bathtubs on water skis and add motors.
18. Since the race in 1981 safety has been watched.
19. In that year the waves were 10 feet high.
20. Mr. Michaels does this sound like fun to you?

Application to Writing

Commas work like yellow caution lights. They slow readers down and prevent "accidents" of misunderstanding. Always edit your work for the correct use of commas. Make sure that you have included all necessary commas, but also watch for any unnecessary commas.

EXERCISE 10 Editing for the Correct Use of Commas

Find the 20 places where commas are missing from this passage. Then rewrite it, adding the commas.

High Jumpers

Listen Terry to this interesting article. The highest jumpers in the world are not people. They are kangaroos. One kangaroo jumped 10½ feet but the best human jumpers can leap only about 7 feet.

Kangaroos are also very fast. Some people in Sydney Australia once held a race. On May 6 1927 a kangaroo raced against a horse. The kangaroo won.

In the wild in Australia kangaroos travel in groups called mobs. Usually a mob of kangaroos includes one large male his mates and several younger animals. Yes it's true. With its front paws the leader of the mob boxes with other male kangaroos.

Adult kangaroos are about 4½ feet tall but their tails are another 3½ feet long. They weigh about 155 pounds. During their entire lives kangaroos grow. Oh the oldest kangaroos must be the biggest ones then.

Kangaroos eat grasses small bushes and other green plants. Here's another interesting fact Terry. In at least one way kangaroos are like camels. For long periods of time they can go without water.

Chapter Review

A **Using Commas Correctly.** Number your paper 1 to 10. Then write each sentence, adding a comma or commas where needed. If a sentence is correct, write *C* after the number.

1. Sheep elephants and camels snore loudly.
2. My sister and her family live in Wichita Kansas.
3. Oh we should wait for Rosa.
4. For approximately six million people in the United States English is a second language.
5. The tiger ran swiftly and chased the hedgehog.
6. Billy do you know the time?
7. We could boil bake or mash the potatoes.
8. The library James is straight down the hall.
9. The Rose Bowl Game is held in Pasadena and the Sugar Bowl Game is held in New Orleans.
10. Columbus first sighted land on October 11 1492.

B **Using Commas Correctly.** Number your paper 1 to 10. Then write each sentence, adding a comma or commas where needed. If a sentence is correct, write *C* after the number.

1. During our trip to Florida we went to Disney World.
2. Well don't you look nice today!
3. Wait for us George.
4. Tin cans first preserved oysters salmon and lobsters.
5. At the park some people were eating their lunches.
6. Santa Fe New Mexico receives an average of 17 more inches of snow per year than Fairbanks Alaska.
7. I poured the soup into a pan stirred it and ate it.
8. On June 12 1985 my older sister got married.
9. Is it nine o'clock yet Mom?
10. A baby kangaroo is called a joey and a baby zebra is called a foal.

C **Editing for the Correct Use of Commas.** Read the following paragraphs and find the 10 places where commas are missing. Then rewrite the paragraphs, adding the commas.

Pedal Power

Bryan Allen of Bakersfield California did something that no one else has ever done. On June 12 1979 he pedaled across the English Channel! For nearly three hours he pumped the pedals that turned the propeller of a small aircraft. The aircraft had no engine and Allen's muscles were its only source of energy.

The aircraft was named *Gossamer Albatross*. The name "Gossamer" refers to something very light and an albatross is a seabird with long wings. The *Gossamer Albatross* looked like a bicycle inside a thin shell. It had a propeller in the back a small control wing in the front and one very long wing overhead. Yes Allen's flight was the longest human-powered flight in history.

*M*astery *T*est

Number your paper 1 to 10. Write each sentence, adding a comma or commas where needed. Then put the correct end mark after each sentence or question.

1. Mr. Reise are you driving us to school tomorrow
2. I ordered chicken mashed potatoes and corn
3. With the light from my flashlight we saw the deer
4. On December 3 1979 a terrible storm hit Boston
5. Yes there are more left-handed males than females
6. Don't go into that deserted mine Patty
7. San Francisco California is a very large city
8. We saw a film had a discussion and took a test
9. Well Paula you made a perfect score on your test
10. The largest state is Alaska and the smallest state is Rhode Island

14

Apostrophes and Quotation Marks

Diagnostic Test

Number your paper 1 to 10. Write each of the following direct quotations. Then add quotation marks and any needed apostrophes.

EXAMPLE   Paul said, This is my dogs old leash.
ANSWER   Paul said, "This is my dog's old leash."

1. That birds nest is very small, Henry stated.
2. We dont have any afternoon classes today, Hannah told everyone.
3. The kindergarten teacher announced, The childrens pictures are hanging on the wall.
4. Where is the librarians desk? Gwen asked.
5. Im not feeling very well, Maggie said.
6. The band members instruments, the director explained, are kept in a locked room.
7. Chris said, This jacket isnt big enough for me.
8. Theyre waiting for us now, Mr. Brown stated.
9. Mom asked, Are those mens suits on sale?
10. My cars tires, Dad stated, are worn out.

*A*postrophes

You probably use apostrophes most often when you write contractions. Apostrophes are also used to show ownership or possession.

Possessive Forms of Nouns

To show ownership, nouns have special forms that include apostrophes. You use these special forms when *of* expressions could be substituted for the nouns.

Elroy's sneakers = the sneakers **of Elroy**
the teachers' coats = the coats **of the teachers**

Possessive Forms of Singular Nouns. To write the possessive form of any singular noun, write the noun just as it is. Do not add or leave out any letters. Then add an apostrophe and an *s*.

14a Add 's to form the possessive of a singular noun.

school + **'s** = school's   I raised the school's flag.
Bob + **'s** = Bob's   This is Bob's handwriting.

*E*XERCISE 1 *Forming Possessive Singular Nouns*

Number your paper 1 to 10. Rewrite each expression, using the possessive form. Then use each expression in a sentence.

EXAMPLE   poem of Linda
ANSWER   Linda's poem   Everyone liked Linda's poem.

1. tail of a fox
2. toys of the baby
3. keys of Mr. Ryan
4. ride of an hour
5. tapes of Vincent
6. friends of David
7. farm of my mother
8. uniform of the sailor
9. howls of the wolf
10. vacation of a month

209

Possessive Forms of Plural Nouns. The plural of most nouns is formed by adding an *s: skates, hours,* and *horses.* There are a few exceptions like *women* and *geese.* These plurals are formed by changing the words. If you are not sure how to form the plural of a noun, look it up in the dictionary.

How the possessive form of a plural noun is written depends on the ending of the noun.

14b ▸ Add only an apostrophe to form the possessive of a plural noun that ends in *s.*

> boys + ' = boys'   The boys' work is excellent.
> [more than one boy]
>
> bears + ' = bears' Bears' dens are often in caves.
> [more than one bear]

14c ▸ Add *'s* to form the possessive of a plural noun that does not end in *s.*

> mice + 's = mice's   I cleaned the mice's cages.
> children + 's = children's The children's film is next.

When you write the possessive of a plural noun, take the following steps. First write the plural of the noun. Then look at the ending of the word. If the word ends in *s,* add only an apostrophe. If the word does not end in *s,* add an apostrophe and an *s.*

PLURAL	ENDING	ADD	=	POSSESSIVE
books	*s*	'	=	books'
boxes	*s*	'	=	boxes'
men	no *s*	's	=	men's

NOTE: The possessive forms of the personal pronouns are *my, mine, your, yours, his, her, hers, its, our, ours, their,* and *theirs.* These pronouns are never written with an apostrophe. Do not put an apostrophe in the possessive form of *its. It's* is a contraction that means *it is* or *it has.*

EXERCISE 2 Forming Possessive Plural Nouns

Number your paper 1 to 10. Rewrite each expression, using the possessive form. Then use each expression in a sentence.

1. coats of the men
2. labels of the boxes
3. soles of the shoes
4. home of the bees
5. tracks of two deer

6. saddles of the horses
7. formation of the geese
8. meeting of the scouts
9. clothes of the children
10. names of the women

EXERCISE 3 Forming Possessive Nouns

Number your paper 1 to 10. Then write each underlined word and add an apostrophe or an apostrophe and an *s*.

EXAMPLE   John is wearing his <u>father</u> watch.
ANSWER   father's

1. The <u>girls</u> gym class has been canceled.
2. All of the <u>farmers</u> barns are full of hay.
3. Timmy is my <u>brother</u> best friend.
4. The <u>kitten</u> toys are all over the living room.
5. The <u>men</u> basketball team won again.
6. Yesterday time moved at a <u>snail</u> pace.
7. Several of my <u>friends</u> apartments are near mine.
8. The <u>children</u> special on TV was funny.
9. There were many diamonds in the <u>king</u> crown.
10. The <u>astronauts</u> suits were carefully checked.

EXERCISE 4 Writing Possessives of Nouns

Number your paper 1 to 5. Then change the *of* expressions into possessive nouns and rewrite the sentences.

1. What are the names of those children?
2. The leaves of the tree fell into a neat pile.
3. I can't remember the license plates of the two cars.
4. Does the face of that boy look familiar?
5. This is the house of the Reynolds.

Contractions

A contraction usually combines two words into one. An apostrophe is added to replace one or more missing letters.

14d Use an apostrophe in a contraction to show where one or more letters have been omitted.

Some contractions combine a pronoun with a verb.

I + am = I'm	I + would = I'd
you + are = you're	they + have = they've
she + will = she'll	that + is = that's
it + is = it's	there + is = there's

Some contractions combine a verb with the word *not*. In this kind of contraction, the apostrophe replaces the *o* in *not*.

is + not = isn't	was + not = wasn't
are + not = aren't	do + not = don't
has + not = hasn't	could + not = couldn't
have + not = haven't	would + not = wouldn't

When you write a contraction, do not add or move around any letters. There is only one common exception: *will* + *not* = *won't.*

Contraction or Possessive Pronoun?   Do not confuse a contraction with a possessive pronoun.

CONTRACTIONS	it's	you're	they're	there's
PRONOUNS	its	your	their	theirs

To avoid any confusion when you write these words, always say to yourself the individual words of a contraction separately.

It's (It is) time for the TV special.

They're (They are) in the gym.

EXERCISE 5 Using Apostrophes with Contractions

Number your paper 1 to 20. Then write the contraction for each pair of words.

1. I am	6. they have	11. you are	16. he is
2. are not	7. could not	12. has not	17. will not
3. it is	8. she will	13. I have	18. they are
4. is not	9. have not	14. was not	19. did not
5. we are	10. I would	15. she has	20. you are

EXERCISE 6 Substituting Words for Contractions

Number your paper 1 to 10. Write each contraction. Then write the words from which each contraction is formed.

EXAMPLE   Today hasn't been such a good day.
ANSWER   hasn't = has not

1. That wasn't a very good movie.
2. We're waiting for the next subway train.
3. They aren't the shirts in the catalog.
4. She's watching her younger brother today.
5. I'm taking my lunch to school every day.
6. They don't look very happy.
7. They're making popcorn for the party.
8. I won't make any promises.
9. You're having dinner with us tonight.
10. It's a good book.

EXERCISE 7 Distinguishing between Contractions and Pronouns

Number your paper 1 to 10. Then write the correct word in parentheses.

1. (It's, Its) 6:30 P.M.
2. (They're, Their) apartment has a lovely view of the park.
3. Did you find (you're, your) jacket in the library or the gym?
4. (There's, Theirs) a fly in this room.

5. How did the dog hurt (it's, its) leg?
6. We will go in (they're, their) car.
7. (You're, Your) the best singer in the chorus at our school.
8. (There's, Theirs) is the house with the white shutters.
9. (It's, Its) fun at the amusement park.
10. (You're, Your) giving your social studies report next.

*T*IME-OUT FOR REVIEW • • • • •

Number your paper 1 to 20. Then correctly write each word that needs an apostrophe.

EXAMPLE   Have you see Johns new computer?
ANSWER   John's

1. I dont know her name.
2. That persons car is parked illegally.
3. Well meet you at the stadium.
4. Have you ever been inside the Morgans house?
5. The fish werent biting at Johnson Pond today.
6. A newspaper reporter spoke to the womens group.
7. They havent gone to the pool yet.
8. Most forest rangers jobs are in national parks.
9. Shes the youngest teacher at the school.
10. I want a dollars worth of oranges.
11. The cat unrolled Moms ball of yarn.
12. Id choose music before art.
13. We waited for the end of the childrens program.
14. This meat doesnt have any taste.
15. The ringmasters voice was very deep.
16. Youve helped me very much.
17. Several drivers taxis have been dented.
18. The oxens load was very heavy.
19. Were taking our dog on vacation with us to Yellowstone National Park.
20. The ponies manes were tangled.

Application to Writing

If you forget to add an apostrophe or if you misplace an apostrophe, a reader may completely misunderstand your meaning. If you forget to add an apostrophe to *we'll*, for example, a reader will read the word *well*. If you want to say that two girls each own one pony and you write *girl's ponies,* a reader will think that only one girl owns more than one pony.

Always edit your work for the correct use of apostrophes so readers will understand *exactly* what you have written.

EXERCISE 8 Editing for the Correct Use of Apostrophes

Read the following paragraphs. Find the 10 words in which apostrophes are missing. Then rewrite the paragraphs, adding the apostrophes.

The Largest Bird

Im writing my science report about ostriches. I couldnt find any information about them. Then the librarians aide showed me this wonderful book. The ostrich is the worlds largest living bird. It may stand 8 feet tall, and its weight may reach as much as 300 pounds. Thats a really big bird!

Ostriches are birds, but they dont fly. Their wings are too small to lift their heavy bodies off the ground. An ostrichs legs, however, move very fast. One ostrich was clocked at 50 miles an hour. Its two-toed feet are good for something else, too. An ostrich can kick very hard. That is a good defense. One kick can break a lions back.

In the 1700s, most womens hats had ostrich feathers on them. Hunters didnt think about anything except money. As a result, ostriches almost became extinct. Now they are plentiful only in East Africa.

Quotation Marks

The more you write, the more you will need to use quotation marks. When you write a report, for example, you should include the exact words from books to support what you are saying. To do this, you need to know how to use quotation marks correctly.

When you write a story, you should often include the conversations of the characters in your story. To improve your writing in this way, you need to know how to use quotation marks correctly.

Direct Quotations

A *direct quotation* is the exact words of a person. Quotation marks go before and after a direct quotation.

14e Use quotation marks before and after a person's exact words.

DIRECT   Lynn said, "Today is Pete's birthday."
QUOTATIONS   She added, "We should give him a party."

If you are writing a one-sentence direct quotation, you can write it in three ways. You can place it before or after a speaker tag such as *she said* or *he asked*. You can also place a speaker tag in the middle of a direct quotation.

In all of these cases, place quotation marks only before and after the person's exact words. The words inside quotation marks should never include a speaker tag.

BEFORE   "For a week I have been jogging," he said.
AFTER   He said, "For a week I have been jogging."
MIDDLE   "For a week," he said, "I have been jogging."
             [Two sets of quotation marks are needed because the speaker tag interrupts the direct quotation.]

216

EXERCISE 9 *Using Quotation Marks with Direct Quotations*

Write each direct quotation, adding quotation marks where needed. In this exercise, the comma or the end mark goes *inside* the closing quotation marks.

Fishy Escapes

1. Many fish simply fool their enemies, she explained.
2. She added, Some fish live along bright corals, and they often have bright coloring.
3. Their color, she said, makes them look like corals.
4. She added, Some fish can change their color.
5. These fish have special color cells, she explained.
6. She said, They can match their backgrounds perfectly.
7. Other fish swallow water, she stated, and puff up.
8. She explained, This action makes them look very big.
9. Some fish, she added, have a bad taste.
10. Other fish always avoid these fish, she concluded.

Capital Letters with Direct Quotations.   Begin each direct quotation with a capital letter.

14f   Capitalize the first word of a direct quotation.

"**T**hese flowers are carnations," he said.

She said, "**T**hey are lovely." [*She* is capitalized because it is the first word of the sentence. *They* is capitalized because it is the first word of the direct quotation.]

"**T**hese flowers," he said, "are for my mother." [*Are* is *not* capitalized because it is in the middle of a sentence.]

"**S**he will like them," he said. "**T**hey are for her birthday." [*They* is capitalized because it starts a new sentence of the direct quotation.]

EXERCISE 10 Using Capital Letters with Direct Quotations

Number your paper 1 to 10. Then write each direct quotation, adding capital letters where needed.

Land of the Dinosaurs

1. "dinosaurs died out millions of years ago," Mr. Chin explained.
2. he added, "they haven't completely disappeared, however."
3. "in some places," he stated, "their bones remain."
4. he said, "one such place is Dinosaur Provincial Park in Canada."
5. "there," he said, "people have found more dinosaur bones than in any other place on earth."
6. "bones from many kinds of dinosaurs were found," he said. "in fact, bones from 30 kinds were found."
7. "during the time of dinosaurs," he said, "the climate on the earth was very different."
8. he explained, "the weather in Canada was like the weather is now in Florida."
9. "the climate was perfect for dinosaurs," he said.
10. he added, "that's why so many kinds lived there."

Commas with Direct Quotations. Commas are used to separate direct quotations from speaker tags.

14g Use a comma to separate a direct quotation from a speaker tag. Place the comma inside the closing quotation marks.

"Monday is the first day of the month," he said. [The comma goes *inside* the closing quotation marks.]

He said, "Monday is the first day of the month." [The comma follows the speaker tag.]

"Monday," he said, "is the first day of the month." [Two commas are needed to separate the speaker tag from the direct quotation: one before and one after the speaker tag. The first comma goes *inside* the closing quotation marks.]

EXERCISE 11 *Using Commas with Direct Quotations*

Number your paper 1 to 10. Then write each direct quotation, adding commas where needed.

The First

1. "In 1978, Naomi Uemura became the first person to reach the North Pole alone " Mrs. Winters told us.
2. She said "His only companions were his sled dogs."
3. "They pulled his sled of supplies " she stated.
4. "He wore polar-bear skins " she explained "for protection from the arctic cold."
5. She added "Once a polar bear raided his camp."
6. "He often cut through huge ridges of ice " she said.
7. She stated "Some ridges were three stories high."
8. "He walked over plates of shifting ice " she said.
9. "Sometimes " she said "the ice would crack open."
10. "In 55 days " she added "he crossed 500 miles."

End Marks with Direct Quotations. A period ends a regular sentence, and a period ends most direct quotations.

14h ▸ Place a period inside the closing quotation marks when the end of the quotation comes at the end of the sentence.

He said, "This is my favorite bat." [inside]

"My dad," he said, "once used this bat." [inside]

Usually, question marks and exclamation points also go *inside* the closing quotation marks.

He asked, "Would you like to use it?" [inside]

She yelled, "Watch out for the ball!" [inside]

When a question or an exclamation comes before a speaker tag, the question mark or the exclamation point is still placed *inside* the closing quotation marks—in place of the comma. Then a period ends the sentence.

"Did you hit that ball?" she asked. [inside]

"That was a fantastic hit!" she exclaimed. [inside]

EXERCISE 12   Using End Marks with Direct Quotations

Number your paper 1 to 10. Then write each direct quotation, adding end marks where needed.

1. She said, "That's my favorite song "
2. "Is Jeffery home " Melinda asked
3. "I have baseball practice this afternoon," he said
4. "Lightning just struck one of our trees " Bart yelled
5. Raymond asked, "What is our math homework "
6. He stated, "Granny Smith apples are green "
7. "Don't go near that boiling water " he screamed
8. "When did you move to South Carolina " she asked
9. "No one knows his name," she stated
10. "I won first prize in the art contest " she exclaimed

TIME-OUT FOR REVIEW • • • • •

Number your paper 1 to 10. Then write each direct quotation, adding quotation marks, commas, end marks, and capital letters where needed.

EXAMPLE   waste products have uses Mr. Shaw said
ANSWER   "Waste products have uses," Mr. Shaw said.

Sawdust

1. he explained every year lumber mills in the United States pile up 15 million tons of sawdust
2. that is a lot of sawdust Rosa Lee exclaimed
3. what do the mills do with it Kathy asked
4. the mills usually sell it Mr. Shaw stated
5. Kim asked who wants it
6. a factory in Oregon Mr. Shaw answered makes oil from sawdust
7. the factory only gets one barrel of oil from three tons of sawdust he added
8. sometimes sawdust is also mixed with cows' feed he continued the sawdust adds bulk to their diets
9. does sawdust taste good asked Vincent
10. Mr. Shaw answered you should ask a cow

220

Writing Dialogue

Dialogue means "a conversation between two or more people." Adding dialogue to a short story often makes the story more interesting. You have to write dialogue in a certain way to let readers know who is speaking.

14i When writing dialogue, begin a new paragraph each time the speaker changes.

In the following dialogue between Pat and Shirley, each sentence follows the rules for direct quotations that you just studied. Notice that a new paragraph begins each time Pat or Shirley speaks.

> Pat asked Shirley, "What should we do after dinner tonight?"
>
> "There's a good movie at Cinema II," Shirley answered. "It starts at seven o'clock."
>
> Pat replied, "I saw that movie last week, and it wasn't very good."
>
> "Let's go skating," Shirley said, "at the park."
>
> "That's a great idea!" Pat replied.
>
> Shirley added, "We should have fun."

EXERCISE 13 Writing Dialogue

Write a short imaginary conversation between a reporter and one of your favorite actors or singers. Punctuate the dialogue correctly, and begin a new paragraph each time the speaker changes.

Writing Titles

When you write a report, sometimes you need to include the title of a book or a magazine that you used as one of your sources of information. However, not all titles are punctuated the same way.

Titles That Are Underlined. Titles of certain kinds of written works—books, magazines, newspapers, and movies—are printed in italics. Italic print is a special kind of print that slants to the right. *It is the kind of print used in this sentence.* Since you cannot write in italics, you should underline any title that would be printed in italics.

14j Underline the titles of books, magazines, newspapers, and movies.

BOOK   I will read the book <u>Sounder</u> by William Armstrong.

MAGAZINE   My sister has a new subscription to <u>National Geographic World</u>.

NEWSPAPER   The <u>Chicago Tribune</u> is delivered every day. [Generally, do not underline *the* before newspaper or magazine titles.]

MOVIE   The movie <u>The Wizard of Oz</u> was on TV.

Titles That Are Enclosed in Quotation Marks. The titles that are underlined are long written works. Most of these long works, however, are made up of shorter parts. A book, for example, might include several short stories or many poems. The titles of these shorter parts are enclosed in quotation marks.

14k Put quotation marks around the titles of stories, poems, articles, and chapters.

STORY   In class we read the story "In a Dim Room" in our textbook <u>Literature of the World</u>.

POEM   I read the poem "Southbound on the Freeway" in the book <u>Poetry of May Swenson</u>.

ARTICLE   The article "Saving Wildlife" was in the last issue of the <u>National Geographic</u>.

CHAPTER   "Searching with a Telescope" is the last chapter in our science book <u>Science Today</u>.

NOTE: For capitalization of titles, see pages 188–189.

EXERCISE 14 Punctuating Titles

Number your paper 1 to 10. Then write and punctuate each title correctly.

EXAMPLE Last night I read the chapter Treasure from the Lagoon in our literature book Our Times.

ANSWER "Treasure from the Lagoon" Our Times

1. For my book report, I read Bridge to Terabithia by Katherine Paterson.
2. Have you ever read the poem The Dream Keeper by Langston Hughes?
3. The Greek Way is the chapter to study in your social studies book.
4. Who was the director of the movie Star Wars?
5. The article Farmers Have Difficult Times was in today's issue of the Washington Post.
6. The Incredible Journey is a wonderful book about a dog.
7. The short story All Summer in a Day is about life on Venus in the future.
8. You can find the poem The Listeners on page 328 in your textbook The World of Literature.
9. Did the movie Fantasia ever win an Oscar?
10. In the magazine Reader's Digest, I read a funny article called Where Socks Go.

EXERCISE 15 Writing Sentences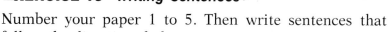

Number your paper 1 to 5. Then write sentences that follow the directions below.

1. Include the title of a book you have read this year or last year.
2. Include the name of a large newspaper in your city or town.
3. Include the name of a poem in your literature book.
4. Include the title of a chapter in your science book.
5. Include the name of a short story in your literature book and include the name of the literature book.

A pplication to Writing

Adding dialogue to stories often makes stories more realistic. After all, people are talking all the time. What people say and how they say it often tell a reader something about the characters in a story. These are only two ways in which dialogue can make your stories more interesting.

If you are going to include any dialogue in your next story, make sure that you punctuate it correctly. Refer to the rules in this section, and check to see if you have written your dialogue correctly. Remember, for example, to begin a new paragraph each time a different character begins to speak. If you forget to do this, your readers may not be able to follow the back and forth conversation of your characters.

EXERCISE 16   *Editing for the Proper Punctuation of Dialogue*

Rewrite the following conversation between Jennie and Greg. Add quotation marks, commas, end marks, and capital letters where needed. Also begin a new paragraph each time Jennie or Greg begins to speak.

The Amazing Mouse

Look at this article about Moonlight Special Jennie said Greg replied what is a Moonlight Special It's a ten-inch robot mouse Jennie answered What did it do Greg asked It competed against other robot mice in the first Amazing Mico-Mouse Maze Contest Jennie answered Each mouse had three chances to run a maze How many mice were in the contest asked Greg There were 16 mice in the race said Jennie Greg asked did Moonlight Special win Unfortunately Jennie said the article doesn't mention that

*C*hapter *R*eview

A **Using Apostrophes.** Number your paper 1 to 10. Then correctly write each word that needs an apostrophe.

1. That gooses feathers are white and brown.
2. All the salespeoples territories cover over 200 miles.
3. Hes running for senator in the next election.
4. Marks canoe just tipped over in the lake!
5. Doesnt the bell ring at 2:20?
6. All the cheerleaders pom-poms are red and white.
7. Shouldnt we take our raincoats?
8. Most teachers parking spaces were full of snow.
9. Theyre waiting for their instructions.
10. The babys cries could be heard across the street.

B **Punctuating Direct Quotations.** Number your paper 1 to 10. Then write each direct quotation, adding quotation marks, commas, end marks, and capital letters where needed.

Glasses

1. do you wear glasses Mrs. Yori asked
2. well she continued people have been wearing glasses since the late 1200s
3. that's a very long time Steve exclaimed
4. Cora asked who invented glasses
5. people in Venice, Italy Mrs. Yori replied
6. for the first 400 years, glasses weren't worn she said they were held up to the eyes
7. Betsy exclaimed   that must have made reading extremely difficult
8. Mrs. Yori continued   finally in the 1720s, a London optician made a new pair of glasses
9. were they like glasses today Cora asked
10. not exactly said Mrs. Yori but they rested on the nose

C **Punctuating Titles.** Number your paper 1 to 10. Then write and punctuate each title correctly.

1. If I Were an Elephant is a funny poem.
2. Who wrote the book A Wrinkle in Time?
3. The short story How the Whale Got His Throat was written by Rudyard Kipling.
4. The magazine Your Big Backyard has wonderful pictures of animals in it.
5. Did you read the chapter The Start of Cities in your social studies book?
6. I like the comics in our newspaper the Grange Herald.
7. We watched the old movie Black Beauty on TV.
8. Healthy Bodies and Minds was an article in Time.
9. I read Eve Merriam's poem At the Edge of the World in a book called Modern Poets.
10. The Scribe is my favorite story in our literature book Reading about the World.

Mastery Test

Number your paper 1 to 10. Each of the following sentences is a direct quotation. Write each one. Then add quotation marks and any needed apostrophes.

1. Todays test is short, Mrs. Franklin told us.
2. Where are the girls uniforms? the coach asked.
3. Weve been practicing for a week, Gail announced.
4. Ellis asked, Havent you made a decision yet?
5. Corey stated, I enjoyed reading Sams story.
6. The mens shirts, the clerk said, are on this floor.
7. Is that Scotts baseball mitt? Otis asked.
8. Ms. Anderson said, Youre our first choice.
9. All citizens rights are guaranteed by law, the lawyer stated.
10. Thats my coat, Bernie said, on the floor!

Standardized Test

Directions: Decide which underlined part in each sentence contains an error in capitalization or punctuation. In the appropriate row on your answer sheet, fill in the circle containing the same letter as the incorrect part. If there is no error, fill in *E*.

SAMPLE   The Brooklyn bridge is a bridge in New York. No error
                    A   B   C   D   E

ANSWER (a) (b) (c) (d) (e)

1. Yesterday i took a picture of Mike. No error
   A   B C   D   E

2. A ruler and two tablets sat on the desk. No error
   A   B   C   D   E

3. We joined the Spanish Club in august. No error
   A   B   C   D   E

4. Natalie asked, "Where is the dinosaur? No error
           A   B   C   D   E

5. I'll bring plates cups and hats for the party. No error
   A   B   C   D   E

6. The senator will meet you at 7:00 p.m.. No error
   A   B   C   D   E

7. "John are you coming with us?" asked Matt. No error
   A   B   C   D   E

8. Nadere's birthday is February 26 1977. No error
   A   B   C   D   E

9. Evan likes the poem *Where the Sidewalk Ends* No error
   A   B   C   D   E

10. We learned about the War of 1776 in school. No error
    A   B   C   D   E

11. Yes, the women's tickets are lost. No error
    A   B   C   D   E

227

12. Meet me at the Esquire Theater at 8:30. No error
    A   B   C   D   E

13. Where is Susans report on Hawaii? No error
    A   B   C   D   E

14. Billy ran to the bus but it had already left. No error
     A   B   C   D   E

15. "I'm glad to meet you," said mayor Wilson. No error
    A B   C   D   E

Directions: Choose the answer that shows the correct way to write the underlined part in each sentence. On your answer sheet, fill in the circle containing the letter of your answer.

SAMPLE The bus leaves at 6 45.
        (A) 6.45:
        (B) 6,45.
        (C) 6:45.

ANSWER Ⓐ Ⓑ Ⓒ

16. Where is Mr Daley?
    (A) Mr. Daley.
    (B) Mr. Daley?
    (C) Mr Daley?

17. The sears tower is the tallest building in the world.
    (A) Sears Tower
    (B) Sears tower
    (C) sears tower

18. Hilde can speak french, German and Spanish.
    (A) french, german, and spanish.
    (B) French, German and Spanish.
    (C) French, German, and Spanish.

19. Paul asked, "where is my belt."
    (A) "Where is my belt"?
    (B) "Where is my belt?"
    (C) "where is my belt?"

20. I borrowed Bettys book.
    (A) Bettys' book.
    (B) Bettys book.
    (C) Betty's book.

Composition

Part One

15

Words

Some writing is so good that readers can almost step into the page and become part of it. Bright, exact words bring writing to life. The following paragraph is from a story about a boy and a bear cub, Kola. Read it carefully. Can you hear the forest sounds?

LIVELY SOUNDS   Next day I took my Kola and started home. Now the whole forest was awake. Cuckoos called and the hoopoe birds chattered back and forth while the rabbits went rushing ahead from bush to bush with the news.

VIVID SIGHTS   From the highest rocks the mountain goats stopped and looked down to see me walking proud with my little bear beside me.

—GEORGE AND HELEN PAPASHVILY, "KOLA THE BEAR," (ADAPTED)

Your Writer's Notebook

Keep a writer's notebook, or journal, to help you think of writing ideas. Every day for a week, write about something in your home. Try to describe it so a reader can see it clearly. Write the day and date of each entry.

Specific Words

Some words are dull and general. They do not call an exact picture to mind. A sentence with dull, general words is like a blurred black-and-white photograph.

GENERAL   In the summer, animals play.

Other words, however, are clear, exact, and descriptive. A sentence with specific words is like a sharply-focused color photograph.

SPECIFIC   In the summer sunshine, growing wolf pups play tag, catch the stick, and romp freely, outdoors.

The box below shows general words and specific words for different parts of speech. Always choose specific words when you write.

	General	Specific	
NOUNS	pet	canary	kitty
		spaniel	puppy
		turtle	gerbil
		goldfish	frog
VERBS	saw	looked	discovered
		noticed	peered
		spied	peeked
		found	spotted
ADJECTIVES	nice	kind	fair
		friendly	loyal
		pleasant	trustworthy
		helpful	steady
ADVERBS	quickly	nervously	swiftly
		hurriedly	hastily
		recklessly	speedily
		eagerly	immediately

231

15a Use specific nouns, verbs, adjectives, and adverbs to help your reader picture exactly what you mean.

EXERCISE 1 *Writing Specific Nouns*

Number your paper 1 to 20. For each general noun, write a specific noun.

EXAMPLE   vehicle
POSSIBLE ANSWER   pick-up truck

1. plant	6. tool	11. thing	16. book
2. game	7. bird	12. school	17. drink
3. machine	8. toy	13. team	18. clothing
4. animal	9. food	14. holiday	19. meal
5. card	10. dish	15. worker	20. sport

EXERCISE 2 *Writing Specific Verbs*

Number your paper 1 to 10. Then write a specific verb that replaces the underlined verb in each sentence.

EXAMPLE   Tania <u>went</u> to the bus stop.
POSSIBLE ANSWER   dashed

1. "Stop bothering me!" <u>said</u> Winona.
2. Because he wanted to win the race, Ian <u>rode</u> his bike at top speed.
3. As the star of the play, Evelyn <u>said</u> her lines with great drama.
4. The baseball player <u>hit</u> the ball all the way out of the park.
5. "I'll clean my room tomorrow," I <u>said</u>.
6. Sheldon <u>went</u> higher and higher on the swing as the other children at the playground watched.
7. The fans <u>said</u> words of support to drive their team on to victory.
8. The door bell <u>sounded</u> suddenly and frightened the young puppy.
9. The lizard <u>went</u> across the floor.
10. "Thanks for everything!" <u>said</u> Tara.

EXERCISE 3   Writing Specific Adjectives

Number your paper 1 to 10. Then use the picture to write a specific adjective that replaces the underlined one.

EXAMPLE   a <u>nice</u> lake
POSSIBLE ANSWER   calm

1. a <u>pretty</u> sky
2. a <u>big</u> mountain
3. <u>interesting</u> trees
4. <u>big</u> trees
5. a <u>nice</u> boat

6. <u>pretty</u> leaves
7. <u>nice</u> clouds
8. <u>good</u> air
9. <u>good</u> water
10. a <u>beautiful</u> sight

EXERCISE 4   Writing Specific Adverbs

Number your paper 1 to 5. Then write a specific adverb that could complete each sentence.

EXAMPLE   The dog barked _____ at the intruder.
POSSIBLE ANSWER   fiercely

1. The clouds hung _____ in the rainy sky.
2. The squirrel nibbled _____ on the peanut.
3. Tom smiled _____ after scoring the point.
4. The toddler peeked _____ around the corner.
5. The motorboat sped _____ across the lake.

*E*XERCISE 5 *On Your Own*

Write five sentences about the zebras in the picture above.
Use as many specific words as possible.

*W*riting Extra

A few well-chosen words can bring a whole world to
life. A Japanese poem called the haiku uses only three
short lines and 17 syllables to paint a picture. Notice the
5–7–5 pattern of the syllables.

SPRING

Playing in the sun,	5 syllables
The first day without jackets.	7 syllables
Oh what muddy shoes!	5 syllables

Try to write your own haiku. Let your words bring to life a
moment in time. The following may give you ideas for
your own haiku.

a drop of dew on a tulip	bare branches in winter
your dog's wagging tail	litter blowing in the wind

Appealing to the Senses

Your five senses—sight, hearing, touch, smell, and taste—are always busy taking in the world. Help your readers see and feel what you do by using words that appeal to their senses.

15b Create vivid pictures by using words that appeal to your reader's senses.

Sight

One of the best ways to help a reader picture something is to describe it. Use words that capture colors, movements, shapes, and sizes just as they appear to you.

Sight Words			
Colors	Movements	Shapes	Sizes
orange	slipped	round	bulky
pink	swaggered	crooked	huge
plum	jumped	wavy	massive
snow-white	slithered	oval	tiny
purple	hopped	stout	baby
lavender	darted	graceful	shallow
sea-green	skipped	tipped	towering

EXERCISE 6 Describing Sights

Answer each question about the photograph on page 236.

1. What colors do you see in this picture?
2. What objects do you see in this picture?
3. What shapes are in this picture?
4. What words describe the movements in this picture?
5. How would you describe the sizes in this picture?

235

EXERCISE 7   *Writing Sentences with Sight Words*

Write five sentences describing the scene in the photo-graph. Use the words you thought of in Exercise 6 to cap-ture colors, movements, shapes, and sizes.

Sound

Stop and listen for a moment. What sounds do you hear? Maybe you hear the click of shoes in the hallway or the sound of a truck motor outside. Notice how the sounds in the following passage wake up your sense of hearing.

SOUND OF ENGINE

SOUND OF WATER AND GULLS

SOUND OF WHISTLE

The engine of the ferry hummed steadily as we took the short trip to the island. Water splashed in rhythm against the boat. Overhead, the gulls soared and called. As we approached the island, the ferry's deep, hollow steam whistle sounded our arrival.

The following words appeal to a reader's sense of hearing.

Sound Words			
rumble	whoosh	clunk	pop
giggle	whimper	groan	boom
drip	bark	squeak	creak
splash	clatter	chatter	trickle
thunder	hum	snicker	rip
clang	crackle	sizzle	whistle

Sometimes people are careless listeners. They fail to hear everyday noises. Practice listening to the silence around you. You may be surprised at what you'll hear.

EXERCISE 8 Describing Sounds

Number your paper 1 to 10. Imagine <u>yourself</u> in the picture on this page. Write ten sounds that you might hear.

EXERCISE 9 Writing Sentences with Sound Words

Write five sentences describing the sounds in the scene on this page. Use the sound words from Exercise 8 to wake up your reader's sense of hearing.

Touch

Your sense of touch tells you how things feel. It will alert you to heat or cold. It will tell you whether something is smooth or rough, soft or scratchy, sticky or slippery. It can also tell you how you are feeling inside, what your emotions and health are.

Like other senses, your sense of touch can come alive through reading. Read the following passage. Try to put yourself into the situation described and feel all the details of touch.

FEELING OF FEATHER COMFORTER

FEELING OF SLEEPINESS

FEELING OF COLD

FEELING OF DOG

FEELING OF LADY'S FUR

That night on the cape was frosty. I pulled the feather comforter up over my shoulders and nestled into the soft bed. My heavy eyes soon gave in to sleep. Hours later I woke with a twitch from a dream. My nose was freezing cold, as was most of my left side. My right side, though, was as warm as an oven. There was Lady, my cousin's dog, curled against my right side, snoring softly. I thought briefly about getting up for a cup of cocoa. I stroked Lady's warm, soft fur and snuggled back under the covers.

Use the following words and others like them to appeal to your reader's sense of touch.

Touch Words

smooth	lumpy	heavy	furry
rough	sleek	gritty	silky
brittle	metallic	flimsy	scratchy
sharp	frozen	steamy	gooey
bumpy	hot	damp	syrupy
moist	warm	clammy	sticky
slippery	cold	dusty	soft
oily	cool	wet	hard

EXERCISE 10 *Writing Sentences with Touch Words*

Try to imagine <u>yourself</u> in the picture on this page. Then write five sentences describing the scene. Be sure to use words that appeal to the sense of touch.

EXERCISE 11 *Describing with Touch Words*

Think about the first day of school each year. What are some of the things you feel on that first day? Maybe you feel the smoothness of a new textbook or the pinch of new shoes. Write five sentences about what you feel on the first day of school. Be sure to use touch words.

Smell

Smells can call powerful memories to mind. For example, what things come to mind when you read the following sentence?

The air was filled with the scent of just-cut grass.

The smell of freshly-mowed grass usually brings to mind thoughts of summer—hot days, cool shade, relaxation. Think about what all the following smell words bring to mind. Use them and others like them to appeal to your reader's sense of smell.

Smell Words

fishy	stale	putrid	rusty
fresh	smoldering	burnt	yeasty
piney	fragrant	stuffy	lemony
moldy	woody	dusty	fruity

EXERCISE 12 Describing with Smell Words

Write five sentences describing the scene in the picture. Be sure to use words that appeal to the sense of smell.

Taste

The following meal may not sound good to you, but it was exactly what Wilbur, a young pig, wanted for dinner.

> TASTE WORDS
>
> It was a delicious meal—skim milk, wheat middlings, leftover pancakes, half a doughnut, the rind of a summer squash, two pieces of stale toast, a third of a gingersnap, a fish tail, one orange peel, several noodles from a noodle soup, the scum off a cup of cocoa, an ancient jelly roll, a strip of paper from the lining of a garbage pail, and a spoonful of raspberry jello.
>
> —E. B. WHITE, *CHARLOTTE'S WEB*

The words in the following chart appeal to a reader's sense of taste. Can you think of any others?

Taste Words

sweet	tangy	rich	doughy
bitter	spicy	creamy	sugary
salty	peppery	sharp	buttery
bland	gooey	mild	fresh
sour	crunchy	stale	tart

EXERCISE 13 Describing with Taste Words

Imagine you own a restaurant where only your favorite food is served. Write a menu for your restaurant. Describe your favorite food in five sentences.

EXERCISE 14 On Your Own

Choose your favorite season of the year. Write ten sentences about it using words that appeal to all five senses. Describe what you see, hear, feel, taste, and smell.

$\mathcal{S}$potlight on Writing

A **Replacing General Words with Specific Words.** You have been asked to rewrite an advertising brochure for your summer camp. Number your paper 1 to 10. Then write a specific noun, verb, adjective, or adverb to replace each general word or phrase.

Camp Mineona

Are you looking for a (1)<u>nice</u> place to spend some time this summer? Come to Camp Mineona, where the air is (2) <u>good</u>, the people are (3) <u>nice</u>, and the food is great.

Boys and girls at Camp Mineona (4) <u>go</u> through the woods, (5) <u>ride</u> boats, and swim every day. They learn valuable (6) <u>things</u> from the counselors. They can (7) <u>be in</u> some of nature's finest splendor. The clean lakes and (8) <u>good</u> forests make a (9) <u>nice</u> summer retreat. Later, campers speak (10) <u>well</u> about their stay at Camp Mineona.

B **Writing Sentences with Specific Verbs.** Write five sentences about the activities you see in the picture. Use specific verbs. Then underline the verbs in your sentences.

C **Writing Sentences with Specific Adjectives.** You have a chance to appear in a movie. Write five sentences to the director describing your face. Try to use specific, unusual adjectives so that your description will catch the director's attention.

D **Listing Words That Appeal to the Senses.** Write the following five headings on your paper. Then add five words to each list.

SIGHT	SOUND	TOUCH	SMELL	TASTE
huge	clang	clammy	sour	salty
green	ring	slimy	rancid	sweet

243

E **Using Words That Appeal to the Senses.** Choose one of the following items. Then write ten sentences to describe it using words that appeal to all five senses.

1. a hayride
2. your block
3. a winter storm

4. lunchtime at school
5. a neighborhood fair
6. a baseball game

F **Writing Imaginative Descriptions.** The following are made-up names of made-up animals. Choose one that appeals to you and think about what it might look like. Draw a picture of it. Then write five sentences describing the animal so that others can picture it. Be sure to use words that appeal to the senses.

Elewolf
Horsebird

Tigaroo
Elfinbear

Dogkitty
Eelsnort

G **Writing from Your Writer's Notebook.** Choose one of the objects you wrote about in your writer's notebook. Then describe it using specific words that appeal to the senses. Exchange papers with a partner. Use the Chapter Summary on page 245 to help you revise your partner's sentences.

Chapter Summary
Words

Specific Words

1. Use specific nouns, verbs, adjectives, and adverbs to help your reader picture exactly what you mean. *(See pages 231–233.)*

Words That Appeal to the Senses

2. Create vivid pictures by using words that appeal to your reader's senses. *(See pages 235–241.)*

16

Sentences

Dull, choppy sentences can make even an interesting subject sound boring.

DULL
SENTENCES
The flying saucers hovered. They were blue. They were also green. They hovered quietly. They hummed. The sound was eerie. I stood. I watched. I would tell people what I saw. Nobody would believe me.

When the writing includes variety, however, readers take interest. Good writing flows as smoothly as a song.

VARIED
SENTENCES
Humming eerily, the blue and green flying saucers hovered. I stood and watched, wondering how I would tell people about what I saw. Nobody would believe me.

This chapter will help you write sentences that sing.

Your Writer's Notebook

Every day for a week, write a memory in your journal. Try to write at least five sentences each day. Then read your writing aloud. Does it flow smoothly? If not, rewrite your sentences to add variety.

Sentence Combining

Good writing has a pleasing rhythm. It avoids the steady drumbeat of short, choppy sentences. Instead, it contains a mix of short and long sentences. One way to write long sentences is to combine several short sentences into one.

16a Combine short sentences into longer, more interesting ones.

Combining Specific Details

Specific, vivid words and phrases help readers "see" clearly. Often specific details can be combined into one sentence instead of spread out over several choppy sentences.

CHOPPY SENTENCES   The spacecraft traveled.
   The spacecraft was **bulky.**
   It traveled **quietly.**
   It traveled **through the solar system.**

The specific details that help you see the traveling spacecraft can all be put in the same sentence.

COMBINED SENTENCE   The **bulky** spacecraft traveled **quietly through the solar system.**

If your combined sentence contains two or more adjectives in a row, use a comma to separate them. Do not put a comma between a single adjective and the noun or pronoun it describes. Study the following example.

CHOPPY SENTENCES   The spacecraft traveled to the **distant** planet Uranus.
   Uranus is **frozen.**

COMBINED SENTENCE   The spacecraft traveled to the **distant, frozen** planet Uranus.

247

EXERCISE 1 Combining Sentences with Prepositional Phrases

Number your paper 1 to 10. Then combine each pair of short sentences into one longer one. Use the underlined prepositional phrases.

EXAMPLE   Voyager 2 was launched. It was launched <u>in 1977</u>.

ANSWER   Voyager 2 was launched in 1977.

Voyager

1. Voyager 2 is traveling. It is going <u>into space</u>.
2. It is a probe to study planets. The planets are <u>in our solar system</u>.
3. Voyager took superb pictures. It took photos <u>of Jupiter's atmosphere and moons</u>.
4. After taking the pictures, Voyager sends them back. It sends them <u>to earth on radio waves</u>.
5. These radio signals fly through space. They travel <u>at a speed of 186,000 miles per second</u>.
6. Voyager completed its pass by Jupiter. It passed Jupiter <u>in 1979</u>.
7. It passed Saturn in 1981. It went by Saturn <u>before beginning its trip to Uranus</u>.
8. Voyager will continue. It will go <u>beyond our sun</u>.
9. This deep space probe is carrying messages. The messages are stored <u>on long-playing records</u>.
10. The probe carries these messages. The messages are <u>for any intelligent beings who may exist</u>.

EXERCISE 2 *Combining with Adjectives and Adverbs*

Number your paper 1 to 10. Then combine each group of short sentences into one longer one.

Voyager and Uranus

1. In 1986, Voyager took pictures of Uranus. The pictures were startling.
2. This planet has baffled scientists for years. The planet is remote. The planet is strange.
3. The pictures showed that Uranus has rings. The rings are thin. The rings are ghostly.
4. Scientists studied the pictures . They looked at them carefully. The pictures were surprising.
5. One of the moons of Uranus is Miranda. Miranda is a large moon.
6. Miranda has a combination of features. This combination is very unusual.
7. Miranda has valleys and hills. The valleys are deep. The hills are shadowy.
8. Another moon, Ariel, has a river . The river is of ice. The river is flowing slowly.
9. The axis of Uranus is tilted. It is tilted greatly.
10. Because of the tilt, darkness on parts of Uranus lasts 20 years. The years are long. The years are frozen.

Combining Sentence Parts

Another way to combine sentences is to join subjects or verbs to form compounds. Use *and, but,* and *or* to form compound subjects and compound verbs. *(See pages 17–18 for a review of compound subjects and compound verbs.)*

COMPOUND SUBJECT	**Luther** made the school team.
	Sandy made the school team.
	Luther and Sandy made the school team.

COMPOUND VERB	Loretta **sings** well.
	Loretta **plays** the piano well.
	Loretta **sings and plays** the piano well.

249

If you combine three or more subjects and verbs, be sure to use commas to separate them. *(See page 199.)*

COMPOUND VERB   In the school play I **danced.** I **sang.** I also **did cartwheels.**

In the school play I **danced, sang, and did cartwheels.**

EXERCISE 3 *Combining Sentence Parts*

Number your paper 1 to 10. Then combine each group of sentences using a compound subject or compound verb. Use *and, but,* or *or.* Remember to use commas where needed.

EXAMPLE   **Words** are used in talking. **Gestures** are used in talking.

ANSWER   **Words and gestures** are used in talking.

Early Writing

1. Sticks were used by early people to communicate. Stones were used too.
2. Notched sticks were used to send messages. Knotted ropes were used the same way.
3. Some bones are scratched in certain patterns, perhaps showing that they were used for calendars. Antlers are also scratched this way. So are stones.
4. Early cave dwellers scratched stones . They also carved pictures on cave walls.
5. Pictographs are symbols in pictures. Ideagrams are also picture symbols.
6. These word pictures tell stories. They also communicate ideas.
7. Ancient Sumerians wrote in pictographs. Babylonians used the same method.
8. Ancient Egyptian writers used hieroglyphics. They wrote on walls.
9. The Phoenicians developed the first real alphabet. They recorded it on stone tablets.
10. The Greeks improved that alphabet and passed it on through history. The Romans improved it also.

Combining by Coordinating

A simple sentence has one subject and one verb.

SIMPLE   **Walter scored** the winning touchdown.
SENTENCES The **crowd cheered** wildly.

When two simple sentences are related, they can be combined to form a compound sentence. You can use the coordinating conjunction *and, but,* or *or* to join two simple sentences. Always put a comma before the conjunction. If the two sentences contain similar ideas, they may be joined with the conjunction *and.*

COMPOUND   Walter scored the winning touchdown, **and**
SENTENCE   the crowd cheered wildly.

If they contain contrasting ideas, they can be joined with the conjunction *but.*

CONTRASTING Walter was tired after the game.
      IDEAS He was proud of the victory.

COMPOUND   Walter was tired after the game, **but** he
SENTENCE   was proud of the victory.

Sometimes two simple sentences will suggest a choice between two ideas. In this case, they could be combined with the conjunction *or.*

  CHOICE   We might have a victory party at the high
 BETWEEN   school gym.
   IDEAS   The coach might give a party at his house.

COMPOUND   We might have a victory party at the high
SENTENCE   school gym, **or** the coach might give a
       party at his house.

When combining by coordinating, choose the conjunction that most clearly shows how the sentences are related. Use *and* for similar ideas, *but* for contrasting ideas, and *or* for a choice between ideas. *(You may want to review simple sentences and compound sentences on pages 99–102.)*

251

EXERCISE 4 Combining by Coordinating

Number your paper 1 to 10. Then use the coordinating conjunction in brackets to combine each pair of sentences into one compound sentence. Remember to use a comma before the conjunction.

EXAMPLE   People have confused fact and fancy many
           times. One time stands out. [but]

ANSWER   People have confused fact and fancy many
           times, **but** one time stands out.

War of the Worlds

1. In 1938, Orson Welles broadcast a radio version of *War of the Worlds*. Radio history was made. [and]
2. The story is by H.G. Wells. A different person wrote the radio script. [but]
3. The radio version started as if it were a program of music. Then a news bulletin which was part of the story interrupted. [and]
4. The made-up bulletin reported disturbances on Mars. Before long, there was another bulletin about spaceships landing on earth. [but]
5. The news bulletins became more and more frequent. Finally they simply took over the music program completely. [and]
6. It was just a radio drama. Some people took it seriously. [but]
7. They must not have been listening carefully. They would have heard four announcements that the show was just a story. [or]
8. People ran to warn friends and family. Streets became crowded with cars as people tried to escape from the cities. [and]
9. No one was hurt. Some people did need to be treated for shock. [but]
10. Orson Welles did not mean to fool anyone. The radio broadcast of *War of the Worlds* became one of the biggest hoaxes ever. [but]

Combining by Subordinating

If the ideas in two short sentences are not equally important, you can combine them into one sentence by *subordinating*. In the combined sentence, you should introduce the less important idea with a subordinating conjunction, as in the examples below.

CHOPPY SENTENCES   Melissa enjoyed the bicycle race. She placed fifteenth.

COMBINED SENTENCE   Melissa enjoyed the bicycle race **even though she placed fifteenth.**

If the less important idea comes first in the sentence, place a comma at the end of that idea.

CHOPPY SENTENCES   Paul was at school. His mother decorated the house for his birthday party.

COMBINED SENTENCE   **While Paul was at school,** his mother decorated the house for his birthday party.
[A comma is placed after the word *school*.]

Subordinating Conjunctions

after	as soon as	since	until
although	because	so that	when
as	before	though	where
as if	even though	unless	while

EXERCISE 5 Combining by Subordinating

Number your paper 1 to 10. Then use the subordinating conjunction in brackets to combine each pair of sentences. Remember to use a comma where needed.

EXAMPLE   I went to Florida last summer. I had never heard of the Florida Everglades. [before]

ANSWER   **Before** I went to Florida last summer, I had never heard of the Florida Everglades.

Majesty
in a
Swamp

1. Everglades National Park is in southern Florida. It seems like a different world. [although]
2. Wildlife is everywhere. Swamp grasses grow in abundance. [since]
3. Visitors can see alligators lying in the sun. They should not try to approach them. [even though]
4. Some ramps have been built above the swamps. People can walk on these to observe the wildlife of the everglades. [because]
5. Visitors drive through the huge park. They can stop in one place and explore. [as]
6. Long-beaked birds bask in the bright, warm sunshine. Huge hard-shelled turtles swim in the clear water. [while]
7. This is a home for all kinds of wildlife. Certain people also often wander through the Everglades. [even though]
8. You see these people with their cameras and lenses strapped around their necks. You instantly recognize them as photographers. [as soon as]
9. Photographers capture graceful birds on film. They cautiously move closer to the water and snap a passing fish. [after]
10. Some swamp creatures are endangered. There are laws to protect them now. [since]

EXERCISE 6 On Your Own

Write ten simple sentences about a recent birthday. Then combine those sentences that are related either by coordinating or subordinating. The following questions may help you think of things to write.

1. How did you celebrate your last birthday?
2. Who was with you on that birthday?
3. What presents did you receive?
4. How would you describe some of the more unusual presents you received?
5. Why did you like one present more than any other?

*W*riting Extra

Good poems, like good sentences, have a pleasing rhythm. Writing poems is one way to experiment with word rhythms that sound good to you.

A cinquain (sin'kān) is a five-line poem that follows a certain pattern of syllables. Read the following cinquain. First read it just for meaning. Then study the pattern of syllables.

Change of Seasons

Summer:	2 syllables
Long days, short nights,	4 syllables
The earth whirling through space	6 syllables
So fast, too fast—oh, wait for me!	8 syllables
Autumn.	2 syllables

Try writing your own cinquain. At first do not worry too much about having the syllables work out exactly. The general rhythm of the lines is more important than the exact number of syllables. The pictures on this page may give you ideas for your poems.

Sentence Variety

Even your favorite food would become boring if you ate it all the time. Overused writing patterns become boring also. Treat your reader to a well-balanced diet of lively, varied sentences.

Varying Sentence Beginnings

A natural way to begin a sentence is with the subject.

SUBJECT FIRST   **Amelia Earhart** was a pioneer of early flight.

If all your sentences started that way, however, a reader would probably stop reading. Notice the varied sentence beginnings in the following passage. It is about Amelia Earhart's flight around the world.

SUBJECT NOT FIRST   **At first** the flight seemed a dream coming true. The view was vast and lovely. **As**

SUBJECT NOT FIRST   **she looked about,** she felt she was gulping beauty. The clouds were marvelous shapes in white, some trailing shimmering veils.

SUBJECT NOT FIRST   **In the distance** the highest peaks of the fog mountains were tinted pink with the setting sun.

—PEGGY MANN, "AMELIA EARHART: FLIGHT AROUND THE WORLD"

Try starting some of your sentences with an adverb or a prepositional phrase.

SUBJECT   The **pilot** carefully checked the gauges.

ADVERB   **Carefully** the pilot checked the gauges.

SUBJECT   The **earth** looked like a model from the sky.

PHRASE   **From the sky** the earth looked like a model.

EXERCISE 7 *Varying Sentence Beginnings*

Number your paper 1 to 10. Then add variety to the following sentences by moving either an adverb or a prepositional phrase to the beginning of each sentence. (*See page 79 for a list of prepositions.*)

A Big Family

1. Elephants are large animals in the mammal family.
2. They browse peacefully on leaves and plants.
3. Elephants could actually live on their own.
4. They live instead in family groups, called herds.
5. The oldest female is at the head of this group.
6. She and the other females patiently teach the young elephant how to use its trunk.
7. They often spray the youngster with water to keep its skin from drying out.
8. Elephants are helpless during their childhood.
9. They need protection in times of danger.
10. Elephants wisely live in groups to help the young.

EXERCISE 8 *Writing Sentence Beginnings*

Number your paper 1 to 10. Write a sentence beginning for each of the following. Use either an adverb or a prepositional phrase as shown in brackets. (*Review the rules for commas on page 200.*)

1. _____ Katy danced across the stage. [adverb]
2. _____ I have a test. [prepositional phrase]
3. _____ the pup peeked around the corner. [adverb]
4. _____ our team lost the last playoff game. [adverb]
5. _____ a fierce wind began howling and school was closed. [prepositional phrase]
6. _____ Sam waited for his test results. [adverb]
7. _____ cars looked like little ants. [prepositional phrase]
8. _____ Mark always carries his lucky penny. [prepositional phrase]
9. _____ the miser counted his money. [adverb]
10. _____ the turtle crawled along. [adverb]

257

*A*voiding Rambling Sentences

A sentence that rambles on and on is hard to follow. In the following example, too many ideas are linked together in one sentence.

RAMBLING There are many stories about how the moon became marked with craters, **and** one of them from India tells of a boy and his father who went out one night and wanted to play with the moon, **and** at that time the moon had a nice clear face and was near to earth, **but** in play the man poked the moon with a pole, **and** the moon didn't like that, **so** it moved far away, **so** in anger the man threw dirt at it and caused the spots that we see on the moon today.

When the ideas are broken up into shorter sentences, the story flows more smoothly.

REVISED There are many stories about how the moon became marked with craters. One of them from India tells of a boy and his father who went out one night and wanted to play with the moon. At that time the moon had a nice clear face and was near to earth. In play the man poked the moon with a pole. The moon didn't like that, so it moved far away. In anger the man threw dirt at it and caused the spots that we see on the moon today.

In the revised example, the ideas are expressed in shorter sentences of their own. Many of the conjunctions have been taken out of the revised sentences. In place of the conjunctions are periods and capital letters that signal a new sentence. Ideas that belong in sentences of their own should not be clumsily strung together.

16c Revise rambling sentences by removing some of the conjunctions. Remember to capitalize and punctuate the new sentences correctly.

EXERCISE 9 Revising Rambling Sentences

Revise each paragraph to eliminate rambling sentences.

1. The Masai people in Africa have stories about the sun and moon, too, and in their story the sun and the moon have a great big fight, and the sun became so mad that it hurt the moon's eye and mouth, so that is why the moon seems to us to have only one eye and a twisted mouth, and according to the legend, the sun's face turned red with shame after the fight and stayed that way.

2. According to myths from Burma, a rabbit lives on the moon in a box, but he doesn't come out fully every night, and instead he just peeks out a little bit at a time, and gradually, as the month wears on, more and more of him comes out, and that is why we see phases of the moon.

EXERCISE 10 On Your Own

Write ten sentences about the moon. Then revise your sentences to be sure you have written varied beginnings and avoided rambling sentences.

Spotlight on Writing

A **Combining Sentences.** Combine each group of short sentences into one longer one with specific details. Use commas where needed.

The Jungle

1. The parrots squawked. They called noisily. They were in the trees.
2. The laughter of chimpanzees rang out. The sound came from across the forest. The forest was thick.
3. A snake slithered by. It was large. It was scaly.
4. A crowd of animals gathered. They were at a watering hole. They were thirsty.
5. A hippopotamus waded. It was in a muddy part of the watering hole. It was huge.
6. Suddenly a sound filled the air. The sound was fearsome. The air was sun-baked.
7. A stampede had begun. The stampede was of antelope. The antelope were fleeing.
8. Lions were hunting. They hunted the antelope on the plains. The lions were hungry.
9. The animals went back to the forest. They were frightened. The forest was dark and safe.
10. Eyes dart . They are bright. They look through the safety of branches. They dart watchfully.

B **Combining Sentences.** Combine each pair of sentences using the coordinating conjunction or subordinating conjunction in brackets. Some sentences can be combined to form a simple sentence with a compound subject or compound verb. Use commas where needed.

East Asian Lands

1. Mountains are a big part of China, Japan, and Korea. Rivers are also a big part. [and]
2. In these countries people live in the fertile valleys. There they also farm. [and]
3. The best farm land is in river valleys. There are other good farm areas too. [although]
4. Minerals are abundant in China and Korea. Japan does not have as many. [while]
5. Japan may lack certain resources. Its waters supply many important things. [but]
6. Japan's waters provide electricity. They also furnish tuna, shrimp, salmon, and other fish. [and]
7. In Chinese farming villages, houses are made of brick. Most of the work is done by hand. [and]
8. Japanese farmers use small machines to do work. Korean workers use small machines also. [and]
9. In East Asian lands, rice dishes replace our familiar potato. Noodles also replace our potato. [and]
10. Japan's industries are known throughout the world. Other countries try to learn the Japanese manufacturing methods. [and]

C **Writing Varied Sentence Beginnings.** Look at the picture of the baseball game on page 262. Write ten sentences about that picture. Make sure that at least three of them begin with a prepositional phrase and three begin with an adverb. Use the lists below to help you select prepositional phrases and adverbs. Read the example sentences on page 262.

ADVERBS	slowly, quickly, suddenly, excitedly, lately
PREPOSITIONAL PHRASES	during the game, behind the plate, on the field

Use the models below to help you write your sentences.

ADVERB **Noisily** the crowd cheered the winning team.

PHRASE **At a baseball game,** the camera is set up to film runners crossing home plate.

D **Revising Rambling Sentences.** Revise the following paragraph to eliminate rambling sentences.

Clever Hans

Clever Hans was a horse that people thought could count. His owner would write out arithmetic problems, and Clever Hans would tap out the answer with his hoof but some people doubted that a horse could do this, so scientists observed Hans and his owner work until one scientist noticed that the owner always raised his eyebrows when Hans was about to reach the right number of taps so he suggested that the test be given with the owner out of the room and sure enough, Hans could not solve the problems correctly.

E **Writing from Your Writer's Notebook.** Choose one memory from your writer's notebook. Then describe it using complete sentences. Exchange papers with a partner. Use the Chapter Summary on page 263 to revise your partner's sentences.

Chapter Summary
Sentences

Sentence Combining
1. Combine short sentences into longer, more interesting ones. *(See pages 247–249.)*
2. Use the conjunctions *and, but,* and *or* to join sentence parts. *(See pages 249–250.)*
3. Use the conjunctions *and, but,* or *or* to join simple sentences. Use a comma before each conjunction. *(See pages 251–252.)*
4. Use subordinating conjunctions to combine ideas of unequal importance. *(See pages 253–254.)*

Sentence Variety
5. Vary the beginnings of your sentences. *(See pages 256–257.)*
6. Break up long, rambling sentences into shorter ones. *(See pages 258–259.)*

Paragraph Structure

Imagine how hard it would be to read a book that had no paragraph divisions. The writing would be one long continuous flow with no breaks. Readers would not know where one idea left off and another began.

Fortunately, paragraph divisions are used. An indented line tells readers that a new idea is starting. When ideas are presented in paragraphs, readers can digest them one at a time and follow them easily.

17a   A **paragraph** is a group of related sentences about one main idea.

Paragraphs that stand alone have three kinds of sentences within them. Study the following chart.

17b

Paragraph Structure	
topic sentence	states the main idea
supporting sentences	expand on the main idea with specific facts, examples, details, or reasons
concluding sentence	adds a strong ending

Read the following paragraph. Notice how each sentence helps to make the main idea clear.

Fire

TOPIC
SENTENCE

SUPPORTING
SENTENCES

CONCLUDING
SENTENCE

Fire is always near us—here and everywhere. It hides in the head of a match and it hums along in electric wires, ready to be of service. It gathers in the distant sky, preparing to crack the earth with lightning. It brews in the earth beneath us, waiting to shoot flame from volcanic mountains. Friendly or unfriendly, human or natural, fire waits for the moment to become flame.

—DOROTHY WILSON, *FIRE PREVENTION*

our Writer's Notebook

A journal is a good place to stretch your imagination. You have just read about fire. How do you think people of long ago first learned about fire? Write a story in your journal about the first human to discover fire. Imagine you are a member of a cave-dwelling family. Every day for a week, write a paragraph about what your life is like.

Topic Sentence

In most paragraphs the main idea is clearly stated in one of the sentences. This sentence is called the topic sentence, since it tells the reader the topic of the paragraph.

17c A **topic sentence** states the main idea of the paragraph.

In most paragraphs the topic sentence is the first sentence. It does not need to be the first sentence, however. It can come anywhere in the paragraph. You can identify the topic sentence by looking for a sentence that tells specifically what the paragraph is about.

TOPIC
SENTENCE

SUPPORTING
SENTENCES

CONCLUDING
SENTENCE

The longest any bird has lived is at least 72 years. This record was set by a male Andean condor named "Kuzya" who died in a zoo in Moscow, USSR, in 1964. He had arrived at the zoo 72 years earlier when he was already an adult. No one knows for sure how old he was, but he was at least 72 years. Zoo workers were sorry to see this old bird go.

—NORRIS MCWHIRTER, *GUINNESS BOOK OF AMAZING ANIMALS*

(ADAPTED)

EXERCISE 1 Identifying the Topic Sentence

Number your paper 1 to 5. Read each paragraph to discover the main idea. Then write each topic sentence.

1. Parrot Talk

Most animals do not talk, but there are some birds that can. Every year in London, England, there is a contest among birds to find the best talker. One bird, a male African gray parrot named Prudle, won the contest every year he was in it. Prudle won the contest for 12 years in a row, from 1965-1976. Prudle knew almost 1,000 words! He talked his way into the record books.

2. Swarming Locusts

The most destructive insect in the world is the desert locust, which lives in the dry regions of Africa, the Middle East, Pakistan, and India. This species of locust can eat its own weight in food every day. Traveling in large swarms, desert locusts can eat all of a village's crops and create a terrible food shortage. The greatest swarm of desert locusts ever recorded blackened the sky over an estimated 2,000 square miles. This swarm, which must have included about 250 billion insects, was seen crossing the Red Sea in 1889. The swarm probably weighed about 550,000 tons. In some parts of the world, no pest is feared more than the locust.

3. Grand Gobbler

Turkeys are not usually very expensive birds. Their price per pound is very low. This was not so, however, for the world's heaviest turkey, which was raised in England and weighed about 79 pounds. In December, 1980, this 79-pound bird was sold in London for more than $5,000. That's more than $60 per pound. The world's heaviest turkey was also the world's most expensive turkey.

4. George the Giraffe

The tallest giraffe ever known lived at the Chester Zoo in England. His name was "George." When he was 9 years old, his head almost touched the roof of the 20-foot-high Giraffe House. George sometimes licked the telephone wires that ran past his pen and made the telephones stop working. Despite the problems he caused, George was a "head-and-shoulders-above" favorite at the zoo.

5. Wealthy Cats

Animals do not usually have any money. However, it does cost people money to care for their animals. Sometimes, when people die, they leave some money for the care of their pets. For example, Dr. William Grier left all of his money to his two cats. When he died in 1963, the cats were 15 years old. Dr. Grier left $415,000 in his will for the two cats. They became two of the richest animals in the world. When the cats died two years later, the money was given to George Washington University in Washington, D.C.

—ALL EXCERPTS FROM NORRIS MCWHIRTER, *GUINNESS BOOK OF AMAZING ANIMALS* (ADAPTED)

EXERCISE 2 Choosing a Topic Sentence

Read each paragraph and the sentences that follow it. Then write the sentence that would be the best topic sentence for the paragraph.

1. Getting to the Root

When we look at a tree, we may see the branches rising 20, 30, 40, or more feet into the air. Under the ground, however, is an equally large system of roots. Roots sometimes spread out as far in width as they do in depth. Next time you gaze at a tree, try to picture the whole tree, underground roots and all, to appreciate its real size.

a. Trees provide shade in hot weather.
b. The roots of most trees extend deep into the ground.
c. Trees as well as bushes have roots.

2. Is it a Bird?

One obvious feature is that birds have feathers. Other body characteristics include an internal skeleton and a constant body temperature. The constant body temperature makes birds warm-blooded. Birds also hatch their young from eggs. Birds are considered to be just below mammals in intelligence. These features set birds apart from other creatures in the animal kingdom.

a. Both wild and tame birds have feathers.
b. Birds are intelligent creatures.
c. Scientists group birds according to certain features.

EXERCISE 3 On Your Own

Write one other possible topic sentence for each paragraph in Exercise 2. Then write a topic sentence for each of the following subjects. Save your work for Exercise 6.

1. school
2. a hobby you enjoy
3. a time you felt proud
4. pets (or a specific pet)

Supporting Sentences

The topic sentence in a paragraph states the main idea in a general way. Often that main idea raises questions in the reader's mind. The supporting sentences answer those questions with specific information. They form the body of the paragraph.

17d **Supporting sentences** explain or prove the topic sentence with specific details, facts, examples, or reasons.

Read the following topic sentence. What will the paragraph discuss? What questions come to mind?

TOPIC SENTENCE   Television performers watch the director for signals about what to do.

This topic sentence tells readers that the paragraph will discuss signals given to television performers. Readers might ask, "What are those signals? What do they mean?" The supporting sentences answer those questions. In the following paragraph, the supporting sentences provide examples to explain the topic sentence. All of the examples relate directly to the main idea.

TOPIC SENTENCE   Television performers watch the director for signals about what to do. A hand raised in the air as if to signal "stop" is really a sign for "stand by." To signal how much time is left before a commercial, a director will hold up one finger for each minute of time. If there is more time than needed, the director will make a motion as if pulling taffy. This signal tells the performer to "stretch" the time to fill it all up. If the director holds up a clenched fist, the performer knows that time is up. These signals help keep a television show running smoothly against the clock.

SUPPORTING SENTENCES

CONCLUDING SENTENCE

270

EXERCISE 4 Identifying Supporting Details

Number your paper 1 to 4. Read the list of details under each topic sentence. Then write the letters of the three details that directly support each topic sentence.

1. Caring for a Puppy

TOPIC
SENTENCE   A young puppy needs special care.

DETAILS   a. Puppies need to be checked by a veterinarian for good health.
b. Puppies need shots to protect them from disease.
c. Puppies need special food.
d. Older dogs sometimes need low-calorie diets.

2. Memory Tricks

TOPIC
SENTENCE   People use different kinds of tricks to help them remember things.

DETAILS   a. Sometimes illness affects a person's memory.
b. Some people tie a string around their finger.
c. Writing things down is a good way to remember them.
d. Taking a clear mental "photo" helps some people remember.

3. Family Fare

TOPIC
SENTENCE   Many adventure stories feature a brother and sister as main characters.

DETAILS   a. In the *Star Wars* movies, Luke and Leia are brother and sister.
b. Two friends team up in *Batman*.
c. He-Man and She-Ra, popular cartoon characters, are brother and sister.
d. A girl and her brother are main characters in *Island of the Blue Dolphins*.

271

4. Bears Fever

TOPIC SENTENCE — In 1986, Super Bowl XX broke several records.

DETAILS —
a. The Chicago Bears beat the New England Patriots by a score of 46-10.
b. Bears' Coach Mike Ditka was once a Bear player himself.
c. The Bears scored more points than any other Super Bowl team.
d. They also won by more points than any other team in Super Bowl history.

EXERCISE 5 *Writing Supporting Sentences*

Write each sentence. Then write three sentences that directly support the main idea of each one.

1. I have several different sides to my personality.
2. My friends have many different interests.
3. There are many things I like about my neighborhood.
4. Without a telephone, I don't know what I would do.
5. I know from experience that "practice makes perfect."

EXERCISE 6 *On Your Own*

Choose one of your topic sentences from Exercise 3. Draw a picture illustrating your main idea. Then write three sentences that could support the topic sentence. Save your paper for Exercise 8.

riting Extra

Thinking of details about a subject is a part of writing poems as well as paragraphs. One kind of poem, called an *acrostic,* spells out the subject of the poem in the first letter of each line. Details about the subject are described in the lines of the poem. Study the following example.

On Guard

Tawny stripes mixed with black,
Inches of sharp, curved teeth ready to strike,
Glaring eyes, daring eyes.
Eyes that catch everything.
Rest easy at night, tiger. Who can hurt you?

Acrostics can also be about people. The following poem gives details about a person named Sandy.

A Childhood Friend

Sometimes silly, sometimes serious,
Asking for less than you give,
Nervous before parties, calm before tests,
Devoted friend.
You will always be part of me.

Try writing your own acrostic poem. Start by writing the letters of the subject one to a line down your paper. Then think of details about your subject that start with each letter.

Concluding Sentence

Paragraphs that stand alone need a concluding sentence to bring the idea to a close. Like the punch line of a joke or the moral of a fable, a concluding sentence adds the finishing touch.

17e A **concluding sentence** adds a strong ending to a paragraph.

The chart below shows four good ways to end a paragraph.

17f

Concluding Sentences

A concluding sentence may
1. summarize the paragraph.
2. state the point of the paragraph.
3. state the main idea in fresh new words.
4. add a thought about the main idea.

Good concluding sentences sound natural. They also add real meaning to the paragraph. Weak endings, on the other hand, sound awkward and repetitious.

Women Wanted

Women were in short supply in the early days of the colonies. Men were often the first to arrive in North America from England. To build strong colonies, whole families were needed. Posters encouraging women to leave England promised a husband and a life in paradise if a woman would set sail for America. Many young women took up the challenge. When they arrived, however, they found a life of hard work. Women were really needed in the colonies.

WEAK
CONCLUSION

The concluding sentence on page 274 is weak because it simply repeats an idea without adding new meaning. The following concluding sentence is weak for a different reason. It suddenly adds new information that does not relate to the paragraph's main idea.

WEAK CONCLUSION   Freedom to worship as they pleased was one reason colonists set off for America.

The following sentences provide a strong ending. Both relate to the main idea and add new meaning.

STRONG CONCLUSIONS   The bravery and strength of these young women helped build the growing nation.

Though disappointed, most set upon their new lives with courage and hope.

EXERCISE 7 Choosing a Concluding Sentence

Read the following paragraph. Then write the best concluding sentence.

Call to Order

The word "chairperson" may seem like a strange term to describe the leader of a group meeting. It actually does make sense, however. In old England, the group's leader was the only person to have a chair to sit on. All the others either sat on stools or stood. The term stayed with the group leader even after everyone had a chair.

a. Once you know the history of a word, you can often understand even a strange term.
b. Chairpeople follow rules when conducting meetings.
c. A chairperson is the leader of a group.

EXERCISE 8 On Your Own

Review your work from Exercise 6. Then write two possible concluding sentences that would add a strong ending to your paragraph.

Spotlight on Writing

A **Writing Topic Sentences.** Write a topic sentence for each of the following paragraphs.

1. Old Time Medicine

A person with a fever might have been given turtle soup or snails to eat, or the longest tooth of a fish to wear. The notion was that such "cold," slow-moving creatures would help reduce fever. For toothaches, people were told to eat a mouse or to inhale the smoke of burning onion seeds. Most important, healers of old told their patients to avoid the night air. Until scientists learned more about diseases, these old fashioned remedies were the only medicine.

—LAURENCE PRINGLE, *THE EARTH IS FLAT—AND OTHER GREAT MISTAKES* (ADAPTED)

2. You Are Getting Sleepy

Some police officers are trained in hypnosis. They have found that people under hypnosis can remember details about a crime they witnessed. Doctors also use hypnosis. Under hypnosis, a person suffering from a problem can remember what happened to create it. Once it is understood, it can be talked about and overcome. Finally, hypnosis is used in entertainment. Trained hypnotists put on a show by having volunteers perform harmless stunts on cue. Once thought to be mysterious, hypnosis is now widely used.

B **Writing Supporting Sentences.** Study the picture on page 277. Write the following topic sentence. Then write at least five supporting sentences that could be used in a paragraph.

Flying in an airplane gives you a bird's eye view of the world below.

C **Writing Concluding Sentences.** The concluding sentence from the following paragraph has been left off. Write two possible concluding sentences for it.

One Third of Your Life

It is surprising how much time is spent in sleep —nearly one third of most lives. Newborn infants spend about 16 hours a day sleeping. Young children sleep about 9 hours a day, and adults sleep 7 or 8. By the age of fifteen, most people will have slept a total of 5 or 6 years. By age thirty, they will have slept for about 8 or 10 years. By the time a person reaches sixty years of age, almost 20 years will have been slept away.

—DAVID SINGER AND WILLIAM G. MARTIN, *SLEEP ON IT: A LOOK AT SLEEP AND DREAMS* (ADAPTED)

277

Chapter Summary
Paragraph Structure

Paragraphs

1. A paragraph is a group of related sentences about one main idea. (*See pages 264–265.*)
2. The topic sentence states the main idea of the paragraph. (*See page 266.*)
3. The supporting sentences back up the main idea with specific details and form the body of the paragraph. (*See page 270.*)
4. The concluding sentence adds a strong ending to the paragraph. (*See pages 274–275.*)

Standardized Test

Directions: Decide which sense each underlined word appeals to. In the appropriate row on your answer sheet, fill in the circle containing the letter of your answer.

SAMPLE The sun was huge and <u>bright</u>.
  A sight
  B sound
  C touch

ANSWER Ⓐ Ⓑ Ⓒ

1. The bell <u>clanged</u> loudly to announce that the game would begin soon.
  A sight
  B sound
  C smell

2. The children held their noses because the spoiled eggs were <u>rancid</u>.
  A sight
  B touch
  C smell

3. They ate the <u>spicy</u> food at the annual neighborhood carnival.
  A sight
  B taste
  C smell

4. His skin was cold and <u>clammy</u>.
  A touch
  B taste
  C smell

5. The snake's skin was not <u>slimy</u> at all.
  A sight
  B sound
  C touch

Directions: Decide which sentence best combines the under-lined sentences. In the appropriate row on your answer sheet, fill in the circle containing the letter of your answer.

SAMPLE The poodle is small. He is grey.
  A The poodle is small, but he is grey.
  B The poodle is small and grey.
  C The poodle is small, and he is grey.

ANSWER Ⓐ Ⓑ Ⓒ

6. Stuart got an A on the test. Richard got an A on the test.
  A Stuart got an A on the test, and Richard did too.
  B Stuart got an A and Richard got an A on the test.
  C Stuart and Richard got an A on the test.

7. The sweater was new. It was red. It looked warm.
  A The new red sweater looked warm.
  B The sweater was new and red, and it looked warm.
  C The new sweater was red, and it looked warm.

8. At recess I jumped rope. I ran. I also skipped.
  A At recess I jumped rope. I also ran and skipped.
  B At recess I jumped rope, ran, and skipped.
  C At recess I jumped rope, and I ran, and I skipped.

9. The dishes are valuable. They are old. They are in the box.
  A The dishes in the box are valuable and old.
  B The dishes are valuable and old, and they are in the box.
  C The dishes are in the box and are valuable and old.

10. Today I studied. I played. I watched TV.
  A Today I studied and played, and I watched TV.
  B Today I studied, and I played, and I watched TV.
  C Today I studied, played, and watched TV.

Composition

Part Two

18

The Writing Process

Leona is writing to her pen pal in Ghana. She is telling about a field trip that her class made to a science museum. She writes for a little while and then stops to read it over. She crosses out a word, adds another word, and reads the letter again. Then she asks her mother to listen as she reads the letter.

"Something doesn't sound quite right here," Leona says to her mother. "Would you listen and tell me what you think? How can I make it better?"

Leona, like other writers, knows that good writing usually takes several tries. Writing is a process of thinking and planning, making choices, and trying again. Most writers go through four main stages in the writing process. This chapter will take you through those stages.

Your Writer's Notebook

Pretend that you have a pen pal from a country of your choice. Give your pen pal a name. Then write a letter to that person in your journal. Describe yourself—your personality, your interests, your opinions. Read your letter aloud. Make changes so the letter will flow smoothly.

Prewriting

The first stage of the writing process is called prewriting. During the prewriting stage, you search for writing ideas. Prewriting activities help you zero in on good subjects. They also help you group your ideas logically so readers will be able to follow.

18a **Prewriting** is the first stage of the writing process. It includes all the planning steps that come before writing the first draft.

Knowing Your Purpose and Audience

When Leona was writing her letter, she was aware of her writing purpose. She was writing to describe the different displays at the science museum.

Leona also knew her audience, the person who would read her letter. She knew that her friend had never visited a science museum in the United States. Leona decided to include extra information so her friend would understand.

18b Writing **purpose** is your reason for writing. **Audience** is the person or persons who will be reading your work.

EXERCISE 1 Identifying Purpose and Audience

Number your paper 1 to 5. Read each situation. After each number, write the purpose and audience.

EXAMPLE   Tim writes a letter to the library requesting information about bears.

ANSWER   Purpose: To request information about bears
          Audience: A librarian

1. Donna writes a note inviting Paula to her party.
2. Ted writes a paragraph for the school newspaper trying to convince the school to sell fruit and yogurt in the cafeteria.
3. Alfonso writes to a department store asking for a refund on a broken baseball bat.
4. Myrna writes a poem for her friend Jenna about the beauty of the Rocky Mountains.
5. Loretta writes a report for her scout troop on how to raise money at bake sales.

Exploring Your Interests

If you are truly interested in a subject, you will enjoy writing about it. Your writing will sparkle, and your readers will feel the spirit behind the writing. Explore your interests and use them as writing ideas.

EXERCISE 2 Interviewing to Explore Interests

Pair up with a classmate. Take turns asking each other the questions below. After each question, write down what your partner says. Exchange papers.

Questions for Interviewing
1. What are your favorite subjects in school?
2. What are your hobbies?
3. What sports or games do you most enjoy?
4. What interests do you share with your friends?
5. What interests do you share with family members?

Freewriting

Another way to unlock writing ideas is freewriting. Freewriting means writing without stopping. If you run out of ideas, write, "I've run out of ideas" until another idea occurs to you. Let your mind relax and don't worry about mistakes.

EXERCISE 3 Freewriting

Write freely for three minutes. Answer the following questions, adding everything that comes to mind.

Who are my heroes and heroines? Why do I admire them?

Brainstorming

Brainstorming also releases ideas from your memory. Brainstorming means listing everything that comes to mind about a subject. Unlike freewriting, brainstorming can be done in spurts. Write down ideas as they occur to you. One idea will lead to another.

EXERCISE 4 Brainstorming

Write down everything that comes to mind when you look at the picture below.

Organizing Your Ideas

After you have thought of ideas, you need to put them in an order that readers can follow. Try to see your ideas from a reader's point of view. Then ask yourself what should come first, second, third, and last.

EXERCISE 5 Using Logical Order

Write an explanation of how Inuits dress to keep warm. Use the picture below as a guide. Arrange your ideas in the order of head to toe.

EXERCISE 6 On Your Own

Brainstorm a list of party games you enjoy playing. Write brief notes about why you like each one. Choose three that are your special favorites. Rank them in order of first choice, second choice, and third choice. Save your work for Exercise 8.

Writing Extra

Everybody's life is a story. When you write the story of your own life, you are writing autobiography. Most autobiographies start at the beginning of someone's life and move forward, giving details about specific events. Read the following passages from the autobiography of Ernie Banks, a famous baseball player.

Most of the kids in the neighborhood raced homemade scooters. The wheels were at opposite ends of a horizontal board attached to a vertical board on the front end. You pushed the scooter with one foot and held on to the vertical board with both hands. As we grew older we would make believe we were racing in the Indianapolis 500 on Memorial Day. . . .

The bicycle made a big change in my life, especially when my parents gave me enough money to buy two used tires, a headlight, and a horn. The first time my mother ever said "no" to me was the night I brought the repaired bike back home and wanted to use the living room as a garage.

"Get it out of here, right now!" Mom ordered. Reluctantly, I found an out-of-sight parking space for it under the outside staircase.

—"MR. CUB," ERNIE BANKS AND JIM ENRIGHT

Write your own autobiography. Every day for a week, write a chapter of your life story. You may use the following titles for the chapters of your autobiography.

1. Birth and Earliest Memories
2. Starting School
3. Good Times Growing Up
4. Highlights in School
5. How I've Changed
6. My Good Friends
7. Next Year and Beyond

Writing the First Draft

After thinking of ideas and organizing them, you are ready to write. Your first try, or draft, does not need to be perfect. Just put your ideas into complete sentences.

18c **Writing the first draft** is the second stage of the writing process. Use your prewriting notes to write complete, flowing sentences that would make sense to a reader.

EXERCISE 7 *Writing a First Draft from Notes*

Use the prewriting notes that follow to write the first draft of a paragraph. The first and last sentences are given.

First sentence: My first stage performance was also my last performance.

NOTES
- it was opening night of our school play
- waited backstage listening for my cue,
- heard my cue, headed onto stage
- caught my costume on hook backstage
- costume ripped down the back
- pretended nothing happened and went out
- forgot my lines and had to be helped by somebody whispering to me from off stage

Last sentence: That night I decided I did belong in the theater—in the audience!

EXERCISE 8 *On Your Own*

Look over your notes from Exercise 6 about party games. Write the first draft of a paragraph telling about them. Use the following phrases.

One of my favorite . . .
Another game I enjoy . . .
The game I enjoy the most . . .

Revising

Revising means "seeing again." Look again at your draft as if you were a reader seeing it for the first time. Ask yourself if it makes sense. If not, rewrite it so that your message comes across loud and clear.

18d   **Revising** is the third stage of the writing process. Revise your draft as often as needed until it is the best you can make it.

Study the following revised paragraph. First read it as if there were no marks on it. Then read the revised version and notice the improvements.

The Pet Fair

Last year our neighborhood held a pet fair. There was a prize for the largest dog and the smallest dog. There was also a prize for the oldest and the youngest dog. The most fun, though, was the pet-owner look-alike contest. Last year there was a pet fair on my cousin's block. I have black curly hair just like my poodle. I placed a red ribbon in my hair and a red ribbon in Gabby's hair. We won the pet look-alike contest and received some free dog food and a good book on dogs. The fair was lots of fun and a good way to know the neighbors better.

When you revise your work, do not try to do everything at once. Instead make changes one at a time. Follow the Revision Checklist on page 290.

289

18e

> ### Revision Checklist
>
> 1. Does your paper state a main idea?
> 2. Do any sentences wander off the subject?
> 3. Are you ideas presented in a logical order?
> 4. Does the composition have a strong ending?
> 5. Is the purpose of your composition clear?
> 6. Is your composition suited for your audience?
> 7. Did you vary your sentences?
> 8. Did you use specific, lively words?

Sharing Your Work

Most writers try their work out on a reader before completing the final copy. Just as Leona asked her mother to listen to her letter, writers look for advice from friends to help them improve their work. However, when you read someone else's work, be sure to comment on good points as well as weak points.

EXERCISE 9   Studying a Revision

Write out a clean copy of the revised paragraph on page 289. Make all the changes shown in the revision. On the back of your paper, do the following.

1. Write the sentence that states the main idea (the topic sentence).
2. Write the two sentences that were combined to make one sentence.
3. Write the sentence that strayed off the main idea.
4. Write the sentence that adds a strong ending.

EXERCISE 10   On Your Own

Exchange papers from Exercise 8 with a classmate and comment on both strong and weak parts of your partner's work. Then use the checklist above to revise your paragraph. Save your work for Exercise 13.

Editing

Sometimes when you write you concentrate so much on your ideas that you make mistakes in grammar, spelling, and punctuation. At the editing stage of the writing process, you can fix those mistakes.

18f **Editing** is the final stage of the writing process. Polish your work by correcting errors and making a neat copy.

The following editing checklist will help you look for and correct any mistakes in your writing. Go over the points one at a time while you are editing your work.

18g

Editing Checklist

1. Are your sentences free of errors in grammar and usage?
2. Did you spell each word correctly? *(See pages 454–465.)*
3. Did you use capital letters where needed? *(See pages 178–192.)*
4. Did you punctuate your sentences correctly? *(See pages 194–225.)*
5. Did you indent your paragraph?
6. Are your margins even?
7. Is your handwriting clear and neat?

Most writers do not try to make a final, neat copy until they have corrected all the mistakes. As a shorthand, they often use proofreading symbols while editing. Proofreading symbols are like another language. Each mark means the same thing each time you see it. These are also the symbols that editors use when marking mistakes before a book is actually printed. (The trial pages that the editors read are called "proofs.") The chart on page 292 shows some commonly used proofreading symbols. Use them while editing your work.

Proofreading Symbols

∧	insert	I waited for you.
ℓ	delete	Tomorrow is my very best friend's birthday.
····	let it stand	I recognized Sue's lilting voice.
#	add space	We made our own icecream.
⌒	close up	See you to night!
∿	transpose	The clwon had a red big nose.
≡	capital letter	I was born in chicago.
/	small letter	Chicago is a Midwestern city.
¶	indent paragraph	We often make mistakes. However, it is important to correct those mistakes.

Cara wrote the following paragraph for her science class. Before making a final copy, she edited the paragraph using the proofreading symbols shown above. The symbols are a quick way for Cara to mark her writing. Notice how she has marked spelling, capitalization, and punctuation errors.

Between Fish and Reptiles

Amphibians are all most like a cross between fish and reptils. Like fish, young amphibians have gills. And take in oxagen from the water. When they grow older. They become more like reptils. They grow lungs and are are able to breath air. The name amphibian tells the story. It is from greek words meaning "having two lives."

EXERCISE 11   Using Proofreading Symbols for Editing

Number your paper 1 to 10. Next to the proper number, write the corrected form of the word.

A Strange Moon

Triton, the largest moon of (1) neptune, is unusual. First, it is very (2) brihgt, which means that (3) its also very big. Second, it has its own (4) atmosfere. Third, it has a (5) see of (6) nitrogin. The sea is probably (7) forzen at the dark pole. Most (8) unusaul is the direction Triton moves. Its (9) orbit around Neptune is opposite the way other moons move. Many (10) deep mysteries still surround Triton.

EXERCISE 12   Editing a Paragraph

Using the Editing Checklist on page 291 to help you correct the errors in the following paragraph. Write the corrected paragraph. Then underline your corrections.

Postage Due

People can do all most anything through the mail. They can keep intouch with friends. They can pay there bills. They can even take classes threw the mail. Chess players can play games through the mail by sending postcards giving each new move. shoppers can buy items from catalogs, some people even make new freinds through the mail. Mail brings poeple and products to gether from all over the world.

EXERCISE 13   On Your Own

Edit your work from Exercise 10 using the checklist on page 291 as a guide. The first time through, use proofreading symbols to mark any mistakes you find. Then exchange papers with a classmate. Mark any mistakes you find with proofreading symbols. When your own paper is returned, make a clean, fresh copy.

_S_potlight on _W_riting

A **Prewriting: Knowing Your Purpose and Audience.** Think of five recent times you have written something. They could include school assignments, letters, or special projects. Write each on your paper. Then tell the purpose and audience of each.

EXAMPLE   report for social studies
           purpose: to describe the Sahara desert
           audience: teacher and classmates

B **Prewriting: Exploring Your Interests.** In groups of three, trace the profiles of your classmates. One person should hold a flashlight. A second person should stand sideways between the light and the wall. A third person should hold a piece of paper against the wall and trace the shadow of the profile. To the left of your profile, write down a list of your interests, hobbies, likes, dislikes, and personality traits.

C **Prewriting: Brainstorming.** Brainstorm a list of details you could use to describe the scene pictured above. Jot down everything you see in the picture.

D **Prewriting: Organizing Your Ideas.** Arrange your brainstorming notes about the marketplace in some logical order—for example, nearest to farthest or one side to another.

E **Writing a First Draft.** Use your prewriting notes about the marketplace to write the first draft of a description. Keep the following purpose and audience in mind as you write.

PURPOSE   To describe a marketplace in Ghana
AUDIENCE   Someone who has never been to one

F **Revising by Sharing Your Work.** Exchange papers with a classmate. As you read your partner's paper, ask yourself the following questions.

- Is the description clear?
- Do the words bring sharp pictures to mind?
- If you hadn't seen the picture, would the description help you "see" the scene?

Tell your partner what was good about the writing. Also tell what could be improved.

G **Revising Based on a Reader's Reaction.** If your partner suggested changes that you think would improve your work, revise your paper to reflect them.

H **Using a Revision Checklist.** Use the Checklist on page 290 to revise your description.

I **Editing Your Work.** Check your description for errors in usage, capitalization, punctuation, and spelling. Use the Editing Checklist on page 291 and the Proofreading Symbols on page 292.

J **Peer Editing.** Exchange papers with a classmate. See if you can find any errors your partner missed.

K **Making a Final Copy.** Copy your description neatly. Be sure to indent your paragraph and leave margins.

Steps for Writing the Writing Process

Prewriting

1. Know your purpose and audience.
2. Think of writing ideas by
   - exploring your interests.
   - freewriting.
3. Brainstorm for details you can use to expand on your subject.
4. Organize your ideas in a logical order.

Writing

5. Use your prewriting notes to write a first draft. Write complete sentences that would make sense to a reader.

Revising

6. Look at your first draft with a fresh eye. Also share your writing with a reader.
7. Use your reader's comments and the Revision Checklist on page 290 to improve your draft.
8. Revise your draft as often as needed.

Editing

9. Polish your work by correcting any errors in usage, capitalization, punctuation, and spelling. Use the Editing Checklist on page 291 and the Proofreading Symbols on page 292.
10. Make a neat final copy.

19

Writing Narrative Paragraphs

If the purpose of your paragraph is to tell a story, you will be writing a narrative paragraph.

19a A **narrative paragraph** tells a real or an imaginary story with a clear beginning, middle, and ending.

A Helping Hand

TOPIC SENTENCE

One bright, sunny Saturday a wild bird flew into my window. I was at my desk doing homework. Suddenly I saw a flutter of wings and heard a big thud. Right away I grabbed a cardboard box and put

BODY

on some heavy gloves. If the bird was hurt, I was going to take it to the vet. Just as I reached down to pick up the

CONCLUDING SENTENCE

bird, it took off with a flutter of wings! I was glad it was only stunned.

*Y*our Writer's Notebook

Most good stories keep readers interested because of the surprises they contain. Use your journal to write about surprising events—big and small—in your life.

Prewriting

The first stage in the process of writing is prewriting. During this stage you think of things to write about and begin to plan your composition. The following activities will help start your ideas flowing.

EXERCISE 1 Freewriting

Use the following starter line. Write freely for three minutes, putting down everything that comes to mind.

There are certain times in my life I will never forget.

EXERCISE 2 Thinking of Subjects from Your Experience

Read each question. Then write answers to each question.

1. If you were making a photo album of important events in your life, what pictures would you include?
2. What has happened to make you laugh lately?
3. Did one of your dreams ever come true?
4. When you think of your childhood, what three events come to mind?
5. What have you lost and found again later?

EXERCISE 3 Thinking of Imaginary Subjects

Use your imagination to write answers to each question.

1. What would happen if a letter from the president arrived for you?
2. What if a raccoon suddenly started talking to you?
3. What if you had the leading role in a new movie?
4. Suppose time stopped for two minutes for everyone but you. What would happen?
5. What would happen if you had a chance to play on your favorite sports team?

Choosing and Limiting a Subject

After thinking of possible subjects, the next step is to choose one. Keep the following guidelines in mind.

19b

Choosing a Subject

1. Choose an event you will enjoy writing about.
2. Choose an event that will interest your audience.
3. Choose an event that has a surprise or two in it.

Sometimes the subject you choose will be too broad to cover in a single paragraph. In those cases you must zero in on a smaller part of the broad subject. This process is called limiting the subject. Study the following examples.

TOO BROAD	MORE LIMITED	LIMITED ENOUGH FOR ONE PARAGRAPH
birthdays	my seventh birthday	finding out about the surprise party
my cat	playing with my cat	time I discovered Tommy's trick
my cousin Chuck	funny things that happened to Chuck	time Chuck reached across table and put elbow in spaghetti

19c Limit your subject so that it can be covered in one paragraph.

EXERCISE 4 Choosing a Subject

a. Number your paper 1 to 4. After each number, write a possible narrative subject. You may use ideas from Exercises 1 and 2.
b. Review the guidelines above. Then circle the subject that best follows all three guidelines.

EXERCISE 5 Identifying Limited Subjects

Number your paper 1 to 10. Then decide whether each subject is limited enough for one paragraph. Write *too broad* or *limited* after the proper number.

EXAMPLE my family
ANSWER too broad

1. our vacation
2. a surprise fire drill
3. the first time I developed film
4. playing outdoors
5. the time my dog was lost in the woods
6. family get-togethers
7. the night I saw seven shooting stars
8. my parakeet
9. the time my parakeet said something funny
10. the first time I tasted a hot pepper

EXERCISE 6 Limiting Subjects That Are Too Broad

All of the following subjects are too broad. For each one, write two events limited enough to be covered in one paragraph. Use your imagination and your own experiences to think of a limited subject.

EXAMPLE forgetting something important
ANSWER time I left my key at home
        forgetting to mail my mom's bills

1. making friends
2. playing volleyball
3. learning something new
4. starting school
5. entering a contest
6. making a mistake
7. taking pictures
8. eating out
9. shopping
10. at the swimming pool

301

Listing Details

When you have a good, limited subject, you can begin listing specific details to use in telling your story. Brainstorming is one good way to think of all the details. Brainstorming means writing down everything that comes to mind when you think about your subject. Use the following brainstorming questions to help you.

Brainstorming Questions
- Who is in the story? List all the people involved.
- Where did the story take place?
- When did the story take place?
- How did you or the other people in the story feel?
- What happened to start things rolling?
- What happened next?
- What is the high point of the story?
- What is the outcome of the story?
- What did you or the other people in the story learn?

19d   Brainstorm a list of details to use in your story.

Suppose you had chosen to write about your first trip to the dentist. Your notes might appear as follows.

Who is in the story?	me, my mother, Dr. Pearlman
Where did it happen?	at home and at the dentist's
When did it happen?	when I was five years old
How did you feel?	very nervous
What happened first?	my mom told me she made a dentist's appointment for me
What happened next?	I tried hiding
What is the high point?	dentist seated me in chair and I tensed up terribly
What is the outcome?	dentist only talked to me and took X-rays
What did you learn?	worst fears are usually wrong

EXERCISE 7 *Listing Details for a Narrative Paragraph*

Write one of the following subjects on your paper. Underneath it, brainstorm a list of details. Use the questions on page 302 to help you think of ideas. Use your own experiences as a guide.

1. the time I first rode a bike
2. the day I met my best friend
3. my first time away from home
4. my proudest day
5. the time I helped someone

EXERCISE 8 *Listing Made-up Details*

Use your imagination to brainstorm a list of details that tell the story in the picture on this page. Use the questions on page 302 to help you think of ideas.

Arranging Details in Time Order

Think of how strange it would be to start reading a story that began, "They all lived happily ever after." You expect to find this sentence at the end of a story, not at the beginning. Readers need to know about a story's events in the order they happened. This order is called time order. Stories that are not in proper time order are hard for readers to follow.

Read the following narrative paragraph. It tells the story of friends exchanging presents. First, they think about what to buy. Then they shop for it. Finally, they exchange gifts. Notice that all the events are told in the order they happened. Words that show time are printed in heavy type.

Grab Bag

Every year my Girl Scout troop has a grab bag. **This year,** my best friend Linda and I picked each other's name out of the hat. I remembered that Linda and I had SCOUT MEETING **once** talked about wanting a set of artist's LATER THAT WEEK chalks for drawing. So **later that week,** my mother took me to an artist's supply store and I bought Linda's gift. I tried to talk my mother into buying me a set too, NEXT SCOUT MEETING but all she said was, "Maybe next time." **At our next scout meeting,** we all exchanged our gifts. **When** Linda opened her present, LINDA'S TURN TO OPEN she started laughing—not the response I expected. **Then** she handed me my present. **As soon as** I opened it, I understood her WRITER'S TURN TO OPEN laughter. Underneath the wrapping was a set of artist's chalks exactly like the one I bought her. Great friends, like great minds, think alike.

19e Check your list of details to make sure that the events are listed in **time order.**

EXERCISE 9 Arranging Details in Time Order

Number your paper 1 to 3. Write the subject. Then write
the details under each subject in proper time order.

1. SUBJECT   neighborhood Olympics
   DETAILS   • first sport was bicycle racing
            • tumbling event was last—I won 1st prize
            • after bike racing was skateboarding

2. SUBJECT   trying out for the basketball team
   DETAILS   • having to play both defense and offense
            • last test was shooting free throws
            • really nervous before starting to play
            • feeling thrilled when I made the team

3. SUBJECT   the day of the flat tire
   DETAILS   • Dad was driving us to movies
            • a woman drove up and offered to help
            • pulled over to side of road
            • Dad fixed tire and picked us up later
            • heard a tharumph, tharumph, tharumph
            • woman turned out to be our neighbor's
              sister, so she drove us to movies

EXERCISE 10 On Your Own

Use the picture on this page to help you choose a subject
for a narrative paragraph. List details and arrange them
in time order. Save your work for Exercise 14.

Writing

Your prewriting notes will help you write the first draft of your paragraph. At this stage, don't worry about spelling or grammar mistakes. Just try to put your ideas into complete sentences that a reader would be able to follow.

Writing a Topic Sentence

The topic sentence states the main idea of a paragraph. (*See pages 266–267.*) In a narrative paragraph, the main idea is the event you are writing about. The steps shown below will help you write your topic sentence.

19f

Steps for Writing a Topic Sentence
1. Look over your prewriting notes.
2. Try to express your main idea in one sentence.
3. Rewrite that sentence until it captures interest.

If you were writing about your first trip to the dentist (*see page 309*), your topic sentence might appear as follows.

WEAK TOPIC
SENTENCE   I was very nervous about my first trip to the dentist.

While that sentence does state the main idea, it lacks interest. The following does a better job of capturing a reader's interest. It makes the reader want to finish the whole paragraph to find out what happened.

IMPROVED
TOPIC
SENTENCE   I had a big surprise the first time I went to the dentist.

Other weak openings are "In this paragraph I will . . ." or "This paragraph will be about . . ." Let your reader focus on the story, not on the writing of the paragraph.

306

EXERCISE 11 Writing Topic Sentences

Each of the following topic sentences could be improved. Read the list of details for each narrative paragraph. Then write an improved topic sentence for each list. Save your work for Exercise 12.

1. This paragraph will be about the time I wrote a poem that was printed in a magazine.

   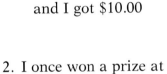

   - poem was for school
   - parents liked it
   - suggested I send it to a magazine
   - two months later reply came
   - poem was printed in the magazine and I got $10.00

2. I once won a prize at a school fun fair.

   - bought ticket with numbers on it
   - forgot I had it as I walked around fair
   - was about to leave when they announced drawing would start
   - watched all the numbers on my ticket match as they read winner
   - won a computer

3. To practice for camp, I spent a night in the backyard in a tent.

   - inflated raft to sleep on
   - pitched tent after dinner
   - unrolled sleeping bag and put inside tent
   - called my dog Rusty to keep me company
   - woke up at midnight soaking wet—storm blew in
   - spent rest of night inside in my own bed
   - Rusty seemed happier

4. I once was a clown in a neighborhood circus.

   - I was 4 years old
   - my part was clown
   - put costume on
   - went out in front of audience
   - people laughed, and I ran behind curtain
   - Dad came backstage and told me clowns were supposed to be funny
   - went back out and finished my part of show proudly

Writing the Paragraph Body

The body of your paragraph will be made up of the events you listed in your prewriting notes. Write about the events in proper time order and use transitions.

19g **Transitions** are words and phrases that show how ideas are related. In time order, transitions show the passing of time.

In the following draft of a paragraph, the transitions are printed in heavy type. Compare the supporting sentences with the prewriting notes on page 302.

TOPIC
SENTENCE

SUPPORTING
SENTENCES
TELL EVENTS
IN ORDER

I had a big surprise the first time I went to the dentist. **One day when I was five,** my mother told me I had to go to the dentist. I was so nervous that I tried hiding in the basement. My mother **finally** found me, though, and off we went to the dentist. **When** Dr. Pearlman placed me in the chair, I really tensed up. To my surprise, though, he didn't even ask me to open my mouth. All he did **that day** was talk to me and take X-rays. None of my fears came to pass.

The following transitions are used often to show time order. Notice how the paragraph about going to the dentist uses transitions. Transitions can appear anywhere in a sentence—at the beginning, in the middle, or at the end.

Transitions for Time Order

before	finally	meanwhile
after	later	after a while
first	soon	the next day
next	at last	last weekend

As you begin to write the first draft of your paragraph, use the following guidelines for help.

19h

Steps for Writing the Body

1. Review your topic sentence and prewriting notes.
2. Write a complete sentence for each supporting detail.
3. Combine sentences that seem to go together.
4. Add transitions to show the passing of time.

EXERCISE 12 *Writing the Body of a Narrative Paragraph*

Choose one of the events from Exercise 11. First copy your improved topic sentence. Then follow the steps above to write the body of your paragraph. Add transitions where necessary. Save your work for Exercise 13.

Writing a Concluding Sentence

Without a concluding sentence, your paragraph will sound unfinished. (*See pages 274–275.*) Finish up your paragraph with an ending that readers will remember. The chart on the following page lists several good ways to end a paragraph.

Writing a Concluding Sentence

The concluding sentence may
1. restate the topic sentence in fresh words.
2. sum up the paragraph.
3. pull the supporting sentences together.
4. state a lesson learned from the experience.

All the following sentences would add a strong finish to the paragraph about going to the dentist. Notice how each uses a different way to end the story. Experiment in your own writing with different kinds of endings.

CONCLUDING
SENTENCES

I sure was expecting something different from my first time at the dentist! [restates topic sentence in new words]

My big surprise at the dentist's office was that the experience could be fun! [sums up the paragraph]

After that first visit, I've never felt nervous about the dentist again. [pulls the supporting sentences together]

I guess the first time for everything is usually less scary than it seems. [adds a lesson from the experience]

EXERCISE 13   Writing Concluding Sentences

Review your work from Exercise 12. Then write two possible concluding sentences for your paragraph. Use one of the guidelines listed in the chart above.

EXERCISE 14   On Your Own

Using your work from Exercise 10, write the first draft of your narrative paragraph. Include a topic sentence, a body of supporting sentences, and a concluding sentence. Save your work for Exercise 16.

riting Extra

Biography—the story of someone's life—is one kind of narrative writing. Short biographies are often collected into one book, called a *biographical reference book.* Examples of these books are *Who's Who, Notable Men and Women of Science,* and *Dictionary of American Biography. (See page 481.)*

You can help your class put together its own biographical reference book. It will be called *Heroes and Heroines of All Time.* Each student will write a short biography of a person he or she admires. The person can be living now or from the past.

Use the library to gather the information you need for your biography. Look up your hero or heroine in the encyclopedia or one of the biographical reference books listed above. Keep the biography one paragraph long. Be sure to present the information in time order and use transitions where appropriate. When all of the biographies are completed, help design a cover for your class book.

Write the following fact sheet on a separate piece of paper. Use it to gather information.

Fact Sheet

Hero or heroine's name:

Birthdate:

Birthplace:

Education:

First major accomplishment:

Other major accomplishments:

Most famous deed:

Date of death:

Revising

Revising means "seeing again." After finishing a draft, put it aside for a while. Later, come back to it and "see it again," looking for ways to improve it. Keep your reader in mind as you make changes. Always try to make your writing as smooth and clear as possible. Ask a friend or relative to point out parts that still need work. Make those improvements.

The following checklist will help you revise your paragraph. Work on your paragraph until you can answer yes to all of the following questions.

Checklist for Revising Narrative Paragraphs

Checking Your Paragraph

1. Does your topic sentence focus attention on the story and raise your reader's interest? (*See page 306.*)
2. Are your supporting details in time order? (*See page 304.*)
3. Did you use transitions to show the passing of time? (*See pages 309–310.*)
4. Do all of your sentences relate to the main idea? (*See pages 270–271.*)
5. Does your concluding sentence bring the story to a close? (*See pages 310–311.*)

Checking Your Sentences

6. Did you combine related sentences to avoid too many short, choppy sentences in a row? (*See pages 247–254.*)
7. Did you vary the beginnings of your sentences? (*See page 256.*)
8. Did you avoid rambling sentences? (*See page 258.*)

Checking Your Words

9. Did you use specific, lively words? (*See page 231.*)
10. Did you use words that appeal to the senses? (*See pages 235–241.*)

313

EXERCISE 15 Revising a Narrative Paragraph

Use the checklist on page 313 to help you revise the following narrative paragraph.

The Party

The first time I gave a party I thought I had everything under control. I mailed out the invitations on Saturday, a week before the party. By Friday night I had the basement decorated just right for the party. Saturday morning my parents and I shopped for the food and drinks. On Wednesday I decided what refreshments to serve and made a shopping list. My friend Rhonda had given a great party a few weeks earlier. Finally the hour arrived and I was all ready. I waited and waited, rearranging the cheese and crackers. No one came for two hours. Just when I was about to give up, the doorbell rang. My first guest gave me the answer. I had written 4:00 on the invitations instead of 2:00.

EXERCISE 16 On Your Own

Revise your work from Exercise 14 using the Revision Checklist on page 313. Save your work for Exercise 17.

314

*E*diting

The final stage of the writing process is editing. During this stage you correct errors in your writing. Use the following checklist to help you edit your work.

Editing Checklist

1. Are your sentences free of errors in grammar and usage?
2. Did you spell each word correctly?
3. Did you use capital letters where needed?
4. Did you punctuate your sentences correctly?
5. Did you indent your paragraph?
6. Are your margins even?
7. Is your handwriting clear and neat?

While editing, you may wish to use proofreading symbols as a shorthand way to show your changes.

Proofreading Symbols

∧	insert	ℯ	delete
····	let it stand	#	add space
⌒	close up space	∿	transpose
≡	capital letter	/	small letter

Use a personal editing chart to help you avoid errors in the future. Make your chart by writing four headings across your paper: *Grammar, Usage, Mechanics, Spelling.* Enter your mistakes in the appropriate column. Refer to your chart each time you edit.

*E*XERCISE 17   *On Your Own*

Edit your work from Exercise 16 using the Editing Checklist on this page.

Spotlight on Writing

A **Writing a Narrative Paragraph for your School Newspaper.** The following notes are out of order. First arrange them in time order. Then use them to write a narrative paragraph for your school newspaper.

PURPOSE   To tell what happened when your class visited the bakery company

AUDIENCE   Readers of your school newspaper

- we all had to put on hair nets before touring factory
- final part of tour was packaging—cakes were wrapped
- whole class went single file through mixing room
- saw huge vats of batter that smelled great
- after that the pans went on a conveyor belt through ovens
- next we saw batter poured into pans
- at very end of tour came the best part—free samples

B **Writing a Narrative Paragraph.** Pretend you are the person in the picture on page 317. Then write a narrative paragraph that suits the following purpose and audience. Use the Steps for Writing a Narrative Paragraph on page 319 as a guide. The following questions will help you brainstorm for ideas.

PURPOSE   To entertain by telling a story

AUDIENCE   Your friends

- Who besides you is involved in the story?
- Where did the event take place?
- When did the event take place?
- How did you feel?
- What happened to start things rolling?
- What happened next?
- What is the high point of the story?
- What is the outcome?

316

C **Writing a True Story.** Write a narrative paragraph to suit the following purpose and audience. Use the Steps for Writing on page 319 as a guide.

PURPOSE   To tell a true story from your life about being patient

AUDIENCE   People younger than you who need to learn patience

D **Revising a Narrative Paragraph.** Revise the following narrative paragraph using the Revision Checklist on page 313.

A Happy Day

One of the happiest days of my life was the day we picked out our puppy at the animal shelter. We had been preparing for a long time. We'd talked about caring for our dog. My brother and I had even worked out a schedule for walking and training the dog. Finally, the day arrived to go to the shelter. The shelter has homeless cats, too. We

317

named our little puppy Raven because he was so black. Right away, my brother and I knew which puppy we wanted. We headed straight for an 8-week-old sleek black puppy. After talking with the shelter workers, we were able to take Raven home. Raven wagged his tail all the way home and hasn't ever stopped. He is now two years old, and he's one of my best friends.

E **Editing a Narrative Paragraph.** Edit the following narrative paragraph using the Editing Checklist on page 315.

Most poeple just watch television, but I was actully on it one time. My boy scout troup raised alot of money for a charity, reporters from the local televeision station came to one of our meetings. Wanting to put us on the air. They brought minicams, small cameras that they helt in there hands. They also had microfones. First they innerviewed our leaders. Then they talked to Ron and Mike, who brought in the most money. Too my suprise, they then came over to to talk to me. The best part of all was watching the troop on television the folowing night. Besides being proud of raising the money. We were also thrilled to see ourselfs on television.

F **Ideas for Writing.** Choose one of the subjects below or one of your own. Write a narrative paragraph using the Steps for Writing on page 319 as a guide.

1. finding a buried treasure
2. meeting a long lost relative
3. helping a stranger
4. surprising yourself
5. learning a lesson
6. being on a team
7. trying as hard as you could
8. overcoming a fear
9. having fun outdoors
10. going on a trip

Steps for Writing a Narrative Paragraph

Prewriting

1. Think about your purpose in writing and consider your audience. *(See pages 283–284.)*
2. Make a list of subjects by jotting down ideas. *(See page 299.)*
3. Choose one subject and limit it. *(See page 300.)*
4. Brainstorm a list of supporting details. *(See page 302.)*
5. Arrange your details in time order. *(See page 304.)*

Writing

6. Write a topic sentence. *(See page 306.)*
7. Write a body of supporting sentences telling the story, event by event. Use transitions. *(See pages 309–310.)*
8. Add a concluding sentence. *(See pages 310–311.)*

Revising

9. Using the Revising Checklist on page 313, check your paragraph for paragraph structure, sentences, and words.

Editing

10. Using the Editing Checklist on page 315, check your spelling, capitalization, punctuation, and form.

20

Writing Descriptive Paragraphs

Sometimes your writing purpose will be to describe. For example, in school you might describe something you see under a microscope. In a letter, you might describe your new bicycle to a friend.

20a A **descriptive paragraph** creates a vivid picture in words of a person, an object, or a scene.

*Y*our Writer's Notebook

Describe each picture below. Every day for a week, write a description of a person, place, or thing.

Descriptive Paragraph Structure

Read the following descriptive paragraph. The structure of the paragraph helps the reader understand the description. Notice how each sentence helps paint the picture.

Coming Home

TOPIC
SENTENCE

From my airplane window, I see my hometown come into view through the dark night sky. Like a sparkling serpent, the street lights wind along the highways.

SUPPORTING
SENTENCES

Squares of lights show the neat patterns of neighborhood streets. Somewhere down there nestled in the glittering lights is my home. As the roar of the airplane engine changes pitch, the ground seems to rise to

CONCLUDING
SENTENCE

meet me. No sight could ever be as beautiful as the home I've missed so much.

When writing a description, you cannot include every single detail about a subject. Instead, decide on the overall feeling you wish to convey. Then choose details that will make the feeling come alive. For example, in the paragraph above, the writer uses lights and the view from an airplane to create a certain mood.

The chart below explains the purpose of each sentence in a descriptive paragraph.

20b

Structure of a Descriptive Paragraph

1. The topic sentence introduces the subject and suggests an overall feeling about it.
2. The supporting sentences give details that bring the picture to life.
3. The concluding sentence sums up the overall feeling of the subject.

EXERCISE 1 Writing Descriptive Topic Sentences

For each descriptive subject, write a topic sentence that conveys an overall feeling.

EXAMPLE   a stormy night
POSSIBLE   The lightning struck,
ANSWER   bringing a feeling of
            doom.

1. a spider
2. a kitten
3. a doctor
4. your room
5. your grandmother

6. a trumpet
7. a picnic
8. a totem pole
9. your favorite outfit
10. a boat

Specific Details

The best way to help a reader picture something is to use specific details that appeal to the senses. *(See pages 235–241.)* If your paragraph is about the beach, show your reader how the sand feels underfoot. Record the sound of waves breaking on the shore. Let your reader smell the salty air. These specific details will wake up your reader's senses and make your writing come alive.

20c Use **specific details** and **words that appeal to the senses** to bring your description to life.

322

Read the following descriptive paragraph. Notice all the specific details that appeal to the senses.

The Food Attic

OVERALL
FEELING

The attic was a lovely place to play. The large, round, colored pumpkins made beau-

COLORS
AND OTHER
SIGHTS

tiful chairs and tables. The red peppers and the onions dangled overhead. The hams and venison hung in their paper wrappings.

SMELLS AND
TASTES

All the bunches of dried herbs, the spicy herbs for cooking and the bitter herbs for medicine, gave the place a dusty-spicy smell.

SOUND

Often the wind howled outside with a cold and lonesome sound. In the attic, though, Laura and Mary played house with the squashes and the pumpkins and everything was snug and cosy.

—LAURA INGALLS WILDER, *LITTLE HOUSE IN THE BIG WOODS*

*E*XERCISE 2 *Listing Specific Details*

Under each subject, list four specific details that appeal to the senses of sight, sound, taste or smell, and touch.

EXAMPLE   playing in football game
POSSIBLE   Sight: opposing players looking at you
ANSWER   Sound: cleats on shoes tapping ground
           Taste: rubbery taste of mouthguard
           Touch: feel of sliding in mud

1. a circus
2. a movie theater
3. the school gym
4. a zoo
5. a busy street
6. a spring day
7. a stormy night
8. a crowded restaurant
9. a bus
10. a deep forest

Space Order and Transitions

To help your reader piece together your descriptive picture, present your ideas in some logical order. One good order for descriptions is space order. For example, you might describe the circus clowns nearest to you before you describe the clowns on the other side of the arena.

20d   **Space order** arranges details according to their location. **Transitions** show the relationship of the details.

The chart below shows different kinds of space order.

SPACE ORDER	TRANSITIONS
near to far (or reverse)	nearest, next to, beyond, farther, across, behind, in the distance
top to bottom (or reverse)	at the top, in the middle, lower, below, at the bottom, above, higher
side to side	at the left (right), in the middle, next to, at one end, to the west
inside to outside (or reverse)	within, in the center, on the inside (outside), the next layer

The following paragraph uses bottom-to-top order. The transitions move from the bottom of the hill to the top.

The House of Mysteries

The old house clung uneasily **to the side of the hill. At the bottom of the hill** an old dirt road ran through clumps of goldenrod and Queen Anne's lace. **Between the road and the hill** lay a field of clover. The hill itself was bare and rocky. **At the very top of the hill** was a thin cluster of trees that looked like either maple or oak. The dark, lonely house seemed in conflict with all living things.

EXERCISE 3 Understanding Space Order

The diagram below shows a side view of the human eye. Look at it carefully. Then write the following paragraph. Fill in the blanks with the correct transitions. Choose the transitions from the following list.

on the outside	behind
between	deeper inside
in the middle	next to

   The human eye is a miracle of living tissues. _____ is the cornea, a thin clear layer of protection. Next is the iris, _____ the cornea. The iris is the colored part of your eye. The pupil is _____ of the iris. The pupil controls how much light enters your eye. _____ the eye is the lens, which sends light images to the retina. The retina is _____ the lens. Nerve cells in the retina send messages to the brain through the optic nerve. The optic nerve is _____ the eye and the brain. These layers of living tissue help the brain "see" the world.

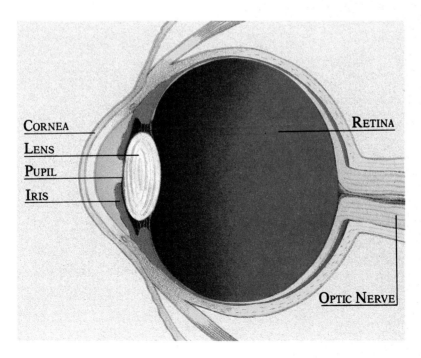

CORNEA

LENS

PUPIL

IRIS

RETINA

OPTIC NERVE

EXERCISE 4 On Your Own

In your Writer's Notebook, write down memorable sights, sounds, smells, tastes, and feelings from each day. These may give you ideas for descriptive paragraphs.

Writing Extra

Another way to express an overall feeling about a subject is to write a poem. In the following activity, you become the subject of your poem. Use strong, simple words to express your feelings about nature. When you finish, give your poem a descriptive title. Read it aloud. Draw a picture that captures the feelings you expressed.

LINE 1 Think of an animal you are most like. Add an adjective to describe that animal.

LINE 2 Think of something in nature you are most like—a lake, a mountain, a tree, a flower. Add an adjective to describe it.

LINE 3 Think of a time of day—morning, noon, evening. Add a color to describe it.

LINE 4 Think of a season of the year and add a descriptive adjective to it.

LINE 5 Complete the following phrase: Boy (or girl) who likes _____.

The following example shows you how to write your own nature poem.

Stillness

Quick squirrel

Majestic tree

Golden afternoon

Chilly fall

Girl who likes silence.

Writing Descriptive Paragraphs

During some parts of the writing process you can let your mind relax and your thoughts run free. At other times you must hold back and think about your reader's needs. Writing is a process that moves back and forth between different kinds of activities. The rest of this chapter will give you practice in the process of writing descriptive paragraphs.

Writing a Newspaper Advertisement

Imagine that you own the bicycle in the picture below. You want to sell it and use the money to buy a new one. Follow the steps below to write a newspaper advertisement for the bicycle.

EXERCISE 5 Describing an Object

Step 1: Prewriting
Look at the picture carefully. Brainstorm a list of details you could use to describe it. Include colors, shapes, feelings, and sounds. Think about what might interest a buyer. Then study your notes and make an organized plan for writing your advertisement.

Step 2: Writing
Use your plan to write an advertisement in the form of a descriptive paragraph. Be sure to present your details in a logical order.

Step 3: Sharing Your Work
Exchange papers with a classmate. Read your partner's paragraph. Tell about the parts you like as well as the parts that could be improved. Does your partner's description get you interested in the bike? When your paper is returned to you, make any changes that would make it better.

Writing a Character Sketch

Think of a character you read about in a book. Complete the following activities to write a one-paragraph description—or sketch—of that character.

EXERCISE 6 Describing a Character

Step 1: Prewriting
Write freely for five minutes. Try to remember details about how the character looks, talks, acts, and thinks. Use your freewriting notes to plan your character sketch. Arrange your details in a logical order.

Step 2: Writing
Use your plan to write the first draft of a paragraph describing your character. Try to make your character come alive through the specific details you show.

Step 3: Sharing Your Work
Exchange papers with a classmate. Read your partner's work carefully. Draw a picture of the character that your partner described. Give the picture and the first draft back to your partner. Then look at the picture your partner drew. Does it show your character the way you tried to describe him or her? Revise your paragraph to make your character easy to picture.

328

EXERCISE 7 *Revising a Descriptive Paragraph*

Use the Revision Checklist that follows to revise one of the descriptive paragraphs from Exercises 5 or 6.

Checklist for Revising Descriptive Paragraphs

Checking Your Paragraph

1. Does your topic sentence introduce the subject and suggest an overall feeling about it? (*See page 321.*)
2. Do your supporting sentences give details that appeal to the senses? (*See pages 322–323.*)
3. Do all of your sentences relate to the main idea? (*See pages 270–275.*)
4. Are your details in either space order or another logical order? (*See page 324.*)
5. Did you use transitions? (*See page 324.*)
6. Does your concluding sentence sum up the overall feeling and add a strong ending? (*See page 321.*)

Checking Your Sentences

7. Did you combine related sentences to avoid too many short, choppy sentences in a row? (*See pages 247–254.*)
8. Did you vary the beginnings of your sentences? (*See page 256.*)
9. Did you avoid rambling sentences? (*See page 258.*)

Checking Your Words

10. Did you use specific, lively words? (*See page 231.*)
11. Did you use words that appeal to the senses? (*See pages 235–241.*)

EXERCISE 8 *Editing a Descriptive Paragraph*

Use the Editing Checklist on page 291 to make a final copy of the paragraph you revised for Exercise 7.

EXERCISE 9 *On Your Own*

In your Writer's Notebook, write a description of a room you especially like.

Spotlight on Writing

A **Describing a Food.** Choose one of the foods in the picture or another of your choice. Brainstorm a list of details that could be used to describe it. Then, without naming your food, write a paragraph describing it. Use the Steps for Writing on page 333 to help you. See if your classmates can guess what you are describing.

PURPOSE To describe a food
AUDIENCE People trying to guess what it is

B **Describing a Character.** Write a description of a cartoon character. Think about how the character looks, moves, talks, and dresses. Describe your character so clearly that a reader would be able to draw a picture.

PURPOSE To describe a cartoon character
AUDIENCE A person younger than you

C **Describing a Place.** If you could have a secret hide-away, where would it be? What would it look like? How would it feel to be in it? Write a description of your hideaway. Use your imagination to think of the details.

PURPOSE   To describe an imaginary hideaway
AUDIENCE   Your classmates

D **Describing to Give Information.** Use the notes that follow to write a descriptive paragraph about Benin City, capital of the ancient African empire. Use the Steps for Writing on page 333 for help.

PURPOSE   To describe the ancient city
AUDIENCE   Social studies classmates

- huge, splendid city
- wide earthen avenue ran through city
- cross streets divided city into squares
- streets were spotless
- houses along street were made of red mud
- houses were also spotless
- center of city was leader's palace
- palace as large as a whole town
- bronze figures adorned walls of great palace
- Benin City was the jewel of the rain forest

E   **Describing to Express Your Feelings.** Choose a subject—a person, place, or thing—that makes you feel very happy. Write a paragraph describing that subject. Use the Steps for Writing on page 333 to help you.

F   **Writing from Your Writer's Notebook.** Choose one of the subjects you listed in your writer's notebook from Exercise 4. Then describe it, using specific details and words that appeal to the senses. Use the Steps for Writing on page 333 to help you. Then exchange papers with a partner. Use the Checklist for Revising on page 329 to help you revise each other's sentences.

G   **Ideas for Writing Descriptive Paragraphs.** Write a descriptive paragraph on one of the following subjects or one of your own. Follow the Steps for Writing a Descriptive Paragraph on page 333.

1. a locker room	6. a concert
2. Thanksgiving	7. a long bus ride
3. Saturday morning	8. a crowded store
4. an attic	9. the flower shop
5. a bowling alley	10. a doctor's office

Steps for Writing
a Descriptive Paragraph

Prewriting
1. Think about your purpose and audience.
2. Make a list of possible subjects including scenes, objects, and persons.
3. Choose a subject that interests you and suits your purpose and audience.
4. Limit your subject so that it can be covered in one paragraph.
5. Brainstorm a list of details that come to mind when you think about your subject.
6. Arrange your notes in space order or another logical order.

Writing
7. Write a topic sentence that expresses an overall feeling about your subject.
8. Use your prewriting notes to write supporting sentences that bring your subject to life.
9. Add a concluding sentence that sums up the overall feeling and adds a strong ending.

Revising
10. Put your paper aside for a while. Then come back to it with a fresh eye. Use the Checklist for Revising Descriptive Paragraphs on page 329 to improve your work.

Editing
11. Use the Editing Checklist on page 291 to prepare a final, polished paragraph.

21

Writing Explanatory Paragraphs

Thousands of books are written each year to explain different subjects to readers. This kind of writing, called explanatory writing, is the kind used in your textbooks. It is also the kind of writing you do most often in school, especially in reports. In one type of explanatory writing the purpose is to give information. A second purpose of explanatory writing is to give directions. Both writing purposes are explanatory.

21a An **explanatory paragraph** explains with facts and examples or gives directions.

Your Writer's Notebook

In your journal, write freely to complete each statement. Put down as many different answers as you can. Use these ideas later when you write explanatory paragraphs.

1. I know a lot about . . .
2. I like to read books about . . .
3. I know how to . . .

Explanatory Paragraph Structure

When you write explanatory paragraphs, you are teaching your readers about something. In the following paragraph, the writer is giving information about killer snakes. The teaching is clear because the writer has a definite plan. The structure of the paragraph helps a reader follow the information easily.

Snakes That Squeeze

TOPIC
SENTENCE
STATES
MAIN IDEA

SUPPORTING
SENTENCES
GIVE DETAILS

CONCLUDING
SENTENCE
SUMS UP

Both of the world's biggest snakes are constrictors, snakes that squeeze their victims. Anacondas and pythons wrap their long bodies around animals. They squeeze so hard that they keep the animal from breathing. In just a few minutes a giant constrictor can kill a large mammal. Although they are not poisonous, these giant snakes are deadly.

The purpose of the following explanatory paragraph is to give directions for making popcorn. Notice how clearly the steps are given.

Fluffy Every Time

TOPIC
SENTENCE
STATES
MAIN IDEA

SUPPORTING
SENTENCES
GIVE STEPS
IN ORDER

CONCLUDING
SENTENCE
SUMS UP

If you want to treat yourself to a bowl of warm, fluffy popcorn, follow these simple steps. First add cooking oil and three kernels of popcorn to a covered pan. Heat over a medium flame until the kernels pop. Then add the rest of the popcorn, only enough to cover the bottom of the pan. Replace the lid and turn the heat up to high. When the popping slows down, remove the pan from the heat and let it sit a few more minutes. While it sits, the last few unpopped kernels will pop. Popcorn cooked by this method will be fluffy every time.

The chart below tells the purpose of each sentence in an explanatory paragraph.

21b

Structure of an Explanatory Paragraph

1. The topic sentence states a main idea based on fact.
2. The supporting sentences provide facts, examples, or steps in a process.
3. The concluding sentence sums up the main idea and adds a strong ending.

EXERCISE 1 *Identifying Explanatory Topic Sentences*

Number your paper 1 to 5. Read each topic sentence. Then write *gives information* or *gives directions* to tell the purpose of each one.

EXAMPLE   Sleet is a combination of snow and rain.
ANSWER   gives information

1. Making ice cream is a fun family project.
2. Halley's comet, a fireball of dust and ice, returns every 76 years.
3. With the right materials and a little patience, you can build a window perch for your cat.
4. We know that there are two types of twins—identical and fraternal.
5. The best way to get to the park is by bus.

Ways to Explain

The types of supporting details you use depend on your writing purpose. What questions does your topic sentence raise? Use details that will answer those questions.

Facts and Examples.   When giving information, you will probably use facts and examples to explain your subject. Study the following topic sentence. Then read the facts and examples used to support it.

TOPIC
SENTENCE
Officials use a set of arm signals to call plays in a football game.

FACTS AND
EXAMPLES
• Raised arms mean a touchdown or field goal.
• Standing sideways with right arm pointed forward means first down.
• Hands touching shoulders mean illegally touched ball.
• Hands crossed over the head mean time out.

21c   Use **facts** and **examples** when giving information.

EXERCISE 2 Listing Facts and Examples

Write each topic sentence. Then, under each one, list three facts or examples to back it up.

EXAMPLE   Wild animals are never far away.
POSSIBLE   Squirrels and wild birds live even in cities.
ANSWER   Many forest preserves contain wild animals.
           Zoos keep wild animals close to cities.

1. Each color on a stoplight means something to drivers.
2. Many holidays have their own special songs.
3. Good nutrition will help you stay healthy.
4. Most television shows take place in cities.
5. The hottest time of the year is August.

Steps in a Process. When your purpose is to give directions, you will be telling your reader what to do step by step. Read the following topic sentence.

TOPIC SENTENCE   You can make a simple stethoscope to listen to your heartbeat.

A reader will wonder, "How can I do this?" The supporting sentences give all the steps in the process. Notice that the steps are given in the order they need to be done.

STEPS IN PROCESS
- Begin by gathering all the materials you will need for this project.
- These are a funnel and rubber tubing.
- The tubing should be long enough to reach from your heart to your ear.
- Attach the rubber tubing to the narrow end of the funnel.
- Place the wide end of the funnel against your chest and listen for your heartbeat.

21d   Use **steps in a process** in the supporting sentences of a paragraph that gives directions.

EXERCISE 3   Listing Steps in a Process

Write each of the following topic sentences on your paper. Under each one, list the steps in the process the reader will have to follow.

EXAMPLE   Everybody can make static electricity.
POSSIBLE ANSWER
- Wait for a day that is not humid.
- Walk across a wool rug, dragging your feet back and forth.
- Touch a metal doorknob for a mild shock.

1. There's a good way to go from my house to school.
2. Just about anyone can draw a good face.
3. Dividing 46 by 4 is not a difficult process.
4. You can make a good hobo's costume from things around the house.

Logical Order and Transitions

Readers will understand and remember more of what you write if you present it in an order that makes sense. In explanatory paragraphs, two kinds of logical order are (1) order of importance or size and (2) sequence order.

Order of Importance or Size. When giving information, many writers arrange their ideas in the order of least to most or most to least. In the following paragraph, the details are arranged in the order of lowest to highest.

Rating the Movies

TOPIC
SENTENCE

ORDER OF
LOWEST
RATING TO
HIGHEST

CONCLUDING
SENTENCE

Movie critics often use stars as a code for rating the movies. When you see movie advertisements in newspapers, look for the rating. A movie given half a star or even one star is usually not worth seeing. A two star movie has some good features but probably as many drawbacks. A three star movie is well worth seeing. It is probably better than most movies made, even though it may be weak in parts. Critics save four stars for only the very best movies. It is the highest rating most critics give. Watching the star rating of movies may save you wasted time and money at the theater.

> **21e** In paragraphs that give information, use **order of importance or size**. Arrange the details in the order of most to least or least to most. Use **transitions** to help your reader follow your logical order.

Transitions Used with Order of Importance or Size		
first	larger	smaller
next	even larger	more important
finally	largest	most important

EXERCISE 4 *Arranging Details in Order of Size*

Write the following topic sentence. Then number your paper 1 to 5. Write the supporting details below in the order of least to most.

The five tallest buildings in the United States are located in Chicago and New York.

- New York's World Trade Center
  —1350 feet (411 m)
- Sears Tower in Chicago
  —1454 feet (443 m)
- Chicago's Amoco Building
  —1136 feet (346 m)
- New York's Empire State Building
  —1250 feet high (381 m)
- John Hancock Building in Chicago
  —1127 feet (343 m)

Sequence Order. When giving directions, the most logical order to use is sequence order. In sequence order, steps are arranged in the order that the reader would do them. The following paragraph is arranged in sequence order. Transitions are printed in heavy type.

How To Bathe a Dog

TOPIC
SENTENCE

STEPS IN
SEQUENCE
ORDER

CONCLUDING
SENTENCE

With a little planning, a dog's bath can go smoothly. **First**, fill the tub about two inches high with warm water. **Next**, place the dog standing in the water. Hold on to the dog gently to make sure he doesn't run off. Using a sprayer attachment, wet the dog with warm water. **Next**, rub on a small amount of dog shampoo and work up a lather. **Then**, rinse the dog completely with a warm water spray. **Finally**, towel dry the dog to remove extra water. Let him stay in a warm place until he is completely dry. Every six months or so, give your dog a bath to keep him sweet and clean.

340

In paragraphs that give directions, use **sequence order** with transitions.

The transitions in the following chart will help your reader follow the steps in order.

Transitions for Sequence Order			
first	before	while	finally
next	after	as soon as	as a last step
then	when	second	now

EXERCISE 5 *Listing Steps in Sequence Order*

The directions below tell how to make a nature mobile. However, they are out of order. Rewrite them so they are in proper sequence. Save your work for Exercise 6.

- Brush a thin coat of glue over each nature item to preserve it.
- Tie the strings to the bottom of a hanger.
- Gather four or five interesting nature items—leaves, cones, nuts, and small branches.
- At the top of each item, attach a piece of string and glue it on.
- Let the items dry.

EXERCISE 6 Adding Transitions

Write a paragraph about how to make a nature mobile. Use your work from Exercise 5 and the following topic and concluding sentences. Add transitions where necessary.

TOPIC
SENTENCE   You can capture the beauty of nature by making a nature mobile.

CONCLUDING   Your completed mobile will make a colorful
SENTENCE   decoration for your room.

EXERCISE 7 On Your Own

Write an advertisement for yourself. Include all the different things you know about and can do. List your ideas in some logical order. Illustrate your ad.

Writing Extra

Sometimes when one thing happens it causes something else to happen. Cause-and-effect paragraphs explain this chain reaction. Read the following.

All For an Untied Shoelace

Everything can be traced back to my left gym shoe with the untied lace. I was walking back from the store when I tripped and dropped a bottle of milk. A dog wandering past stopped and licked up the milk. That day cost me the price of the milk, a week's pain in my ankle, and a lot of embarrassment. There was one good result, though. The dog followed me home and stayed!

Try writing your own cause-and-effect paragraph. The following ideas may help you think of subjects.

1. the reasons you do well in school
2. how a friend or family member has changed your life
3. money you've earned and how you've spent it

Writing Explanatory Paragraphs

You will be asked to write explanations or instructions many times in your life, especially in school. The following activities will give you practice in explaining.

Writing a Newspaper Feature Story

A simple news story gives only the facts about an event. It answers the questions *Who? What? When? Where? Why?* and *How?* A feature story, in contrast, contains more in-depth information. It often tells the personal side of the news, called human interest. Writing a feature story is good practice in explaining.

EXERCISE 8 Writing a Human Interest Story

Imagine you have been asked to write a human interest story for your school newspaper. The theme is "Someone You Should Know." Follow the steps below.

Step 1: Prewriting
Think about people you know who are special. Maybe they stand out because they have a special talent or a handicap they overcame. Choose one person who stands apart from all the others. Write his or her name and list all the things about that person that a reader might like to know. Arrange your details in order of importance.

Step 2: Writing
Write a topic sentence that introduces your special person to your readers. Then use your notes to write the paragraph body. Add a concluding sentence.

Step 3: Sharing Your Work
Exchange papers with a partner. After reading your partner's work, tell him or her the things you liked about the paragraph. Also tell what could be improved.

Writing a How-To Paragraph

Giving your directions clearly and in order is the key to writing good how-to paragraphs. Practice writing directions with the following activity.

EXERCISE 9 *Writing to Give Directions*

You have thought of a secret code for your club. You must now explain the code to the club members and show them how to use it to write secret messages. Follow the steps below to write your paragraph.

Step 1: Prewriting
The key to this code is simple. The words in the secret message are those that come *after* the name of an animal. Other words are added just to make the code confusing. These are called misleads. Study the example below. The real message is printed in blue. In your notes, jot down the steps for writing messages with this code.

Step 2: Writing
Use your notes to write a paragraph that gives directions on how to use the code.

Step 3: Sharing Your Work
Show your paragraph to someone who has not seen the example in this book. Are your directions clear enough to follow? If not, revise your work until it makes sense.

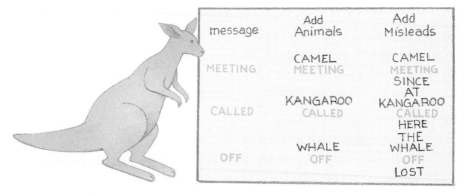

message	Add Animals	Add Misleads
MEETING	CAMEL MEETING	CAMEL MEETING SINCE AT
CALLED	KANGAROO CALLED	KANGAROO CALLED HERE THE
OFF	WHALE OFF	WHALE OFF LOST

*E*XERCISE 10 *Revising Explanatory Paragraphs*

Use the following checklist to revise your paragraphs from Exercises 8 and 9.

Checklist for Revising Explanatory Paragraphs

Checking Your Paragraph

1. Does your topic sentence state a main idea based on fact? (*See page 336.*)
2. If your paragraph gives information, did you use facts and examples? (*See page 337.*)
3. If your paragraph gives directions, did you use steps in a process? (*See page 338.*)
4. Are your details arranged in order of importance or size, sequence order, or some other logical order? (*See pages 339–341.*)
5. Did you use transitions? (*See pages 339–341.*)
6. Does your concluding sentence sum up the paragraph and add a strong ending? (*See page 336.*)

Checking Your Sentences

7. Did you combine short, choppy sentences into longer, more interesting ones? (*See pages 247–254.*)
8. Did you vary the beginnings of your sentences? (*See page 256.*)
9. Did you avoid rambling sentences? (*See page 258.*)

Checking Your Words

10. Did you use clear, specific words? (*See page 231.*)

---

*E*XERCISE 11 *Editing Explanatory Paragraphs*

Use the Editing Checklist on page 291 to edit your revised paragraphs from Exercise 10.

*E*XERCISE 12 *On Your Own*

Write an explanatory paragraph on a subject from your science, health, or social studies class. Follow the Steps for Writing an Explanatory Paragraph on page 349.

345

*S*potlight on *W*riting

A **Understanding Explanatory Paragraphs.** Tell what kind of supporting details you would use with each of the following topic sentences. Give your answer by writing *facts and examples* or *steps in a process* after each number.

1. You can teach a parakeet to talk if you follow a few simple steps.
2. Through history, volcanoes have caused great destruction all over the world.
3. If you want to develop strong arm muscles, go through the following set of exercises five times a week.
4. Some plants as well as some animals are in danger of becoming extinct.
5. There are many different styles of telephones and each has a different use.

B **Using Logical Order and Transitions.** Use the topic sentence and the notes below to write an explanatory paragraph. First arrange the details in the order suggested in the topic sentence. Then write the paragraph using complete sentences and transitions. Add a concluding sentence to complete your paragraph.

TOPIC SENTENCE   The three main types of clouds are called cirrus, cumulus, and stratus.
- stratus clouds are low
- cumulus clouds are low
- stratus clouds appear as layers
- cirrus clouds are high in the sky
- cumulus clouds look like fluffy popcorn
- cumulus clouds have flat bottoms
- cirrus clouds are sometimes called "mare's tails" because of their shape

C **Writing a Paragraph to Give Information.** Use the facts provided to write an explanatory paragraph that suits the following purpose and audience.

PURPOSE To explain how a koala bear climbs a tree
AUDIENCE People who have never seen a koala

Notes
- koalas have strong hand-like paws
- sharp claws dig into branch
- second finger is almost like second thumb—lets them grab branches
- when climbing, koala reaches front legs up and grabs tree trunk
- then brings hind legs up
- from then on pushes off from hind legs

Step 1
Make front approach.

Step 2
Execute pike position.

Step 3
Extend and enter water.

D **Writing a Paragraph to Give Directions.** Study the pictures and notes above. Use them to write an explanatory paragraph for the following purpose and audience.

PURPOSE   To give directions for making a dive
AUDIENCE   Someone who does not know how to dive

E **Ideas for Explanatory Paragraphs.** Write an explanatory paragraph on one of the following subjects or one of your own. Follow the Steps for Writing an Explanatory Paragraph on page 349.

1. what makes it rain
2. the rules of a club you belong to
3. how work is shared around your house
4. how to earn money during the summer
5. what happens to a letter after you mail it

348

Steps for Writing
an Explanatory Paragraph

Prewriting
1. Consider your purpose and audience.
2. Make a list of possible subjects and choose one that interests you the most.
3. Limit your subject so that it can be adequately covered in one paragraph.
4. Write down everything that comes to mind when you think about your subject. If your purpose is to give information, list facts and examples. If your purpose is to give directions, list steps in the process.
5. Arrange your notes in logical order.

Writing
6. Write a topic sentence suited to your purpose.
7. Use your prewriting notes to write the supporting sentences.
8. Add a concluding sentence that summarizes the main idea and adds a strong ending.

Revising
9. Put your paper aside for a while. Then use the Checklist for Revising Explanatory Paragraphs on page 345 to make it as clear as possible.

Editing
10. Use the Editing Checklist on page 291 to prepare a final, polished paragraph.

22

Writing Opinion Paragraphs

People often write to express opinions. For example, citizens write to elected officials to state an opinion on a current event. Also, a cousin may write you a letter giving his or her opinion about a new movie. When you write an opinion paragraph, your goal is to let others know how you think. You also want to persuade them that your opinion is reasonable.

22a ▸ An **opinion paragraph** states an opinion and uses facts, examples, and reasons to persuade readers.

Your Writer's Notebook

To help you think of opinions to write about, complete each of the following statements. Include as many answers as you can.

1. It's really unfair when . . .
2. If I could, I'd change . . .
3. Some good things about television are . . .
4. The best places for vacations are . . .
5. The best radio stations are . . .

Understanding Opinion Paragraphs

Your purpose in writing opinion paragraphs is to persuade. Of course you do not need to persuade people who already agree with you. Your job in writing opinion paragraphs, then, is to try to persuade those who *disagree* with you. Clear thinking and strong reasons will help you convince your readers.

The purpose of the following paragraph is to persuade young athletes to concentrate on schoolwork. The opinion is expressed in the first sentence. The rest of the paragraph backs up the opinion with reasons. The concluding sentence sums up and adds a strong ending.

Young Athletes

TOPIC
SENTENCE

THREE
GOOD
REASONS
GIVEN
IN
SUPPORTING
SENTENCES

CONCLUDING
SENTENCE

Students who excel in a sport should get a good education and not count on a career in sports. First of all, very few people actually play professional sports. Second, even those lucky enough to become professionals may not be able to play for long. An injury may cut their career short. Finally, even a healthy sports career does not usually last a lifetime. A good education will prepare an athlete for a rewarding job after sports.

The chart below describes the role of each sentence in an opinion paragraph.

22b

Structure of an Opinion Paragraph

1. The topic sentence states an opinion.
2. The supporting sentences use facts, examples, and reasons to back up the opinions.
3. The concluding sentence sums up the paragraph and adds a strong ending.

EXERCISE 1 *Writing Topic Sentences for Opinion Paragraphs*

Number your paper 1–10. For each subject, write a topic sentence stating an opinion.

EXAMPLE   the library
POSSIBLE   Our city's public library should stay open for
ANSWER   longer hours.

1. pets
2. earning money
3. taking lessons
4. growing up
5. camping
6. pollution
7. pool safety
8. computers
9. wild animals
10. commercials

Facts and Opinions

Challenge your readers' opinions by offering good solid facts, examples, and reasons as proof.

22c ▸ **Facts** are statements that can be proven. **Opinions** are judgments that vary from person to person.

The proper place for an opinion is in the topic sentence. After that, avoid trying to use opinions as proof.

22d ▸ Use **facts and examples,** not opinions, to convince readers.

EXERCISE 2 *Recognizing Facts and Opinions*

Number your paper 1 to 5. For each statement write *F* if it is a fact and *O* if it is an opinion.

1. *White Fang* is a better book than *Call of the Wild*.
2. I think polluted air looks ugly.
3. George Lucas directed *Star Wars*.
4. Bicyclists should always wear helmets.
5. Abraham Lincoln was the sixteenth president of the United States.

Order of Importance and Transitions

Most opinion paragraphs use order of importance to arrange the supporting points. The most convincing reasons are presented either first or last.

22e Arrange your supporting points in **order of importance.** Use **transitions** to show the importance of each idea.

Transitions for Order of Importance

also	for example	more important
another	in addition	most important
finally	in the first place	second of all
first	in the same way	third

In the paragraph below, does the most important idea come first or last? Check the transitions in heavy type to find out which is the most important idea.

Put Out That Fire!

TOPIC
SENTENCE:
OPINION

SUPPORTING
POINTS IN
ORDER OF
IMPORTANCE

CONCLUDING
SENTENCE:
GOOD ENDING

Everyone using the forest should try to prevent a forest fire. **First of all,** forest fires cost time and money to put out. **Second,** forest fires can destroy valuable timber along with other plants important in the forest. **Most important,** forest fires kill wild animals and wipe out their homes. If everyone were more careful in the forest, 76,000 fires a year could be prevented.

353

EXERCISE 3 On Your Own

Bring in an advertisement from a magazine. Be prepared to identify all the opinions in the ad. Also point out any facts it may contain. Explain how the advertiser is trying to persuade you to buy the product.

Writing Extra

Think of an opinion you hold. Then think of someone you know who would disagree with it. Imagine a conversation between you and that person. Write out that conversation in the form of a short play. The following example may give you ideas for your scene.

A Zoo Story

ME: It isn't right to put wild animals in cages.

STAN: Well, at least here they don't have to worry about getting eaten or dying of hunger.

ME: But that's not why we have zoos. We have them because we like to look at the animals.

STAN: Well, would you like it if there were no zoos?

ME: No, but maybe we could watch them on film.

STAN: I guess we just disagree, huh?

ME: I guess.

Writing Opinion Paragraphs

The ability to state opinions and back them up will help you convince people throughout your life. Build your persuasive powers with the following activities.

Writing a Review

A review is an opinion about the quality of something. Reviews usually discuss both strong and weak points. They also usually make a recommendation, telling readers whether or not they should see a movie, buy a book, or eat at a certain restaurant.

EXERCISE 4 Writing a Restaurant Review

Imagine that you have been asked to write a review of a restaurant. Follow the steps below.

Step 1: Prewriting
Think of a restaurant where you have eaten. Jot down your overall impression of it. Then make two columns on your paper. In the first column, write all the things you liked about the restaurant. In the second column, list the restaurant's weak points. Think of the following: tastiness and quantity of the food, service, price, and décor.

Step 2: Writing
Use your notes to write your restaurant review. Include a topic sentence that states an overall opinion of the restaurant. Let your supporting sentences tell the strong and weak points. Your concluding sentence should tell whether you recommend the restaurant or not.

Step 3: Sharing Your Work
Exchange papers with a partner. Tell your partner whether his or her review was convincing. Listen to the comments about your review. Make any necessary improvements on your paper.

Writing a Newspaper Editorial

Newspapers pride themselves on sticking to the facts. They do, however, include a special section for opinions, called the editorial page. Editorials are short pieces that express opinions and back them up with facts.

*E*XERCISE 5 *Writing an Editorial*

Write an editorial for your school or local newspaper. Follow the steps outlined below.

Step 1: Prewriting
Look at the picture on this page. What opinions does it bring to mind? Write out as many opinions as you can. Then choose the one you feel strongest about. Jot down reasons for your opinion. Arrange your reasons in order of importance.

Step 2: Writing
Use your notes to write an editorial expressing your opinion and backing it up with reasons.

Step 3: Sharing Your Work
Exchange papers with a partner. Check your partner's work to be sure that facts, examples, and reasons rather than opinions are used to back up the topic sentence. Make any necessary changes to your paper.

EXERCISE 6 Revising an Opinion Paragraph

Use the following checklist to revise your paragraphs from Exercises 4 and 5.

Checklist for Revising Opinion Paragraphs

Checking Your Paragraph

1. Does your topic sentence state an opinion? (*See page 351.*)
2. Did you use facts, examples, and reasons to back up your opinion? (*See page 352.*)
3. Are your supporting points organized in order of importance or another logical order? (*See page 353.*)
4. Did you use transitions? (*See page 353.*)
5. Does your concluding sentence add a strong ending? (*See page 351.*)

Checking Your Sentences

6. Did you combine short, choppy sentences into longer, more interesting ones? (*See pages 247–254.*)
7. Did you vary the beginnings of your sentences? (*See page 256.*)
8. Did you avoid rambling sentences? (*See page 258.*)

Checking Your Words

9. Did you use specific words? (*See page 231.*)
10. Did you use words that appeal to the senses? (*See pages 235–241.*)

EXERCISE 7 Editing Opinion Paragraphs

Use the Editing Checklist on page 291 to edit your paragraphs from Exercises 4 and 5.

EXERCISE 8 On Your Own

Look for editorials you strongly agree or disagree with, and clip them out of the newspaper. Keep them to use as ideas for opinion paragraphs.

Spotlight on Writing

A **Recognizing Facts and Opinions.** Some of the following statements are opinions. Others are facts. Number your paper 1 to 10. For each statement write *F* if it is a fact and *O* if it is an opinion.

1. Solids, liquids, and gases are the three states of matter known to science.
2. Glass is made from sand.
3. Some insects are poisonous.
4. Everyone should have a chance to be a scout.
5. All new cars today have seat belts.
6. Everybody should wear a seat belt because seat belts save lives.
7. I think there are black holes in space.
8. Bananas grow in clusters on trees.
9. Hospitals should use more volunteers to help care for patients.
10. Winter is the best season.

B **Writing an Opinion Paragraph.** The following notes give information about exercise. Read the information to form an opinion. Then write an opinion paragraph to suit the following purpose and audience.

PURPOSE   To recommend ways to stay healthy
AUDIENCE   People who do not now exercise

BENEFITS
- vigorous exercise keeps heart and lungs healthy
- exercise burns calories to help control weight
- exercise releases chemicals in the brain that make you feel good

DRAWBACKS
- exercise takes time
- overly difficult exercises can damage muscles and cause pain
- exercise can be harmful for people with certain health problems

C **Writing a Royal Decree.** Imagine that you have been appointed king or queen of the world for one day. You can make one change in the world and one change only. Write an opinion paragraph telling what you would decree (make into law) with your royal power.

PURPOSE   To tell about a change that needs to be made
AUDIENCE   Your loyal subjects around the world

D **Writing from Your Writer's Notebook.** Choose one of the opinions you wrote about in your writer's notebook. Then write an opinion paragraph backing it up with facts, examples, or reasons.

E **Ideas for Writing an Opinion Paragraph.** Write an opinion paragraph on one of the following subjects or one of your own. Follow the Steps for Writing an Opinion Paragraph on page 360.

1. why manners are important
2. the right amount of homework
3. great television shows
4. the best kind of music
5. kindness to animals
6. bicycle safety
7. school rules
8. friendship
9. allowances
10. school vacations

Steps for Writing
an Opinion Paragraph

Prewriting

1. Think about your purpose and audience.
2. List some opinions on subjects you feel strongly about.
3. Choose a subject that interests you and that suits your purpose and audience.
4. Limit your subject so that it can be covered in one paragraph.
5. Brainstorm a list of facts, examples, and reasons that could support your opinion.
6. If necessary, find information in the library.
7. Arrange your notes in order of importance.

Writing

8. Write a topic sentence that states an opinion.
9. Use your prewriting notes to add supporting sentences with clear transitions.
10. Add a concluding sentence that sums up and provides a strong ending.

Revising

11. Put your paper aside for a while. Then pretend you disagree with your own opinion as you read over the paper. Use the Checklist for Revising Opinion Paragraphs on page 357 to improve your paragraph.

Editing

12. Use the Editing Checklist on page 291 to prepare a final, polished paragraph.

Standardized Test

Directions: Decide which order is best for the sentences in each group. In the appropriate row on your answer sheet, fill in the circle containing the letter that shows the best order.

SAMPLE (1) Last, let the soup simmer for an hour.
(2) This is how to make soup.
(3) Next, put in soup mix and vegetables.
(4) First, boil a quart of water.

      A 1 - 3 - 4 - 2   **C** 2 - 3 - 4 - 1
      B 2 - 4 - 3 - 1   **D** 3 - 4 - 1 - 2

ANSWER Ⓐ Ⓑ Ⓒ Ⓓ

1. (1) Today was a hard day.
   (2) Then, I was late to school.
   (3) First, I woke up late.
   (4) Later, I was even late for dinner.

       A 1 - 3 - 2 - 4   **C** 3 - 2 - 1 - 4
       B 2 - 4 - 3 - 1   **D** 4 - 3 - 2 - 1

2. (1) Next, start the engine.
   (2) With the engine running, put it in gear.
   (3) Finally, look both ways and pull out.
   (4) To drive a car, first put on your seat belt.

       A 1 - 4 - 3 - 2   **C** 4 - 1 - 2 - 3
       B 2 - 1 - 3 - 4   **D** 1 - 2 - 4 - 3

3 (1) After math comes science.
   (2) Math is my first class.
   (3) After science, I go to gym.
   (4) At the end of the day, I have French.

       A 1 - 3 - 4 - 2   **C** 3 - 1 - 2 - 4
       B 2 - 1 - 3 - 4   **D** 4 - 1 - 2 - 3

4 (1) Then the phone rang again at 7:00 A.M.
   (2) I hung up the phone and went back to bed.
   (3) The phone rang at 6:00 A.M.
   (4) I talked on the phone until 6:15 A.M.

       A 1 - 4 - 3 - 2   **C** 4 - 1 - 2 - 3
       B 2 - 1 - 3 - 4   **D** 3 - 4 - 2 - 1

361

5. (1) Next pull the loose threads off the edges.
   (2) This is how to make a place mat.
   (3) First cut a square piece of burlap.
   (4) Finally, iron the place mat.

   A 2 - 3 - 1 - 4   **C** 3 - 2 - 1 - 4
   B 1 - 2 - 3 - 4   **D** 4 - 3 - 1 - 2

Directions: Decide which sentence would be the topic sentence for the sentences in each list. Fill in the appropriate circle on your answer sheet.

SAMPLE **A** Dolphins have helped lost sailors.
        B Dolphins are friendly to people.
        C Swimmers have been aided by dolphins.
        D Once a dolphin gave a drowning man a ride.

ANSWER Ⓐ Ⓑ Ⓒ Ⓓ

6. **A** Mice are destructive
   B Mice eat farmers' crops
   C They chew holes in walls.
   D Mice also eat holes in food containers.

7. **A** Coal is an efficient fuel.
   B It is relatively easy to find.
   C Coal is widely used for several reasons.
   D Compared with other fuels, coal is inexpensive.

8. **A** It has ten speeds.
   B I bought a new bike.
   C The spokes are extra thin.
   D The whole bike weighs only ten pounds.

9. **A** Bakers are the large brown potatoes.
   B Sometimes potatoes are called taters.
   C In Idaho they are called spuds.
   D There are many names for potatoes.

10. **A** The sun is 93 million miles from the earth.
    B The sun is really a star.
    C Here are some facts about the sun.
    D It is a ball of hot gases.

Composition

Part Three

23

Writing Stories

Without stories, life could be dreary. Made-up stories take us to faraway lands. Stories based on real life introduce us to brave people and stir our feelings. A character facing a problem, a particular time and place, a sudden surprise—these are the ingredients of a story.

23a A **story** is a true or made-up account of a character facing and resolving a problem.

Your Writer's Notebook

In your journal, write about who came knocking at *your* door.

Some One

Some one came knocking
  At my wee, small door;
Some one came knocking,
  I'm sure—sure—sure;
I listened, I opened,
  I looked to left and right,
But nought there was
  a-stirring
  In the still dark night;

Only the busy beetle
  Tap-tapping in the wall,
Only from the forest
  The screech-owl's call,
Only the cricket whistling
  While the dew drops fall,
So I know not who came
  knocking,
  At all, at all, at all.

—WALTER DE LA MARE

Understanding Stories

What happens when you read a story? First you meet the characters and learn the time and place in which the story is set. Then you discover the problem or conflict facing the character and become involved in the character's struggles. Finally when you come to the end you see how everything works out.

Even though stories can range from fantasies set in the future to timeless folktales, all stories have the same basic parts. The chart below shows the structure of a story.

The Structure of a Story

1. The **beginning** of the story introduces the characters, the time and place of the story, and the problem or conflict.
2. The **middle** of the story tells the events in the order in which they happened. It includes the climax, the high point of the action.
3. The **ending** shows how the problem or conflict was resolved.

The following is an old story from Turkey. It is about the Hodja, a learned man who often acts foolishly. As you read it, look for the three main parts of a story.

The Hodja and the Moon

BEGINNING   One evening, the Hodja was drawing water when he saw the reflection of the moon at the bottom of the well.

"The moon has fallen down my well," said

MIDDLE   the Hodja. "If I do not get it out, it will be the end of the world, and everyone will blame me!"

He tied a large iron hook to the end of a piece of rope and let it down the well. When

he judged that he could hook the moon, he began to pull on the rope. The hook, however, had caught under a stone on the bottom of the well. The Hodja strained and pulled, until the hook suddenly dislodged the stone and flew up the wellshaft. The Hodja fell flat on his back.

ENDING "Allah be praised!" he said, seeing the moon in the sky. "It was a great effort, but I have got it back where it belongs!"

—CHARLES DOWNING, *TALES OF THE HODJA*

EXERCISE 1 *Studying a Story*

Reread the story of the Hodja. Then write answers to the following questions.

1. At what time of day does this story take place?
2. How many characters are in the story?
3. What does the Hodja think his problem is?
4. In your own words, tell what happens in this story.
5. How can you tell which parts of this story are the character's spoken words?

*C*haracters

In a movie, you can see how characters look, dress, and act. You can hear their voices. When you read a story, though, you rely on the writer's words and your own imagination to picture the characters. The chart below shows several ways you can paint a portrait of a person with words.

Ways to Describe Characters

1. To describe your character's appearance, use details that appeal to the senses.
2. Describe your character's actions.
3. Tell what your character is thinking and feeling.
4. Compare your character to something else.

Read the following portrait of Margot, a young girl in a short story by Ray Bradbury.

DETAILS THAT APPEAL TO THE SENSES

COMPARISON

ACTIONS

Margot stood alone. She was a very frail girl who looked as if she had been lost in the rain for years and the rain had washed out the blue from her eyes and the red from her mouth and the yellow from her hair. She was an old photograph dusted from an album, whitened away, and if she spoke at all her voice would be a ghost. Now she stood, separate, staring at the rain and the loud wet world beyond the huge glass.

—RAY BRADBURY, "ALL SUMMER IN A DAY"

*E*XERCISE 2 *Writing a Character Sketch*

Think of someone you know or have read about, or make up a character. Draw a sketch of that character in words. Start by comparing your character to something else. Then describe your character's appearance, actions, and feelings.

Dialogue

When you read the actual words that characters speak, the characters spring to life. Conversations between characters in a story are called dialogue. Read the story below. Notice how natural the dialogue sounds. Also notice the punctuation. (*See pages 216–224 for a review of using quotation marks.*)

Two Liars

A traveler liked to tell strange, wonderful tales—a new one every night.

"I once saw a ship in a foreign port," said the traveler one evening, "and it was sooooo enormous you couldn't even imagine its size if you tried! Why, a young boy who set out from one end would arrive at the other end an old, white-haired man!"

"Oooooooh!" gasped the audience.

"What is so wonderful about that?" asked a woodcutter, who was getting annoyed with these nightly bragging sessions. "In the forest not far from here, I once saw some trees so huge, sooo old, soooo tall that a bird that had been flying for ten years hadn't even reached halfway to the top."

"Liar!" cried the traveler. "Trees like that don't exist."

The woodcutter smiled. "Then where do you suppose the carpenters found the wood for your ship's mast?" he asked.   —VIETNAMESE FOLKTALE, BEATRICE TANAKA (ADAPTED)

23d Use natural-sounding **dialogue** to bring characters to life.

EXERCISE 3 *Writing Dialogue*

Write ten lines of conversation between Seiji, a shy new boy at your school, and Marianne, an outgoing girl trying to make friends with him. Use the following starter lines.

"Hi! My name is Marianne. What's yours?"

"My name? Oh, uh, it's, uh, Seiji," the boy answered shyly.

Setting

The setting of a story is the place and time in which it happens. Choose a setting for your story that matches the action and the mood. Then add details to make it seem as real as possible. If you were writing a scary story, your notes about the setting might appear as follows.

PLACE   in a run-down farmhouse
- creaky doors
- broken windows
- no other houses nearby

TIME   autumn night
- wind howling
- leaves blowing around
- drizzling rain

23e Create a **setting** by deciding on the place and time of your story. Add details to bring the setting to life.

EXERCISE 4 Creating Settings

Use your imagination to add at least three details to each of the following places and times for a story.

EXAMPLE   Place: roller skating rink
                 Time: winter weekend

POSSIBLE   Place: • rink was crowded
ANSWERS   • loud music
                • gaudy decorations
           Time: • Saturday night
                • freezing rain outside
                • 8:00 P.M.

1. Place: top of tall building
   Time: early morning
2. Place: bus stop
   Time: afternoon
3. Place: Alaska
   Time: summer
4. Place: a small town
   Time: a hundred years ago
5. Place: Venus
   Time: next century

EXERCISE 5 Matching Characters to Settings

Create two characters who would fit in the picture below. Write a brief sketch of those characters. Include their names, ages, occupations, and general personalities.

Plot

The plot of the story is the most important part. It tells what happens to the characters in the given setting. When thinking of a plot for your story, answer the following questions.

Questions for Thinking of Plots

1. What is the conflict or problem facing the characters?
2. What happens to start the story rolling?
3. What happens next? Next? Next?
4. What is the climax, or high point, of the story?
5. What finally happens to resolve the conflict?
6. How does the story end?

You can use the questions above to outline the plot of a story. The outline should follow time order. The plot outline of the story of the Hodja and the moon (*see pages 365–366*) would be as follows.

Problem:	Hodja thinks moon has fallen into well
First event:	goes to the well and sees the moon's reflection in the water
Next:	attaches hook to rope
Next:	tries to pull moon out
Next:	hook catches on stone—Hodja thinks he's got moon
Climax:	pulls so hard that stone is dislodged and Hodja goes flying
Resolution:	Hodja lands on his back and sees the moon in the sky
Outcome:	Hodja thinks he's pulled the moon out of the well

List all the events in your story in **time order.** Include the event that starts the story rolling, the climax of the story, the resolution of the problem, and the outcome.

EXERCISE 6 Thinking of Plots

Choose one of the following subjects. Then use the questions on page 371 to list the events that make up the story. Use your imagination.

1. the day a mysterious package was delivered
2. the time you tried skiing
3. a giant who came to town
4. a car with a mind of its own

EXERCISE 7 On Your Own

Think of a story you want to tell. It could be a true story or an imaginary one. It could be one you've heard before or one you make up on your own. Complete the following story chart in your writer's notebook.

Setting:
Characters and brief description:
Conflict or problem:
Plot outline: (See page 371.)

Writing Extra

In some stories, the storyteller is a character in the story and calls himself or herself "I." In other stories, the storyteller is not involved in the action. He or she just tells what happens to others.

Fairy tales are told in this way. The storyteller writes, "The prince searched for the beautiful girl with the glass slipper." Try writing a fairy tale in which you are a character. Tell the story from your own point of view. Write the whole story using "I." For example, if you were the prince in Cinderella, you might write, "I searched for the beautiful girl with the glass slipper."

Writing Stories

Stories come in many different forms. Jokes are stories, cartoon strips are stories, legends and myths are stories. No matter what form they use, however, story writers know one important rule: They must keep their readers interested from the very first sentence. A good beginning will make readers want to read on.

Writing a Fable

One popular kind of story is the fable. A fable is a story in which animal characters act like people to teach a lesson or moral. Read the following fable from India.

The Crow and the Partridge

SETTING A crow flying across a dusty road saw a partridge strutting along the ground.

PROBLEM "What a beautiful walk that partridge has!" said the crow. "I must try to see if I can walk like him." She landed behind the

EVENTS TOLD IN ORDER partridge and tried for a long time to learn to strut. At last the partridge turned around and asked what she was doing.

"Do not be angry with me," replied the crow. "I have never seen a bird who walks as beautifully as you can, and I am trying to learn to walk like you."

"Foolish bird," responded the partridge.

CLIMAX "You are a crow and should walk like a crow. You would look silly if you were to strut like a partridge."

But the crow went on trying to strut, until she had finally forgotten her own way

OUTCOME of walking. Now, she could neither walk like a partridge nor a crow.

MORAL Be yourself if you want to be your best.

373

EXERCISE 8 *Writing a Fable*

Step 1: Prewriting

Use one of the following famous sayings as the moral of your fable.

1. Haste makes waste.
2. People in glass houses shouldn't throw stones.
3. Beauty is only skin deep.
4. Every journey begins with the first step.
5. To know a person, you must stand in his or her shoes.

Next think of animal characters to act out a story that shows the truth of your saying. Also think of a setting. Then sketch out all the events of the plot in the order in which they happen. Use the questions on page 371 to write a plot outline.

Step 2: Writing

Use your prewriting notes to write your fable. Remember that the beginning of a story introduces the characters, the setting, and the problem. The middle tells the story event by event, leading up to the climax. The ending tells the outcome. Be sure to include dialogue in your story. Leave the moral of your story out for now.

Step 3: Sharing Your Work

Exchange papers with a classmate. After they read your fable, ask them to guess which saying you chose. If they cannot figure it out, revise your story as needed to make the moral clear. Add the moral to your revised copy.

Step 4: Revising

Use the Checklist for Revising Stories on page 377 to revise your fable.

Step 5: Editing

Use the Editing Checklist on page 291 to edit your fable.

Step 6: Publishing

Make a neat copy of your story. Also make illustrations to go with it. Show your fable to your family and friends.

Writing a Folktale

Another popular kind of story is the folktale. Folktales are stories that were told aloud long before they were written down.

One kind of folktale is called the "why" story. This kind of story explains something by telling how it started. The following folktale explains why we have Spanish moss.

Gray Moss on Green Trees

SETTING

There was an Indian mother working in the field along the river. Nearby, her two children played. Suddenly, cold Wind came racing in the air through the trees. Then Rain came on, sharp rain. Water in the river rose, high and cold.

PROBLEM

The mother saw that they would have to climb a tree to stay away from the flood.

EVENTS TOLD IN ORDER

Carrying her younger child, she climbed a thick oak tree. Her older child followed. Soon they were high up, away from the flood.

Then the Rain stopped, but cold Wind still ran wildly through the trees.

"Mother, I am cold. My feet are cold."

"Mother, my hands are cold and I can't hold on to the branches."

Moon came out over the black, flying clouds. Its light was sharp and bright.

"Moon in the Sky," the mother prayed, "my children are very cold and will die. I

CLIMAX

am very cold and can't keep them warm. Be kind to us, and don't let us die."

RESOLUTION

Moon spoke to Clouds and to Wind. They listened. Moon shone strong on the mother and the children, and they fell asleep. Then Moon wove and wove and wove. . . .

Morning came. The sky was clear and warm. The Indian mother and her children

375

OUTCOME

awoke and were warm. They looked on the branches and saw something new. All over the trees was a thick green-gray blanket that had covered them.

"Mother," cried the older boy, "it's a blanket that kept us warm. Moon heard you pray and tore up the clouds to make a blanket for us."

The mother and her children came down from the tree and went home.

The "Cloud-Cloth" is now called Spanish moss. It has been on trees ever since.

—M. A. JAGENDORG, "GREY MOSS ON GREEN TREES"

EXERCISE 9   Writing a "Why" Story

Step 1: Prewriting

Choose one of the following subjects (or one of your own) to explain in a "why" story.

1. why the rain comes
2. why rabbits have long ears
3. why a cat purrs
4. why the earth spins

Next, use your imagination to think of a story explaining the event. Start by choosing a setting and some characters. Then brainstorm a list of possible events that could lead to the ending you want. Once you have an idea of your plot, list the events in time order.

Step 2: Writing

Use your prewriting notes to write your "why" story. Be sure to include the setting, the event that sets the story in motion, all the events in the story, and the climax and resolution. Add dialogue to your story.

Step 3: Sharing Your Work

Read your story aloud to the class. Ask for comments about what your classmates liked. Also ask them to tell you about parts that could be improved. Make any needed changes.

Step 4: Revising Your Story

Use the following checklist to revise your "why" story.

Checklist for Revising Stories

1. Does the beginning of your story give the setting, introduce characters, show the problem or conflict, and capture attention?
2. Does the middle of your story show the problem or conflict and tell, in time order, how the characters try to solve it?
3. Does your story have a climax?
4. Did you use dialogue and description to help make the characters and the problem believable?
5. Does the ending show how the problem or conflict was resolved?

Step 5: Editing Your Story

Use the Editing Checklist on page 291 to edit your story.

EXERCISE 10 On Your Own

Try writing a humorous "why" story for future generations. Instead of explaining something in nature, write a story explaining something modern. Some ideas include how washing machines came to be, or why a television set looks like a big eye. For a funny effect, keep a serious mood to your writing.

Spotlight on Writing

A **Writing Character Sketches.** Look at the picture below. Then write a brief character sketch of each person. Include all the following information about each. Use your imagination.

Name   Age   Appearance   Personality   Favorite activities

B **Writing Dialogue.** Write a dialogue between two of the people in the picture below. Use your character sketches to help you think of the kinds of things they would say. Remember to punctuate and indent correctly.

C **Describing a Setting.** Look at the settings pictured above. Choose one of the settings and write a brief description to fit the people pictured on page 378.

D **Thinking of Plots.** Use your imagination to think of a plot involving the characters on page 378. Answer all the questions given on page 371.

E **Writing a Story.** Use your ideas from Exercises A–D to write a story about your characters. Use the Steps for Writing a Story on page 381 as a guide.

379

F **Writing a Rescue Story.** The picture on this page shows a rescue situation. Use it to give you ideas for writing a dramatic rescue story. Try to make your story as suspenseful as possible.

G **Writing from Your Writer's Notebook.** Use ideas from your journal to write a story. Follow the Steps for Writing a Story on page 381.

H **Writing Ideas.** Write a story on one of the following subjects or one of your own. Use the Steps for Writing on page 381 as a guide.

1. the day that clocks went on strike
2. how the skunk got its white stripe
3. why the moon appears in phases
4. a lost starship
5. a hungry grizzly bear
6. the big race
7. the surprise of your life
8. the day you became famous
9. the wishing well
10. riding on a cloud

Steps for Writing a Story

Prewriting

1. Using your own experiences and your imagination, make a list of events for possible stories.
2. Choose one subject that would make the best story.
3. Write a brief character sketch for every person in your story. (*See page 367.*)
4. Create a setting for your story. (*See pages 369–370.*)
5. List all the events in your story in time order. (*See page 371.*)

Writing

6. Write the beginning of your story. Be sure to capture attention, introduce characters, give the setting, and start the story rolling. (*See page 365.*)
7. Write the middle of your story. Tell the events in time order with transitions. Use dialogue and description to bring the story to life. Show how the characters are trying to resolve the problem. (*See page 365.*)
8. Write the ending of your story. Tell how the problem is solved and bring the story to a close. (*See page 365.*)

Revising

9. Use the Checklist for Revising Stories on page 377.

Editing

10. Use the Editing Checklist on page 291 to polish your final draft.

24

Writing Reports

Sometimes you will be writing about subjects beyond your own experience. Maybe you want to write about sharks or the eruption of Mt. Vesuvius. Maybe you want to write about making movies or traveling in outer space. For these topics, you will find information in books, magazines, television shows, and newspapers. You can also find information by interviewing people who know the subject well. When you write about what you have learned from these sources, you are writing a report.

24a A **report** is a composition of three or more paragraphs that uses information from books, magazines, and other sources.

Like a paragraph, a report has three main parts. Study the following comparison chart.

Sentences in Paragraph	Paragraphs in Report
Topic Sentence: states the main idea	**Introduction:** contains sentence stating main idea
Body: gives specific information to back up main idea or topic sentence	**Body:** supports main idea with specific information from sources
Concluding Sentence: sums up and adds strong ending	**Conclusion:** sums up and adds strong ending

In addition to the three main parts, a report also has a title and a listing of sources. The title suggests what the report is about and should make the reader interested enough to read on. The listing of sources comes at the end of the report. It shows all the books, magazines, encyclopedias, and other sources you used.

Writing reports is an important part of your schoolwork. You will be surprised how well you know a subject once you have written a report on it.

Your Writer's Notebook

Answer the following questions as completely as you can. Your answers should give you good ideas to use as subjects for a report.

1. What television shows have I seen about plants, animals, and nature?
2. What magazines do I like to read or look through? What subjects do their articles cover?
3. What informational books have I read?
4. What topics in the news interest me?

Prewriting

Most reports stick to telling the facts about a subject, without adding opinions. Be aware of the difference between fact and opinion. Focus on the facts as you prepare your report.

Choosing a Subject

To write a report, you will need to use library sources for your information. The subject "My Dog Pete" would not be a good report subject since information about Pete is stored in your head—not in the library. However, the subject "Dogs That Save Lives" would be good for a report. For this subject you would need to find library sources telling about dogs that rescue people.

24c Choose a subject for which you will need to use the library or other sources to gather information.

EXERCISE 1 Identifying Good Report Subjects

Number your paper 1–10. Decide whether each subject is based on someone's personal experience or whether it requires library work. Then write *experience* or *library work* after each number.

1. my "flying up" ceremony in Girl Scouts
2. Girl Scout uniforms through the years
3. how buildings are torn down
4. ways to make friends
5. how Martin Luther King, Jr. Day was started
6. songs to sing around a campfire
7. how to ride a bicycle
8. the world's tallest trees
9. the first public library in North America
10. theories about what happened to the dinosaurs

Limiting a Subject

In a short report, you need to limit your subject. For example, you cannot possibly write all there is to know about sharks or about volcanoes. The more specific your subject, the better you will be able to cover it. Break down a broad subject into smaller parts. Study the following examples.

TOO BROAD	MORE LIMITED	SUITABLY LIMITED
sharks	habits	feeding habits
baseball	baseball players	stories about Babe Ruth
actors	movie stars	child movie stars

24d Limit your subject to a suitable size.

EXERCISE 2 Limiting a Subject

For each broad subject, write a limited subject that would be suitable for a short report.

> EXAMPLE China
> POSSIBLE ANSWER languages spoken in China

1. whales
2. stars
3. computers
4. foods
5. cars
6. the Olympics
7. national parks
8. careers in medicine
9. polar bears
10. toys

Gathering Information

When you gather information on a subject, you need a plan. Write out a list of questions you want to answer. The answers will become part of your report.

Suppose you had decided to write a report on Koko the gorilla, an animal you read about in *National Geographic* magazine. Your library questions might look like the ones on the following page.

- Why are people so interested in Koko?
- How did Koko learn sign language?
- When did Koko first get her pet cat?
- What name did Koko give her cat?
- How did Koko and her cat get along?
- What happened to the cat?

With your questions in hand, you can begin looking for books and other sources to help you answer them. Use the following steps to find library information.

24e

Steps for Gathering Information

1. Check an encyclopedia for a general study of your subject. It might also list books or other encyclopedia articles containing more information.
2. Use the subject cards in the card catalog to find more information. (*See page 477.*)
3. Look up your subject in *The Readers' Guide to Periodical Literature*. Find some recent magazine articles.
4. Make a list of all your sources. Include the author, title, and the date of publication.

After gathering information about Koko the gorilla, you might prepare a list of sources like the one below. Try to include several types of sources.

ENCYCLOPEDIA   "Gorillas," *World Book Encyclopedia,* 1986 edition.

BOOK   *Koko's Kitten* by Francine Patterson, 1985.

MAGAZINE   "Koko's Kitten," *National Geographic,* Jan. 1985, pp. 110–113.

EXERCISE 3 *Gathering Information*

Use the library to list three sources for each subject below. No more than one source may be an encyclopedia.

1. Bigfoot
2. forest fires
3. basketball
4. the sinking of the *Titanic*
5. money

Interviewing is another way to gather information. During an interview, ask questions and listen carefully to the answers. Follow these steps when interviewing.

Conducting an Interview

1. Call or write ahead to arrange the interview.
2. Prepare a list of questions you want to ask.
3. During the interview, take notes. (You may also tape record the interview with permission.)
4. If necessary, politely ask the person to repeat something you did not understand.
5. Thank the person for the interview.

Writing Extra

Practice your interviewing skills by talking with a family member about his or her job. Follow the steps above to conduct an interview.

Taking Notes

You will need to take notes to help you remember what you learn from your sources. Index cards are handy for this purpose. A folder with pockets along with rubber bands and paper clips are other useful supplies.

At the library, find your information sources. Then locate a space with plenty of room for you to spread out your supplies.

Always use your own words when taking notes. As you read, write your own ideas about the information. The words and ideas of authors are protected by law. Using them as your own is a serious offense, called plagiarism.

The following guidelines will help you take well-organized notes.

24f

Taking Notes

1. Write the title of your source in the upper right-hand corner of your index card.
2. Write a heading in the upper left-hand corner to tell the part of the subject being discussed.
3. Begin a new card for each new part of your subject.
4. Summarize the main points in your own words.
5. Write down the page number from which your information is taken.

Read the following selection about Koko from *National Geographic,* page 110. Then compare it with the note card on the following page.

Can a kitten raised by a dog find happiness with a 230-pound gorilla who converses in American Sign Language? Well, you can ask Koko, a 13-year-old female lowland gorilla who for a dozen years has been the focus of the world's longest ongoing ape language study, sponsored by the Gorilla Foundation of California with past support from the National Geographic Society. According to Dr. Francine "Penny" Patterson, Koko uses more than 500 signs regularly and knows some 500 others in American Sign Language, or Ameslan—the hand language of the deaf. That's how Koko came to tell Penny that she wanted a cat—a word she signs by pulling two fingers across her cheeks in the manner of whiskers.

SAMPLE NOTE CARD

HEADING   SOURCE

background info   Nat'l Geog.

— Koko 13 years old, 230 pounds, lowland gor.

— been part of study for 12 years

— uses 500 signs of Ameslan (Am. sign lang. used by deaf) and knows as many more

p. 110

IDEAS
TOLD
IN NEW
WORDS

PAGE NUMBER

EXERCISE 4 Taking Notes

The following information about the appearance of the octopus is from page 508 of *World Book Encyclopedia*. Make a note card for it. Use the card above as a model. Remember to list your source and to use you own words.

Some people call octopuses *devilfish*, probably because of the animal's frightening appearance. An octopus has large, shiny eyes, and strong, hard jaws that come to a point like a parrot's bill. The octopus uses its arms to catch clams, crabs, lobsters, mussels, and other shellfish, and to break the shells apart. It cuts up food with its horny jaws. Some kinds of octopuses inject a poison that paralyzes their prey. Octopuses rarely attack people.

Outlining

After you have found all the answers you need, you can make an outline to help you plan your report. An outline is a skeleton of the body of your report. It contains specific information to support your main idea.

When you draft your report later, you write out your outline in flowing sentences. Use the following guidelines to help you prepare your outline.

24g

Preparing an Outline

1. Use the headings on your note cards to group the cards into a few categories.
2. Save cards that do not fit into any categories. You may be able to use the ideas on these cards in your introduction or conclusion.
3. Make a list of your categories. Then use Roman numerals (I., II., III.) to arrange your categories in some logical order.
4. Use the categories as main topics in your outline.
5. Using your note cards, list subtopics under each main topic. Use capital letters with subtopics.

Remember that an outline is for the body of your report only. The following outline is for the body of a report about Koko the gorilla.

SUBJECT	Koko and her pet kittens
MAIN TOPIC	I. Koko and her kitten All Ball
SUBTOPICS	A. How she got All Ball
	B. How she cared for All Ball
MAIN TOPIC	II. All Ball's death
SUBTOPICS	A. How it happened
	B. Koko's reaction
	C. Public's reaction
MAIN TOPIC	III. Koko's next kitten
SUBTOPICS	A. How she got and named it
	B. How she treats it

After finishing your outline, check its form. Be sure you used Roman numerals for main topics and capital letters for subtopics. Also, if you used subtopics, be sure you have at least two—never just one alone. Finally, check your capitalization and indentation.

EXERCISE 5 Practicing Outlining

Use the subtopics below to complete the following outline. Place each subtopic under the proper main topic.

SUBJECT the Great Wall of China

   I. Size of wall
     A.
     B.
  II. Materials used
     A.
     B.
 III. Number of workers
     A.
     B.
     C.

SUBTOPICS
- 300,000 people hired in A.D. 446
- stones and pebbles used in mountain areas
- 6000 kilometers long
- over one million workers in A.D. 607–608
- sand and twigs in desert region
- 1.8 million peasants in A.D. 555
- 8.5 meters high

EXERCISE 6 On Your Own

Follow the steps below to plan a report. Save your work for Exercise 9.

STEP 1 Choose and limit a subject for a report.
STEP 2 Gather information from library sources and take notes on cards.
STEP 3 Organize your notes into categories.
STEP 4 Write an outline for the body of your report.

391

Writing

Using your outline as a guide, write the first draft of your report. Think about your readers and what they need to know to understand your subject.

Writing the Introduction

The introduction to your report should accomplish three goals. The chart below shows the goals of a strong introduction.

Writing an Introduction

A strong introduction
1. captures the reader's attention.
2. provides any needed background information.
3. contains a sentence stating the main idea.

Read the following two versions of an introduction to the report about Koko.

Introduction 1

Koko is a 13-year-old gorilla who has learned to use sign language. She is part of an experiment at Stanford University. Dr. Francine Patterson teaches Koko and cares for her. According to Patterson, Koko knows about 1000 signs. On her 12th birthday, Koko used her language to ask for a special present—a pet cat. This is the story of Koko and her kitten.

Introduction 2

Koko is a very interesting gorilla. She told her human friend Penny Patterson that she wanted a cat. Koko loved the cat and treated it well. Koko got another cat later. Koko uses sign language.

Exercise 7 Studying Introductions

Read the two introductions again. Then write answers to the following questions.

1. Which introduction accomplishes the three goals shown on page 392?
2. What background information is given in the first introduction? Is that information necessary?
3. What sentence expresses the main idea in the first introduction?

*W*riting the Body

When you write the body of your report, you can use your outline as a guide. Write a paragraph for each Roman numeral you included in your outline. Be sure to use transitions to show your reader how ideas are related. (*See* page 395.)

24i Use your outline to write the paragraph in the **body** of your report. Write a paragraph for each main topic.

Read the following body of a report. Notice that it follows the order of the outline on page 390.

Several months after she first asked for it, Koko got her cat. A worker arrived with three kittens who had been left by their mother and raised by a dog. Koko chose a tabby cat that had no tail. Because he looked like a ball when he curled up, Koko named him All Ball. Koko treated All Ball just like a baby of her own. She carried him around on her back. She groomed him. She fed him milk from a small bottle. All Ball was never afraid of this gentle gorilla.

When All Ball was seven months old, he got out and was hit by a car. Koko cried. She understood All Ball was not coming back. She signed, "Sleep Cat," and "cry, sad, frown." Thousands of people who had read about Koko in magazines heard of All Ball's death and sent letters and cards. Everybody thought Koko should get a new kitten.

394

For months Patterson tried to get Koko another kitten. The kind Koko wanted, tailless like All Ball, was hard to find. Finally Koko got her kitten. All Ball's mother had another litter. Koko chose a loving, gray female and named her Smokey. She cradled and rocked her new kitten. She treated her just as gently as she had treated All Ball.

EXERCISE 8   Recognizing Transitions

Reread the body of the report on pages 394–395. Then write answers to the following questions.

1. What transitional phrase starts the first paragraph?
2. How much time passes between the first and second paragraphs? How do you know?
3. What transition leads into the third paragraph?
4. Write another transition used in the third paragraph.

Writing the Conclusion

Following are a few good ways to end a report.

24j

Writing a Conclusion

1. Tell the importance of your subject.
2. Use an idea from the introduction.
3. Restate the main idea in new words.

Read the following conclusion. Notice how strong an ending it provides.

> Koko has had many teachers who have helped her learn her language. She has also been a teacher herself. She taught many people that gorillas are smart enough to learn language. She has also shown that gorillas are gentle enough to care for a tiny, furry kitten. Once Koko was asked to tell a story about All Ball. She said, "Koko love Ball." Those words say it all.

At the end of your report, be sure to list all the sources you used. Include the author, title, and date. Add the page number if your source is a magazine article. (*See page 388.*)

EXERCISE 9   On Your Own

Use your outline from Exercise 6 to write the first draft of your report. Remember that your outline is for the body of the report. You may find ideas for your introduction and conclusion in the notes you did not use in your outline. Save your work for Exercise 10.

Revising and Editing

After your first draft is finished, put it away for a while. When you read it later, you will be able to see what needs improvement. Use the following checklist as a guide. When you are satisfied with your revisions, you can edit your work and make a neat, final copy.

Checklist for Revising Reports

Checking Your Report

1. Does your introduction capture attention, give background information, and state the main idea?
2. Does the body of your report give specific facts and examples to support the main idea?
3. Did you use your own words?
4. Did you use transitions?
5. Does your conclusion add a strong ending?
6. Does your report have a title?
7. Did you list the sources you used?

Checking Your Paragraphs

8. Does each body paragraph have a topic sentence?
9. Does each paragraph stick to the topic?
10. Does one paragraph lead smoothly to the next?

Checking Your Sentences and Words

11. Are your sentences varied? (*See page 256.*)
12. Did you use specific, lively words? (*See page 231.*)

EXERCISE 10 Revising Your Report

Use the checklist above to revise your report.

EXERCISE 11 On Your Own

Use the Editing Checklist on page 291 to edit your report and prepare a final copy.

Writing Book Reports

In school, you will be asked to write book reports.

24I ▶ A **book report** offers a brief summary of the book and an opinion about the quality of the book.

24m ▶

Structure of a Book Report

INTRODUCTION
- gives title of book and author's name
- tells what the book is about
- gives time and place of fictional story

BODY
- tells highlights of the book
- gives specific details from book

CONCLUSION
- gives your opinion of the book
- adds a strong ending

Read the following book report. Notice that the writer does not try to tell the whole story, just some highlights.

The Phantom Tollbooth

INTRODUCTION: GIVES TITLE, AUTHOR, SUBJECT, AND SETTING

The Phantom Tollbooth by Norton Juster is the story of Milo, a young boy who is bored with life. Nothing interests him. One day he comes home after school feeling very glum. To his surprise he finds a huge package with a tollbooth and a mysterious map inside. Not expecting much, Milo gets in his toy car and sets off on a unique journey.

BODY: GIVES SPECIFIC HIGHLIGHTS

Along the way Milo teams up with a dog named Tock and an insect named the Humbug. Together they go to strange places. In Dictionopolis they see words bought and sold like vegetables in a market. Later they discover a symphony orchestra that creates colors instead of sounds. They also go to a silent place where sounds have been banned. They reach Digitopolis, ruled by the Mathemagician. Then they head out on a dangerous mission to free Rhyme and Reason from the Castle in the Air.

CONCLUSION: SUMS UP AND GIVES OPINION

At times, the writer turns familiar sayings, like "jump to conclusions," into actions. For example, Milo suddenly finds himself leaping to an isolated island named Conclusions when he makes up his mind too fast about something. These clever adventures are fun to read. As Milo travels through this strange land, he learns to love and appreciate his life. He sees things more clearly and is no longer bored. *The Phantom Tollbooth* is a fun book that makes you think as well as laugh.

When writing a book report, assume that your readers have not read the book you are writing about. Be careful, though, that you do not try to tell too much of the story.

EXERCISE 12 On Your Own

Choose a book for a book report. Read it carefully. Then jot down answers to the following questions. Save your work for the Spotlight on Writing.

1. What do you like or dislike about the book?
2. What characters and scenes stand out in your mind?
3. What are the high points of the story?
4. Would you recommend this book to someone else? Why or why not?

Spotlight on Writing

A **Taking Notes.** Imagine that you are planning a report on life in the ocean. Prepare a note card using the following information from *Heath Science*, page 226. Use the card on page 389 as a model.

What kinds of living things can be found in the dark parts of the ocean? We know that plants cannot grow in very deep water, because they need sunlight. But some kinds of animals are able to live there. Many of these animals feed on matter that sinks down from the ocean's surface. Some animals in the dark ocean feed on the other animals that live there.

Some animals, such as the flashlight fish, have organs that give off light. These light organs help the fish see to find food and communicate with others of its own kind. If it needs to get away from an enemy, the flashlight fish can even turn off its light organs.

B **Using Your Own Words.** Using your note card from Exercise A, write what you learned about animals in the deep ocean in your own words.

C **Checking an Outline.** The following outline for a report on life in the ocean uses incorrect form. Revise it, using the model on page 390 as a guide.

I. Life near the surface
A. plants
B. fish
II. Mammals in the ocean
III. life in the dark parts
a. types of creatures that live there
b. how they feed
3. how they live in darkness
4. how scientists study them

D **Writing a Research Report.** Write a research report on one of the following subjects or one of your choice. (Review your writer's notebook for ideas.) Follow the Steps for Writing a Report on page 402.

1. dinosaurs
2. Helen Keller's teacher
3. Egyptian hieroglyphics
4. Indian sign language
5. how dolphins communicate

6. constellations
7. cars of the future
8. guide dogs
9. coyotes
10. bicycle racing

E **Writing a Book Report.** Write a book report, using your ideas from Exercise 12. Follow the Steps for Writing a Book Report on page 403.

Steps for Writing a Report

Prewriting

1. Choose a subject requiring library work and limit it to a suitable size. (*See pages 384–385.*)
2. Gather information from library sources and interviews. (*See pages 385–387.*)
3. Take notes on note cards. (*See pages 387–389.*)
4. Organize your notes into categories and use them to outline the body. (*See pages 390–391.*)

Writing

5. Write an introduction that includes a sentence stating the main idea. (*See pages 392–393.*)
6. Use your outline to write the body in your own words. (*See pages 394–395.*)
7. Add a concluding paragraph. (*See page 396.*)
8. Add a title.
9. List the sources you used at the end of your report. (*See page 396.*)

Revising

10. Use the Revision Checklist to check your report for good organization, well-organized paragraphs, and lively sentences and words. (*See page 397.*)

Editing

11. Use the Editing Checklist to check your grammar, spelling, mechanics, and form. (*See page 291.*)

Steps for Writing a Book Report

Prewriting

1. Briefly summarize the story in your own words.
2. Describe in a sentence or two the book's overall effect on you. How did you feel when you read it? Bored? Fascinated? In suspense? Amused?
3. Skim the book, jotting down specific details that led to your overall feeling about the book.

Writing

4. Write an introduction that tells the title, the author, the subject, and the setting of the story.
5. Write the body. Tell the plot of the story briefly, giving highlights and specific details.
6. Write a conclusion. Give your opinion about the book. Be sure your opinion is backed up by the details you mention in your book report.

Revising

7. Did you summarize the story briefly?
8. Did you offer a specific opinion with details to back it up?

Editing

9. Did you check your report for errors in grammar, spelling, punctuation, and capitalization?
10. Did you make a final, neat copy of your report?

25

Writing Letters

When did you last receive a letter? Before you opened it, you probably felt a tingle of excitement. What news would it contain? Letters can inform us, amuse us, instruct us, and persuade us. They can also take care of business. You can order goods or request information. This chapter will give you practice in writing different kinds of letters.

Your Writer's Notebook

In a letter to his 11-year-old daughter at camp, the writer F. Scott Fitzgerald wrote the following:

Things to worry about:
Worry about courage
Worry about cleanliness
Worry about efficiency
Things not to worry about:
Don't worry about popular opinion
Don't worry about growing up
Don't worry about anybody getting ahead of you

In your journal, write a letter to yourself giving advice. Tell what is worth worrying about and what isn't.

Friendly Letters

You are sitting in your sitting room tatting when you hear the news that Sir Lancelot unexpectedly encountered a tremendous dragon and that sorcerers and surgeons are being rushed to the scene. Whereupon you pick up your pen, and this is what you write:

A Get-Well Note

> *The Royal Palace*
> *Camelot, England*
> *February 28, 1962*
>
> *Dear Dragon,*
> *This little note is to tell you that I am thinking about you and hoping that you will soon feel better.*
>
> *Most Sincerely,*
> *Your friend Gwen*

—SESYLE JOSLIN AND IRENE HAAS, *text and note from* DEAR DRAGON (ADAPTED)

Your friendly letter to the dragon expresses get-well wishes. You can also use letters to thank someone for a gift, invite someone to a party, or congratulate someone. All friendly letters have five main parts.

25a   The parts of a friendly letter are the **heading, greeting, body, closing,** and **signature.**

Correct Form for a Friendly Letter

heading

355 W. 24th St.
Fox, OK 73435
March 6, 1987

greeting

Dear Margaret,

    I am having a party next Saturday (March 11) at 2:00 to celebrate my eleventh birthday. We will have cake and ice cream, and there will be music for dancing. I hope you will be able to come.

body

closing   Your friend,

signature   Starr Ann

- The **heading** includes your full address with zip code. Write the full name of your state or use the abbreviation. (*See page 411 for a full listing.*) Always include the date after your address. Remember to capitalize proper nouns and use commas correctly in addresses.

- The **greeting** is a way to say hello. Capitalize the first word and all nouns. Use a comma after the greeting.

  Dear **A**unt **E**sther,   **D**ear **D**ad,

- The **body** is your message. Remember to indent each paragraph.

  The **closing** should be brief. Capitalize the first word only. Use a comma after the closing.

  Your best friend,   **L**ove,

- The **signature** should be handwritten below the closing.

EXERCISE 1 Understanding the Parts of a Friendly Letter

Write the get-well note from page 405 on your paper. Then label the five parts of a friendly letter. Use the letter on page 406 as a guide.

EXERCISE 2 Writing a Friendly Letter

Write a letter to a friend. In it, refresh your friend's memory about how the two of you met. Use the correct form for a friendly letter.

Thank-you Notes

Whenever you are not able to thank someone in person, you should write a thank-you note. In your note, mention the gift and tell how you plan to use it. Include all five parts of a friendly letter.

Thank-you Note

5521 Planter Road
Flat Rock, NC 28731
May 15, 1987

Dear Mrs. Benton,

Thank you so much for the subscription to *National Geographic Explorer*. The first issue arrived today, and it was filled with great pictures and interesting stories. Thanks again for a thoughtful birthday gift.

Yours truly,
Marc

EXERCISE 3 *Writing a Thank-you Note*

Think of a gift you would like to receive. Then pretend that someone you know gave it to you. Write a thank-you note telling how much you appreciate the gift. Make sure that your completed letter uses the correct form.

EXERCISE 4 *On Your Own*

Pretend you are best friends with a famous movie star. Write a friendly letter congratulating him or her on the success of a recent movie.

Writing Extra

Think of the characters you learned about in mythology. Then think of something that they have or use. Zeus, for example, was lord of the sky. He is often pictured carrying a lightning bolt. Once you have thought of your god or goddess and a thing he or she uses, write a friendly letter. Tell the character that you have found the thing he or she lost. Make arrangements for returning it. Then answer your own letter, pretending you are the god or goddess.

*B*usiness Letters

Business letters need a sixth part—the inside address. It gives information about who is to receive the letter. Many letters are removed from their envelopes when they reach a business. The inside address makes sure the letter reaches the right person or department.

25b The six parts of a business letter are the **heading, inside address, greeting, body, closing,** and **signature.**

- The **heading** is the same as for a friendly letter. (*See page 406.*) If you abbreviate the state in the heading, use an abbreviation in the inside address also.

- The **inside address** starts two to four lines below the heading. Write the name of the person who will receive the letter. Use *Mr., Ms., Mrs.,* etc., before the name. If the person has a title, such as *Manager,* write it on the next line. Then write the receiver's address. Follow the rules for capitalizing and punctuating.

- The **greeting** starts two lines below the inside address. In a business letter, use a colon after the greeting. If you do not know the person's name, use Sir or Madam.

   Dear **M**r. Timberlake: **D**ear **S**ir or **M**adam:

- The **body** begins two lines below the greeting. Skip a line between paragraphs and indent each one.

- The **closing** of a business letter lines up with the left-hand edge of the heading. Capitalize the first letter only and use a comma.

   Sincerely,   **V**ery truly yours,

- The **signature** in a business letter appears twice. First type or print your name four lines below the closing. Then sign your name between the closing and your printed name.

When you write a business letter, always use plain white paper. Leave margins at least one inch wide on all sides.

Correct Form for a Business Letter

heading
```
2311 Maplewood
Wilmette, IL 60091
January 15, 1987
```

inside address

White Water Rafting
927 Ridgemont
Loveland, CO 80537

greeting

Dear Sir or Madam:

My family is interested in taking a rafting trip down the Colorado River next summer. We understand that you have group trips. Please send us a brochure or any other information to help us plan our trip. Also please include information about prices. Thank you very much.

body

closing   Sincerely yours,

signature   *Nancy Lapallonia*

Nancy Lapallonia

The Envelope

The model on page 411 shows the correct form for an envelope. Print your own name and address in the upper left-hand corner. The receiver's address is the same as the inside address. It is centered on the envelope. Use the postal abbreviation for the state and the ZIP code.

Correct Form for a Business Envelope

Nancy Lapallonia   your name
2311 Maplewood   your address
Wilmette, IL 60091

receiver's
address

White Water Rafting
927 Ridgemont
Loveland, CO 80537

State Abbreviations

Alabama	AL	Montana	MT
Alaska	AK	Nebraska	NE
Arizona	AZ	Nevada	NV
Arkansas	AR	New Hampshire	NH
California	CA	New Jersey	NJ
Colorado	CO	New Mexico	NM
Connecticut	CT	New York	NY
Delaware	DE	North Carolina	NC
District of Columbia	DC	North Dakota	ND
Florida	FL	Ohio	OH
Georgia	GA	Oklahoma	OK
Hawaii	HI	Oregon	OR
Idaho	ID	Pennsylvania	PA
Illinois	IL	Puerto Rico	PR
Indiana	IN	Rhode Island	RI
Iowa	IA	South Carolina	SC
Kansas	KS	South Dakota	SD
Kentucky	KY	Tennessee	TN
Louisiana	LA	Texas	TX
Maine	ME	Utah	UT
Maryland	MD	Vermont	VT
Massachusetts	MA	Virginia	VA
Michigan	MI	Washington	WA
Minnesota	MN	West Virginia	WV
Mississippi	MS	Wisconsin	WI
Missouri	MO	Wyoming	WY

EXERCISE 5 Using the Correct Form for Writing a Business Letter

Use the following information to write a business letter in the proper form. The information on page 409 and the model on page 410 will help you.

Heading: your address, and today's date
Inside address: Healthy Pet Foods, 342 Kennel Lane, Richmond, Kansas 66080
Greeting: Dear Sir or Madam
Body: I would like to teach my dog how to catch a flying disc. I saw in a magazine article that you have a free pamphlet with instructions. I would appreciate receiving a copy of this pamphlet. Thank you very much.
Closing: Sincerely yours
Signature: your name

Letters of Request

Requesting information is one common purpose for writing a business letter. The letter on page 410 is an example of a letter of request. To receive exactly what you want, be as specific as possible in asking for information. Also, be sure to check your letter for errors in grammar, usage, and spelling.

EXERCISE 6 Correcting Errors in a Letter of Request

In the following letter, each line preceded by a number contains an error. Rewrite the letter, correcting each mistake. Then underline the corrections you made. (*See pages 409 and 410 for help.*)

1   2220 Hawthorne road
2   Lakeview Oregon 97630
3   march 11, 1987

4   mr. Akiro Tanaka
5   Karate institute
   477 W. Belmont
6   Chicago IL 60600

7   Dear Mr. Tanaka,

8   I am interested in karate and have taken some lessons. I understand that you have many books on the subject that are for sale. If you have a list of these books, I would appreciate receiving it. Thank you.

9   yours truly,

10

   Mickey Santora

EXERCISE 7 On Your Own

Write a business letter to a famous person in the past. Request information that only he or she would have. Use your imagination to make up the inside address.

413

Filling Out Forms

From time to time you will need to complete a form. You may be applying for a library card, ordering something, or joining a club or organization. Follow these guidelines when completing a form.

Completing Business Forms

1. Read all directions carefully before you begin.
2. Check both sides of the form to make sure you do not miss any questions written on the back.
3. Do not leave blanks. If a question does not apply to you, write NA (not applicable) in the space.
4. Always use blue or black pen.
5. Be sure to print neatly and clearly.
6. Remember to sign the form if needed.
7. Check your work when you are finished.

When you shop, you can go to a store or order items from a store's catalog. Suppose you wanted to order the following items from a catalog. You would fill out the order form as shown on page 415.

> 1 music box, #9877, $4.50
>
> 3 pens, #452, $1.50 each
>
> 1 lap table, #221 $4.65

EXERCISE 8 On Your Own

On separate paper, draw a blank copy of the same order form. Fill out your form, ordering the following. Use your name and address, and pay with a check or money order.

> 1 telephone, #607, $14.50
>
> 10 erasers, #2, $.10 each
>
> 3 notebooks, #1012, $1.50 each

SEND TO:

Name *Mary Thundercloud*
Address *467 Cliff Bend*
City *Big Sky* State *MT* Zip *59716*

Check Payment Method

☑ Check or money order

☐ VISA ☐ MASTERCARD ☐ AMERICAN EXPRESS

Card Number _____
Expiration Date _____
Signature _____

How Many	Item No.	Description of Item	Unit Price	Total
1	9877	music box	4.50	4.50
3	452	pens	1.50	4.50
1	221	lap table	4.65	4.65

Postage and handling:		
Up to $20.00 . . . . $3.95	Merchandise total	13.65
$20.01 to $30.00 . . . . $4.95		
$30.01 to $40.00 . . . . $5.95	Postage and handling	3.95
Over $40.00 . . . . $6.95		
	Grand Total	17.60

Spotlight on Writing

A **Writing a Friendly Letter.** Follow the steps below to write a friendly letter. Choose one of the following purposes for your letter.

- inviting someone to a party
- accepting an invitation to a party
- congratulating someone on a job well done
- thanking a relative for taking you and your friends to a concert.
- sending someone a get well wish

Step 1: Prewriting
Think about what you want to say in the body of your letter. Jot down ideas and notes.

Step 2: Writing
Look over the correct form for a friendly letter on page 406. Then write your letter. Use your notes to help you write the body.

Step 3: Revising
Read your letter over as if you were receiving it instead of sending it. Is the message clear? If not, rewrite it until it is.

Step 4: Editing
Check the form of your letter line by line against the model letter on page 406. Make sure your punctuation and spelling are correct. Make a neat copy.

B **Writing a Thank-you Note.** You have just received the item pictured on page 417 as a birthday gift. Use your imagination about who gave it to you, what it is, and how you will use it. Write a thank-you note for the gift. Remember to include all five parts of a friendly letter.

416

C **Writing a Letter of Request.** Write a letter to a local television station. Request information about a news story reported on that station. Use the phone book to look up the station's address.

D **Writing from Your Writer's Notebook.** Look over the letter you wrote to yourself. Write a letter of advice to a younger brother, sister, or friend. Tell them a mistake you made that you want them to avoid.

417

Steps for Writing a Letter

Friendly Letters

1. Use the proper form for a friendly letter. (*See pages 405–406.*)
2. Edit your letter for errors in usage, capitalization, punctuation, and spelling.
3. Recopy your letter if necessary for neatness.
4. Include a return address on the envelope. (*See pages 410–411.*)

Business Letters

1. Jot down notes and ideas about what you need to include in your letter.
2. Use the proper form for a business letter. (*See pages 409–410.*)
3. Use a formal greeting and a proper closing for a business letter. (*See pages 409–410.*)
4. Express your message briefly and clearly in the body of your letter.
5. Follow the correct form for the signature. (*See pages 409–410.*)
6. Edit your letter for errors in usage, capitalization, punctuation, and spelling.
7. Use white paper and leave one inch margins.
8. Address the envelope correctly. (*See pages 410–411.*)

Standardized Test

Directions: On your answer sheet, fill in the circle of the line in each group that contains an error. If there is no error in the group, fill in the circle containing *4*.

SAMPLE
1)   4825 Douglas Street

2)   Sioux City, Iowa 51104

3)   November 3, 1986

4) (No error)

ANSWER   ① ② ③ ④

1.
1)   1592 LaSalle Avenue

2)   Evergreen, CO

3)   October 6, 1986

4) (No error)

2.
1)   Dear Uncle Sid

2)   I really like the airplane model

3)   you sent me for my birthday last week.

4) (No error)

3.
1)   I've been collecting models for

2)   two years. This is one I have always

3)   wanted. I don't know how you knew.

4) (No error)

4.
1)   Thank you for a great present.

2)   Love

3)   *Carl*

4) (No error)

Directions: Decide which subject in each group is limited enough for a short report. Fill in the appropriate circle on your answer sheet.

SAMPLE **A** Animals
         B Mammals
         C Foxes

ANSWER Ⓐ Ⓑ Ⓒ

5. **A** The Universe
   B The Planet Jupiter
   C Stars

6. **A** Energy Sources
   B Electricity
   C How Coal Is Mined

7. **A** Planting Corn
   B How Food Is Grown
   C Crops of North America

8. **A** Musical Instruments
   B History of the Violin
   C Orchestras

9. **A** Bones of the Hand
   B The Human Body
   C Bones

10. **A** Birds
    B Pelicans
    C Reptiles

Related Language Skills

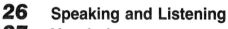

26

Speaking and Listening

Words make communicating with others clear and easy. Words alone, however, do not guarantee that communication is taking place. Communication depends on two important things happening at the same time. First, a person's words must send a clear message. Second, someone must listen and understand that message.

Speaking in Everyday Situations

Although people spend much of their time talking, the purposes of their conversations change constantly. Among the purposes of most conversations is sharing information, ideas, and opinions. You have much information that other people do not have. How to share that information—and your ideas and opinions—effectively is what you will learn in this chapter.

Giving Directions

During a week you give more directions than you probably realize. *Where's the office? Where's your locker? Where's the dog's leash? Where's the nearest subway stop? Where did you put Sunday's newspaper?* Your ability to give clear directions in these and many other situations is very important to the people who ask you the questions. Read the two following sets of directions. Which set of directions would you rather follow if you were in a strange city?

UNCLEAR   You want to get downtown? Just walk a few blocks that way and take a bus at the corner. The bus will get you there.

CLEAR   Where do you want to go downtown? Oh, the State Theater. Walk two blocks straight ahead, past the library to Main Street. After you cross Main Street, wait at the bus stop for number 42 bus. Ask the driver to let you off at State Street. The theater is on the corner of State and Main.

The second set is clearer because it gives exact distances, street names, and other important details, such as the number of the bus.

Following are some important things to keep in mind when you are giving directions.

Giving Directions

1. Ask questions, if necessary, to make sure you know exactly where the person you are directing wants to go.
2. Use words like *left, right,* and *straight ahead.* Avoid *north, south, east,* and *west.*
3. Use street names or highway numbers if you know them.
4. Name buildings, statues, parks, or other landmarks.
5. Give the exact or approximate number of blocks or miles.
6. If the directions are complicated, write them down or draw a map.
7. If you are unsure of the right directions, direct the person to someone who might know.
8. Repeat the directions or have the other person repeat them to you.

EXERCISE 1 Giving Directions

Think of a place you often go to—a park, a movie theater, or a store. Then write directions to get there from your school. Follow the guidelines on page 423. Be prepared to read your directions aloud.

Group Discussions

Group discussions are very important. They are often used to solve a problem or a disagreement. Most of the time, however, discussions are used to share and exchange ideas and information. Following are some guidelines you should remember the next time you become involved in a group discussion—at home or at school.

Guidelines for Group Discussions

1. Keep to the subject of the discussion.
2. Listen carefully to what others have to say and do not interrupt.
3. Ask questions if you do not understand something.
4. If you disagree with someone, do it politely and explain why you disagree.
5. Support your ideas and opinions with facts if you can.
6. Try to reach a decision or a conclusion.

EXERCISE 2 Having a Group Discussion

Your teacher will divide the class into groups of four to six students. Then each group should choose one of the following topics (or one of its own). When the discussion is over, each group should decide how well the discussion followed the guidelines in the box.

1. Making the school day longer or shorter
2. The advantages and disadvantages of television
3. The necessity of having an allowance
4. The advantages and disadvantages of school uniforms

Giving an Oral Report

During your school years, you will have to give many oral reports. You might give a book report for your English class or reports for your science or social studies classes. This section will show you how you can give your next oral report with confidence. It will show you how an oral report is much the same as a written report. They are both prepared the same basic way. The main difference, of course, is that you deliver your oral report aloud to an audience. This section will also show you how to overcome most of your nervousness when you are standing in front of an audience.

Knowing Your Audience and Purpose

Before you start to plan your oral report, you need to think about who your audience will be. At school, it usually will be your classmates. Once in a while, however, you may be asked to speak to adults at a school open house or to a group of younger students. You need to be sure that the report or speech you give is right for your audience.

Following are some questions you should ask yourself about your audience. The answers to these questions will help you plan an oral report or a speech that your audience will understand and enjoy.

Knowing Your Audience

1. What age group will my audience be—my age, older, or younger?
2. What are the interests of my audience? Are they the same as my interests?
3. What will my audience already know about the subject I would like to talk about?

You also need to think about your report's purpose. The purpose of most oral reports is to inform. Other speeches you give, however, may have different purposes.

Purposes of an Oral Report or Speech

Purpose	Examples
TO INFORM	• to explain what was learned from the moon rocks brought to Earth • to explain how farmers grow rice
TO ENTERTAIN	• to tell about the first time you tried to ice skate • to tell about the surprise party you held for a friend who didn't show up
TO PERSUADE	• to convince students to join a club • to convince students to keep their lockers clean throughout the year

---

Using Reasons to Persuade. To win your audience over to your side in a persuasive speech, you must present a convincing argument. To do this, you should include at least three reasons to explain your position. These reasons should be facts, not opinions. Remember that a fact is a statement that can be proven, while an opinion is a personal judgment about something. (*See page 352 for information about facts and opinions.*) Each reason that you state should also be supported by facts, specific figures or details, and examples.

Suppose, for example, that you wanted to give a speech to persuade your classmates to keep your school clean. Your reasons might include the following:

1. Clean-up costs money that could be spent on important things like better sports equipment.
2. Keeping the school clean shows respect for property that belongs to others.
3. A clean school is a better place to learn in than a dirty, messy school.

EXERCISE 3 *Determining Purpose*

Number your paper 1 to 10. Then label the purpose of each oral report: *to inform, to persuade,* or *to entertain.*

1. to tell about the time you made popcorn and it popped all over the kitchen
2. to explain how the first emperor of China united the country for the first time
3. to convince people to take the newspaper you deliver
4. to explain how to make figures of birds and other animals by folding sheets of paper
5. to explain how some schools are using computers to help students learn math more easily
6. to tell the story of a book you read
7. to convince students to collect aluminum cans
8. to persuade your classmates to vote for you as president of your school's student council
9. to tell about camping at a state park
10. to explain why different parts of the country have different kinds of weather

Choosing and Limiting a Subject

The next step in preparing an oral report or a speech is to choose a subject. Begin by making a list of subjects you know something about. Then pick one you think will interest your audience. For example, an oral report about *the different kinds of horses* might interest your science club. A better subject for your social studies class might be *how horses have changed in history.*

Once you have chosen a topic, think about how much time you have to give your report. If you have only a few minutes, you cannot cover a large subject. You will have to limit your subject. To do this look at the parts of the larger subject. Then choose one of the parts. For example, *Mexico* would be too much to talk about, but you could choose *exports of Mexico* or *weather in Mexico.*

427

EXERCISE 4 Finding a Subject

Number your paper 1 to 5. Then write a subject for an oral report that could be included in each area. If your teacher permits, share your ideas with your classmates.

EXAMPLE   personal experience
POSSIBLE ANSWER   my first day at a new school

1. personal experience
2. current events or issues
3. how to do something
4. how to make something
5. past events or people

EXERCISE 5 Limiting a Subject

Number your paper 1 to 10. Then limit each subject so it will be good for a six-minute report or speech.

EXAMPLE   women in science
POSSIBLE ANSWER   Madame Curie's work

1. the Olympic Games
2. United States presidents
3. dinosaurs
4. exploring the moon
5. South America
6. famous musicians
7. forecasting weather
8. pets
9. educational television
10. mystery stories

Gathering Information

The next step in preparing an oral report or a speech is to gather information about your subject. The encyclopedia is a good place to look for information. Use things you know about your subject to help you find things you do not know. For example, if you selected *horseback riding* as your subject, you probably know that most people who ride horses use either an English or a Western saddle. This may lead you to wonder whether there are other kinds of saddles. You can find out by going to the library and looking up *saddle* in an encyclopedia. Questions about many topics can be answered this way.

Gathering Information

1. List what you already know about your subject.
2. List things you want to learn about your subject.
3. Examine encyclopedias and other books and magazines at the library. (*See pages 472–482.*)
4. Find interesting examples or quotations you can use in your speech.
5. Write the information on note cards. (*See page 470.*)

EXERCISE 6 *Gathering Information*

Choose and limit a subject for a six-minute report. Write what you already know about it on note cards. Then go to the library and find more information about the subject. Get enough for at least three more note cards. Save your note cards for Exercise 7.

Making an Outline

After you have gathered information about your subject, you must organize it. To do this, make an outline, as you do before writing a report. (*See pages 390–391.*) Use the following guidelines to help organize your information.

Organizing Information

1. Make an outline of your oral report. (*See page 390.*)
2. The introduction of your report should get the attention of your audience. It should also include the main idea of your report. (*See pages 392–393.*)
3. The body of your report should include all of your supporting points. (*See page 270.*) Arrange your points in a logical order. (*See page 339.*) Use transitions to connect your ideas. (*See page 340.*)
4. The conclusion of your report should summarize your main ideas. (*See page 274*).

EXERCISE 7 *Making an Outline*

Take the note cards with the information you gathered in Exercise 6. Use them to make an outline for an oral report. Save your outline for Exercise 8.

Practicing Your Oral Report

Before you give your report before an audience, you should practice it aloud by yourself several times. First, practice it alone. Then give your report before members of your family or some friends, and ask them for suggestions. If you can, make a tape recording of a practice session. Then play the tape for yourself, listening for the following major problem areas.

A Variety of Words. As you listen to yourself, do you find that you are using the same words over and over again? If you are, use a *thesaurus,* which is a special dictionary that gives you several words with the same meaning. For example, if you repeatedly use words such as *nice, good, bad,* or *okay,* replace them with words that produce clearer images in the minds of your readers. (*See pages 231–241 for more information about specific words.*)

Clear, Expressive Words. As you listen to yourself, also notice how clearly you are pronouncing your words, how fast you are speaking, and how loudly you are speaking. Your audience will never understand your speech if you mumble your words, speak too fast, or speak too softly. Listen also for bad habits, like saying "um" or "uh" between sentences or overusing words like *and* and *like.*

Physical Movement. If possible, practice in front of a mirror and watch your movements—or lack of movement. Look especially for any nervous movements such as switching back and forth from one foot to the other. Your movements should be as natural as possible.

The more you practice your report aloud, the more confident you will feel when you deliver it to an audience. Following are some helpful suggestions to think about as you practice.

Practicing Your Oral Report

1. Read your complete outline several times, until you are familiar with all the information.
2. Make only a few notes to use as you begin to practice aloud. You want to talk about your subject, not read about it.
3. Practice in front of a long mirror so that you can see how you will look to your audience.
4. Practice looking around the room as you talk. Good eye contact with your listeners is important.
5. Time your report. If it is too long, decide what information you can leave out. If it is too short, find information that you can add to make it both longer and more interesting.
6. Practice your report several times over a period of several days.

EXERCISE 8 *Practicing Your Oral Report*

Your teacher will have you work with another student in class. With your partner practice giving the report you outlined in Exercise 7. Then discuss it with your partner. Listen to your partner's report and discuss that report as well.

Delivering Your Oral Report

You may feel a little nervous before you begin to give your report. Most speakers do. If you are well prepared and have practiced your report, you will be far less nervous. Keep the following suggestions in mind when you deliver your report.

Delivering Your Oral Report

1. Be well prepared and have all of your materials ready.
2. Wait until your audience is quiet and settled.
3. Take a deep breath and begin.
4. Stand with your weight evenly divided between both feet. Avoid swaying back and forth.
5. Speak slowly, clearly, and loudly enough to be heard.
6. Use gestures and facial expressions to stress your main points.
7. Look directly at the people in your audience, not over their heads. Try to make eye contact with them.
8. Use pictures, models, or other aids to get and hold the attention of your audience.

EXERCISE 9 *Delivering Your Oral Report*

In front of a group of four to six students from your class, present the report you practiced with a partner in Exercise 8. After you have given your report, write a short evaluation of how you spoke. Think about how you looked and sounded to your audience. Make a list of the things you think you did well when you gave your report. Then make a list of the things you would like to do better.

Evaluating Oral Reports

Throughout your school years, you will be asked to evaluate the oral reports of others. Sometimes you will have the chance to work with another student as you prepare your reports. Most of the time, however, you will be asked to evaluate the oral reports of other students as they are formally giving them. The purpose of evaluating another person's speech is to help that person improve in future speeches. You will be most effective if you are always polite and constructive. Following are several ways in which to be positive in evaluating speeches.

Clarifying. Point out areas in which students could have made parts of their speech clearer or easier to understand. Perhaps they should have defined certain terms; described some things, people, or actions; or given more examples.

Qualifying. Alert the speaker to any opinions he or she states that were not supported by reasons and examples. Listeners tend to dismiss ideas that are not backed and qualified with specific facts.

Extending Ideas. Tell the speaker any questions that were raised during the speech but remained unanswered at the end of the speech. Often answers to questions like these would have made the speech more satisfying and enjoyable to the audience. You also might tell the speaker which ideas in the speech you thought were most interesting. This kind of information will help the speaker keep the listeners in mind more in future speeches.

Evaluating Oral Reports

1. Does the speaker need to clarify any terms?
2. Has the speaker qualified his or her opinions?
3. Does the speaker need to extend his or her ideas?

EXERCISE 10 Evaluating Oral Reports

Listen carefully as the other students in your small group give their reports. As you listen, pay special attention to how each report is given.

As each student finishes his or her report, make a list of five things that you thought were well done. When all of the reports have been given, make a list of five things in any of the reports that could be improved. Then have a group discussion about each report. Point out the strong points of each report as well as areas that could be improved.

Listening

Stop reading for a minute and listen. What do you hear? If the room is quiet, you might answer that you hear nothing. Listen more carefully. Maybe you can hear someone turning a book page or a car going down the street. You will be surprised at how much you can hear when you are really listening. This section will help you become a better listener.

Listening for Main Ideas

A good way to understand a report you are hearing is first to listen carefully for the speaker's main ideas. Long reports can have several main ideas, while a short report should have only one main idea. Most often that main idea will be stated in the form of a declarative topic sentence. Be alert, however, because a main idea may also be expressed as a question, a quotation, or a personal example. Suppose you were listening to a report in which you heard the following.

> People often say that lightning never strikes twice in the same place. Nothing could be more wrong. Lightning *can* strike the same place more than one time. In fact, it often does. Lightning usually hits the tallest thing around. In a storm, some tall buildings are hit by lightning bolts again and again.

When you read this paragraph, you can skim over it more than once and easily find the main idea in the third sentence. When you listen, however, you must listen carefully to catch the speaker's main ideas.

Once you have identified the speaker's main ideas, you must then listen for supporting details and examples. The types of supporting details the speaker uses depend on his or her purpose. These details may be incidents or events, quotations, or facts and examples. For instance, if the speaker's purpose is to persuade you to support efforts to save the rain forests, he or she would relate incidents or facts and examples as supporting details.

At the beginning of the report, the speaker may even alert you to the number of supporting details by using a statement such as *You can help in five ways.* Knowing the keyword is *five*, you can then listen carefully for transitional words and phrases—such as *first, next, most important,* or *as the last step.* Listening for specific clues like these will help you follow the logical organization of an oral report.

EXERCISE 11 Finding a Main Idea

You know interesting facts about various subjects—such as ballet, baseball, computers, or cooking. Choose a subject and write a paragraph. Include an interesting fact as the main idea of the paragraph. Be sure to use your fact in the topic sentence of the paragraph. (*See page 266.*) Finally, work with a classmate. Take turns reading your paragraphs aloud and listen for each other's main ideas.

Taking Notes

Usually you will not have any trouble remembering the main idea of a very short report. However, you should take notes when you must remember several points. Following are some guidelines for taking notes.

Taking Notes

1. Use short phrases. Do not write everything down.
2. Write the main idea of the speaker's introduction.
3. Use outline form for your notes. (*See page 390.*)
4. Listen for clues (such as "There are three reasons why . . .") that will help you organize your notes.
5. Write the restatement of the main idea in the conclusion of the report.

As you take notes and add to your outline, never try to write everything down. Write only the necessary information that you need to remember accurately.

EXERCISE 12 Listening and Taking Notes

Prepare an explanation of how to do something such as wrap a package. Then take notes as each student presents his or her explanation to the class. After each presentation, compare your notes with the notes of other students to see if everyone included the same ideas.

Listening Critically

You must listen critically as well as carefully. Critical listening will help you sort out misleading information from facts.

Motive, Point of View, and Bias.   Listening critically means understanding the speaker's words and deciding whether you agree or disagree with the speaker's ideas. You can do several things to develop your critical listening skills. First, as you listen to the speaker, think about his or her *motive*, or reasons, for selecting the topic. In addition, listen for clues to the speaker's *point of view*—how he or she feels about the topic. As you listen, be aware of any signs that the speaker shows a *bias*, which is a viewpoint based purely on personal feelings rather than facts. The key is to listen for loaded words—words that express the speaker's emotions, as in the following.

BIASED   The food in the school cafeteria is **awful.**
UNBIASED   The school cafeteria should offer more fruits and vegetables.

BIASED   The plan for the new library is **ridiculous.**
UNBIASED   The plan for the new library needs to provide an access for the disabled.

436

To detect bias, you should also listen carefully for other clues. Ask yourself what tone of voice the speaker is using. Most often a biased speaker cannot hide the fact that he or she is approving, angry, or sarcastic.

Even a speaker's facial expressions or gestures may indicate bias. Political speakers, for example, use approving gestures and expressions when referring to candidates of their own party. In such cases the speaker's facial expression is a sure sign of bias. Such clues will help you understand the speaker's message.

Hasty Generalizations. Hasty generalizations are one kind of misleading information. A hasty generalization is a broad statement based on only a few examples. It does not take exceptions into account.

HASTY   All boys like football.
GENERALIZATIONS   Doctors and lawyers are always rich.

Listen for words such as *all, always, never, everyone, no one,* and *nobody.* Such words often signal a hasty generalization. *Most* boys (and a lot of girls, too) may like football. That does not mean that *all* boys like football. In the same way, *some* doctors and lawyers are rich, but not every single doctor and lawyer in the world is rich.

Watch out for hasty generalizations. Listen critically so that you can tell when a speaker is saying something that sounds truthful but really is not.

EXERCISE 13   *Rewriting Hasty Generalizations*

Number your paper 1 to 5. Then rewrite the following hasty generalizations so that they are not misleading.

1. Boys are better at math than girls are.
2. Everyone likes dogs better than cats.
3. All teenagers like rock music.
4. Everyone will be watching the Super Bowl.
5. Radio station WROK never plays the kind of music teenagers like.

*C*hapter *R*eview

A **Giving Directions.** Rewrite each sentence so that its directions are clearer. Add details as needed.

1. Walk several blocks straight ahead.
2. Turn that way and go two blocks. Then turn south.
3. Go as far as the big street about a mile ahead.
4. I don't know where the place is, but if you keep going that way you might find it.
5. Go two blocks that way. Then turn and go two more.

B **Improving Directions.** Find the errors in the following directions. Then rewrite them. Use details of your own to improve them.

You want King Avenue and 23rd Street? Drive that way for a few minutes; then turn north. Go a few more blocks, and turn east at a traffic light. Then drive a few more blocks until you get there.

C **Analyzing a Group Discussion.** Number your paper 1 to 5. Then read the group discussion. Follow the guidelines in the box on page 424 to answer the questions.

BETH   For our field trip, we could go to the aquarium, the art museum, or the high school science fair.
JOE   The aquarium is a stupid idea.
PAT   Joe is stupid for saying the aquarium is stupid.
LEE   I've never been to the aquarium. What is it like?
SUE   The high school science fair wouldn't cost much.
PHIL   Last year we went to a nearby ranch.

1. What was the topic of the discussion?
2. What rule did Joe and Pat break?
3. Who broke rule number 1?
4. What rule did Sue follow?
5. What rule did Lee follow?

D **Knowing the Purpose of an Oral Report or Speech.**
Each of the following sentences is the first sentence of a report or speech. Tell what you think is the purpose of each one: *to inform, to persuade,* or *to entertain.*

1. Did you ever glue your fingers together?
2. I want to tell you the many reasons why you should vote for Julia Chin as our homeroom representative.
3. When we introduced our new kitten to our dog, the fun began!
4. Have you ever wondered how a refrigerator works?
5. The Sahara is the largest desert in the world.
6. Everyone must cooperate in keeping the school grounds neat and clean.
7. Everyone must get out and vote today.
8. It was a stormy night in late summer when I thought I saw a ghost.
9. Here are some tips on how to study.
10. We should all support our soccer team.

E **Limiting a Subject.** Limit each topic below so that it is suitable for a six-minute speech.

1. Africa
2. World War II
3. great cities in Europe
4. famous explorers
5. our solar system
6. jungle birds
7. the tsars of Russia
8. medical discoveries
9. great inventions
10. radio

F **Giving an Oral Report.** Choose one of the limited topics you wrote for Exercise E. Prepare a six-minute oral report about it. Your teacher may ask you to give your report in class.

G **Listening and Taking Notes.** Listen as your teacher reads a paragraph from a book or magazine. Take notes as you listen. Then use your notes to write five questions about the subject of the paragraph. See if some of your classmates can answer your questions.

439

27

Vocabulary

How many words do you know? If you are like most sixth graders, you probably know between 7,000 and 8,000 words. You will probably add another 1,000 words to your vocabulary each year you are in school.

The more words you know and use correctly, the more successful you will be—in school and out. A large vocabulary will help you read and write well. It will also help you listen and speak accurately. With a good vocabulary, you can find exactly the word you need to express your thoughts and feelings.

As you study this chapter, you will learn 60 new words to add to your vocabulary. You will also learn ways that you can build your vocabulary every day.

*E*XERCISE 1 *Previewing the Vocabulary List*

Turn to the vocabulary list on page 451. The words on the vocabulary list will be used in this chapter. Look over the words to see how many of them you already know. If you do not know a word's meaning, use a dictionary for help. Then number your paper 1 to 5. Choose five words from the list and write a sentence using each one.

The Growth of English

Languages have histories, just as countries do. A language can grow, just as human beings grow. The English language has a history that goes back hundreds of years. English has grown and changed in that time.

Borrowed Words

Many of our words have come from other languages. This is one way English has grown. For example, *kindergarten* was originally a German word. Kindergarten classes were first started in Germany. When people in the United States began kindergarten classes, they took both the idea and the name from Germany. Following are some words borrowed from other languages.

ARABIC   zero, giraffe, sugar, alcohol
FRENCH   garage, crime, restaurant, barber, art
GERMAN   house, nickel, noodle, poodle, waltz
ITALIAN   piano, violin, volcano, umbrella, pizza
SPANISH   patio, tuna, corral, rodeo, stampede

EXERCISE 2   Using Words from Latin

Many words about government came to us from Latin, the language of ancient Rome. Number your paper 1 to 5. Then write a sentence using each underlined word. Use a dictionary if you do not know a word's meaning.

Words from Rome

1. republic—from *res publicus,* "public affairs"
2. govern—from *gubernare,* "to pilot (a ship), direct"
3. senate—from *senex,* "old, aged" (In early Rome, the senators were a council of elders.)
4. candidate—from *candidatus,* "white robed" (A Roman wore his whitest robe when running for office.)
5. emperor—from *emperator,* "commander"

441

Words from Names

Many words added to the English language have come from names. For example, the *Ferris wheel* is named for George Ferris, the man who invented it. The sports coat we call a *blazer* is modeled after a coat first made for sailors on the British ship *Blazer*.

EXERCISE 3 Using Words from Names

Number your paper 1 to 5. Write a sentence using the word that came from each underlined word below.

1. Ground meat took its name from <u>Hamburg</u>, a German city.
2. Another German city, <u>Homburg</u>, is where a certain kind of hat was first made.
3. Rudolph <u>Diesel</u> invented a new kind of engine.
4. A type of wool cloth was first made in Scotland, near the <u>Tweed</u> River.
5. Allessandro <u>Volta</u> made early studies of electricity.

Compound Words

Compound words are made by combining two words into one. For example, *pine* plus *apple* gives *pineapple*. *Down* plus *stairs* makes *downstairs*. Many new words have been added to English in this way.

EXERCISE 4 Making Compound Words

Number your paper 1 to 10. Then write ten compound words. For each compound, use one word from list A and one from list B. Use each list word only once.

LIST A	book	head	news	play	through
	every	land	over	rail	wind
LIST B	board	ground	lord	paper	shield
	body	keeper	out	quarters	way

Word Meaning

Suppose you come across a new word in your reading. You will need to know what the word means. You can find out by looking it up in a dictionary. You may also use some other ways to unlock the meanings of new words. This section will help you learn some ways in which you can discover word meanings.

Context Clues

Looking for context clues is one way to learn what a new word means. The *context* of a word is the sentence, the surrounding words, or the situation in which a word is used. Look at the following example.

CONTEXT   Tom made a good **adjustment** to his new school,
CLUES   fitting in and making new friends quickly.

The clues in that sentence will help you to see that *adjustment* means something like "a change of circumstances." You can still look it up in a dictionary later, but you will not have to stop reading.

Following are some examples of context clues.

DEFINITION   A **metropolis** is a very large city.

EXAMPLE   Fish, seals, and whales are **aquatic** animals.

SYNONYM   A crowd began to gather in the **foyer.** Soon, the outer hall was filled with people.

In the first example above, the word *metropolis* is defined in the sentence. The whole point of the sentence is to tell what the word means. In the second example, the names of animals that live in the water are given. Naming these animals lets you know that *aquatic* has to do with something that lives or grows in water. In the third example, *outer hall* is the clue. It is a synonym (a word or phrase that means about the same thing) for *foyer.*

443

EXERCISE 5 *Using Context Clues*

Number your paper 1 to 10. Then write the letter of the word or phrase that is closest in meaning to the underlined word in each sentence.

1. After they <u>demolish</u> the old school, they will start building a new one in the same place.
   (A) decorate   (B) improve   (C) build
   (D) destroy   (E) complete

2. The letters *A*, *B*, and *C* can be used to label the sides of a <u>triangle</u>.
   (A) rectangle   (B) circle   (C) three-sided figure
   (D) four-sided figure   (E) box

3. We are having the <u>annual</u> fourth of July picnic at the park this year.
   (A) daily   (B) yearly   (C) usual   (D) short
   (E) enjoyable

4. You will get <u>drenched</u> if you go out in this storm without an umbrella.
   (A) dirty   (B) blown over   (C) hit by lightning
   (D) frozen   (E) very wet

5. To avoid an accident, you should be extra <u>cautious</u> when you drive in bad weather.
   (A) helpful   (B) fast   (C) careful   (D) clever
   (E) tricky

6. The <u>miniature</u> house was so small you could hold it in your hand.
   (A) smaller than life-size   (B) fancy   (C) brick
   (D) old-fashioned   (E) bigger than usual

7. Because we like carrots, we <u>frequently</u> eat them.
   (A) never   (B) often   (C) rarely   (D) honestly
   (E) regretfully

8. Even though all the tickets were sold, many seats in the auditorium were <u>vacant</u> during the concert.
   (A) wooden   (B) filled   (C) empty   (D) crowded
   (E) broken

9. The <u>coarse</u> shirt made my skin itch and turn red.
   (A) rough   (B) fine   (C) old   (D) thin   (E) tiny

10. I <u>assume</u> from seeing your big smile that you had a good time at the party.
(A) know for a fact   (B) wonder   (C) expect
(D) do not know   (E) suppose

Prefixes and Suffixes

Another way to find the meaning of a new word is to break it down into its parts. For example, you might come across the word *distrust*. You probably know what *trust* means. This part is called the root. A *root* is the part of a word that carries its basic meaning. The roots of the following words are in heavy type.

ROOTS   dis**like**   re**move**   un**expect**ed   **skill**ful

EXERCISE 6   Finding Roots

Number your paper 1 to 10. Then write each word and underline its root.

1. repay
2. uneasy
3. painful
4. review
5. unhappy
6. research
7. unusual
8. replace
9. thankful
10. disagree

Prefixes.   A prefix is a part of a word that comes before a root. In *distrust*, the prefix is *dis-*. If you know that *dis-* means "not," you can figure out that *distrust* means "not trust." Following are some common prefixes and their meanings.

PREFIX	MEANING	EXAMPLE
dis-	not	dis + ease = disease
mis-	bad or wrong	mis + behave = misbehave
re-	again	re + pay = repay
un-	not	un + cover = uncover

*E*XERCISE 7 *Using Prefixes*

Number your paper 1 to 10. Write the prefix that has the same meaning as the underlined word. Then write the complete word that has the meaning after the equal sign.

EXAMPLE   <u>not</u> + happy = sad
ANSWER   un-, unhappy

1. <u>wrong</u> + spell = to make a spelling mistake
2. <u>not</u> + like = to not like someone or something
3. <u>again</u> + turn = to come back or bring back
4. <u>not</u> + easy = feeling worried about something
5. <u>again</u> + place = to put or bring something back
6. <u>not</u> + courage = to try to persuade someone not to do something
7. <u>again</u> + search = make a careful study of something
8. <u>bad</u> + fortune = bad luck
9. <u>not</u> + expected = something surprising
10. <u>not</u> + guise = something that hides who you are

Suffixes. A suffix is the part of a word that comes after a root. Like a prefix, a suffix can change a word's meaning. A suffix can also change a word's part of speech. In the following examples, the suffixes are in heavy type.

EXAMPLES   agree**ment**   skill**ful**   govern**or**

Following is a list of some common suffixes.

SUFFIX	MEANING	EXAMPLE
-able	fit for	wash + able = washable
-en	make or become	sharp + en = sharpen
-er	one who	teach + er = teacher
-ful	full of, having	care + ful = careful
-ment	state of	equip + ment = equipment
-or	one who	act + or = actor
-ous	full of	danger + ous = dangerous

EXERCISE 8 Using Suffixes

Number your paper 1 to 10. Write the suffix that has the same meaning as the underlined words. Then write the complete word defined after the equal sign.

EXAMPLE   use + <u>full of</u> = having uses
ANSWER   -ful, useful

1. read + <u>fit for</u> = able to be read
2. tight + <u>make or cause</u> = to make tighter
3. amaze + <u>state of</u> = feeling of wonder
4. poison + <u>full of</u> = very harmful, deadly
5. skill + <u>full of</u> = having or showing skill
6. photograph + <u>one who</u> = one who takes pictures
7. thank + <u>full of</u> = glad, pleased
8. accept + <u>fit for</u> = able to be accepted
9. edit + <u>one who</u> = person who edits
10. length + <u>make or become</u> = to make longer

EXERCISE 9 Using Prefixes and Suffixes

Number your paper 1 to 10. Add a prefix, a suffix, or one of each with the same meaning as the underlined word or words. Write only the complete word that has the meaning after the equal sign.

1. <u>bad or wrong</u> + lay = to put in the wrong place
2. respect + <u>full of</u> = showing respect
3. agree + <u>state of</u> = state or act of agreeing
4. <u>not</u> + usual = something that is strange
5. power + <u>full of</u> = very strong
6. adjust + <u>state of</u> = a correction
7. <u>not</u> + accept + <u>fit for</u> = something that cannot be accepted
8. advertise + <u>state of</u> = something that advertises
9. <u>again</u> + search + <u>one who</u> = person who searches for information
10. <u>again</u> + turn + <u>fit for</u> = able to be brought back

Synonyms

A big dictionary may contain over 600,000 words. No one would use that many different words in a lifetime. Still, you can express your ideas exactly by using the best possible words in a given situation. For example, how often have you heard someone say, "It was a good movie"? Think of all the other words you could use to describe a movie you liked.

A word that has nearly the same meaning as another word is called a *synonym*. In the following sentences, the words *huge* and *gigantic* are synonyms, but *gigantic* gives a better picture of something very big.

EXAMPLE   The King Ranch in Texas is **huge**.
IMPROVED   The King Ranch in Texas is **gigantic**.

Dictionaries often give synonyms for words. They may also explain the differences in meanings of synonyms. In writing, look for words that will express your ideas exactly and colorfully. Use a dictionary for help.

EXERCISE 10   Recognizing Synonyms

Number your paper 1 to 10. Write the letter of the answer that is closest in meaning to the word in capital letters. Then check your work in a dictionary.

1. AMAZE   (A) fast   (B) astonish   (C) heavy
   (D) pretty   (E) slippery
2. VACANT   (A) better   (B) warm   (C) full
   (D) empty   (E) modern
3. RAPID   (A) slight   (B) sure   (C) fast
   (D) mighty   (E) tall
4. EXPENSIVE   (A) costly   (B) excellent
   (C) shocking   (D) dainty   (E) huge
5. BRIEF   (A) long   (B) slide   (C) make
   (D) help   (E) short

6. OBTAIN   (A) try   (B) enjoy   (C) get
   (D) discourage   (E) move
7. GORGEOUS   (A) pleasant   (B) beautiful
   (C) slender   (D) happy   (E) distrustful
8. CONTRIBUTE   (A) toss   (B) whirl   (C) take
   (D) give   (E) hurry
9. QUANTITY   (A) answer   (B) skill   (C) choice
   (D) quality   (E) amount
10. TREMENDOUS   (A) lovely   (B) average
    (C) vacant   (D) huge   (E) slow

EXERCISE 11   Choosing the Better Word

Number your paper 1 to 10. Then write the synonym in
parentheses that best fits the meaning of each sentence.

EXAMPLE   We had to make a (sore, painful) decision.
 ANSWER   painful

1. Running the obstacle course in gym class is a (test,
   quiz) of skill.
2. The twins were dressed in (similar, uniform) jeans
   and shirts.
3. Try to (conclude, stop) your report with a brief
   summary of the main ideas.
4. The cat's behavior was (uneasy, doubtful) and
   restless.
5. The actor completed the disguise by adding the
   (untrue, false) nose.
6. I disagree with your (argument, fight) about the
   need for a new school building.
7. The wreckers arrived and began to (demolish,
   eliminate) the old building.
8. We need to (return, replace) the broken steps with
   new ones.
9. The students all went to the library to (obtain, fetch)
   information for their reports.
10. It is (ordinary, normal) to be a little nervous during
    try outs for the talent show.

Antonyms

An *antonym* is a word that means the opposite of another word. Dictionaries list antonyms for some words. The following pairs of words are antonyms.

long—short expensive—cheap
never—always gorgeous—ugly

EXERCISE 12 Recognizing Antonyms

Number your paper 1 to 10. Write the word that is most nearly the opposite of the word in capital letters.

1. CAUTIOUS poor guess careless imitation
2. WEALTHY poor rich old funny
3. GRACEFUL slender careful curved clumsy
4. CONCLUDE help begin walk end
5. ABSENT tardy prepared without present
6. VICTORY win weak tired defeat
7. INCREASE add uncover decrease replace
8. RAPID add slow more less
9. SIMILAR false guess different normal
10. COARSE bumpy moist tight smooth

EXERCISE 13 Using Antonyms

Number your paper 1 to 5. Then rewrite each sentence using an antonym for the underlined word. Choose the antonyms from the following list.

brief conclude ordinary uneasy
skillful frequently tidy vacant

1. The painter was very clumsy.
2. Speakers seldom use notes.
3. Begin your speech with your main idea.
4. Try not to make your speech too long.
5. Meg's room always looks messy.

Vocabulary Building

You can work at building your vocabulary every day. When you come across a new word, try to figure out its meaning from the context in which you read or hear it. Write the word down so that you can look it up in a dictionary later. If you cannot figure out the meaning, look it up right away.

Keep a notebook of new words, and add new words and their meanings as you come across them. Look over your list from time to time to refresh your memory. Try to use the new words in your speaking and writing so they become familiar to you.

Vocabulary List. The following list contains words that you may come across in your reading. All of the words have appeared earlier in the chapter. Write any word you don't know the meaning of in your vocabulary notebook. Use a dictionary to look up the meaning.

Vocabulary List

absent	diesel	misfortune	respectful
adjustment	discourage	normal	senate
advertise	disguise	obtain	similar
agreement	distrust	overboard	skillful
amazement	drench	painful	thankful
annual	editor	photographer	throughout
assume	emperor	poisonous	tidy
bookkeeper	expensive	powerful	tremendous
brief	frequent	quantity	triangle
candidate	gorgeous	quiz	uneasy
cautious	govern	railway	unexpected
coarse	graceful	rapid	vacant
conclude	headquarters	replace	victory
contribute	increase	republic	wealthy
demolish	miniature	research	windshield

Chapter Review

A **Recognizing Word Origins.** Number your paper 1 to 10. Then write the letter that tells how each word came into the English language. Use a dictionary if you need help.

(A) borrowed from another language
(B) taken from a person's name
(C) taken from the name of a place
(D) compound—made from two other words

1. rodeo
2. tweed
3. senate
4. railway
5. throughout

6. republic
7. diesel
8. hamburger
9. windshield
10. headquarters

B **Using Context Clues.** Number your paper 1 to 10. Then use context clues to figure out each missing word. Choose the best word for each sentence from the following list.

candidate   editor   obtain   replace
contribute   gorgeous   painful   similiar
disguise   normal   powerful   uneasy

1. Having a tooth pulled can be very _____.
2. If you lose your book, you will have to _____ it.
3. After waiting in line for hours, I was able to _____ two free tickets for the concert.
4. Our coats were so _____ I could not tell them apart.
5. Which _____ will you vote for?
6. Some people feel nervous and _____ the first time they speak before an audience.
7. She wore a _____ so no one would recognize her.
8. You can _____ your old toys to Toys for Tots.
9. The flower garden was really _____.
10. A newspaper _____ should know how to use words.

C **Using Prefixes and Suffixes.** Number your paper 1 to 10. Add a prefix, a suffix, or both to each underlined word to make the sentence read correctly. Write the new word only. Hyphens show where to add word parts.

1. The photograph- asked us to smile before she took the picture.
2. DeVito will -place the injured quarterback.
3. I found out about the sale from an advertise-.
4. I -placed my book and couldn't find it for days.
5. The govern- of our state was once a high school teacher.
6. We were surprised by your -expected visit.
7. My brother tried to -courage me from taking on such a difficult project.
8. Her messy room was really -grace-.
9. If you can short- it by a few inches, we can fit it into the smaller box.
10. Their mother told the boys to stop arguing and settle their -agree-.

D **Recognizing Synonyms.** Number your paper 1 to 10. Write the word in each line that is a synonym for the word in capital letters.

1. POWERFUL   normal   strong   coarse   huge
2. CAUTIOUS   careless   untidy   careful   respected
3. DRENCHED   moist   damp   dry   soaked
4. QUANTITY   amount   lots   few   several
5. DEMOLISH   build   repair   wreck   throw
6. EXPENSIVE   pay   cheap   afford   costly
7. THANKFUL   graceful   grateful   generous   glorious
8. NORMAL   tidy   averge   rich   powerful
9. TIDY   neat   coarse   skillful   vacant
10. RAPID   race   slow   forward   fast

E **Finding Antonyms.** Number your paper 1 to 5. Using the words in part D, find five words in capital letters that have an antonym in the same line. Write the word and its antonym.

28

Spelling

You want readers to concentrate on what you are saying in your writing. If they are distracted or confused by spelling errors, they may not understand you. This chapter will help you improve your spelling so your meaning can shine through.

*E*XERCISE 1 *Spelling Warm-up*

Number your paper 1 to 10. Then write the correct spelling of each underlined word.

Unusual Birds

Most people think of birds as flying (1) <u>creetures</u> that live in trees and eat seeds and insects. While this is true of most types of birds, other birds practice many (2) <u>diffrent</u> ways of life. The ostrich is an (3) <u>intresting</u> bird. It (4) <u>wieghs</u> more than 300 pounds and cannot fly at all. (5) <u>It's</u> home is the dry, treeless desert. The penguin is also a bird. It lives in the cold ocean. It can't fly (6) <u>ether</u>, but it can stay underwater for an hour and often (7) <u>remanes</u> at sea for months at a time. It almost (8) <u>allways</u> lives on fish (9) <u>insted</u> of seeds. Many kinds of birds make (10) <u>there</u> living from the water.

Spelling Rules

You can spell hundreds of words correctly by learning a few spelling rules. Write the rules in your spelling notebook with examples to help you remember them. Also write down any exceptions. Reviewing these rules often will help you conquer many spelling demons.

Spelling Patterns

You have probably heard the rhyme that helps you spell words with *ie* or *ei*.

Put *i* before *e*
Except after *c*
Or when sounded like *a*
As in *neighbor* and *weigh*.

The following examples show this rule in action.

I BEFORE *E*	EXCEPT AFTER *C*	SOUNDED LIKE *A*
believe	ceiling	eight
mischief	conceit	freight
niece	deceive	sleigh
piece	perceive	veil
thief	receipt	weight

Following are some exceptions to this rule.

either	foreign	height	ancient
leisure	protein	their	conscience
neither	seize	weird	species

Some other words that cause spelling problems are those that end with a "seed" sound. This sound can be spelled *-cede*, *-ceed*, or *-sede*. Almost all words ending with the "seed" sound are spelled with the *-cede* ending. The chart on the following page shows the only words that have the other endings.

-SEDE	-CEED	-CEDE
supersede	exceed	all others
	proceed	
	succeed	

EXERCISE 2 Using Spelling Patterns

Number your paper 1 to 20. Then write each word, adding
either *ie* or *ei*.

1. f____ld
2. misch____f
3. rec____ve
4. dec____ve
5. v____l
6. w____gh
7. conc____t
8. r____gn
9. br____f
10. n____ce

11. n____ther
12. sl____gh
13. n____ghbor
14. prot____n
15. ____ght
16. c____ling
17. bel____ve
18. rec____pt
19. for____gn
20. y____ld

EXERCISE 3 Using Spelling Patterns

Number your paper 1 to 10. Then write each word, adding
-sede, *-ceed*, or *-cede*.

1. pre____
2. inter____
3. ex____
4. pro____
5. re____

6. ac____
7. super____
8. suc____
9. con____
10. se____

Plurals

The following rules will help you form the plurals of
nouns correctly. When in doubt about an exception, check
a dictionary.

Regular Nouns. To form the plural of most nouns, simply add *s*. If a noun ends in *s, ch, sh, x,* or *z,* add *es* to form the plural.

SINGULAR	dog	lamp	apple	notebook
PLURAL	dog**s**	lamp**s**	apple**s**	notebook**s**
SINGULAR	di**sh**	fox	mo**ss**	chur**ch**
PLURAL	di**sh**es	fox**es**	mo**ss**es	chur**ch**es

EXERCISE 4 Forming Plurals

Number your paper 1 to 10. Then write the plural of each noun.

1. march
2. pencil
3. boss
4. wish
5. trace

6. box
7. match
8. reflex
9. room
10. waltz

Nouns Ending in y. Add *s* to form the plural of a noun that ends in a vowel and *y*.

SINGULAR	bo**y**	pla**y**	to**y**	tra**y**
PLURAL	bo**ys**	pla**ys**	to**ys**	tra**ys**

Change the *y* to *i* and add *es* to a noun that ends in a consonant and *y*.

SINGULAR	coun**try**	assem**bly**	wor**ry**	batte**ry**
PLURAL	coun**tries**	assem**blies**	wor**ries**	batte**ries**

EXERCISE 5 Forming Plurals

Number your paper 1 to 20. Write the plural of each noun.

1. donkey
2. caddy
3. witch
4. class
5. lady

6. city
7. loss
8. decoy
9. wax
10. spy

11. dish
12. box
13. ash
14. fly
15. lass

16. birch
17. journey
18. canary
19. perch
20. discovery

457

Nouns Ending in o. Add *s* to form the plural of a noun that ends in a vowel and *o*.

SINGULAR ster**eo**   cam**eo**   kangar**oo**   tatt**oo**
PLURAL stereo**s**   cameo**s**   kangaroo**s**   tattoo**s**

The plurals of nouns that end in a consonant and *o* do not follow a regular pattern.

SINGULAR toma**to**   mot**to**   ha**lo**   ze**ro**
PLURAL tomato**es**   motto**es**   halo**s**   zero**s**

Add *s* to form the plural of a musical term that ends in *o*.

SINGULAR sol**o**   alt**o**   pian**o**   banj**o**
PLURAL solo**s**   alto**s**   piano**s**   banjo**s**

Check the dictionary if you are unsure about how to form the plural of a noun that ends in *o*. If the plural is not formed by simply adding *s*, the dictionary will show the correct spelling. (*See page 486.*)

EXERCISE 6 *Forming Plurals*

Number your paper 1 to 10. Write the plural of each noun.

1. potato
2. radio
3. tornado
4. hero
5. ratio
6. cello
7. mosquito
8. soprano
9. volcano
10. zoo

Nouns Ending in f or fe. To form the plural of some nouns that end in *f* or *fe*, simply add *s*.

SINGULAR roo**f**   belie**f**   gira**ffe**   fi**fe**
PLURAL roof**s**   belief**s**   giraffe**s**   fife**s**

To form the plural of other nouns that end in *f* or *fe*, change the *f* to *v* and add *es*.

SINGULAR li**fe**   hal**f**   lea**f**   kni**fe**
PLURAL li**ves**   hal**ves**   lea**ves**   kni**ves**

There is no sure way to tell how to form the plural of nouns that end in *f* or *fe*. When you write these words, you need to use a dictionary to check the plural forms.

EXERCISE 7 *Forming Plurals*

Number your paper 1 to 10. Write the plural of each noun.

1. loaf
2. shelf
3. calf
4. gulf
5. thief

6. sheaf
7. bluff
8. self
9. knife
10. safe

Other Plural Forms.   The following box lists examples of nouns that do not form the plural by adding *s* or *es*. Study these words so that you will remember them when you want to use them in your writing.

Irregular Plurals		
tooth, teeth	child, children	ox, oxen
foot, feet	woman, women	die, dice
goose, geese	man, men	mouse, mice
Same Form for Singular and Plural		
Chinese	sheep	scissors
Swiss	moose	series
English	fish	politics

EXERCISE 8 *Forming Plurals*

Number your paper 1 to 10. Write the plural of each noun. Then check your answers in a dictionary.

1. wolf
2. studio
3. series
4. tooth
5. sheriff

6. woman
7. mouse
8. Chinese
9. duo
10. tomato

459

Prefixes and Suffixes

A *prefix* is one or more syllables placed in front of a root to form a new word. When you add a prefix, do not change the spelling of the root.

mis + spell = misspell   re + phrase = rephrase
mid + night = midnight   im + patient = impatient

One or more syllables placed after a root is called a *suffix*. In many cases, you simply add the suffix. In others, however, you must change the spelling of the root before adding the suffix. The following rules will help you spell words with suffixes.

Words Ending in e

Drop the final *e* before a suffix that begins with a vowel.

close + est = closest   true + ism = truism

Keep the final *e* before a suffix that begins with a consonant.

peace + ful = peaceful   amuse + ment = amusement

Note the following exceptions to these rules.

change—changeable   judge—judgment   wise—wisdom

Words Ending in y

To add a suffix to most words that end in a vowel and *y*, keep the *y*.

enjoy + able = enjoyable   annoy + ing = annoying

To add a suffix to most words that end in a consonant and *y*, change the *y* to *i* before adding the suffix.

happy + ness = happiness   fly + er = flier

EXERCISE 9 Adding Prefixes and Suffixes

Number your paper 1 to 10. Then write each word, adding the prefix or suffix shown. Remember to make any necessary spelling changes.

1. dis + appoint
2. im + mature
3. re + enter
4. nerve + ous
5. state + ment

6. joy + ful
7. save + ing
8. un + done
9. rely + able
10. judge + ment

Doubling the Final Consonant

The final letter in a word is sometimes doubled before a suffix is added. Before you double a consonant, check to make sure the word meets both of the following tests.

- The word has only one syllable or is stressed on the final syllable.
- The word ends in one consonant preceded by one vowel.

run + ing = running   prefer + ed = preferred
dip + er = dipper   forget + able = forgettable

- Do not double the final letter if it is preceded by two vowels.

meet + ing = meeting   beat + er = beater
rain + ed = rained   train + able = trainable

EXERCISE 10 Adding Suffixes

Number your paper 1 to 10. Then write each word, adding the suffix shown. Remember to make any necessary spelling changes.

1. begin + ing
2. hit + ing
3. repeat + ed
4. boat + er
5. skip + ing

6. clean + ing
7. regret + able
8. jog + er
9. benefit + ed
10. knit + ed

461

*H*omophones and Homographs

Homophones are words that sound alike but have different meanings and spellings.

Commonly Confused Homophones

its	belonging to it [possessive pronoun]
it's	it is or it has [contraction]
their	belonging to them [possessive pronoun]
there	at a certain place [adverb]
they're	they are [contraction]
theirs	belonging to them [possessive pronoun]
there's	there is [contraction]
to	in a direction toward [preposition]
too	excessively; also [adverb]
two	a number [adjective]
whose	belonging to whom [possessive pronoun]
who's	who is [contraction]
your	belonging to you [possessive pronoun]
you're	you are [contraction]

In contrast, *homographs* are words that are spelled alike but have different meanings and sometimes different pronunciations.

HOMOGRAPH	PRONUNCIATION	MEANING
light	līt	illumination
light	līt	not heavy
wound	wound	past tense of *wind*
wound	wünd	injury
present	pre′sent	not absent
present	pre·sent′	give

*E*XERCISE 11 *Using Homophones*

Write the correct form of each homophone.

1. I don't know if (their, there, they're) going.
2. The dog buried (its, it's) bone.
3. Pat and I are going (to, too, two) my cousin's house.
4. Nobody knew (whose, who's) notebook it was.
5. The Nelsons are selling (their, there, they're) car.
6. Do you think (your, you're) going to the play?
7. (Theirs, There's) a track meet tomorrow.
8. The music is (to, too, two) loud.
9. (Its, It's) going to be dark soon.
10. (Whose, Who's) the best swimmer in your class?

*E*XERCISE 12 *Using Homographs*

Number your paper 1 to 10. Write a sentence to show each meaning of the homographs listed below.

EXAMPLE   lead (lĕd) a metal; lead (lēd) to guide
ANSWER   The pipes are made out of lead.
         Mr. Stewart will lead the parade.

1. object (ob′ject) a thing; object (ob·ject′) to protest
2. pen (pen) a cage for animals; pen (pen) an instrument for writing
3. palm (päm) a tropical tree; palm (päm) the inner part of the hand
4. live (līv) alive; live (liv) to inhabit
5. wound (wound) past tense of *wind*; wound (wünd) an injury
6. duck (duk) a water bird; duck (duk) to dodge
7. post (pōst) a heavy beam; post (pōst) to put up a notice
8. light (līt) illumination; light (līt) not heavy
9. bow (bou) to bend the body forward; bow (bō) a type of knot
10. present (pre′sent) not absent; present (pre·sent′) to give

Spelling Demons

The words in the following list are often spelled incorrectly. Study the words carefully, following the suggestions on page 455.

Spelling Demons

absence	cooperate	heiress	probably
ache	corral	immigrant	pursuit
achievement	courageous	increase	quiet
acquaint	courtesy	instead	quiver
address	coyote	interested	raisin
aerial	daily	interrupt	raspberry
again	deceive	irregular	receipt
aisle	definition	irrigation	reference
allegiance	dependent	jealous	reign
all right	different	knapsack	remain
altogether	disguise	label	remembrance
always	drought	license	responsibility
analyze	easel	lightning	rhythm
anniversary	eighth	mileage	scenery
assignment	embarrass	miniature	sear
assistance	emphasize	mischievous	seize
ballet	environment	misspell	siege
bargain	especially	monitor	science
beautiful	familiar	necessary	separate
believe	fascinate	neighbor	similar
boulevard	feud	nickel	skillful
brief	fiery	niece	squawk
business	forty	occasion	stretch
busy	fourth	occurrence	sufficient
calendar	friend	opponent	thief
campaign	gauge	ordinary	throughout
carriage	genuine	pamphlet	truly
chord	guess	paralyze	unique
complexion	guilty	particle	vehicle
condemn	handicap	phantom	weight
convenient	height	pitiful	weird

Chapter Review

A   **Using Spelling Patterns.** Number your paper 1 to 10.
Write the word that is spelled correctly in each pair.

1. believe, beleive
2. recieve, receive
3. wiegh, weigh
4. niether, neither
5. preceed, precede

6. radios, radioes
7. dishs, dishes
8. citys, cities
9. potatos, potatoes
10. leaves, leafs

B   **Adding Prefixes and Suffixes.** Number your paper 1 to
10. Then write each word, adding the prefix or suffix
shown. Remember to make necessary spelling changes.

1. noisy + er
2. courage + ous
3. dis + appoint
4. true + ly
5. im + mature

6. grace + ful
7. il + legal
8. run + ing
9. re + view
10. happy + ness

C   **Using Homophones and Homographs.** Number your
paper 1 to 10. Then write the word or the pronunciation that fits the meaning in each sentence.

1. Is Maria coming (to, too, two)?
2. I gave my brother a (pres'ent, pres·ent') for his
   birthday.
3. (Whose, Who's) glasses are those?
4. Larry (wünd, wound) his watch.
5. Is (their, there, they're) any fruit left?
6. Have you ever seen a metallic (ob'ject, ob·ject') like
   this before?
7. What color is (your, you're) new shirt?
8. Cheryl expects to (led, lēd) the team in rebounds.
9. (There's, Theirs) a good book about archery in the
   library.
10. They have (liv, līv) tigers at the zoo.

Study Skills and Library Skills

You will study many subjects in school. Good study skills will help you remember what you have learned. Good library skills will help you find new ideas. Skills you learn now will stay with you throughout your life. This chapter will help you build those skills.

*E*XERCISE 1 *Previewing the Chapter*

Start now to develop good study habits. Number your paper 1 to 10. Read each question below. Then find the answer by looking in the chapter.

1. On what page does the chapter end?
2. Does this chapter explain the Dewey decimal system?
3. What page shows you a sample author card?
4. What will the SQ3R method help you do?
5. What pages tell you about notetaking?
6. Which comes first in this chapter, library skills or dictionary skills?
7. On what page is there a chart called "Kinds of Reference Materials?"
8. What page tells you about definitions?
9. What is the title of Exercise 18?
10. On what page does the Chapter Review begin?

Reading a Textbook

Most of the books you use in school are textbooks. Many of your tests are based on information from these books. Knowing how to read your textbook carefully is a key to success in school. The more you can remember from your books, the better you will do.

The SQ3R Method

One of the best reading aids is the SQ3R method. This stands for *Survey, Question, Read, Recite, and Review.* If you use this method, you will be able to remember many things from your reading. Your notes will also help you study later.

The SQ3R Method

SURVEY First get a general idea of what the chapter or selection is about. Start by reading titles and other words set off by size or color. Look at the illustrations.

QUESTION Figure out which questions you should be able to answer after reading the selection. To do this, look at the study questions in the textbook. Write down other questions that come to mind as you survey.

READ Now you are ready to read. As you read, try to answer the study questions. Find the main idea in every section. Look for important ideas not covered by your questions. Take notes. (*See page 470.*)

RECITE Answer each question in your own words. Recite or write down the answers.

REVIEW Answer the questions again without looking at the book or your notes. Check your answers. Review until your answers are correct.

EXERCISE 2 *Reading a Textbook*

Use the SQ3R method to study the following selection about tooth care.

1. Survey the selection. What gives you the general idea of what it is about?
2. Write down questions to answer later.
3. Read the passage and take notes.
4. Recite or write down answers to your questions.
5. Review your answers by writing them down without looking. Check your answers with the selection.

Tooth Doctors

A person specially trained to take care of your teeth is called a *dentist*. The **dentist** is a type of doctor who treats problems with teeth and gums. These problems include caries, or cavities, in the teeth. Often the dentist tells you ways to avoid problems, including brushing your teeth and not eating foods that contain sugar.

Some children and some adults need braces put on their teeth to straighten them. An **orthodontist** is a dentist with additional training who measures and fits the braces over your teeth.

The Parts of a Book

Books include many different parts that can help you find information in them easily. The key parts of a book are the title page, the copyright page, the table of contents, and the index.

The title page is at the beginning of the book. It contains the complete title and the authors' names. The title page also gives the name of the publisher and the city in which the book was published.

The copyright page gives the year the book was published. Some kinds of books, especially in science and health, can contain old ideas that have been disproved. If the book is too old it will not be helpful to you for studying.

For a good introduction to the book, look at the table of contents. It is in the front of the book near the copyright page. The table of contents lists the title of each chapter and usually the major divisions of the chapter and the pages on which each starts. Always read the table of contents carefully. Each book on the same subject is different. The table of contents will show you what is important in each book.

Textbooks and many other nonfiction books contain an index. Look in the back for the index. Subjects are listed alphabetically, with page numbers showing each place a subject is discussed. A social studies textbook may discuss American Indians ten times or more. You can find all the passages on American Indians by using the index.

EXERCISE 3 *Exploring Books*

Following is a list of things you may look for in books. Number your paper 1 to 10. Write down where you would find each item in a book.

1. the starting page number for the chapter on weather and climate
2. a book published in London, England
3. all the passages about food in a health book
4. the starting page number for the last chapter of the book
5. the names of the authors
6. all the passages about Martin Luther King, Jr., in a book on black history
7. in a group of books about space exploration, the one that is newest or most recent
8. the first time the earth is discussed in a geography textbook
9. the name of the first chapter in a book
10. in a group of books about animals, the one published by the Smithsonian Institution

Taking Notes and Summarizing

Once you are familiar with how a textbook is organized, you can study one of its passages or chapters in detail. Taking notes in your own words is one good way to study. By writing notes, you help yourself remember the most important ideas of what you have read. By using your own words, you make yourself think carefully about what the book is saying.

You also need notes on your reading to help you review information for studying. As you know, taking notes is an important part of the SQ3R method of studying. This method is very effective. SQ3R stands for *Survey, Question, Read, Recite, and Review. (See page 467.)*

Strategies for Taking Notes

1. Read the selection once. Then review it, taking notes in your own words.
2. Write down only the main ideas and important details you need to remember.
3. Write key words or phrases; do not write complete sentences.
4. Look for important words that are printed in a different type, size, or color.
5. Look for words that go with main points, such as *first, another important, then, finally.*
6. Review the notes soon after you write them, so you can make important changes right away.

Summarizing means listing the most important points in a passage or chapter. After you take notes and review them, go back and summarize the main points. For example, suppose a book you are reading says that five inventions led to the invention of the automobile. After you take notes on each invention, go back and make a list of the five. Your list will help you remember what you need to know.

EXERCISE 4 *Taking Notes*

Following is a passage about living and working in Hawaii. Follow the directions below, and take notes on the passage.

1. Read the passage once.
2. Write the title of the passage.
3. Write the words that appear in dark type.
4. Find and write one phrase that marks an important point.
5. Write two abbreviations that you might use in your notes.
6. Using the note-taking strategy on page 470, take notes on the passage.

Working in Paradise

Think about Hawaii and what it might be like. Most people think about golden beaches, warm sunshine, palm trees, and surfboarding. Hawaii has these beautiful features, but what is life like for ordinary families who live and work there? Most of them are involved with Hawaii's three main industries: *tourism,* the *military,* and *agriculture.*

Tourism is the business of travel. It includes all the money travelers spend when they visit a place. Many people who live in Hawaii work for hotels, restaurants, airlines, and bus and tour companies.

The **military** is the part of the government that defends the country and fights wars when necessary. The United States Army and the United States Navy each keep large bases in Hawaii. Many soldiers and sailors are stationed there for a year or more. Also, many local people work for the military.

Last but not least, **agriculture,** or farming, is an important industry in Hawaii. Farming contributes a third of the state's income each year. Many people work on farms. Main crops are sugar cane, pineapple, and coffee. Many people work on cattle ranches too.

The Library

Your school library contains a variety of resources. You can use them when you need to write a book report, prepare a social studies report, or do a science project. All libraries are arranged according to the same basic filing system.

Library Arrangement

A library is arranged to help you find books easily. Books of fiction are in alphabetical order in one section. Nonfiction books are marked with numbers and put in another section.

Fiction. Books called fiction are stories of imaginary people and events. Fiction includes novels and short stories. Fiction books are filed in alphabetical order by the author's last name. The following rules will help you find fiction books by authors whose last names are sometimes hard to put in alphabetical order:

- Two-part names are alphabetized by the first part of the name, for example, **O'**Connor and **Van** Leeuwen
- Names that start with *Mc* or *St.* are alphabetized as if they began with *Mac* and *Saint*.
- Books by the same author are also alphabetized by their title. Skip *a, an,* and *the* at the beginning of the title.

EXERCISE 5 Arranging Fiction

Number your paper 1 to 10. Then write the novels in the order they should be filed on the shelf.

The Mysterious Island, Jules Verne
I Am the Cheese, Robert Cormier
Frank and Stein and Me, Kin Platt
The Luckiest Girl, Beverly Cleary
The Trumpeter of Krakow, Eric P. Kelly
Ramona the Pest, Beverly Cleary
A Tale of Two Cities, Charles Dickens
The Land of Oz, Frank Baum
Roll of Thunder, Hear My Cry, Mildred D. Taylor
Anastasia on Her Own, Lois Lowry

EXERCISE 6 Solving Shelving Problems

Number your paper 1 to 10. Then write the following fiction authors in the order that they should appear on the shelf.

Eloise T. McGraw	Lester Del Rey
Will James	Mary Rodgers
Madeleine L'Engle	Meindert DeJong
William MacKellar	Brian Daley
Walter D. Edmonds	Scott O'Dell

Nonfiction. Books that contain facts about real people and real events are called nonfiction. Many libraries use the Dewey decimal system to arrange nonfiction books on shelves. In this system, each book receives a number according to its subject. The Dewey decimal system has ten general subject categories. (*See page 474.*)

The Dewey decimal system was developed more than 100 years ago, but it still works well today. The system was set up so that the basic ten categories could be stretched to fit new topics as knowledge grew. Thus, Dewey numbers are available for the computers and lasers of today as well as the discoveries of tomorrow.

Dewey Decimal System

000–099	General Works (reference books)
100–199	Philosophy
200–299	Religion
300–399	Social Science (law, education, economics)
400–499	Language
500–599	Science (mathematics, biology, wildlife)
600–699	Technology (medicine, inventions, energy)
700–799	Fine Arts (painting, music, sports)
800–899	Literature
900–999	History (biography, geography, travel)

The Dewey decimal number is written on the spine of the book, the part that faces you when it stands on the shelf. The books are arranged in numerical order, so books on the same topic are near each other. For example, the study of dinosaurs is part of science. Therefore, books on dinosaurs are assigned a number between 500 and 599. When you locate one book on dinosaurs, you will see other books on the same subject nearby on the shelves.

EXERCISE 7 Understanding the Dewey Decimal System

Number your paper 1 to 10. Read the following list of book titles. For each title, write the range of numbers and the category it falls under in the Dewey decimal system.

EXAMPLE *Electricity Made Simple*
ANSWER 600–699 Technology

1. *Speak Spanish in Two Weeks*
2. *The Law and Women*
3. *Philosophy and Life*
4. *Soccer Today*
5. *Climbing Mount Everest*
6. *Understanding Shakespeare*
7. *Encyclopedia of Encyclopedias*
8. *Religions of the World*
9. *Fact Book of Dolphins*
10. *Good Health for Teens*

EXERCISE 8 Solving Shelving Problems for Nonfiction Books

Number your paper 1 to 10. Then write the following Dewey decimal numbers and book titles in order as the books would appear on the shelves in the library. Remember that nonfiction books are arranged numerically, not alphabetically.

1. 598.2 *Birds of Asia*
2. 597.3 *Sharks in the Caribbean*
3. 582.3 *Tropical Flowers*
4. 591.9 *Polar Bears*
5. 590.7 *National Zoo in Photos*
6. 593.9 *Jungles of Brazil*
7. 581.4 *Redwood Forests of California*
8. 595.7 *Killer Bees*
9. 594.6 *Book of the Squid*
10. 586 *Plants of the Ocean*

The Card Catalog

The card catalog is a cabinet of small file drawers. It holds a file card for every book in the library. The drawers may also hold cards for other types of materials, such as tapes or records. The card catalog is arranged in alphabetical order. Each drawer is labeled to show what part of the alphabet it includes.

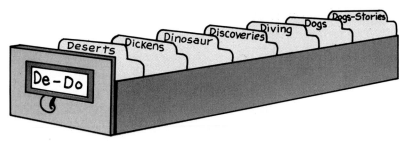

There are three cards for each book in the card catalog. Each book is listed on an *author card,* a *title card,* and a *subject card.*

Author Cards. Sometimes you know the author of a book but not the title. Look in the card catalog under the author's last name. For example, to find a book by Pamela Wood, look in the drawer for the letter *W.*

AUTHOR CARD

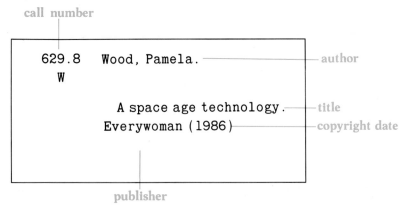

Title Cards. Perhaps you know the title of a book but not the author. You will find the book by looking up the first word in the title, except for *a*, *an*, and *the*. For example, to find *A Space Age Technology,* look in the drawer for the letter *S*.

TITLE CARD

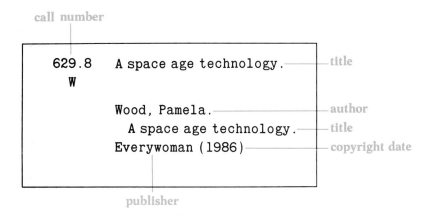

Subject Cards. When you need to find books for a report, you will use subject cards more than title or author cards. For example, if your subject is space exploration, you would look in the drawer for the letter *S*. There you would find cards for all the books about space in your library.

SUBJECT CARD

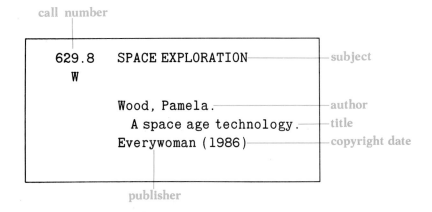

Look again at all three cards for *A Space Age Technology*. Notice that they all contain the same information. To find the book on the shelves, look at any one of these cards and write down the number listed in the upper left corner.

EXERCISE 9 *The Card Catalog*

Number your paper 1 to 10. Here is a list of items you can find in a library. For each one write whether you would look in the card catalog under author, title, or subject.

1. a book by Isaac Asimov
2. recent information on robots
3. information on the White House
4. *The Call of the Wild*
5. information about the life of Mark Twain
6. a book by Alan Alda
7. *My Side of the Mountain*
8. *The Phantom Tollbooth*
9. short stories by O. Henry
10. short stories in American literature

Cross-Reference Cards.   Another type of card in the card catalog is the cross-reference card. This card gives you "see" and "see also" listings. A "see" card means that the subject you are looking for is not filed in that part of the card catalog. The "see" card tells you where to look instead. For example, you may look under "air pollution" and find a card that says "air pollution *see* pollution."

A "see also" card gives you other subjects to look under. For example, you may look under "pollution" and find a card that says "pollution *see also* environment." This means that both headings will have books on your subject.

Guide Cards.   The card catalog also contains guide cards, which look like the ones shown on page 476. Each has a word or letter at the top. The guide cards divide the file drawer into alphabetized sections. The guide cards will help you find the cards you are looking for.

Steps for Finding Books

1. Look for an author card, title card, or subject card in the card catalog.
2. Read the card carefully to see if the book might have the information you need. Check the copyright date to see how new the book is.
3. On a piece of paper, copy the call number, title, and author's name for each book you want to find.
4. Go to the shelves and look for the book by its call number or author. Fiction books will often be marked with an F. Nonfiction books will have a Dewey number.

---

*E*XERCISE 10 *Using the Card Catalog*

Number your paper 1 to 10. Then write the letter or letters of the drawer in which you would find each of the following in the card catalog.

EXAMPLE *The Incredible Journey*
ANSWER He-I

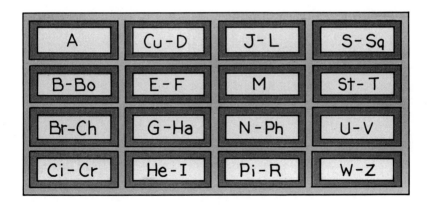

1. the Constitution
2. China
3. Arthur C. Clarke
4. poetry
5. *The Alfred Summer*
6. skiing
7. Susan Hunt
8. oceans
9. *Peter Pan*
10. *A Very Young Dancer*

*R*eference Materials

Reference books are books that you use when you want to look up specific facts. Reference books include the encyclopedia, thesaurus, biographical dictionary, atlas, almanac, yearbook, and dictionary. Usually reference books are kept in a separate section in the library and cannot be checked out of the library. Most libraries put a table and chairs near the reference section so you will have a place to use these books.

Encyclopedias. When you write reports, you will often begin to look for information in an encyclopedia. An encyclopedia is a collection of facts about a variety of subjects, usually arranged alphabetically by subject. In most cases, an encyclopedia is a set of books, rather than just one. On the spine of each volume in an encyclopedia set, you will find letters of the alphabet or words showing which subjects are found in that book.

If a subject is new to you, a good way to begin learning about it is to read an encyclopedia article. You can also use the encyclopedia to find specific facts to use in a report. Make notes of the facts you find on a piece of paper. Remember to include where you found the information. Never copy material directly from an encyclopedia or any other book without crediting the source.

Also remember to use the index in the encyclopedia. The index is in the last volume in most sets. It tells you where to find additional information about your subject in the encyclopedia. You may miss some important information if you do not use the index.

Thesaurus. A thesaurus is a special dictionary that gives you several words with the same meaning. If you are writing a paper, try not to use the same word again and again. A thesaurus will help you find other words similar to the one you have in mind. For example, look up *hurry* and you will find *rush* and *speed up.*

480

Kinds of Reference Materials

REFERENCE MATERIAL	WHAT IT CONTAINS	EXAMPLES
encyclopedia	information about many subjects, arranged A to Z by subject	*Encyclopedia Britannica, World Book Encyclopedia*
biographical reference	information about famous people, arranged alphabetically	*Current Biography, Webster's Biographical Dictionary, Who's Who in America*
atlas	maps and related information about geography	*Collier's World Atlas and Gazetteer, Hammond World Atlas, Rand McNally Road Atlas*
almanac or yearbook	various facts such as world records, awards and prizes, current events	*Information Please Almanac, World Almanac and Book of Facts, Guinness Book of World Records*
dictionary	words—their pronunciation, their definition, their origin	*Scott, Foresman Advanced Dictionary*
specialized dictionary	entries of only one type or on only one subject	*Compton's Illustrated Science Dictionary, The New Roget's Thesaurus in Dictionary Form, Webster's New Dictionary of Synonyms*
Readers' Guide to Periodical Literature	index to popular magazine articles, arranged alphabetically by author and subject	
vertical file	file folders by subject, containing newspaper clippings, pamphlets, and catalogs	

EXERCISE 11 *Using Reference Materials*

Number your paper 1 to 20. Following is a list of items you might need to look up in the library. For each one write the best source of reference materials. Choose the best source from this list.

encyclopedia	dictionary
biographical reference	specialized dictionary
atlas	*Readers' Guide*
almanac or yearbook	vertical file

1. world record for passing a football
2. article from your local newspaper telling which American Indians lived in your area in the 1700s
3. general information on Puerto Rico
4. facts about the life of John Glenn, who has been an astronaut and United States senator
5. the meaning of the word *serendipity*
6. articles in *Time* and *Newsweek* about the election campaign for president of the United States
7. map of Canada showing each province with its capital and other major cities
8. person with world's longest fingernails
9. the meaning of the word *hologram* with a diagram that shows how one is made
10. details of battles fought during the war of independence for Texas
11. pamphlet on basic food groups
12. states that border on Nevada
13. early life of the new vice-president
14. general history and other information about aviation
15. words that mean the same as *noble*
16. pronunciation of *odometer*
17. major rivers of Mexico
18. recent magazine articles on heart surgery
19. pamphlet of tips for babysitters
20. winner of last year's Nobel prize for literature

*T*he Dictionary

Most people use the dictionary more often than any other reference. A dictionary tells how to spell a word correctly, what it means, how to pronounce it, and much more.

SPELLING — **but ton** (but′n), *n.* **1** a round, flat piece of metal, bone,
DEFINITIONS — glass, plastic, etc., fastened on garments to hold them closed or to decorate them. **2** knob used as a handle or a catch to take hold of, push, or turn so that it holds or closes something.
WORD ORIGIN — [<Old French *boton* < *bouter* to thrust] —**but′ton less,** *adj.*
RELATED FORMS — —**but′ton like′,** *adj.*
PRONUNCIATION — **buy** (bī), v., **bought, buying,** *n.*—*v.t.* **1** get by paying a
PART OF SPEECH — price, usually in money; purchase: *You can buy a pencil for ten cents.* See synonym study below. **2** get in exchange for something else, or by making some sacrifice.
Syn. *v.t.* **1 Buy, purchase** mean to get something by paying a price. Buy is the general and informal word: *A person can buy anything in that store if he or she has the*
SYNONYMS — *money.* Purchase, a somewhat more formal word, suggests buying after careful planning or negotiating or on a large scale: *The bank has purchased some property on which to construct a new building.*
ABBREVIATIONS — **B.W.I.,** British West Indies.
bx., pl. bxs. box
PROPER NOUN — **Byrd** (berd), *n.* **Richard Evelyn,** 1888-1957, American
HYPHENATED — naval officer, aviator, and polar explorer.
COMPOUND — **by-street** (bī′strēt′), *n.* a side street.

From SCOTT FORESMAN ADVANCED DICTIONARY by E. L. Thorndike and Clarence L. Barnhart. Copyright © 1983, 1979, 1974 by Scott, Foresman & Co. Reprinted by permission.

*W*ord Location

A dictionary lists words in alphabetical order so that you can find them quickly. Guide words help you find the page your word is on.

Guide Words. At the top of each dictionary page, two words or phrases are printed in heavy type. These are the guide words. They show the first and last words defined on that page. For example, the guide words **bullfrog** and **bundle** tell you that *bumblebee* is listed on that page. *Bungle*, however, would appear on the next page.

EXERCISE 12 *Using Guide Words*

Make two columns on your paper. Write the guide words
handler/hanging at the top of the first column. Then write
hangnail/harbor at the top of the second column. Now
write each word below in the correct column. Refer to the
rules for alphabetizing that are explained below.

happy	handwriting	harangue	hangar
hang glider	handyman	hang	hansom
handshake	hang nail	hang up	Hanover
happen	handy	handspring	hand set
hanger	Hannibal	harass	hand made

Alphabetical Order. When you find the page you need,
locate the word by looking at the alphabetical order letter
by letter. Words that start with the same letter are
alphabetized by the first letter in each word that is
different. Compound words are alphabetized as if they
were one word with no hyphen or space between them.
Note the alphabetized list below.

close	SINGLE WORD
close call	TWO-WORD COMPOUND
closemouthed	ONE-WORD COMPOUND
close-up	HYPHENATED COMPOUND

All dictionary entries are listed in alphabetical order,
including abbreviations. However, abbreviations are alphabetized letter by letter, not by the word they stand for.
For example, the abbreviation *St.* for *street* falls between
squirrel and *stadium*, several pages away from *street*.

EXERCISE 13 *Alphabetizing Words*

Number your paper 1 to 10. Then arrange the underlined
words in each phrase in alphabetical order.

EXAMPLE   a <u>rabbit</u> on <u>Richmond</u> <u>Rd.</u>
ANSWER   rabbit, Rd., Richmond

Long and Short of It

1. <u>fullback</u> moves <u>fifty</u> <u>ft.</u>
2. <u>mountaintop</u> of <u>Mt.</u> <u>McKinley</u>
3. <u>Mary</u> got <u>M.A.</u> from <u>Maryland</u> College near Maryville, Maryland
4. <u>Incas</u> only 10 <u>in.</u> from <u>Indies</u>
5. <u>famous</u> <u>files</u> of the <u>FBI</u>
6. <u>G-suit</u> and <u>gravity</u> in the late afternoon high over Guatemala
7. <u>noon</u> in <u>New York,</u> <u>NY</u>
8. <u>public</u> meeting of <u>Pomona</u> <u>P.T.A.</u>
9. ten <u>lb.</u> <u>lamb</u> with <u>potatoes</u> and a crisp green vegetable salad
10. <u>any</u> week, <u>anytime</u> in the A.M.

EXERCISE 14 Alphabetizing Words

Make two columns on your paper. Then write the words in each column below in alphabetical order. Use the rules for alphabetizing you have just studied.

1.	2.
full-grown	top-secret
full blast	top kick
full-scale	topmost
fully	topcoat
full-length	topflight
fullback	top-drawer
full-blown	topsoil
full-time	top-heavy
Fullerton	top hat
full	top-notch

Information in an Entry

The information given for each word in the dictionary is called an entry. Entry words are printed in heavy type. The entry has four main parts: (1) the entry word, (2) the pronunciation, (3) the definitions, and (4) the word origin. The entry for *athlete* that follows on page 486 shows these four main parts.

485

ENTRY WORD
PRONUNCIATION
ath lete (ath′lēt′), **n.** person trained to do physical exercises
DEFINITION — of agility and strength, especially one who participates or
competes in games requiring physical skill and stamina.
WORD ORIGIN — [<Greek athlētēs <athlein compete for a prize <athlon prize]

From SCOTT FORESMAN ADVANCED DICTIONARY by E. L. Thorndike and Clarence L. Barnhart. Copyright © 1983, 1979, 1974 by Scott, Foresman & Co. Reprinted by permission.

Entry Word. The entry word provides you with three kinds of information. It shows (1) the spelling of the word, (2) the word's capital letters, if any, and (3) how to divide the word into syllables.

First, the entry word tells how to spell a word correctly. Some words have more than one correct spelling. The most common spelling, or *preferred spelling,* is shown first. The second spelling is called the variant spelling. Always use the preferred spelling of a word in your writing.

PREFERRED SPELLING
ax or **axe**
VARIANT SPELLING

Second, if a word should be capitalized, its entry word will begin with a capital letter. If a word is capitalized only some of the time it is used, the word will be shown with a capital letter near the definition that needs capitalization.

CAPITAL
LETTERS

east (ēst), *n.* **1** direction of the sunrise; direction just opposite west. **2** Also **East**, the part of any country toward the east. **3 the East, a** the part of the United States to the east of the Allegheny Mountains, especially New England. **b** the part of the United States that lies to the east of the Mississippi River, especially the states north of Maryland and the Ohio River. **c** the countries in Asia as distinguished from those in Europe and America; the Orient. **d** the Soviet Union and its satellites in eastern Europe. **4 down East, a** New England. **b** the eastern part of New England: Maine. **c** in, to, or toward New England. —*adj.* **1** toward the east; farther toward the east. **2** coming from the east. **3** in the east.—*adv.* **1** toward the east. **2 east of,** further east than. [Old English *ēast*]
East Anglia, early Anglo-Saxon kingdom in SE England, comprising modern Norfolk and Suffolk.

From SCOTT FORESMAN ADVANCED DICTIONARY by E. L. Thorndike and Clarence L. Barnhart. Copyright © 1983, 1979, 1974 by Scott, Foresman & Co. Reprinted by permission.

Third, the entry word shows how to break a word into syllables. If you need to divide a word at the end of a line, you must break it as shown in the dictionary.

long • horn   smug • gle   cat • tle

EXERCISE 15 Dividing Words into Syllables

Number your paper 1 to 10. Using a dictionary, write each word with a small dot between the syllables.

1. gridiron
2. familiar
3. urgent
4. begin
5. pressure

6. information
7. among
8. liter
9. dynamite
10. usually

Related Forms of the Word.   Entries in the dictionary also give the plurals of nouns, the principal parts of verbs, and the comparative and superlative forms of adjectives and adverbs. However, these are listed only if the form or spelling is irregular.

cit y (sit′ē), *n., pl.* **cit ies**   NOUN PLURAL

clap (klap), *v.,* **clapped, clap ping**   PRINCIPAL PARTS

cloud y (klou′dē), *adj.,* **cloud i er,**   COMPARATIVE
cloud i est   AND
                                                       SUPERLATIVE

Sometimes words are made by adding a prefix or suffix to the entry word. These related forms are shown at the end of the entry and are called derived words.

PRINCIPAL PARTS ——— **bridge** (brij), *n.,v.,* **bridged, bridg ing.**—*n.* **1** structure built over a river, road, railroad, etc. so that people, cars, trains, etc., can get across. **2** platform above the deck of a ship from which the officer in command directs the course of the ship.—*v.t.* **1** build a bridge over; *The engineers bridged the river.* **2** form a bridge over; extend over; span: *A log bridged the brook.* [Old English *brycg*]—**bridge′** DERIVED WORDS ——— **a ble,** *adj.*—**bridge′ · like,** *adj.*

From SCOTT FORESMAN ADVANCED DICTIONARY by E. L. Thorndike and Clarence L. Barnhart. Copyright © 1983, 1979, 1974 by Scott, Foresman & Co. Reprinted by permission.

EXERCISE 16 Checking Spelling

Number your paper 1 to 20. Spell each word correctly with the ending shown in parentheses. Use a dictionary to check the spelling.

EXAMPLE help(er)

ANSWER helper

1. thief(s)	11. referee(ed)
2. dangle(ing)	12. valley(s)
3. crazy(est)	13. pledge(ing)
4. yourself(s)	14. crabby(est)
5. file(ing)	15. life(s)
6. run(ing)	16. risky(er)
7. itchy(est)	17. handicap(ed)
8. activity(s)	18. develop(ed)
9. wavy(er)	19. money(s)
10. big(er)	20. tug(ed)

Pronunciation. A phonetic spelling shows how to pronounce a word correctly. In the dictionary a phonetic spelling is shown in parentheses after the entry word.

knot (not)   **kum quat** (kum′kwot)

Each dictionary provides a complete pronunciation key to help you understand the letters and symbols used in phonetic spellings. Usually the complete key is in the front of the dictionary. Most dictionaries also give you a short form of the key on every page or every other page.

PARTIAL PRONUNCIATION KEY

a hat	i it	oi oil	ch child	a in about
ā age	ī ice	ou out	ng long	e in taken
ä far	o hot	u cup	sh she	ə = { i in pencil
e let	ō open	ů put	th thin	o in lemon
ē equal	ô order	ü rule	ŦH then	u in circus
ėr term			zh measure	< = derived from

From SCOTT FORESMAN ADVANCED DICTIONARY by E.L. Thorndike and Clarence L. Barnhart. Copyright © 1983 Scott, Foresman and Company. Reprinted by permission.

In the pronunciation key on page 488, some vowels have marks over them. The marks are diacritical marks and show different vowel sounds.

e as in let   **ē** as in equal   **ė** as in term

Sometimes vowels are pronounced as if they were spelled *uh*. A dictionary uses the symbol ə to represent this sound. The symbol is called a schwa.

cus tom (kus′təm) **fun gus** (fung′gəs) **wom an** (wùm′ən)

An accent mark (′) shows which syllable to stress when you pronounce the word.

un bolt (un bolt′)   **Hou di ni** (hü dē′nē)

Some words have two accent marks. The darker one tells you which syllable gets more stress.

bas ket ball (bas′kit bôl′)

E XERCISE 17 Marking Pronunciation

Number your paper 1 to 10. Use a dictionary to write the pronunciation for each word. Include diacritical marks.

1. wolf
2. nice
3. earth
4. quarter
5. bamboo
6. hoop
7. survive
8. decide
9. long
10. truth

E XERCISE 18 Placing Accent Marks

Number your paper 1 to 10. Use a dictionary to write the pronunciation for each word. Mark all accents.

1. anymore
2. legendary
3. sympathetic
4. folklore
5. wildlife
6. definition
7. musketeer
8. follow-through
9. Tuscarora
10. boomerang

Definitions. Most words have more than one meaning. The following entry for *coat* gives five definitions.

> **coat** (kōt), *n.* **1** an outer garment of cloth, fur, etc., with sleeves. **2** a natural outer covering: *a dog's coat of hair.* **3** a thin layer covering a surface; coating: *a coat of paint.* —*v.t.* **1** cover with a thin layer: *The old books were coated with dust.* **2** provide with a coat. [<Old French *cote*] —**coat′less,** *adj.*

To find the definition that fits the meaning you have in mind, read all the definitions and examples very carefully.

Dictionaries use the following abbreviations to show parts of speech.

n.	noun	*pron.*	pronoun
v.	verb	*prep.*	preposition
adj.	adjective	*conj.*	conjunction
adv.	adverb	*interj.*	interjection

Many words can be more than one part of speech. Then, as in the entry for *coat,* two or more abbreviations will appear in one entry. Make sure that you find the right part of speech when you read the definitions.

Words with similar meanings are called synonyms. Some dictionaries list synonyms at the end of an entry and explain how the meaning differs from that of the entry word. As in the following example, the abbreviation *syn.* is often used for synonyms.

> **spe cial** (spesh′əl), *adj.* **1** of a particular kind; distinct from others; not general. See synonym study below. **2** more than ordinary; unusual; exceptional: *Today's topic is of special interest.* **3** for a particular person, thing, purpose, etc.: *The railroad ran special trains on holidays.* **4** held in high regard; great; chief: *a special friend, a special favorite.*—*n.* **1** a special train, car, bus, etc. **2** any special person or thing. **3** a special edition of a newspaper. **4** a specially featured product, service, etc. **5** a television show, produced especially for a single broadcast, usually out of the pattern of regular daily or weekly programs. [<Latin *specialis* <*species* sort, kind, species]
>
> **Syn.** *adj.* **1 Special, particular** mean belonging or relating to one person, thing, or group, as distinguished from others. **Special** implies being different from others of its kind: *Babies need special food.* **Particular** implies being or treated as being unique: *the particular meaning of a word.*

SYNONYMS

EXERCISE 19 Choosing an Appropriate Meaning

Number your paper 1 to 10. Using the dictionary entry for
coat on page 490, write the definition that applies to each
of the following sentences.

EXAMPLE   They *coat* the berries with honey.
ANSWER   cover with a thin layer

1. The horse's *coat* shone in the moonlight.
2. Maria put on her new purple *coat.*
3. Evan *coats* his birdhouse with varnish.
4. A heavy *coat* keeps you warm.
5. A fine *coat* of sand lay on the floor.
6. The wolf's *coat* was covered with mud.
7. Next *coat* each shelf with paint.
8. The *coat* was so short that it did not even cover his
   knees.
9. They wanted to find out how to *coat* the model with
   plastic.
10. Harvey tried not to step on what looked like a *coat*
    of water on the floor.

EXERCISE 20 Finding Different Meanings of Words

Number your paper 1 to 10. Find the entry or entries for
down in your dictionary. Write the correct part of speech
for *down* as it is used in each sentence.

1. A small dog rode *down* the escalator.
2. The quarterback tried for a first *down.*
3. Two linemen dragged *down* the quarterback.
4. Please do not go up the *down* staircase.
5. After playing baseball in the hot sun, we *down* our
   milk quickly.
6. During the fire drill, the children walked *down* the
   fire escape carefully.
7. My pillow is filled with *down.*
8. I threw *down* my pillow.
9. Joe felt *down* after he got a low grade on the test.
10. "Look *down* the hill," LaToya yelled.

*C*hapter *R*eview

A **The Parts of a Book.** The following questions are the kinds of questions that you might need to answer when you are working with books. Number your paper 1 to 10. Then choose the part of a book that would best help you answer each question. Use the list of parts of a book below.

    title page
    copyright page
    table of contents
    index

1. The library has three almanacs on the shelf. Which one is most recent?
2. Which social studies textbook was written by a teacher from your school?
3. Does this textbook contain information about punctuation, and what pages is it on?
4. In your social studies textbook, how can you quickly find the title of the chapter on the Industrial Revolution?
5. Where was your science textbook published and who is the publisher?
6. How many pages of information can you find in your health textbook that deal with physical fitness and exercise?
7. What is the correct name of the chapter on the Civil War in your social studies textbook?
8. The library has four books about the National Aeronautics and Space Administration (NASA). Which one was written and published first?
9. Does your health textbook have information on vision?
10. In a book about poetry, is there a chapter about the work of Carl Sandburg?

B **The Library.** Number your paper 1 to 10. Write the following authors in the order they appear in the card catalog of your library.

1. MacPherson
2. Espinoza
3. St. Gaudens
4. McBride
5. Selvey

6. DeGrandis
7. Wong
8. Grandville
9. DeWinter
10. Derry

C **The Library.** Use the Dewey Decimal list on page 474 in this chapter. Number your paper 1 to 5. For each of the following book titles, write the range of numbers and the category it falls under in the Dewey decimal system.

1. *Butterfly Migration*
2. *Getting Started in French*
3. *The Life of Mark Twain*
4. *American Folk Music*
5. *Webster's Dictionary*

D **The Dictionary.** Find the word *dress* in the dictionary. The entry in the dictionary shows more than one part of speech for this word. Recall the exercise in this chapter using the word *coat*. Think of it as an example of a word that can be used as more than one part of speech. Write the following about the word *dress*.

1. guide words at top of the dictionary page
2. pronunciation, including any accents and diacritical marks
3. definitions
4. one part of speech—for example, noun
5. a sentence using the word in that part of speech
6. a second part of speech
7. a sentence using the second part of speech
8. the principal parts listed at beginning of the entry

Test Taking

There are skills involved in just about everything you do, including taking tests. Once you master the skills of test taking, you can concentrate on what your tests are about, not on how to take them. When you know how to take tests, you do better on them. This chapter will help you learn some basic test-taking skills.

EXERCISE 1 Test-taking Skills

Number your paper 1 to 5. Read the statements about test taking in the following list. Then write *True* if you think a statement is true. Write *False* if you think a statement is false. All the answers can be found in this chapter.

1. You should skim test directions instead of reading them carefully.
2. If any part of a true–false statement is false, then the statement is false.
3. It is not necessary to read all the choices for a multiple-choice question.
4. Short-answer questions don't indicate what kind of answer to give.
5. You should not spend too much time on any one question on a standardized test.

Classroom Tests

Classroom tests often include two basic types of questions: objective questions and essay questions. An *objective question* is one that has only one correct answer. Common types of objective questions include true–false, multiple-choice, and short-answer questions. An *essay question* has more than one correct answer. To answer an essay question you may have to write one or more paragraphs.

True–False Questions

A true–false question is a single statement. You must decide if the statement is true or false.

EXAMPLES   China is on the continent of Asia.
North America is one of five continents.

You would probably have no trouble with the first item. It is true. The second item might fool you. North America *is* a continent, so you might be tempted to answer *true*. However, notice that the statement says "one of five continents." There are seven continents, not five. Therefore, the statement is false.

Hints for Answering True–False Questions

1. Read every word carefully. Just one word can make a statement false.
2. Look for words such as *always, never, all,* or *none.* They mean that there are no exceptions.
3. Look for words such as *many, some, sometimes, usually,* or *may.* They mean that the statement can have exceptions and still be true.
4. Think carefully about each part of the statement. If *any* part is false, then the statement is false.

EXERCISE 2 *Answering True–False Questions*

Number your paper 1 to 10. Then write *T* if the statement is true and *F* if it is false. Look in other parts of this book for the answers.

1. Listening is not important in a group discussion.
2. All proper nouns must be capitalized.
3. Every sentence must end with a period.
4. Adjectives name people, places, or things.
5. A verb must agree with its subject.
6. An opinion is different from a fact.
7. *He* and *she* are examples of pronouns.
8. All of the words in a title must be capitalized.
9. The words *synonym* and *antonym* are synonyms.
10. An added suffix can change a word's meaning.

Multiple-choice Questions

A multiple-choice question gives several possible answers. You must choose the best one.

EXAMPLE   On which continent is the country of China?
   a. India   c. North America
   b. Antarctica   d. Asia

In the example, a question is asked. You must pick the right answer from the choices given. You may be able to choose the right answer right away. If not, you can often find it by deciding which choices you know are wrong. For instance, India is a country, not a continent. Antarctica is a continent that has *no* countries on it. You can reject those two choices. That leaves only North America and Asia. Since you live on the North American continent, you know that China is not a near neighbor. Therefore, the answer must be Asia.

Here is another kind of multiple-choice item.

EXAMPLE   North America is one of _____ continents.
   a. five   c. seven
   b. six   d. eight

496

In this example, an incomplete statement is given. You must complete the statement by choosing the answer that best fits in the blank space.

A multiple-choice test may include either of the two types of questions—or both. Read the directions for the test carefully to see what you are asked to do.

Hints for Answering Multiple-choice Questions

1. Read the directions carefully.
2. Read each question or statement carefully.
3. Read all of the choices before answering.
4. Eliminate choices you know are wrong.
5. Choose the best answer from the remaining choices.

EXERCISE 3 *Answering Multiple-choice Questions*

Number your paper 1 to 10. Then write the letter of the correct answer or the answer that best completes the statement.

1. Which word is misspelled?
   a. international   c. inspection
   b. irigation   d. catalog
2. Which pair of words are antonyms?
   a. graceful, grateful   c. weary, tired
   b. disgrace, shame   d. proceed, halt
3. Who was the first president of the United States?
   a. John F. Kennedy   c. George Washington
   b. Benjamin Franklin   d. Abraham Lincoln
4. What is the state capital of Texas?
   a. New York City   c. Austin
   b. Los Angeles   d. Washington, D.C.
5. Which bird does not fly?
   a. parrot   c. penguin
   b. sparrow   d. parakeet
6. An example of a possessive pronoun is _____.
   a. its   b. it's   c. we   d. they

7. The events of a story make up its _____.
   a. main idea   c. characterization
   b. meaning   d. plot
8. A _____ gives the main idea of a paragraph.
   a. topic sentence   c. declarative sentence
   b. compound sentence   d. defining sentence
9. Water freezes at _____.
   a. 32°C   b. 0°F   c. 32°F   d. 100°C
10. The number 30 + 7 is the same as _____.
   a. 6 × 6   b. 25 + 8   c. 40 − 2   d. 8 + 29

Short-answer Questions

A short-answer question is just what its name suggests. It requires a short answer—a word, a phrase, or a short sentence. Your answer comes from things you have learned in your class or from studying for the test.

EXAMPLE   What part of speech is the word *and*?

Read short-answer questions carefully to make sure you know exactly what kind of answer is required. In the example, the words "What part of speech" tell you the answer should be a word that names a part of speech. Your answer should be *conjunction*.

EXERCISE 4   Understanding Short-answer Questions

Number your paper 1 to 5. Read each question. Then write *word, phrase,* or *short sentence* to tell what kind of answer is required.

1. Who was the first U.S. citizen to set foot on the surface of the moon?
2. Name three professional sports that involve teams of six or more players.
3. In what direction must you look to see the sunrise?
4. Where does the sun set?
5. Why do plants die if you leave them in a dark room for a long time?

Standardized Tests

Standardized tests are printed tests given to students all over the country. They measure knowledge and skills in various subjects—reading, mathematics, social studies, science, and others.

You cannot study for a standardized test. You can, however, prepare for one by keeping up with your schoolwork. You can also prepare for one by becoming familiar with the types of questions standardized tests include. This part of the chapter will help you understand standardized test questions.

Hints for Taking Standardized Tests

1. Listen carefully to the instructions of the person who is giving the test. Follow those instructions exactly.
2. Read the directions and sample questions for each part of the test carefully. Be sure you understand them before you begin.
3. Read each question carefully. Then read all of the choices before answering a question.
4. Do not spend too much time on any one question. If you are unsure of an answer, go on to the next question. Answer all the questions you know first. You can come back to your unanswered questions if there is time.
5. You may write on the test booklet, but always mark your answers on the separate answer sheet. Most tests ask you to shade or darken the circle that contains the letter of your answer.
   ANSWER SHEET Ⓐ Ⓑ Ⓒ Ⓓ Ⓔ
6. Most standardized tests are scored by machine. Therefore, you must mark only one answer for each question and make sure your mark is dark. If you need to change an answer, erase your first choice.
7. Be sure the number on the answer sheet matches the number on the question.
8. Check your answers if you have time.

Vocabulary Tests

One type of vocabulary test question asks you to select a word that is either a synonym or an antonym for another word. You learned about this type of question in Chapter 27. (*See pages 448–450.*)

Analogies. An *analogy* is a type of vocabulary question that requires you to decide what relationship you see between two pairs of words.

EXAMPLE   hat : head :: shoe : foot

You would read the example question this way: *Hat* is to *head* as *shoe* is to *foot*.

Notice that the analogy can be split into two parts, each part containing one pair of words.

FIRST PART   hat : head
SECOND PART   shoe : foot

When the analogy is in question form, one of the parts will have a word missing.

EXAMPLE   car : gas :: people : _____

To complete the analogy, decide what the relationship is between the words in the first pair. (A car needs gas to keep going.) The second pair should show the same kind of relationship. (People need what to keep going? *Food.*)

To answer an analogy question correctly, you must know what each of the words means. You must also understand how they relate to each other.

ANALOGIES   cat : kitten :: cow : calf
hot : cold :: fast : slow

In the first example, the relationship is a mother–child relationship. Cats have kittens, and cows have calves. In the second example, each pair contains opposites, or antonyms. *Cold* is the opposite of *hot*, and *slow* is the opposite of *fast*.

EXERCISE 5 Completing Analogies

Number your paper 1 to 10. Then write the letter of the word that completes each analogy.

1. boy : man :: girl :: _____
   (a) child   (b) female   (c) mother   (d) woman
2. warm : hot :: cool : _____
   (a) tepid   (b) summer   (c) cold   (d) ice
3. snake : bite :: bee : _____
   (a) bite   (b) hurt   (c) sting   (d) slap
4. actor: theater :: doctor : _____
   (a) shots   (b) disease   (c) patient   (d) hospital
5. photograph : photographer :: book : _____
   (a) library   (b) writer   (c) picture   (d) pencil
6. finger : hand :: toe : _____
   (a) foot   (b) leg   (c) ear   (d) body
7. fuel : airplane :: _____ : lamp
   (a) bulb   (b) electricity   (c) wire   (d) switch
8. bacteria : microscope :: star : _____
   (a) astronaut   (b) moon   (c) telescope   (d) sun
9. railway : train :: _____ : truck
   (a) plane   (b) diesel   (c) highway   (d) garage
10. assemble : construct :: brave : _____
    (a) scared   (b) build   (c) astonish   (d) courageous

Tests on Mechanics and Usage

Standardized tests often use a special style to test your knowledge of mechanics and usage. In that style, a test item might look something like this:

Scientist's were sure they would soon find a cure for
   A   B   C
the disease. No error
   D   E

You must read the sentence and find the error in it if there is one. Each item will have either no error or one error—never more than one.

501

Begin by reading the entire sentence. Then look at each underlined part to see if it contains an error. If there is no error, mark choice *E* on your answer sheet. If there is an error, mark the letter of the part that contains the error. In the example on page 501, for instance, you would mark *A. Scientists* is a plural, not a possessive, and should contain no apostrophe.

Hints for Taking Tests on Mechanics and Usage

1. Watch for missing or unneeded capital letters.
2. Notice missing, misplaced, or unnecessary punctuation.
3. Examine the subjects and verbs in sentences. There may be lack of agreement between subject and verb.
4. Watch for lack of agreement between pronoun and verb or between pronoun and antecedent.
5. Examine the sentence for wrong verb tenses.
6. Notice wrong or misspelled words.

E*XERCISE 6* *Answering Questions on Mechanics and Usage*

Number your paper 1 to 10. Then write the letter of the underlined part that has an error. If there is no error, write *E*.

1. Where <u>was</u> you on April <u>17, 1986? No error</u>
      A   B   C   D   E

2. Id<u>a,</u> Sar<u>ah,</u> and <u>I</u> will head the proje<u>ct.</u> <u>No error</u>
      A   B   C   D   E

3. <u>uncle</u> Dan <u>will arrive</u> on the nine <u>o'clock</u> fli<u>ght.</u> <u>No error</u>
      A   B   C   D   E

4. Stop<u>!</u> <u>you're</u> <u>going</u> the wrong wa<u>y.</u> <u>No error</u>
          A B   C   D   E

5. <u>Ms.</u> P<u>o's</u> car <u>doesn't</u> start on cold <u>morning's.</u> <u>No error</u>
     A B   C   D   E

6. <u>All of them</u> forgot to <u>bring</u> <u>they're</u> boo<u>ks.</u> <u>No error</u>
        A   B   C   D   a

7. I told <u>you,</u> <u>"You</u> would enjoy seeing that movie, did<u>n't</u> <u>I?</u>
       A   **B**   **C D**
  <u>No error</u>
    E

8. <u>Close</u> the <u>window,</u> <u>Sal.</u> <u>It's</u> getting cold. <u>No error</u>
   A   **B**   **C D**   **E**

9. <u>Each one</u> of <u>us</u> <u>are</u> going to perform in the school
    A   **B C**
  <u>play, which</u> we all helped to write. <u>No error</u>
     D   **E**

10. She answered, <u>"Alaska, California,</u> and Texas are the three
                A   **b**
  largest <u>States</u> in the <u>country."</u> <u>No error</u>
        C   **D**   **E**

Tests of Writing Ability

To test your writing ability, a standardized test may ask you to read some paragraphs and answer questions about them. For example, you might be asked to put several sentences in the right order to make a good paragraph. Another question may ask you to find the topic sentence of a paragraph. Read the instructions carefully so you know exactly what to do. The sentences will be numbered, so you can refer to them by number.

EXERCISE 7 Answering Questions on Writing

Number your paper 1 to 5. Then write the letter that answers each question.

1. Which sentence order makes the best paragraph?
    (1) Close the door tightly.
    (2) Finally, start the dishwasher.
    (3) Put all the dishes into the dishwasher.
    (4) Then add the dishwashing powder.
    (5) Do not pile the dishes tightly together.

    (A) 1, 2, 3, 4, 5   (D) 3, 5, 4, 1, 2
    (B) 4, 5, 1, 2, 3   (E) 4, 3, 1, 5, 2
    (C) 5, 1, 4, 2, 3

Questions 2–4 below are based on the following paragraph. Read the paragraph, then answer the questions.

(1) It is not difficult to get a library card. (2) All you have to do is go to the library and fill out a simple form. (3) You also need to bring proof of who you are and where you live. (4) A recent gas bill with your family's name and address on it will serve as proof. (5) Some people use electricity instead of gas for cooking and heating. (6) Think of all the good books you will be able to read once you have your library card.

2. Which sentence does not belong in the paragraph?
   (A) sentence 2   (D) sentence 5
   (B) sentence 3   (E) sentence 6
   (C) sentence 4

3. Which sentence contains the paragraph's main idea?
   (A) sentence 1   (D) sentence 5
   (B) sentence 3   (E) sentence 6
   (C) sentence 4

4. Which sentences add supporting details to the main idea or topic sentence?
   (A) sentences 1, 2, 3   (D) sentences 2, 3, 4, 5
   (B) sentences 2, 5, 6   (E) sentences 3, 4, 5, 6
   (C) sentences 2, 3, 4

5. What is the topic sentence of the following paragraph?

(1) Long ago, when two armed male strangers met by chance, their meeting could lead to trouble. (2) To show that he was friendly, one of the two would stretch out his empty sword hand. (3) The other would do the same, and the two would clasp hands. (4) While each was holding tightly to the other's hand, neither man could draw his sword. (5) This is how the custom of shaking hands began.

(A) sentence 1   (D) sentence 4
(B) sentence 2   (E) sentence 5
(C) sentence 3

Chapter Review

A **Answering True–False Questions.** Number your paper 1 to 10. Then write *T* if the statement is true and *F* if it is false.

Using
the
Library

1. Your local library is a good place to go to for information.
2. Every school and every town has a library.
3. All the books in a library are shelved in alphabetical order by title.
4. Libraries usually have encyclopedias.
5. You can get a library card by looking in the card catalog.
6. You should never ask a librarian for help.
7. Encyclopedias often have more than one volume.
8. Taking notes will help you remember information.
9. Any book in a library can be taken home if you show your library card.
10. To take out a book, remove a card from the card catalog and exchange it for the book you want.

B **Completing Analogies.** Number your paper 1 to 5. Then write the letter of the word that best completes each analogy.

1. hand : arm :: foot : _____
   (a) toe   (b) leg   (c) elbow   (d) shoe
2. whale : ocean :: monkey : _____
   (a) desert   (b) seashore   (c) air   (d) jungle
3. mansion : cottage :: _____ : town
   (a) family   (b) estate   (c) skyscraper   (d) city
4. blunder : error :: need : _____
   (a) require (b) secure (c) own (d) encouragement
5. pronunciation : speaking :: handwriting : _____
   (a) reading   (b) writing   (c) sentence   (d) essay

C **Answering Questions on Writing.** Number your paper 1 to 10. Then write the letter of the underlined part that has an error. If there is no error, write *E*.

1. Do you think <u>governor</u> <u>Rodriguez</u> will run for office
                 A   **B**
   <u>again</u> next year? <u>No error</u>
     C   **D**   **E**

2. Sally was born <u>at</u> <u>midnight</u> on June <u>1,</u> <u>1975.</u> <u>No error</u>
                A   **B**   **C**   **D**   **E**

3. Dic<u>k,</u> <u>Sue,</u> and <u>me</u> will come to the <u>game.</u> <u>No error</u>
       A   **B**   **C**   **D**   **E**

4. "<u>What</u> are the three main parts of an oral repor<u>t?</u>"
    A   **B**
   <u>The</u> teacher aske<u>d.</u> <u>No error</u>
    C   **D**   **E**

5. Without even thinkin<u>g,</u> I answere<u>d,</u> "<u>They</u> are parts one,
                    A   **B**
   tw<u>o,</u> and <u>three."</u> <u>No error</u>
     C   **D**   **E**

6. <u>Neither</u> Anne <u>nor</u> Richard <u>have</u> turned in a written
     A   **B**   **C**
   <u>report</u> yet. <u>No error</u>
     D   **E**

7. Do you have a school holiday on Veterans<u>'</u> <u>Day</u> or
                                 A B
   Presidents<u>'</u> <u>day?</u> <u>No error</u>
         C D   **E**

8. <u>Leave</u> your coat with Tina or <u>I</u> before enterin<u>g,</u> then find a
     A   **B**   **C**
   <u>seat</u> and wait for instructions. <u>No error</u>
     D   **E**

9. All of the Smit<u>h's,</u> including the small childre<u>n,</u> were at
                 A   **B**
   the <u>New</u> <u>Year's</u> Day party. <u>No error</u>
       C   **D**   **E**

10. Jo<u>hn,</u> ask the Mill<u>ers</u> if <u>their</u> planning a surprise party for
        A   **B**   **C**
    Martha. <u>No error</u>
      D   **E**

Standardized Test

Directions: Choose the word that is most nearly the *same* in meaning to the word in capital letters. In the appropriate row on your answer sheet, fill in the circle containing the same letter as your answer.

SAMPLE BRIEF (a) long (b) smart (c) able (d) short

ANSWER (a) (b) (c) (d)

1. TIDY (a) pretty (b) neat (c) messy (d) old
2. COARSE (a) dark (b) smooth (c) rough (d) unsure
3. TREMENDOUS (a) huge (b) ugly (c) complete (d) empty
4. MINIATURE (a) electric (b) large (c) imitation (d) tiny
5. GORGEOUS (a) happy (b) useful (c) beautiful (d) helpful
6. DRENCH (a) open (b) soak (c) pull (d) break
7. ANNUAL (a) yearly (b) rare (c) often (d) young
8. RESPECTFUL (a) useful (b) common (c) skillful (d) courteous
9. THANKFUL (a) happy (b) grateful (c) playful (d) religious
10. SIMILAR (a) different (b) smiling (c) alike (d) frowning
11. QUANTITY (a) amount (b) surplus (c) character (d) playfulness
12. FREQUENT (a) unusual (b) often (c) rarely (d) normal
13. RAPID (a) slow (b) angry (c) pleased (d) swift
14. RESEARCH (a) investigate (b) learn (c) follow (d) repeat
15. EXPENSIVE (a) broad (b) thoughtful (c) costly (d) cheap

Directions: Decide the correct meaning for each word by looking at its prefix or suffix. In the appropriate row on your answer sheet, fill in the circle containing the same number as the correct meaning.

SAMPLE teacher
  1) fit for teaching
  2) state of teaching
  3) one who teaches
  4) teach again
  5) not teaching

ANSWER ① ② ③ ④ ⑤

16. repay
  1) one who pays
  2) pay again
  3) not pay
  4) full of pay
  5) fit for paying

17. skillful
  1) one who is skilled
  2) wrong skill
  3) not skilled
  4) full of skill
  5) cause to be skilled

18. dislike
  1) not like
  2) like again
  3) one who likes
  4) full of likes
  5) become liked

19. uneasy
  1) full of ease
  2) not easy
  3) ease again
  4) become easy
  5) state of ease

20. dangerous
  1) fit for danger
  2) wrong danger
  3) not danger
  4) danger again
  5) full of danger

Index

518

Superlative degree, 163–164
Supporting sentences, 265, 270
Syllable division, 487
Symbols, proofreading, 292, 315
Synonyms, 443, 483, 490

T

Taking notes, 387–389, 435, 470
teach, learn, 122
Tense of verbs, 124
Tests
  classroom, 495–497
  essay, 495
  mechanics and usage, 501–503
  multiple-choice, 496–497
  short-answer, 498
  standardized, 111–112, 175–176,
    227–228, 279–280, 361–362,
    419–420, 507–508
  true-false, 495–496
  vocabulary, 500–501
  of writing ability, 503–504
Textbook, reading of, 467–470
Thank-you note, 407
Thesaurus, 430, 480
this, that, these, those, 65
Time expression, colon with, 196
Time order, 304, 310, 371
Title
  capitalization of, 188–189
  quotation marks with, 222, 386
  underlining (italics) for, 222, 386
Title cards in card catalog, 477
Topic sentence, in paragraph, 265,
  266, 306
Transitions, 309
  list of, 310
  with order of importance, 339
  with sequence order, 340–341
  with space order, 324
True-false tests, 495–496

U

Underlining (italics), 222, 386
Understood subject, 15

V

Variety in sentences, 74, 85, 256
Verb phrase, 12, 43, 152
Verbs, 10, 91
  action, 41
  agreement of subjects with,
    147–157
  complements of, 45, 47, 52, 66, 133
  compound, 17, 99, 108, 202,
    249–250
  helping, 12, 43, 115, 152
  irregular, 116–119
  linking, 50, 52, 66, 133
  number, 148
  principal parts, 115–119
  regular, 115
  state-of-being, 50
  tense, 124
Vocabulary
  analogies, 500–501
  antonyms, 450
  borrowed words, 441
  context clues, 443
  list, 451
  prefixes, roots, suffixes, 445–446,
    487
  synonyms, 443, 490
  words from names, 442
Vocabulary tests, 500–501

W

well, good, 170
Word choice
  sensory words, 235–241, 322–323
  specific adjectives, 69
  specific nouns, 34
  specific verbs, 57
Word meaning, 443–446
Word origin in dictionary, 483
Writing, process of
  brainstorming, 285, 302
  editing, 127, 143, 159, 172, 191, 205,
    215, 258, 291, 292, 315, 397
  first draft, 288, 392–396
  freewriting, 285

Glossary of Terms

A

Abbreviation An abbreviation is a shortened form of a word. Many abbreviations begin with a capital letter and end with a period. (*See page 196.*)

Action verb An action verb tells what action a subject is performing. (*See page 41.*)

Adjective An adjective is a word that modifies, or describes, a noun or a pronoun. (*See page 61.*)

Adverb An adverb is a word that modifies, or describes, a verb, an adjective, or another adverb. (*See page 70.*)

Antonym An antonym is a word that means the opposite of another word. (*See page 450.*)

Audience The audience is the person or persons who will read your work or hear your speech. (*See pages 283 and 425.*)

B

Brainstorming Brainstorming means listing everything that comes to mind about a subject. (*See page 285.*)

Business letter The six parts of a business letter are the heading, inside address, greeting, body, closing, and signature. (*See page 409.*)

C

Complete predicate A complete predicate includes all the words that tell what the subject is doing, or that tell something about the subject. (*See page 6.*)

Complete subject A complete subject includes all the words used to identify the person, place, thing, or idea that the sentence is about. (*See page 6.*)

Compound sentence A compound sentence is made up of two simple sentences, usually joined by a comma and a coordinating conjunction. (*See page 100.*)

Compound subject A compound subject is two or more subjects that have the same verb and are joined by a conjunction. (*See page 17.*)

Compound verb A compound verb is two or more verbs in one sentence that have the same subject and are joined by a conjunction. (*See page 17.*)

Concluding sentence A concluding sentence adds a strong ending to a paragraph. (*See page 274.*)

Contraction A contraction is a word that combines two words into one. It uses an apostrophe to replace one or more missing letters. (*See page 212.*)

Coordinating conjunction A coordinating conjunction connects single words or groups of words. (*See pages 86, 100, and 251.*)

D

Declarative sentence A declarative sentence makes a statement or expresses an opinion. It ends with a period. (*See page 4.*)

Descriptive paragraph A descriptive paragraph creates in words a vivid picture of a person, an object, or a scene. (*See page 320.*)

Dialogue A conversation between two or more persons is called a dialogue. (*See page 221.*)

Direct object A direct object is a noun or pronoun that answers the question *What?* or *Whom?* after an action verb. (*See page 45.*)

Direct quotation A person's exact words are quoted in a direct quotation. Quotation marks are used before and after a direct quotation. (*See page 216.*)

Double negative   A double negative is the use of two negative words to express an idea when only one is needed. (*See page 169.*)

E

Editing   Editing is the final stage of the writing process when writers polish their work by correcting errors and making a neat copy. (*See page 291.*)

Exclamatory sentence   An exclamatory sentence expresses strong feeling. It ends with an exclamation point. (*See page 4.*)

Explanatory paragraph   An explanatory paragraph explains with facts and examples or gives directions. (*See page 334.*)

F

Fable   A fable is a story in which animal characters act like people to teach a lesson or moral. (*See page 373.*)

Facts   Facts are statements that can be proved. (*See page 352.*)

Fiction   Books called fiction are stories of imaginary people and events. Fiction includes novels and short stories. (*See page 472.*)

First draft   Writing the first draft is the second stage of the writing process. Writers use their prewriting notes to get their ideas on paper as quickly as possible. (*See page 288.*)

Folktales   Folktales are stories that were told aloud long before they were written down. (*See page 375.*)

Freewriting   Freewriting means writing nonstop in a relaxed way, without worrying about mistakes. (*See page 285.*)

Friendly letter   The parts of a friendly letter are the heading,

greeting, body, closing, and signature. (*See page 405.*)

H

Helping verb   A helping, or auxiliary, verb works with the main verb in a verb phrase. (*See page 12.*)

Homographs   Homographs are words that are spelled alike but have different meanings and pronunciations. (*See page 462.*)

Homophones   Homophones are words that sound alike but have different meanings and spellings. (*See page 462.*)

I

Imperative sentence   An imperative sentence makes a request or gives a command and ends with either a period or an exclamation point. (*See page 4.*)

Indirect object   An indirect object is a noun or pronoun that answers the question *To or for whom?* or *To or for what?* after an action verb. (*See page 47.*)

Interjection   An interjection is a word that expresses strong feeling. (*See page 86.*)

Interrogative sentence   An interrogative sentence asks a question. It ends with a question mark. (*See page 4.*)

Irregular verb   An irregular verb does not form its past and past participle by adding -*ed* or -*d* to the present. (*See page 116.*)

L

Linking verb   A linking verb links the subject with another word that renames or describes the subject. (*See page 50.*)

N

Narrative paragraph   A narrative paragraph tells a real or an imaginary story with a clear beginning, middle, and ending. (*See page 298.*)

Nonfiction   Books that contain facts about real people and real events are called nonfiction. (*See page 473.*)

Noun   A noun is a word that names a person, place, thing, or idea. A common noun gives a general name. A proper noun names a specific person, place, or thing and always begins with a capital letter. (*See pages 31 and 32.*)

O

Object pronouns   Object pronouns are used for direct objects, indirect objects, and objects of prepositions. (*See pages 135–136.*)

Opinion paragraph   An opinion paragraph states an opinion and uses facts, examples, and reasons to persuade readers. (*See page 350.*)

Opinions   Opinions are judgments that vary from person to person. (*See page 352.*)

Order of importance   Order of importance is a way of organizing information by arranging details in the order of *most to least* or *least to most* important. (*See page 339.*)

Outline   An outline organizes information about a subject into main topics and subtopics. (*See page 390.*)

P

Paragraph   A paragraph is a group of related sentences about one main idea. (*See page 264.*)

Plot   The plot of a story tells what happens to the characters in a given setting. The plot contains the climax, or high point, the resolution of the conflict, and the outcome, or ending. (*See page 371.*)

Possessive pronouns   Possessive pronouns are used to show ownership or possession. (*See page 139.*)

Predicate adjective   A predicate adjective is an adjective that follows a linking verb and modifies, or describes, the subject. (*See page 66.*)

Predicate nominative   A predicate nominative is a noun or a pronoun that follows a linking verb and identifies, renames, or explains the subject. (*See page 52.*)

Prefix   A prefix is a word part that is added to the beginning of a word and changes the basic, or root, meaning of that word. (*See page 445.*)

Preposition   A preposition is a word that shows the relationship between a noun or a pronoun and another word in the sentence. (*See page 79.*)

Prepositional phrase   A prepositional phrase is a group of words made up of a preposition, its object, and any words that describe the object. (*See page 80.*)

Prewriting   Prewriting is the first stage of the writing process. It includes all the planning steps that come before writing the first draft. (*See page 283.*)

Principal parts of a verb   The principal parts of a verb are the *present*, the *past*, and the *past participle*. (*See page 115.*)

Pronoun   A pronoun is a word that takes the place of one or more nouns. (*See page 35.*)

Proofreading symbols   Proofreading symbols are a kind of shorthand that writers use to correct their mistakes while editing. (*See page 292.*)

Purpose   Writing purpose is your reason for writing. (*See page 283.*)

R

Regular verb A regular verb forms the past and the past participle by adding *-ed* or *-d* to the present. (*See page 115.*)

Report A report is a composition of three or more paragraphs that uses information from books, magazines, and other sources. (*See page 382.*)

Revising Revising is the third stage of the writing process, when a writer changes a draft as much as needed to improve it. (*See page 289.*)

Root A root is the part of the word that carries its basic meaning. (*See page 445.*)

Run-on sentence A run-on sentence is two or more sentences that are written as one sentence. They are separated by a comma or have no mark of punctuation at all. (*See page 104.*)

S

Sentence A sentence is a group of words that expresses a complete thought. (*See page 3.*)

Sentence fragment A sentence fragment is a group of words that does not express a complete thought. (*See page 21.*)

Setting The setting is the place and time of a story. (*See page 369.*)

Simple predicate A simple predicate, or verb, is the main word or phrase in the complete predicate. (*See page 10.*)

Simple sentence A simple sentence is a sentence that has one subject and one verb. (*See page 99.*)

Simple subject A simple subject is the main word in the complete subject. (*See page 8.*)

Space order Space order arranges details according to their loca-tion. Transitions show the rela-tionship of the details. (*See page 324.*)

Story A story is a true or made-up account of a character facing and resolving a problem. (*See page 364.*)

Subject pronouns Subject pro-nouns are used for subjects and predicate nominatives. (*See page 132.*)

Subordinating conjunction A sub-ordinating conjunction is used in a sentence to introduce an idea of less importance than the main idea. (*See page 253.*)

Suffix A suffix is a word part that is added after a word and chang-es its basic, or root, meaning. (*See page 446.*)

Synonym A synonym is a word that has nearly the same meaning as another word. (*See page 448.*)

T

Tense The present, past, and fu-ture tenses are forms a verb takes to show time. (*See page 124.*)

Thesaurus A thesaurus is a special dictionary that gives several words with the same meaning. (*See page 480.*)

Time order Time order is a way of organizing details according to when they happened. (*See page 304.*)

Topic sentence A topic sentence states the main idea of the para-graph. (*See page 266.*)

Transitions Transitions are words and phrases that show how ideas are related. (*See pages 309, 310, 324, 339, and 353.*)

V

Verb phrase A verb phrase is a main verb plus one or more help-ing verbs. (*See page 43.*)

Acknowledgments

The authors and editors have made every effort to trace the ownership of all copyrighted selections found in this book and to make full acknowledgment of their use. Grateful acknowledgment is made to the following authors, publishers, agents, and individuals for their permission to reprint copyrighted materials.

Page 230. George and Helen Papashvily, "Kola the Bear" from *Thanks to Noah*. Copyright © 1951 by George and Helen Papashvily. Reprinted by permission of Harper & Row, Publishers, Inc.

Page 241. Extract from p. 75 in *Charlotte's Web* by E. B. White. Copyright © 1952, 1980 by E. B. White. Reprinted by permission of Harper & Row, Publishers, Inc.

Page 256. From *Amelia Earhart: First Lady of Flight* by Peggy Mann. Copyright © 1970 by Peggy Mann. Reprinted by permission of Coward, McCann, Geoghegan, Inc.

Page 265. From *Fire Prevention* by Dorothy Wilson. Copyright © 1965 by Franklin Watts, Inc. Reprinted by permission.

Pages 266–268. From *Guinness Book of Amazing Animals*. Copyright © 1981 by Sterling Publishing Co., Inc., New York, NY. Reprinted by permission of the publisher.

Page 276. Adaptation of "Early Remedies" from *"The Earth is Flat"—And Other Great Mistakes* by Laurence Pringle. Copyright © 1983 by Laurence Pringle. Adapted by permission of William Morrow & Co.

Page 277. From *Sleep On It: A Look at Sleep and Dreams* by David L. Singer and William G. Martin. Copyright © 1969 by David L. Singer and William G. Martin. Reprinted by permission of Prentice-Hall, Inc.

Page 287. From *Mr. Cub* by Ernie Banks and Jim Enright. Copyright © 1971 by Rutledge Books, Inc. and Jim Enright and Ernie Banks. Reprinted by permission of Allyn and Bacon.

Page 323. Adapted from p. 20 in *Little House in the Big Woods* by Laura Ingalls Wilder. Copyright © 1932 by Laura Ingalls Wilder; copyright renewed 1959 by Roger L. MacBride. Reprinted by permission of Harper & Row, Publishers, Inc.

Page 324. From *The House of Dies Drear* by Virginia Hamilton. Copyright © 1968 by Virginia Hamilton. Reprinted by permission of Macmillan Publishing Co., Inc.

Page 338. From *Mr. Wizard's Supermarket Science* by Don Herbert. Copyright © by Don Herbert. Reprinted by permission of Random House, Inc.

Page 344. "Jungle Jumble" from CODES FOR KIDS by Burton Albert, Jr. Text © 1976 by Burton Albert, Jr. Used by permission of Albert Whitman & Company.

Page 364. Walter de la Mare, "Some One," from *Collected Poems: 1901–1918*. Copyright © 1948 by Walter de la Mare. Reprinted by permission of The Literary Trustees of Walter de la Mare and The Society of Authors as their representative.

Pages 365–366. Reprinted with permission from *Tales of the Hodja*. Copyright © 1964 by Charles Downing. Published by David McKay Company, Inc.

Page 367. From "All Summer in a Day" by Ray Bradbury. Copyright © 1954 by Ray Bradbury. Reprinted by permission of Don Congdon Associates, Inc.

Page 368. Beatrice Tanaka, "Of Ships and Trees" from *World Treasury*. Reprinted by permission of the author.

Page 373. Arthur Ryder, translator, "The Crow and the Partridge," from *Tales of the Panchatantra*. Copyright © 1925 by The University of Chicago Press. Reprinted by permission of the University of Chicago Press.

Pages 375–376. M. A. Jagendorf, "Gray Moss on Green Trees" from *Folk Stories of the South*. Copyright © 1972 by M. A. Jagendorf. Reprinted by permission of Vanguard Press, Inc.

Page 388. From "Koko's Kitten" by Jane Vessels, *National Geographic*, January, 1985.

Credits

Editorial Development, Art Direction, and Production: Ligature, Inc.

Photos

Unit 1: **1:** Lou Jones

Unit 2: **113:** Robert Llewellyn

Unit 3: **177:** William Smith

Unit 4: **229:** J. E. Fogle (The Picture Cube). **Chapter 15: 233:** Photri (Marilyn Gartman Agency). **234:** Mike Andrews (Photo Trends). **236:** Jawitz (The Image Bank). **237:** Cezus (Click/Chicago). **239:** Richard Heinzen (PhotoUnique). **240:** Anthony Galvan (Taurus Photo) **243:** Focus West. **244:** Brian Seed (Click/Chicago). **Chapter 16: 248:** NASA. **255:** Bullaty Lomeo (The Image Bank). **259:** Grant Heilman (Grant Heilman). **260:** R. Hayo (The Image Bank). **262:** Jim Pickerell (Click/Chicago). **Chapter 17: 272:** Carl Sissac (Nawrocki Stock Photo). **277:** John Shelton.

Unit 5: **281:** John Stuart. **Chapter 18: 283:** Pam Hasegawa (Taurus Photos). **285:** Focus West. **286:** Lael Morgan (Click/Chicago). **295:** Marvin Newman (The Image Bank). **Chapter 19: 301:** Jeffrey Meyers (FPG). **303:** Martin Rogers (Click/Chicago). **305:** Ken Sexton (Nawrocki Stock Photo) **309:** Jeffrey Meyers (FPG). **317:** Jeffrey Meyers (FPG). **Chapter 20: 320:** *l* Harald Sund (The Image Bank), *c* C. Stevenson (Earth Scenes), *r* Vince Streano (Click/Chicago). **322:** *l* Jay Freis (The Image Bank), *r* Ted Levin (Animals, Animals). **323:** Hans Wendler (The Image Bank). **326:** B. Mitchell (The Image Bank). **330:** *l* Oudi (Manhattan Views), *r* M. Breskin (FPG). **331:** Marilyn Houlberg. **332:** Jeffrey Myers (FPG). **Chapter 21: 340:** Will Rhyins (West Light). **347:** Dallas and John Heaton (Click/Chicago). **348:** Kirk Schlea (Focus West). **Chapter 22: 354:** Larry Reynolds (Reynolds Photography). **356:** Grant Heilman (Grant Heilman).

Unit 6: **363:** Robert Llewellyn. **Chapter 23: 369:** Jeffrey Sylvester (FPG). **370:** *t* Bob Rashid (Click/Chicago), *b* Peter Fronk (Click/Chicago). **378:** *tl* Tom Stack (Tom Stack & Associates), *tr* Spencer Swanger (Tom Stack & Associates), *bl* Joe Craighead (Click/Chicago), *br* Beebe (The Image Bank). **379:** *t* Robert Farber (The Image Bank), *b* Jim Wright (Nawrocki Stock Photo). **380:** Judy Griesedieck (Black Star). **Chapter 24: 389:** Jeff Rotman. **391:** Travelpix (FPG). **393:** Ronald Cohn (The Gorilla Foundation). **395:** Ronald Cohn (The Gorilla Foundation). **400:** Steven Arnam (Marilyn Gartman Agency). **401:** Jeff Rotman. **Chapter 25: 412:** L. Grant (FPG). **417:** *t* William Nawrocki (Nawrocki Stock Photo), *b* Jeffrey Myers (FPG).

Unit 7: **421:** Robert Llewellyn

Illustrations

5, 14, 18, 32, 36, 41, 51, 58, 62, 68, 81, 83, 92, 96, 103, 109, 121, 126, 151, 186, 190, 195, 204, 217, 225: Rhonda Voo. **242, 265.** Yoshi Miyake. **266, 268, 273:** Rhonda Voo. **289, 292:** Rich Lo. **294:** Yoshi Miyake. **302:** Rich Lo. **307, 308:** Rhonda Voo. **314:** Yoshi Miyake. **322:** Rhonda Voo. **325:** Rich Lo. **327:** Yoshi Miyake. **336:** Rhonda Voo. **337, 338:** Yoshi Miyake. **341:** Rhonda Voo. **344:** Rich Lo. **353:** Rhonda Voo. **359, 366:** Yoshi Miyake. **372:** Rhonda Voo. **376, 382:** Yoshi Miyake. **386:** Rhonda Voo. **389, 392-396:** Rich Lo. **398:** Yoshi Miyake. **405-407:** Rich Lo. **408:** Yoshi Miyake. **472, 474, 476, 479:** Rich Lo.